DEMOCRACY AND ITS LIMITS

Robert S. Pelton, C.S.C.
Small Christian Communities
Imagining Future Church (1998)

Víctor E. Tokman and Guillermo O'Donnell, eds.
Poverty and Inequality in Latin America: Issues and New Challenges (1998)

Brian H. Smith
Religious Politics in Latin America, Pentecostal vs. Catholic (1998)

Tristan Anne Borer
Challenging the State: Churches as Political Actors in South Africa, 1980–1994 (1998)

Guillermo O'Donnell
Counterpoints: Selected Essays on Authoritarianism and Democratization (1999)

Juan E. Méndez, Guillermo O'Donnell, and Paulo Sérgio Pinheiro, eds.
The (Un)Rule of Law and the Underprivileged in Latin America (1999)

Howard Handelman and Mark Tessler, eds.
Democracy and Its Limits: Lessons from Asia, Latin America, and the Middle East (1999)

DEMOCRACY AND ITS LIMITS

Lessons from Asia, Latin America, and the Middle East

Howard Handelman and Mark Tessler, editors

UNIVERSITY OF NOTRE DAME PRESS

NOTRE DAME, INDIANA

Library of Congress Cataloging-in-Publication Data

Democracy and its limits : lessons from Asia, Latin America, and
   the Middle East / Howard Handelman and Mark Tessler, editors.
        p.   cm. — (Titles from the Helen Kellogg Institute for
International Studies)
    Includes bibliographical references and index.
    ISBN 0-268-00891-4 (pa. : alk. paper)
    1. Democracy—Developing countries.   2. Democratization—
Developing countries.   3. Developing countries—Politics and
government.   I. Handelman, Howard, 1943-   .   II. Tessler,
Mark A.   III. Series: Title from the Helen Kellogg Institute for
International Studies.
JC421.D4625   2000
320.9172′4–dc21   99-35184

*The paper used in this publication meets the minimum requirements
of the American National Standard for Information Sciences—
Permanence of Paper for Printed Library Materials,
ANSI Z39.48-1984.*

Contents

Acknowledgments

THIS BOOK BEGAN WITH a conference on "Democracy and Its Limits" held at the University of Wisconsin—Milwaukee on May 2–3, 1997. That conference was sponsored by UWM's Center for Latin America and Center for International Studies and included all of the contributors to this volume, with the exceptions of Augustus Richard Norton and Jeffrey Riedinger, who joined the project later. We would like to express our appreciation to the U.S. Department of Education's Title VI program for its support of the two aforementioned national resource centers at UWM. The Title VI NRC program offered financial support both to the conference and to the subsequent publication of this book. We would also like to thank the Helen Kellogg Institute for International Studies at the University of Notre Dame and its director, Scott Mainwaring, for their support of the book's publication.

In addition to those represented in this volume, our thanks also go to a number of other scholars who participated in the conference—either as presenters, discussants, or panel chairs—and contributed to the book's intellectual content: David Buck (UWM), David Garnham (UWM), Dru Gladney (University of Hawaii), Uk Heo (UWM), Evelyne Huber (University of North Carolina—Chapel Hill), Jodi Nachtwey (UWM), Richard Kagan (Hamline University), Garth Katner (St. Norbert College), Mohammed Muslih (Long Island University), Marvin Weinbaum (University of Illinois), and Keith Yanner (Central College).

The success of any project of this size depends on careful preparation and follow-up. Consequently, we are very grateful to the staffs of our two centers for their hard work, skill, and dedication. In particular we thank Cheryle Darmek, Julie Kline, and Amy Langsdon Warner (all of the Center for Latin America) and Anne Banda, Joanne Hemb, Jodi Nachtwey, Claire Thompson, Amy Kuether, and Laura Sayles (all of the Center for International Studies).

Finally we express our appreciation to James Langford of the University of Notre Dame Press for his support.

Introduction

IT IS NOW nearly three decades since "The Third Wave of Democratization" began (Huntington 1991). Since that time, democracy has spread with varying speed and intensity to a significant portion of the Third World. Beginning with transitions from military to elected, civilian government in Ecuador and Peru at the close of the 1970s, procedural, if not necessarily substantive, democracy has expanded across Latin America with particular strength. As that region approaches the end of the twentieth century, all of its governments save Cuba's appear to be either democratic or semidemocratic. To be sure, there have been important setbacks, including President Alberto Fujimori's "autocoup" in Peru and renewed military intervention in Haiti. And democratic institutions and values remain weak in countries such as Guatemala, Nicaragua, and Paraguay. Still, in the past two decades Latin America has enjoyed the most pervasive and sustained period of democratic rule in its entire history. While undoubtedly there will be additional regression, the region finally seems to be escaping the pendular swings between democracy and authoritarianism that have plagued it in the past (Pastor 1989).

Asia's experience has been more varied (Friedman 1994), including significant democratic transitions in South Korea, the Philippines, and Taiwan, but, until recently, only liberalization in Indonesia, and little or no change to date in China, Myanmar, and Vietnam. Inheriting dynamic economies, high educational levels, and comparatively equitable distributions of land and income, the new democratic governments of Taiwan and South Korea enjoyed many of the socioeconomic prerequisites for democracy that are so often lacking in other developing countries. Even in the wake of East Asia's recent financial crisis, that region retains its high educational levels and substantial income equality. At the same time, however, as the chapters by Sunhyuk Kim and Jeffrey Riedinger note, patronage politics, closed political networks, and government cor-

ruption in countries such as South Korea and the Philippines have sub-
verted the objectives of procedural and substantive democracy.

Several countries in the Middle East and North Africa achieved pal-
pable political liberalization and even limited democratization during the
late 1980s. Algeria, Jordan, Tunisia, and Egypt were in the forefront of
change. But more recently, Mark Tessler laments, democratic change has
been sidetracked or, in cases such as Algeria, completely aborted. Thus
in most of the Middle East and North Africa the transition to democracy,
much less democratic consolidation, remains elusive. On the other hand,
Farhad Kazemi and A. Richard Norton maintain that ongoing economic
liberalization, strengthening of civil society, and increased popular demands for government accountability all offer hope for future democratic openings.

Following the euphoria that greeted the Third World's early transitions from authoritarian rule, scholars and democratic reformers alike
increasingly have recognized important limits to democratization. This
book will focus on two distinct types of limitation:

1. Institutional, cultural, ideological, and leadership factors that
   have limited democratic transition and consolidation or, in the
   cases of China and many Middle East states, prevented even
   substantial political liberalization.
2. Limits on the capacities of emerging democracies in Asia, Latin
   America, and the Middle East to create representative political
   institutions, equal opportunities for political participation, honest and efficient bureaucracies and court systems, or a measure
   of social and economic justice.

As Eric Hershberg observes, "democratization remains partial and
uneven, and at least so far it has enjoyed only minimal success in addressing some of the most pressing [socioeconomic and institutional] issues
facing Latin American [and other Third World] societies." Excepting
Uruguay, Latin America has seen already sharp income disparities widen
throughout the region during the recent florescence of democratic government. Jeffrey Riedinger's and Sunhyuk Kim's chapters describe how
corruption and insider politics have persevered, and even flourished, during Philippine and South Korean democratization. And, in his analysis of
Brazil, Barry Ames demonstrates how similar corrupting forces create a
"permanent governability crisis," undermining the very foundations of
democracy.

In short, in most third-wave democracies the glass is both half full
and half empty. Much has been accomplished and much remains to be

done. In our analysis, we define democracy as polyarchy (Dahl 1971), focusing on procedural requisites such as contested elections for major political posts (or, at least, contestation for most of them), near universal suffrage, realistic possibilities of alternating government control among contending political parties, fundamental civil liberties, and the absence of external controls over elected officials by nonelected actors such as economic elites and the military (Dahl 1971; Mainwaring 1992; Schmitter and Karl 1991).

In countries as far-flung as South Korea, South Africa, Brazil, and Chile, former police states have been dismantled, political prisoners have been freed, and civil society has been revived. Even erstwhile critics of liberal democracy have come to recognize the inherent value of civil liberties, electoral contestation, pluralism, and a vibrant civil society, regardless of the nature of substantive policy outcomes. That is, political (procedural) democracy is now widely appreciated for its inherent value even if it fails to bring with it social democracy—i.e., social justice and improved economic equality (O'Donnell and Schmitter 1986: 3–14).

Still, the very incompleteness of democracy as it now exists in much of the developing world, the vastly unequal political resources available to different individuals and social classes, extensive corruption and other inequities in the judicial system, and the failure of many democratic regimes to address severe social and economic injustices, all undermine procedural democracy itself and threaten its survival. Often political authority has been delegated to democratically elected but all-powerful presidents who reject checks by countervailing forces within their government (O'Donnell 1993 and 1994). Corrupt bureaucracies, unresponsive judiciaries, and irresponsible political parties also frequently undermine democratic legitimacy.

PROSPECTS FOR DEMOCRATIZATION: CULTURAL AND IDEOLOGICAL INFLUENCES

In his discussion of Latin America, Scott Mainwaring notes that the region, until recently, has not experienced the usual correlation between socioeconomic modernization (as measured by per capita GNP and rate of literacy) and democratic government. But Latin America's exceptionality is matched in other regions. Rapid economic growth and modernization in China and the petroleum-producing Arab states also have not produced concomitant levels of democratization or, in cases such as China and Iraq, even liberalization. For Mainwaring, the answer lies, in part, in the somewhat independent roles of political culture and political leadership, an explanation supported by Howard Handelman's analysis of lingering authoritarian values in Mexico's "culture of fear."

Ideology and cultural factors, including religion, also may inhibit (or promote) liberalization and democratization. But the precise ways in which particular ideological or cultural variables influence a nation's democratic potential are often difficult to measure and open to competing interpretations. In China, Leninist definitions of democracy (encompassing no semblance of polyarchy) and Maoist contempt for bourgeois democratic institutions precluded even moderate political liberalization prior to the 1980s. Today, however, as Joseph Fewsmith argues convincingly, Marxist-Leninist-Mao Zedong thought is no longer taken very seriously by China's leadership. Instead, other factors now stand in the way of political liberalization, with ideology acting largely as a smoke screen.

Similarly, Mark Tessler's discussion of Islam and democracy warns against overemphasizing cultural influences such as religion in evaluating the Middle East's prospects for democracy. On the one hand, he notes, support for (militant) political Islam grows in significant measure out of popular longings for more responsive government, rather than from any mass aspirations for public law and policy based on the strict interpretation of religious codes. Thus, the current Islamist (fundamentalist) resurgence in many ways expresses popular protest against authoritarian secular regimes.

At the same time, while Islamist governments have themselves been highly authoritarian, Tessler notes that there is no necessary contradiction between Islamic values and democratic principles. Islam contains diverse traditions and differing legal interpretations, and those that value pluralism, tolerance of diversity, and political accountability are as authentic as those that emphasize conformity, hierarchy, and submission to authority.

In some regions, political liberalization has allowed the mobilization of formerly repressed groups who do not share democratic values. Consequently, factors permitting the political activation of those groups may inhibit the rights of another. For example, the inclusion of Islamist actors in the political arena often results in exclusionary policies toward women. But here again, Laurie Brand notes, a more nuanced interpretation is in order. The quality of past interactions between government and the Islamist opposition, and the nature of earlier government social policies help determine whether a particular Islamist political movement offers a greater threat to women's political and social rights (Tunisia) or a lesser one (Jordan).

STRUCTURAL CONSTRAINTS AND INDUCEMENTS

Like cultural and ideological variables, structural factors may also either inhibit or encourage democratization. At times they may do both. In the Middle East, note Kazemi and Norton, statist economic institutions have produced rentier states in which favored groups resist sharing their gains. Not surprisingly, the most important opposition to political liberalization in the region comes from those who have benefited most from the political and economic status quo. Although the authors remain guardedly optimistic about the long-term possibilities for democracy in the Middle East, they concede that concern for the protection of rentier privilege has induced many regimes to abandon experiments in liberalization that seemed so promising a decade ago. Sunhyuk Kim describes a similar, though less intense, pattern of corruption in South Korea.

Prospects for democracy are better in Latin America, but not entirely hopeful. Howard Handelman observes that Mexican neoliberal reforms have limited the resources available to the state-party regime and thereby reduced opportunities for rents. But the still-potent state bureaucracy and corporatist official party continue to raise barriers to further democratization. And in Brazil, Barry Ames argues, political institutions—most notably a distorting electoral system, weak political parties, a feeble national legislature, and a powerful presidency that normally lacks a congressional majority—undermine democratic consolidation by promoting massive corruption and unbridled pork-barrel politics, thereby limiting government's capacity to solve pressing national problems.

Small wonder that Edward Friedman insists that the struggle to achieve and consolidate democracy is continuous and never-ending. "Democratization is so revolutionary," he asserts, "as to be a fortuitous process full of vicissitudes and set-backs anywhere and everywhere, including the West." To be sure, empirical evidence suggests that the longer procedural democracy has been in place in a given country, the greater are its chances for continued survival. But the collapse of Latin America's two most enduring democracies, Chile and Uruguay, in 1973 and the emergence of repressive, bureaucratic-authoritarian regimes in those countries highlights the fragility of even apparently consolidated democracies.

Against this background, the contributors to *Democracy and Its Limits* assess problems and opportunities associated with democratic transition and consolidation. However, they do more than offer a catalogue of what has been accomplished and what remains to be done, or merely identify the problems that are most likely to be consequential in the future. Rather, taken together, these chapters also offer broad and potentially generalizable theoretical insights about the factors that promote and retard progress toward democratization.

Further, these concerns are addressed within an explicitly cross-regional and comparative framework. The book tries to identify generalizable insights on the one hand and, on the other, conditionalities associated with assessments that apply in some regions or countries but not in others. Given the important differences between Asia, Latin America, and the Middle East, observations and conclusions that appear to be applicable to all three world regions are likely to be generalizable elsewhere. The diversity encompassed by those three regions, as well as the diversity within each region, means that common insights will have been shown to apply under widely differing conditions. This diversity constitutes a "most different systems" research design.

Alternatively, those insights that apply in some countries or regions but not in others teach us something about their locus of applicability. More specifically, characteristics and experiences of the regions or countries in which they apply may be incorporated as conditionalities into hypotheses that seek to account for variance in the salience, as well as the nature, of processes and problems relating to democratization.

OVERVIEW

Scott Mainwaring's chapter on "Democratic Survivability in Latin America" asks why the widely observed correlation between socioeconomic modernization and political democracy has until recently been less apparent in Latin America (and in China as well). He examines the roles of both structural and cultural correlates of democracy and suggests that political and socioeconomic changes in recent decades have transformed Latin America's political culture, increasing the likelihood of democratic survivability.

In their analysis of "Hardliners and Softliners in the Middle East," Farhad Kazemi and A. Richard Norton discuss the structural and cultural obstacles to political liberalization in that region. Explaining why democratization has lagged, they argue that the rentier nature of many governments induces political officials to oppose liberalization. They also note, however, that societal pressures for democratization persist today in many Middle Eastern countries. Accordingly they identify several factors that may produce future movement in this direction.

Each of the five country-specific chapters that follow (China, South

Korea, Brazil, the Philippines, and Mexico) stresses structural constraints on liberalization and democratization. Some also suggest reforms that may facilitate further advancement.

Joseph Fewsmith ("Institution Building and Democratization") is cautiously optimistic about China's chances for political liberalization despite limited progress to date, and sees evidence of some breakthroughs toward creating political institutions capable of sustaining democracy. Economic growth, the emergence of a substantial nonstate economic sector, and the regime's diminished ideological legitimacy have created pressure for institutional reform in the political arena. Following Tiananmen Square and a period of hard-line retrenchment, Jiang Zemin has "rationalize[d] and regularize[d] politics at the highest level." But while the political system has been transformed from totalitarian to authoritarian, further progress toward democratization is uncertain. "To the extent that the economic and public spheres and the realms of Party and state are [still] conflated," Fewsmith warns, "it is difficult at best for . . . a vital civil society to emerge."

South Korea seems to have successfully negotiated its democratic transition and consolidation. But, Sunhyuk Kim's chapter, "Patronage Politics as an Obstacle to Democracy," warns that the persistence of patronage politics, clientelism, and corruption undermines the country's chances for substantive democracy. Fortunately, Kim Dae Jung's election as president improves prospects for curtailing patronage networks. Reform is by no means certain, however, and will require a reactivation of civil society.

Barry Ames ("Institutions and Democracy in Brazil") notes that some of Brazil's most important political institutions are highly dysfunctional for democracy—most notably its electoral system, weak national legislature, and weak political parties. Despite the president's substantial political powers, these factors limit his ability to fashion a workable legislative majority and contribute to the problems of political patronage, pork-barrel politics, and corruption (not unlike in South Korea). Despite the country's highly capable political leadership in recent years, in the person of President Fernando Henrique Cardoso, Ames is pessimistic about the future of political reform. In its absence, Brazil's new democracy will be hard-pressed to address the country's most important social and economic problems.

In his discussion of Philippine politics, "Caciques and Coups," Jeffrey Riedinger contrasts Dahl's definition of *electoral* democracy with Diamond's (1996) more demanding standards of *liberal* democracy. While the "People Power Revolution" of 1986 helped secure the former, the country has a long way to go before achieving the latter. The political system, like Brazil's, is plagued by weak political parties, personalism, and governance by local and regional strongmen (*caciquismo*). Unlike Latin America's military, whose political involvement has diminished during that region's democratic transformation, the Philippine armed forces have become increasingly politicized, particularly under President Fidel Ramos. Armed communist and Muslim insurgencies, and accompanying human rights abuses by the military, have further undermined liberal democracy. In varying degrees, some progress has been made toward addressing most of these problems, but much remains to be done.

Howard Handelman's discussion of Mexico's emerging democracy, "Waiting for Democracy in Mexico," focuses on both institutional and cultural dimensions. Neoliberal economic reforms since the mid-1980s have greatly reduced the state's economic resources and, consequently, its ability to co-opt major groups in society. The decline of patronage politics has, in turn, undermined the official party's (PRI's) corporatist structure. At the same time, recurring economic crises since 1982 have made civil society more insistent upon electoral reforms and opened the door to major electoral gains by the opposition parties. Equally important, as Mexicans have emerged from their "culture of fear"—a political culture that associated political change and opposition-party challenges with the chaos and violence of the revolutionary era—they have become more committed to democratic transformation. But, as Mexico cautiously democratizes, it must create institutions and procedures that balance the need to decentralize and to reduce presidential authority with the dangers of transferring power to regional political bosses who are more authoritarian than the chief executive.

Laurie Brand's examination of political change in the Middle East and North Africa, "Arab Women and Political Liberalization," indicates that liberalization has often been a two-edged sword, liberating formerly repressed groups but also unleashing authoritarian movements into civil society. Thus, while political liberalization in Jordan and Tunisia has presented women with new opportunities, it has also mobilized Islamist forces opposed to women's political and social rights. As we have noted earlier, the magnitude of that Islamist threat depends on the nature of earlier state social policies and past government relations with Islamist political movements.

While several authors in this volume stress the obstacles that authoritarian cultural values present to democratization, Mark Tessler ("Democratic Concern and Islamic Resurgence") cautions against misrepresenting Islamic political values (which, to be sure, contain both progressive and reactionary strands) or overstating the antidemocratic underpinnings of Islamist mass support. "Islam and democracy," Tessler insists, "are not of necessity incompatible." Indeed, democratic currents in the Middle East have strong domestic roots and are not merely a response to global trends. Even in the face of political repression, civil society is maturing in many parts of the region. And, while Islamist leaders often reject political and social pluralism, many of their supporters are primarily attracted to the movement's vocal opposition to elitism and political corruption, not to its authoritarian political values.

Eric Hershberg's chapter on "Democracy and Its Discontents" first notes that only a few of Latin America's new democracies fully fit the requirements of polyarchy. The rest are either "pseudo," "diminished," or "tutelary" democracies. As such they fail to satisfy completely the essential state obligations of sovereignty, citizen participation, accountability, and viable economic policy. In a region historically known for its low accountability and limited political participation, new democracies can achieve their promise only by enhancing their concept of citizenship, thereby overcoming Latin America's tradition of exclusionary politics.

Finally, Edward Friedman ("The Painful Gradualness of Democratization") reminds us that the very definition of democracy is ever-changing, ever-evolving. For example, most historians would classify mid-eighteenth-century America as democratic. But it persecuted Native Americans, enslaved African-Americans, and denied women the franchise, hardly conforming to today's standards. Given its fluidity over time, he argues, democracy is never fully consolidated and never fully secure. In that sense, the study of all democracies, fledgling or advanced, is an exercise in "transitology."

REFERENCES

Dahl, Robert A. 1971. *Polyarchy: Participation and Opposition*. New Haven: Yale University Press.

Diamond, Larry. 1996. "Is the Third Wave Over?" *Journal of Democracy,* 7, no. 3 (July): 20–37.

Friedman, Edward, ed. 1994. *The Politics of Democratization: Generalizing East Asian Experiences*. Boulder: Westview Press.

Huntington, Samuel P. 1991. *The Third Wave*. Norman: University of Oklahoma Press.

Mainwaring, Scott. 1992. "Transitions to Democracy and Democratic Consolidation: Theoretical and Comparative Perspectives," in *Issues in Democratic Consolidation*, ed. Scott Mainwaring, Guillermo O'Donnell, and J. S. Valenzuela. Notre Dame: Notre Dame University Press, pp. 294–341.

O'Donnell, Guillermo. 1993. "On the State, Democratization, and Some Conceptual Problems." *World Development*, 21, no. 8 (August).

———. 1994. "Delegative Democracy." *Journal of Democracy,* 5, no. 1 (January).

O'Donnell, Guillermo, and Philippe C. Schmitter. 1986. *Transitions from Authoritarian Rule: Tentative Conclusions about Uncertain Democracies.* Baltimore: Johns Hopkins University Press.

Pastor, Robert A. 1989. *Democracy in the Americas: Stopping the Pendulum.* New York: Holmes and Meier.

Schmitter, Philippe, and Terry Karl. 1991. "What Democracy Is, and Is Not." *Journal of Democracy,* 2 (Summer).

1
Democratic Survivability in Latin America

Scott Mainwaring

IN THIS CHAPTER, I document a sharp increase in the number of democracies and a decline of authoritarianism in Latin America in the period since 1978. This has been an unprecedented time of democracy in Latin America. At the beginning of the period, Latin America had only three democracies: Colombia, Costa Rica, and Venezuela. By 1990, virtually every government in the region was democratic or semidemocratic. Moreover, in contrast to what occurred in earlier waves of democratization in Latin America, this wave has lasted much longer and has been broader in scope.

This is not to present an apologetic view of the quality of democracy in Latin America or to suggest that most of these democracies are consolidated. Many of the democratic and semidemocratic governments in the region have serious shortcomings. However, these shortcomings should not obscure the sea change that has occurred in Latin American politics. A region that throughout its history was overwhelmingly authoritarian has become mostly democratic and semidemocratic.

The question of why this shift has occurred is linked to the age-old issue of the social conditions favorable to democracy, around which a robust literature has revolved. Although there have been many fine analyses of the erosion of authoritarian regimes in Latin America (e.g., Stepan 1988), of transitions to democracy in the region (e.g., O'Donnell, Schmitter, and Whitehead 1986), and of democracy in individual countries or sets of countries, little has been written about why democracy has proven to be more enduring since 1978 than ever before in the region. In addition to being intrinsically important, the question of why democratic

11

survivability has increased in Latin America can help shed light on the broader issue of what conditions favor democracy.

I claim that three factors help explain the vicissitudes of democracy in Latin America, including why the region has become mostly democratic since 1978. The first explanation revolves around the structural transformations unleashed by modernization: urbanization, growing literacy, greater wealth, a larger working class, and the gradual reduction of the political power of the landed elite. These structural changes were favorable to democratization even though they do not fully explain it. In previous decades, lower rates of education, wealth, and urbanization provided less fertile breeding ground for democracy.

Second, from the left to the right of the spectrum, political attitudes changed in Latin America in the 1980s, toward a growing valorization of democracy. This development permitted a change away from the polarized atmosphere of the 1960s and 1970s. Finally, international support for democracy, especially from the United States, increased in the second half of the 1980s. In an era of growing internationalization in Latin America, new institutional mechanisms have formed to help protect democracy. Here, too, the contrast with earlier decades is significant.

DEMOCRACY AND AUTHORITARIANISM IN LATIN AMERICA, 1940–96

My first purpose is to trace the historical record of democratic survivability in Latin America in the period since 1940. A tremendous amount has been written on political regimes in different Latin American countries, but relatively little has been written on democracy in the region as a whole. The main exceptions are Diamond and Linz (1989), who discuss the region as a whole but not individual countries; Rueschemeyer, Stephens, and Stephens (1992), who systematically categorize regime types for South America but not for Central America; Hartlyn and Valenzuela (1994), who mostly confine their analysis to eight major countries (Argentina, Brazil, Chile, Colombia, Costa Rica, Peru, Uruguay, and Venezuela); and Collier and Collier (1991), who analyze the relationship between the labor movement and political regimes in eight countries (Argentina, Brazil, Chile, Colombia, Mexico, Peru, Uruguay, and Venezuela). Remmer (1996) compares the sustainability of democratic and authoritarian regimes in South America but does not analyze in depth the conditions favorable to democracy.

Because these are important contributions, it is worth briefly noting some of the differences in my work vis-à-vis theirs. I pay more attention to international factors than these previous works. The international dissemination of ideas and changing orientations of international actors toward democracy have been a key part of the demise of authoritarianism and heightened democratic survivability in Latin America. Except for Whitehead (1986, 1991, 1996), none of the main overviews of Latin American democracy has highlighted these considerations.

I emphasize structural underpinnings of democracy, especially the level of development, more than Hartlyn and Valenzuela (1994) or Diamond and Linz (1989), but less than Rueschemeyer, Stephens, and Stephens (1992). For Latin America, the level of development increases or diminishes the odds that democracy will be implemented and survive, but it far from determines regime types. Like Hartlyn and Valenzuela (1994), I focus more on the attitudes of political elites than Rueschemeyer, Stephens, and Stephens (1992). Political attitudes are relatively independent of the level of development, and they are crucial in understanding prospects for democracy.

Dealing with nineteen countries represents an intermediate research strategy between studies that deal with one country or a few countries and larger n studies that examine democracy or political regimes for the Third World (e.g., Hadenius 1992; Power and Gasiorowski 1997) or the entire world (e.g., Bollen 1980; Bollen and Jackman 1985; Dahl 1971; Przeworski and Limongi 1997; Vanhanen 1990). This intermediate strategy has some compelling advantages. The much larger n than single-country case studies enables us to examine some relationships (e.g., between level of development and regime type) in a more systematic manner than a single case would allow. At the same time, the n is sufficiently small that an analyst can make somewhat informed judgments about all nineteen cases. Moreover, the number of official languages is small enough (Spanish and Portuguese except for Haiti) that an analyst can be informed by the academic debates in the countries in question. Holding constant some of the major factors that affect prospects for democracy, because these cases share some common features, reduces the normal disadvantages of a medium-sized n (too many variables and too few cases) compared to a larger one.

One final advantage of the intermediate n strategy has to do with the fact that this particular set of countries is found in a region of the world with distinctive regional dynamics and strong influences from one country to the next. Latin America has had waves of democracy, and these waves have both been influenced by and significantly shaped the global waves that Huntington (1991) analyzed. However, the interesting contrasts between democratic survivability in Latin America and at a global level suggest that regions are an important unit of analysis.

Thematically, the closest studies to this one are Przeworski et al.

(1996) and Przeworski and Limongi (1997). These works deal with a much larger set of countries—the great majority of countries in the contemporary world. While following some of the methodologies used by Przeworski and his collaborators, this chapter delves more into the specifics of one region. It also focuses more on changing values and changes in the international system in explaining democratic survivability. Finally, many of the substantive results for Latin America diverge from the findings that Przeworski et al. report for their broader set of countries.

Regime Classification

I classified governments as democratic, semidemocratic, or authoritarian for the period from 1940 until 1997. To be classified as democratic, a government must meet four criteria: (1) the president and legislature are chosen in open and fair competitive elections;[1] (2) these elected authorities have the real governing power, as opposed to a situation in which elected officials are overshadowed by the military or by a nonelected shadow-figure; (3) civil liberties are respected; and (4) the franchise includes the sizable majority of the adult population.[2] For the 1940s, less stringent criteria for the inclusiveness of the franchise are warranted. During this period, a government could be democratic even if women or the illiterate were not yet enfranchised. I included Chile as democratic despite the exclusion of the illiterate until 1970 because this exclusion probably did not appreciably alter electoral outcomes. The notion and practice of democracy are somewhat historically contingent, and imposing the participatory standards of today on the 1940s would not be fully appropriate. This is not, of course, to condone the exclusion of women or those not fortunate enough to read or write.

A semidemocratic government or restricted democracy refers to a civilian government elected under reasonably fair conditions, but with significant restrictions in participation, competition, and/or the observance of civil liberties. An authoritarian regime has little effective political competition. Most authoritarian regimes also impose restrictions on political participation and civil liberties.

This analysis focuses on nineteen Latin American countries. I excluded the English-speaking countries of the Caribbean, Surinam, and Belize in order to focus on countries that have been independent for a longer time than these. In addition, several scholars have argued that British colonization has a positive independent effect on the likelihood that a country will be democratic (Domínguez 1993; Weiner 1987;

Bollen and Jackman 1985). Restricting the analysis to countries of Latin heritage eliminated the need to control for differences in colonial background. I excluded Cuba because of difficulties in obtaining GNP per capita data comparable with that for the other countries.[3]

Table 1 indicates the coding of the nineteen countries from 1940–97. A wide array of sources was useful in making decisions about how to categorize regimes. Many cases are consensual, but others involve complex borderline judgments, reflecting the hybrid (mixed authoritarian and democratic) nature of several Latin American political regimes.

Figure 1 shows the number of democratic, semidemocratic, and authoritarian governments in Latin America for every year between 1940 and 1996. To avoid having to get exact months or dates of regime changes, I treated the year of a regime transition as belonging to the new regime. Thus, 1973 (the year of the military coups) counts as part of the authoritarian period for Chile and Uruguay. In a few cases, there were two regime transitions in the same year. For example, in the Dominican Republic, a short lived democratic government took office in early 1963 but fell prey to a coup later that year. I have coded such cases as belonging half to one category and half to the other.

The increase in the number of democracies since 1978 is dramatic, and the demise of authoritarianism even more so. The magnitude of this change is striking even to those who are familiar with the evolution of political regimes in Latin America. In 1940, only one of these nineteen countries (Chile) was a democracy, and only four others (Colombia, Costa Rica, Ecuador, and Peru) were semidemocratic. This situation improved slightly as the later phases of World War II gave rise to a brief period of political liberalization and democratization in several countries. In 1942, Uruguay reestablished democracy, with democratic experiments following in Guatemala (1944–54), Venezuela (1945–48), and Costa Rica (1949–present). Argentina and Brazil shifted from the authoritarian to the semidemocratic camp in 1946.

But the progress of democratization proved ephemeral. As the cold war set in, the U.S. government and militaries, oligarchies, and conservatives in Latin America proved intolerant of progressive-leaning reformist regimes. For the U.S. during the cold war, national security interests usually took precedence over democracy (Packenham 1973); much the same was true for conservatives in Latin America. Democracy broke down in Venezuela in 1948 and in Guatemala in 1954. It quickly eroded in Argentina as Juan Perón (1946–55) became the first democratically elected leader of an authoritarian regime in the twentieth century. The number of authoritarian regimes, which had decreased from 14 in 1940–41 to 10 by 1946–47, increased back to 13 by 1951. After the 1954 coup

Scott Mainwaring

TABLE 1
Classification of Latin American Governments, 1940–97

D = democratic
S = semidemocratic
A = authoritarian

Argentina	1930–46	A		Guatemala	1839–1944	A
	1946–51	S			1944–54	D
	1951–58	A			1954–85	A
	1958–61	S			1986–97	S
	1962–63	A		Haiti	1815–1991	A
	1963–66	S			1991	S
	1966–73	A			1991–97	A
	1973–76	D		Honduras	1838–1957	A
	1976–83	A			1957–63	S
	1983–97	D			1963–81	A
Bolivia	1825–1952	A			1982–97	S
	1952–64	S		Mexico	1821–1988	A
	1964–82	A			1988–97	S
	1983–97	D		Nicaragua	1838–84	A
Brazil	1822–1945	A			1984–97	S
	1946–64	S		Panama	1903–56	A
	1964–85	A			1956–68	S
	1985–97	D			1968–89	A
Chile	1932–73	D			1990–94	S
	1973–90	A			1994–97	D
	1990–97	D		Paraguay	1918–89	A
Colombia	1936–49	S			1989–97	S
	1949–57	A		Peru	1939–48	S
	1958–74	S			1948–56	A
	1974–90	D			1956–62	S
	1990–97	S			1962–63	A
Costa Rica	1918–49	S			1963–68	D
	1949–97	D			1968–80	A
Dominican Rep.	1930–62	A			1980–90	D
	1963	D			1990–92	D
	1963–78	A			1992–94	A
	1978–94	D			1995–97	S
	1994–97	S		Uruguay	1933–42	A
Ecuador	1940–44	S			1942–73	D
	1944–48	A			1973–84	A
	1948–61	S			1985–97	D
	1961–68	A		Venezuela	1830–1945	A
	1968–70	A			1945–48	D
	1970–79	A			1948–58	A
	1979–97	D			1958–97	D
El Salvador	1931–84	A				
	1984–92	S				
	1992–97	D				

Sources: Among others, Diamond, Linz, and Lipset (1989); Gasiorowski (1993); Mainwaring and Scully (1995); Rueschemeyer et al. (1992); Hartlyn and Valenzuela (1994); and some individual country studies. For the post-1972 period, I also consulted the annual publications of Freedom House.

FIGURE 1
Democratic Governments in Latin America, 1940–96
Number of Governments in Each Category

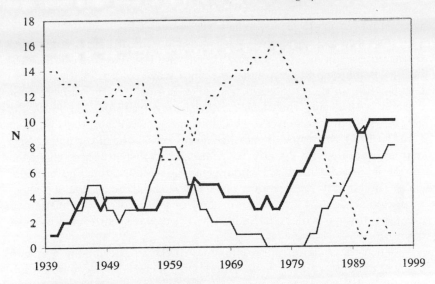

- - - - - Authoritarian ——— Semidemocratic ——— Democratic
Sources: Table 1 and Freedom House, *Freedom in the World*, various years.

in Guatemala, only Chile, Costa Rica, and Uruguay remained in the democratic camp, and only three others (Bolivia, Brazil, and Ecuador) were semidemocratic.

In 1958, a new wave of democratization began as Venezuela switched back to the democratic camp. That same year, Colombia established a semidemocratic regime (political competition was restricted until 1974). Argentina also instituted a semidemocratic government in 1958; the Frondizi government was elected in competitive elections with broad participation; civil liberties were respected, but the Peronist party—Argentina's largest—was proscribed.

As had occurred with the brief wave of democratization in 1942–48, this one proved fragile. In the aftermath of the Cuban revolution, politics became deeply polarized in much of the region. The 1960s and 1970s witnessed a succession of democratic breakdowns. Military coups toppled elected governments in Peru in 1962, Bolivia and Brazil in 1964, Argentina in 1966, and Peru again in 1968. The two oldest democracies in the region, Chile and Uruguay, succumbed to breakdowns in 1973, leading to highly repressive military regimes. Another coup occurred in Argentina in 1976, spawning an even more brutal military dictatorship.[4]

By 1977, only Colombia, Costa Rica, and Venezuela were democratic. The other 16 countries were ruled by patently authoritarian governments. In the post-1940 period, this was the zenith of authoritarianism in Latin America. Paradoxically, it was also toward the beginning of what Huntington (1991) has called "democracy's third wave."[5]

As the world's attention was focused on the atrocities committed by the generals in Argentina, Brazil, Chile, and Uruguay and on the revolutionary upheaval in Nicaragua, the third wave of democratization began in 1978 in the Dominican Republic, a small, comparatively poor country with deeply entrenched authoritarian traditions. In 1979, the generals relinquished power in Ecuador, and one year later they did so in Peru. By 1980, the region already had more democratic governments (six) than ever before, and the number continued to increase throughout the rest of the decade. In 1981, Honduras inaugurated a civilian government chosen in fair and free elections. Thus, whereas the third wave of democratization at a global level began in some of the wealthiest nondemocracies (Spain in particular), in Latin America it was spearheaded by poor countries.

Then the cycle of military regimes in the southern cone began to exhaust itself, starting with the Argentine generals' bellicose misadventure in the Falklands/Malvinas in 1982, which paved the way to a transition to democracy the following year. The military regime in Bolivia eroded, giving way to democratic elections in 1982. Democratic governments took office in Uruguay in 1984 and Brazil in 1985, replacing military regimes in both countries.

Several countries experienced their first-ever taste of democracy in the mid and late 1980s. Even the poor Central American countries savaged by civil wars in the early 1980s enjoyed more open elections than before. Civilian presidents elected in reasonably fair circumstances took office in Guatemala in 1986 and El Salvador in 1985. They did not end the atrocities of the civil wars until the 1990s, but they gradually curbed the scale of human rights violations. In view of the relentless history of authoritarianism in both countries and the brutal repression and bloody civil wars of the 1980s, this accomplishment is significant. The U.S. invasion of Panama in 1989 deposed dictator Manuel Noriega and initiated a long process of establishing democracy. A 1989 coup ousted long-time dictator Alfredo Stroessner in Paraguay and began a process of liberalization and democratization. The 1990 election in Nicaragua, resulting in the Sandinistas' defeat, paved the way to peace negotiations in El Salvador and Guatemala. By 1990, the only patently authoritarian government in the region was the Haitian. By 1994, no authoritarian governments except Cuba and Haiti remained. The shift away from authoritarianism has been dramatic.

When the unexpected comes to pass, analysts easily forget how unlikely such an outcome seemed. So it is with democratization in Latin America. Today, we take it for granted that competitive political regimes have survived, but when these transitions to democracy or semidemocracy took place, many analysts saw little chance that democracy would endure. Enumerating factors that worked against democracy in Latin America, Wiarda (1986: 341) argued that "(T)he prospects for democracy are hardly encouraging. . . . None of these economic conditions is encouraging to the cause of democracy in Latin America, nor do they help established democracies in the region to survive. . . . Given rising expectations, competition for control of the fewer resources that do exist becomes intense, polarized, and violent. . . . Liberal-pluralist democracy is difficult to sustain under such conditions." Many analysts from diverse political and theoretical orientations concurred.

It is no great surprise that democracy has survived in Uruguay since 1984 or in Chile since 1990. Both countries had fairly strong democratic traditions prior to the 1973 breakdowns, and Chile's economy was in good condition when General Pinochet relinquished the presidential sash. However, these two countries are the exception rather than the norm. Elsewhere, democracy (or even restricted democracy) faced daunting challenges: weak democratic traditions and institutions, egregious social disparities, and parlous economic conditions.

Bolivia's democratic stability of the post-1982 period epitomizes the surprises. Prior to 1982, Bolivia had been plagued by a long history of instability and chronic coups. The country had precarious democratic traditions, having never experienced democracy prior to 1982, and a semidemocratic regime only for a twelve-year interregnum (1952–64) and for several months during the chaotic 1978–82 period. Hernán Siles Suazo, the new democratic president (1982–85), inherited disastrous economic conditions and proceeded to make them worse through mismanagement. Inflation hit 8171 percent in 1985, and per capita income slid downward throughout most of the first decade of democracy. This economic decline exacerbated poverty in one of the poorest countries in Latin America. Per capita income in 1982 stood at 759 dollars (in 1980 dollars), less than one-fourth the level of the region's wealthiest countries (Argentina and Venezuela). Bolivia has one of the most ethnically divided societies in Latin America, with an indigenous majority that for centuries has been exploited by a ladino (of white origin) minority. The country also had a long history of military coups. All of these conditions augured poorly for democracy.

The democratic regime tottered during its first years. By the mid-1990s, however, democracy appeared to be remarkably stable. Free and fair elections occurred in 1982, 1985, 1989, 1993, and 1997, resulting in alternations in power in 1985 and 1993. The Bolivian congress became accustomed to institutionalizing power-sharing arrangements. The Bolivian case is a remarkable example of democracy surviving despite formidable structural and economic circumstances (Mayorga 1997). It is, however, not the only case of a democracy surviving in the face of daunting challenges.

Most Latin American countries experienced their longest period ever of democracy in the 1980s and 1990s. Table 2 shows the longest period of full democracy that Latin American countries have enjoyed. Only three countries—Chile (1932–73), Guatemala (1944–54), and Uruguay (1942–73)—previously enjoyed longer periods of continuous democracy than they have in the post-1978 period.

That democracy has survived despite poor social and economic results makes this achievement all the more noteworthy. Democratization in Latin America roughly coincided with the debt crisis and later with a transition from state-led development to market-oriented policies. Both factors led to short-term disruptions and imposed high costs on national economies. For the region as a whole, per capita income was flat in the long period between 1980 and 1995. In 1983, few analysts would have predicted that democracy in Bolivia, Argentina, and Brazil would be able to withstand annual inflation rates that reached 8171%, 4923%, and 2489%, respectively, or that Bolivia and Ecuador, with their long histories of political instability, would witness a succession of democratically elected presidents. Similarly, the gruesome repression associated with El Salvador's "reactionary despotism" (Baloyra 1983) in the early 1980s gradually gave rise to a succession of semidemocratic governments by the 1990s.

Democracy as a Continuous Variable

So far I have treated democracy as a trichotomous variable, but it can usefully be thought of as a continuous variable (Bollen 1980; Coppedge and Reineke 1990; Dahl 1971; Hadenius 1992; Vanhanen 1990). There are two advantages to analyzing democracy as a continuous variable. Conceptually, this option is sensible because countries can be more or less democratic within a wide range that cannot be fully captured by a trichotomous classification. In addition, continuous measures allow for more satisfactory treatment of some quantitative relationships.

The question is how to operationalize a continuous measure of democracy. So far, there have been three main approaches to this problem: (1) scholars who have developed scores based on data that are readily

TABLE 2

Longest Period of Uninterrupted Democracy by Country

COUNTRY	YEARS
Argentina	1983–98
Bolivia	1982–98
Brazil	1985–98
Chile	1932–73
Colombia	1974–90
Costa Rica	1949–98
Dominican Republic	1978–94
Ecuador	1979–98
El Salvador	1992–98
Guatemala	1944–54
Haiti	*
Honduras	*
Mexico	*
Nicaragua	*
Panama	1994–98
Paraguay	*
Peru	1980–90
Uruguay	1942–73
Venezuela	1958–98

* No period of full democracy has taken place.

available, such that it is relatively simple to give each country a score for a longer time-period; (2) scholars who have constructed more sophisticated measures, but based on data that are not readily available for a longer time; and (3) Freedom House scores.

Vanhanen (1990) is an example of the first approach. Following Dahl (1971), he argued that democracy has two dimensions: competition and participation. He measured competition by subtracting the largest parties' share of the vote from 100, and participation by taking the percentage of the total population that voted. He then multiplied these two indicators to derive an index of democracy. This measure has serious drawbacks, however. The measure of competition is flawed; it is too highly correlated with party-system fragmentation. A system in which the largest party wins 50% is not necessarily less democratic than one in which the largest wins 35%. The measure of participation depends too much on the age structure of the society; it discriminates against countries with youthful populations in which a large share of the population have not yet reached voting age. Moreover, for democracy, the crucial point is that legal barriers and human rights conditions be such that the adult population *can* participate, not that it actually does so. Higher rates of electoral participation may reflect compulsory voting laws rather than a more participatory environment. Most important, Vanhanen's measure fails to incorporate any assessment of civil liberties and political rights.

Coppedge and Reineke (1990) and Hadenius (1992: 36–71) constructed multidimensional, sophisticated measures of democracy,[6] but both measures require substantial qualitative information that is not readily available for a longer time-span. Not coincidentally, both restricted their measure to a single year (1985 for Coppedge and Reineke, 1988 for Hadenius).

Given these shortcomings of the easily operationalized measures of democracy and the difficulties of obtaining data to reproduce Coppedge and Reineke or Hadenius for long periods, I used Freedom House scores for 1972–96. Beginning with 1972, for each year, Freedom House has ranked all independent countries from 1 (the best score) to 7 on civil liberties and on political rights. These scores implicitly incorporate the three dimensions of democracy: free and fair competition, broad participation, and civil liberties and human rights. For 1985, Freedom House scores correlated very highly (.934 to .938) with Coppedge and Reineke's polyarchy scale (Coppedge 1997: 180). Given this high correlation to a sophisticated measure of democracy, plus their ready availability, Freedom House scores represent a reasonable measure. The advantages of a measure that can be readily obtained and used for a substantial period of time are compelling. This explains the growing use of Freedom House scores as a measure of democracy (e.g., Diamond 1996).

The combined scores for political rights and civil liberties create a scale ranging from 2 to 14. The Freedom House combined scores correlate strongly with my evaluations of which governments are democratic. Scores from 2 through 5 generally correspond to my classification of democracies. A score of 7 usually falls in my category of semidemocratic governments, and scores from 9 through 14 usually correspond to what I classified as authoritarian governments. Scores of 6 (democratic or semidemocratic) and 8 (semidemocratic or authoritarian) are borderline, such that they easily correspond to either category. For the 1972–96 period, of 475 cases (19 countries times 25 years), 68 Freedom House scores (14.3%) diverged from my assessment.[7] Most of the divergences resulted from cases I coded as authoritarian but that had Freedom House scores of 7 or better (e.g., Brazil 1979–84, Dominican Republic 1972–77, El

Salvador 1972–77, Guatemala 1972–76, Honduras 1980–81, Mexico 1973–84).

Freedom House scores have two shortcomings as a measure of democracy. First, they seem harsher on leftist governments than others. For example, in 1984, El Salvador was more repressive than Nicaragua, and it is not clear that the Salvadoran elections were fairer than those held in Nicaragua. Yet Freedom House scores indicate a markedly more democratic government in El Salvador (a combined score of 6) than in Nicaragua (a combined score of 10). Second, some scores of the 1970s and early 1980s are too lenient compared to scores in the 1990s. For example, Mexico received a score of 6 to 8 throughout the authoritarian 1970s and 1980s. Colombia, the Dominican Republic, El Salvador, and Guatemala received lower scores than they should have in the 1970s, dipping as low as 4 for Colombia (1972–74) when competition was quite restricted, 5 for the Dominican Republic (1972–73) during an authoritarian regime, 5 for El Salvador (1972–75) during an authoritarian regime, and 4 for Guatemala (1973) during an authoritarian period. Freedom House scoring became more stringent in the 1990s; thus, the same score in the 1990s often reflects more democratic conditions than it would have in the 1970s or early 1980s. For example, Mexico's political system was clearly more democratic in 1990 than it had been a decade earlier, but Freedom House's 1980 combined score (7) is slightly better than the 1990 score (8). Political rights improved in Brazil between 1984, when the military was still in power, and the early 1990s, but Freedom House scores indicate the opposite. The human rights situation improved substantially in El Salvador between the grizzly mid-1980s and the mid-1990s, but Freedom House scores reflect no change. By 1994, the insurrectional FMLN, the object of brutal repression throughout the 1980s, felt secure enough to participate in the electoral process.

For present purposes, neither of these shortcomings constitutes an overwhelming problem. Nicaragua (1979–90) and Chile (but just for 1972) are the only leftist governments in the sample, so discrepancies in how they were evaluated do not affect the overall conclusions. The main use here of Freedom House scores is not comparison over time (though I briefly undertake this comparison), but rather comparison across countries: are more economically developed countries more democratic? For this purpose, as long as Freedom House judgments have remained consistent across countries, if standards have become more stringent over time, it matters less.

Freedom House scores indicate a marked improvement in political rights and civil liberties in the region, from 8.7 in 1977 to an all time best of 5.7 in 1989. These means understate the actual improvement because the scores have been more stringent in recent years than was the case in the 1970s through the mid-1980s.

LIMITS TO DEMOCRATIZATION

Although the transformation in Latin American politics is profound, the process of democratization has had some serious shortcomings. These shortcomings have been analyzed in detail elsewhere, so a brief discussion will suffice here.

The powerful tide against authoritarianism has not ushered in an equally powerful trend in favor of unrestricted democracy. Many of the elected governments in the region are better described as semidemocratic than democratic. The 1990s have witnessed some erosions from democracy to semidemocracy: Colombia, the Dominican Republic, and Peru (before Fujimori's palace coup in 1992).

As Schmitter and Karl (1993) have argued, democracy revolves around the notion of citizenship, that is, on the right and ability of the people to participate effectively in politics. People must be able to make somewhat informed choices when they go to the ballot box, and other forms of participation must not be formally blocked or restricted because of widespread fear. For some marginalized groups, effective citizenship is still an elusive goal in Latin America.

This problem of uneven citizenship varies across countries and regions (Diamond 1996; Karl 1995; O'Donnell 1993, 1998). In the countries with histories of virtually uninterrupted authoritarianism until the 1980s, large sectors of the population do not enjoy full citizenship. The indigenous, black, and rural populations now enjoy the formal rights of citizenship throughout Latin America, but in practice these groups are frequently marginalized.

Related to this uneven fulfillment of the promise of citizenship is one of weak democratic institutions and limited rule of law in many countries (O'Donnell 1998). Weak judiciaries and personalistic control prevail in the backwards regions of virtually every country in the region (Hagopian 1996b). Party systems are weak in much of the region and, as a result, accountability is limited and personalism sometimes unchecked (Mainwaring and Scully 1995). Democracy has endured with weak institutions and fettered citizenship, but it has had serious shortcomings.

In several countries, fear remains an important ingredient in politics. In most of the countries ravaged by civil wars—Peru in the second half of the 1980s, Guatemala, El Salvador until the signing of the peace agreement in 1992, Colombia in the 1990s—those suspected of leftist sympathies were subjected to harassment, torture, and death. In these countries, the revolutionary left also used fear as a tool, sometimes forcefully impressing citizens into their side of the fray. Under these conditions, political expression and participation were severely hampered. Even when elections were held and votes were counted fairly, the left could not participate, and the circumstances surrounding the elections diminished their democratic credentials. The signing of peace accords in El Salvador, Guatemala, and Nicaragua has not fully resolved this problem. The military is not entirely under civilian control in many countries, including Chile, which has some of the region's strongest democratic traditions and institutions.

These limitations to democratic practice are so significant that one can properly question whether the glass is half full or half empty. Both ways of looking at the problem have merit. Latin America is more democratic than ever before, but there are serious problems of democratic practice in most countries in the region. However, even if the glass is half empty, the region is still more democratic than ever. The biggest surprise is not that democracy has had serious shortcomings, but that it has survived. Democracy has not fully triumphed, but dictatorship is much less pervasive than ever before. In fact, full-fledged dictatorship has virtually disappeared for the time being.

MODERNIZATION AND DEMOCRACY

The second major purpose of this chapter is to account for the increase in democracy and the demise of authoritarianism in Latin America. The Latin American experience is not only interesting and important in and of itself, it can also illuminate the broad issue of why democracy exists in some countries but not others.

Many factors including religion (Huntington 1991: 72–85), British colonial experience (Weiner 1987; Domínguez 1993) and degree of ethnic fragmentation (Horowitz 1985; Lijphart 1977) affect democratic survivability. One advantage of focusing on Latin America is that it holds constant several such factors. All of the countries in Latin America are predominantly Catholic and have been so for centuries, so differences in the dominant religious preference do not account for why democracy has flourished in some countries more than others. With rare exceptions, Latin American democracies have had presidential systems, so presidentialism does not explain regime differences (i.e., democratic or not) across countries or across time. All but Haiti have Iberian colonial experience, so colonial background (understood in this very broad sense) does not account for differences in regime.[8] With the exception of Panama, which gained independence in 1903, the countries under consideration here became independent in the first half of the nineteenth century, so they all have been independent for roughly similar lengths of time. These commonalties reduce the number of independent variables and thus facilitate the explanatory process.

In explaining the growth of democracy in the period since 1978, idiosyncratic factors come into play in every country, but there nevertheless has been a region-wide trend toward democracy. Therefore, rather than accounting for the region-wide trend on the basis of developments in individual countries, I seek a more general explanation. I examine variance across countries, but within the framework of arguing that there has been a region-wide trend with some common factors driving it.

One possible explanation for the greater prevalence of democracy since 1978 is that the brisk pace of modernization in the decades preceding, roughly, 1980 helped promote democratization. Between 1950 and 1980, the pace of modernization in Latin America was spectacular. Table 3 shows that economic growth in most of the nineteen Latin American countries was vigorous from 1950 until 1979. Per capita income more than tripled in the region's largest and most populous country, Brazil. Partially because of Brazil's phenomenal growth, per capita income for the region as a whole increased 116 percent. Per capita income more than doubled in Costa Rica, the Dominican Republic, Ecuador, Mexico, Panama, and Venezuela. Only in a few small countries did per capita growth increase less than 50 percent in these three decades.

The Literature

Many analysts (Bollen 1980; Bollen and Jackman 1985; Coppedge 1997; Coulter 1975; Dahl 1971: 62–80; Diamond 1992; Lipset 1960; Lipset et al. 1993; Przeworski et al. 1996; Przeworski and Limongi 1997; Rueschemeyer et al. 1992) have shown a strong correlation between per capita income and the existence of democracy at a global level. However, Coulter (1975: 69–84) and Collier (1975) observed little correlation between democracy and per capita income in Latin America, even while acknowledging the strong correlation at the global level.[9] Moreover, as Dahl (1971), May (1973), Przeworski et al. (1996), and others have reported, even at the global level the association between level of development and democracy is not linear. Some scholars (Arat 1988) have even questioned the fundamental premise of the modernization school, suggesting that the relationship between modernization and democracy is

TABLE 3

Per Capita Income, Latin America, 1950–79
constant 1970 dollars

	1950	1960	1970	1979	% CHANGE 1950–79
Argentina	817	912	1,208	1,405	72.0
Bolivia	231	192	296	362	56.7
Brazil	233	332	450	773	231.8
Chile	576	679	850	937	62.7
Colombia	370	425	508	728	96.8
Costa Rica	347	474	656	895	157.9
Dominican Republic	230	294	351	483	110.0
Ecuador	247	296	355	532	115.4
El Salvador	265	319	397	436	64.5
Guatemala	293	322	417	525	79.2
Haiti	119	117	99	126	5.9
Honduras	232	250	289	294	26.7
Mexico	486	627	893	1,066	119.3
Nicaragua	215	271	394	300	39.5
Panama	459	549	868	932	103.1
Paraguay	305	293	353	532	74.4
Peru	313	415	525	561	79.2
Uruguay	851	875	905	1,142	34.2
Venezuela	653	914	1,180	1,380	111.3
Latin America	396	490	648	857	116.4

Source: *Statistical Abstract of Latin America, 1983* vol. 22, pp. 282–83.

weak or spurious. Therefore, it is not obvious *ex-ante* whether a higher level of development contributed to democratization in Latin America. Before we reach that conclusion, we need more evidence than the global correlations and the strong growth performance of the 1950–80 period. We can examine the relationship between modernization and democracy both by cross-sectional analysis (i.e., by looking at whether the wealthier countries have been more likely to be democracies) and by longitudinal analysis (i.e. by verifying whether modernization over time fostered a larger number of democracies).

Per capita income is a reasonable proxy for modernization. Literacy may be a better univariate surrogate for modernization than GDP per capita, but for Latin America literacy figures are not available on an

TABLE 4

Likelihood of Democracy by Income Category,
19 Latin American Countries, 1945–96

GDP/CAPITA (1980 U.S. DOLLARS)	REGIME-YEARS (N)	% REGIME-YEARS DEMOCRATIC	% REGIME-YEARS SEMIDEMOCRATIC	% REGIME-YEARS AUTHORITARIAN
0 to 399	58	0.0	0.0	100.0
400 to 799	340	10.9	30.6	58.5
800 to 1,199	196	23.0	21.4	55.6
1,200 to 1,799	176	58.0	13.1	29.0
1,800 to 2,399	91	40.7	6.6	52.7
2,400 to 3,199	53	22.6	30.2	47.2
3,200 or more	74	77.0	0.0	23.0
Total (%)	988	290 (29.4)	191 (19.3)	507 (51.3)

annual basis. In any case, GDP per capita correlates fairly highly with literacy in Latin America. In 1950, the correlation between literacy and per capita income for the nineteen countries was .605; in 1980, it was .552.

Cross-Sectional Analysis

If a higher level of development fostered democratization, then one would expect that the countries with higher per capita incomes would be more likely to be democracies. Table 4 presents data to verify whether this is the case. Following Przeworski et al. (1996) and Przeworski and Limongi (1997), each country is coded for every year; thus, there are 988 cases (52 years x 19 countries).

At the low- and high-income categories, the data are consistent with the argument that wealthier countries are more likely and poor countries are less likely to be democracies. The likelihood that a very poor country would be democratic is zero; the poorest countries are overwhelmingly authoritarian. And the other low-income categories ($400 to $799 and $800 to $1,199) are also unlikely to be democracies. The significance of the lowest income category is questionable because of the 58 cases; Haiti alone counts for 52 and thus could skew results. But the data for both the $400 to $799 and $800 to $1,199 categories come from 13 different countries, and no single country accounts for a dominant share of the cases.

In the highest income category, the likelihood of democracy peaks at 77.0%. But the relationship between income category and democracy is far from linear. The likelihood of democracy increases to 58.0% in the $1,200–$1,799 per capita range, but then plummets to 40.7% in the $1,800–$2,399 category and to 22.6% in the $2400–$3199 category. Five different countries were not democratic in the fairly high $2400–$3199 income level: Argentina (1946–51, 1953–57, 1958–61, 1962, 1963–65, and 1966), Chile (1981 and 1989), Mexico (1980–86, 1992–94, 1996), Uruguay (1980–81), and Venezuela (1948–53). Similarly, the high share of nondemocratic regimes in the $1,800–$2,399 category is a result of six different countries: Argentina (1945 and 1952), Brazil (1978–83), Chile (1973–80, 1982–88), Mexico (1970–79), Panama (1982–83, 1985–87, 1993), and Uruguay (1974–79, 1982–84). Thus, the high proportion of nondemocratic cases in these income categories cannot be attributed to a single or even a few outliers, as could conceivably occur with time-series cross-section data.

Nor is the seeming anomaly of a high proportion of democracies in the $1,200–$1,799 per capita category a result of one or two outliers. Chile (1945–62), Colombia (1978–81, 1983–90), Costa Rica (1970–96), the Dominican Republic (1981, 1993–94), Ecuador (1979–96), Panama (1995), Paraguay (1993–96), Peru (1981), and Uruguay (1945–53, 1958–72) all qualified. The Latin American pattern diverges from what Przeworski and Limongi (1997) found at a global level; they showed an almost linear relationship between per capita income and likelihood of democracy. In Latin America, this pattern is far from linear.

Another way of examining the relationship between per capita income and democracy is that the democracies should be more likely to have higher per capita incomes if modernization analysis is correct. To verify whether this has been the case, figure 2 indicates the mean country level per capita income of the democracies, semidemocracies, and authoritarian governments for every year from 1940 to 1996. To illustrate how the figure should be read, consider the data for 1980. The six democracies (Colombia, Costa Rica, the Dominican Republic, Ecuador, Peru, and Venezuela) had per capita incomes in 1980 dollars of $1,207, $1,552, $1,130, $1,415, $1,190, and $3,377, respectively. The mean of these six figures is $1,645. Since this mean is not weighted by population size, it does not constitute a mean income for the individuals living in those countries.

A change in any category from one year to the next can result from

FIGURE 2
Mean Country Per Capita GDP by Regime Type by Year
(1980 Dollars)

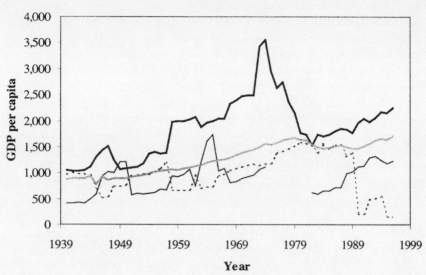

- - - - - Authoritarian ———— Semidemocratic ———— Democratic ———— Latin America

Sources:

1940–79:	Statistical Abstract of Latin America, vol. 22, 1983
1980–82, 84:	Statistical Yearbook for Latin America 1991
1983:	Statistical Yearbook for Latin America, 1987
1985–92:	Statistical Yearbook for Latin America, 1993
1993–95:	Statistical Yearbook for Latin America, 1996
1996:	Statistical Yearbook for Latin America, 1997

All figures are 1980 dollars. Figures for 1940–79 were originally in 1970 dollars and have been corrected by an inflator figure for each country, equal to that country's 1970 per capita GNP in 1980 dollars divided by that country's 1970 per capita GNP in 1970 dollars. An analogous procedure was applied to 1993–96 figures originally expressed in 1990 dollars.

changes in the countries that are in that category and/or from changes in the per capita income of the countries. A sharp increase from one year to the next (say, from $715 in 1987 to $986 in 1988 for the semidemocratic regimes) does not primarily reflect high growth rates in certain countries, but rather Mexico's shift from the authoritarian to the semidemocratic category.

As expected, the mean per capita income for the democratic countries is almost always higher than the mean for the authoritarian and semidemocratic countries. This result is consistent with the widespread finding that countries with higher per capita incomes are more likely to be democracies. Only in one of fifty-seven years (1982) did the mean for the countries ruled by authoritarian regimes exceed that of the democracies, and the mean for the semidemocratic countries was always lower. However, the mean per capita income of the democracies has not always been significantly higher than that of the authoritarian governments. In fact, the gap has been narrow during some periods.

In the mid-1970s, when democracy was the exception, higher per capita income was favorable to democracy, but this was partially because Venezuela, with the region's highest per capita income, was one of only three democracies. In the late 1970s and early 1980s, some comparatively poor countries (Bolivia, the Dominican Republic, Ecuador, and Peru) initiated the series of transitions to democracy. From 1976 to 1983, most of the region's wealthiest countries (Argentina, Brazil, Chile, Mexico, Uruguay) remained bogged down in authoritarian rule. At the same time, after 1979, several countries with per capita incomes below the regional average were democratic. Honduras, Bolivia, Peru, and the Dominican Republic were democratic or semidemocratic; in 1985, they had the second, third, seventh, and eighth lowest per capita GDPs in the region. As a result, from 1979 to 1986, per capita income in the democracies was never more than 24% higher than in the authoritarian regimes. If one eliminated Haiti, the region's poorest country and a persistently authoritarian one until 1991, in the early and mid-1980s the authoritarian countries usually had a higher per capita income than the democracies.

Argentina in 1983, Uruguay in 1985, and Brazil in 1985 underwent transitions to democracy. Because these three countries had per capita incomes among the six highest in the region in 1983–85, these transitions substantially increased the mean income of the democracies and reduced that of the authoritarian regimes. By the end of the 1980s, a large gap opened between the democratic and authoritarian groups. By then, all of the region's more developed countries were democratic or semidemocratic. Some poor countries (Bolivia, the Dominican Republic, and Peru until 1990) remained in the democratic category, but all of the authoritarian countries except Mexico were poor.

To see whether using a continuous measure of democracy rather than the simple democratic/semidemocratic/authoritarian distinction would change these results, the correlations between Freedom House scores and per capita income for 1972–96 are relevant. If modernization theory applied to Latin America, one would expect a significant negative

TABLE 5

Correlation Between Freedom House Scores and Per Capita Income

1972	−.25	1984	−.35*
1973	−.25	1985	−.32*
1974	−.25	1986	−.32*
1975	−.27	1987	−.35*
1976	−.15	1988	−.39*
1977	−.14	1989	−.44**
1978	−.17	1990	−.47**
1979	−.10	1991	−.52**
1980	−.17	1992	−.47**
1981	−.22	1993	−.40**
1982	−.08	1994	−.51**
1983	−.30	1995	−.50**
		1996	−.51**

*Significant at .10
** Significant at .05

correlation between Freedom House scores and per capita income since a high Freedom House score indicates less democracy. Table 5 shows the results.

The information in table 5 reinforces the analysis associated with table 4 and figure 2. During the late 1970s and early 1980s, the correlations between Freedom House scores and per capita income were weak, dipping as low as −.08 in 1982. The correlation remained constantly low, at or below −.30 until 1984. By 1989, the correlation had become more robust (−.51). The correlation remained moderately strong through 1996. Even the highest correlation (−.52 in 1991), however, is lower than what Coulter (1975: 22) reported for 85 countries; he obtained a powerful correlation of .67 between per capita income and his measure of liberal democracy. The correlations between per capita income and Freedom House scores in Latin America between 1972 and 1996 are usually much lower.

The Freedom House scores reinforce two conclusions. First, the democracies have generally been wealthier than the nondemocracies.[10] Second, compared to the robust correlations between democracy and higher per capita income reported by other scholars for the global level, for Latin America between 1972 and 1996 this correlation ranged from weak to moderate. If there were a linear relationship between modernization and democracy, one would expect the democratic countries to be among the most economically developed. For some periods, this holds true, but for others the pattern is mixed.

Comparativists working on the relationship between per capita income and democracy at a global level have avoided treating economic development as a force that would automatically produce democracy. The need for such caution is clear for Latin America. Along with Eastern Europe, it is one of two regions in the world where the correlation between higher living standards and democracy has been most tenuous (Collier 1975; Coulter 1975; Diamond 1992). Economic development did not act as a demiurge that automatically led to democracy.

If one expected a linear relationship between higher per capita income and democracy, Latin America would present three anomalies. First, several comparatively wealthy countries have had long periods of authoritarian rule. For much of the post-1950 period, Argentina stands out as a democratic underachiever in light of its high per capita income and quality of life. Throughout the entire 1940–83 period, Argentina had the highest or second highest per capita income in the region. Yet until 1983, the country oscillated between semidemocratic (1946–51, 1958–62, 1963–66) and patently authoritarian (1940–46, 1955–58, 1962–63, 1966–73, 1976–83) periods. Argentina's per capita income in 1950 was already double the 1979 income of several poor countries that underwent democratic transitions and remained mostly democratic in the 1980s. Mexico is also an outlier: authoritarian until 1988 (when it became semidemocratic) despite having one of the higher per capita incomes in the region. Similarly, Chile and Uruguay, with their comparatively high standards of living, should not have experienced democratic breakdowns in 1973.

The second anomaly is the fact that some poor countries have sustained democracy for a considerable time in the 1980s and 1990s. From the low level of development, one would not expect democracy or semidemocracy to survive in Bolivia, El Salvador, Honduras, or Nicaragua. Yet these countries have not experienced regime breakdowns. Nor would one expect poor countries such as the Dominican Republic, Ecuador, and Peru to be at the forefront of the wave of democratization that began in 1978.

If there were just a few anomalies in an overall discernible pattern, one could dismiss them as exceptions to the rule. In Latin America, however, there have been periods when the correlation between democracy and per capita income broke down. And even when the democracies had higher per capita incomes, the correlation is not overwhelming.

The final anomaly is that the country mean per capita income of the authoritarian regimes is frequently higher than that of the semidemocracies. In twenty-nine years, this was the case compared to twenty-one years when the semidemocratic countries had a higher per capita income. (In seven years, there were no semidemocratic regimes.) If the relationship between per capita income and democracy were linear, one would expect the semidemocratic countries in Latin America to usually be wealthier than the authoritarian ones.

Longitudinal Analysis

The discussion so far has compared across countries at a given moment in time. In addition, if the modernization argument applied in linear fashion, the number of democracies would increase as countries attained a higher level of development. Periods of economic growth would be followed by a burgeoning of democracy, and periods of substantial economic decline might lead to authoritarian regressions. The actual record is checkered. Declining standards of living in the 1980s prompted fewer authoritarian involutions than any of Latin America's previous waves of democratization. Conversely, the authoritarian involutions of the 1960s and 1970s occurred on the heels of the rapid growth of the 1950s and 1960s. If economic growth had a linear impact on democracy, then one would have expected more democracies in 1976 than in 1960. In fact, the opposite was the case; there were more democracies between 1958 and 1967 than in 1973–74 and 1976–77. Moreover, the incidence of patently authoritarian regimes was greater in the mid-1970s than in the period between 1958 and 1963. Yet the region as a whole had a substantially higher standard of living in the mid-1970s than it did in 1960.

To be sure, democratic breakdowns in Brazil in 1964, Argentina in 1976, and Chile and Uruguay in 1973 occurred at moments of economic problems (O'Donnell 1973). However, these problems should not obscure the overall growth performance of the 1950s and 1960s. The dominant viewpoint today is that economic problems were not the principal factor behind most of those earlier coups (Collier 1979; Santos 1986; Stepan 1971). Rather, political radicalization, the intransigence of some actors, and poor leadership were the key problems. Much worse economic performances in the 1980s than those of the 1960s and 1970s did not lead to regime breakdown.[11] Moreover, some breakdowns of democratic or semidemocratic regimes occurred during periods of economic expansion, as was the case in Argentina in 1966.

In sum, although economic development was a contributing factor, it does not fully account for Latin America's turn to democracy. The fact that the correlation between per capita income and democracy has been weak during lengthy periods suggests that modernization does not tell the whole story. Although economic growth in the decades prior to the third wave contributed to the likelihood of democratic longevity, polyarchy has survived in Latin America's poor and intermediate income countries alike, suggesting that modernization alone does not explain the democratic stability of the post-1978 period.[12] These observations do not constitute a wholesale dismissal of the modernization hypothesis. Until the 1980s, the region's poorest countries were extremely unlikely to be democratic. Yet for Latin America, changes in attitudes have been more important than structuralists have recognized.

STABILITY AND BREAKDOWN RATES OF DIFFERENT REGIMES AT DIFFERENT LEVELS OF DEVELOPMENT

In a recent pathbreaking work, Przeworski and Limongi (1997) argued that developed countries are more likely to be democracies because, once established, democracy in these countries is less vulnerable to breakdown. They show that the process of modernization per se does not explain this correlation. Does this argument apply to Latin America?

The simple answer is no (table 6). The Latin American experience runs counter to what one finds at a broader comparative level. Within the per capita income categories used in this chapter, democracy in Latin America has not been less vulnerable to breakdown and erosion at higher levels of development until one reaches the $3,200 per capita level.

The data initially appear to be consistent with O'Donnell's (1973) bureaucratic-authoritarian argument. O'Donnell argued that at a certain level of development in the 1960s and 1970s, modernization produced pressures against democracy, so one should expect, exactly as occurs, a dip in the likelihood of democracy as per capita income increases. Interestingly, in view of the fact that the data are consistent with O'Donnell's argument, most of the subsequent literature has disagreed with him.

A closer examination supports part of O'Donnell's argument but not its entirety. Democracy broke down virtually everywhere in Latin America in the 1960s and 1970s. The more developed countries were not particularly vulnerable to breakdown, so it is not clear whether modernization generated distinctive pressures that led to breakdown. That may have been the case in some countries, but it does not tell the story for the region as a whole. Moreover, several analysts (D. Collier 1979) have cast doubt on the causal linkage O'Donnell postulated between a certain phase of industrialization and democratic breakdown. Radicalization and polarization in the context of the cold war were the primary fac-

TABLE 6

Likelihood of Regime Transitions by Regime Type and Income Category, 19 Latin American Countries, 1945–96

GDP/capita (1980 U.S. dollars)	No. of Democratic Cases	Breakdown and Erosion Rate of Democracies	No. of Semi-democratic Cases	Transition Rate of Semi-democracies*	No. of Authoritarian Cases	Transition Rate of Authoritarian Regimes	Transition Rate of All Regimes
0 to 399	0	—	0	—	58	0.0	0.0
400 to 799	37	2.7	104	6.7	199	5.5	5.6
800 to 1,199	45	4.4	42	11.9	109	5.5	6.6
1,200 to 1,799	102	2.9	23	4.3	51	5.9	4.0
1,800 to 2,399	37	2.7	6	16.7	48	8.3	6.6
2,400 to 3,199	12	8.3	16	18.8	25	16.0	15.1
3,200 or more	57	1.8	0	—	17	17.6	5.4
Total	290	3.1	191	8.9	507	6.1	5.8
# Transitions / # Regime Years		(9/290)		(17/191)		(31/507)	

* Includes transitions to democracies and reversals to authoritarian regimes.

Note: Every year counts as a separate case for every country. Regime transitions lasting less than one year were not coded into the dataset.

tors behind these breakdowns (Linz and Stepan 1978; Santos 1986; A. Valenzuela 1978). Nevertheless, consistent with O'Donnell's argument, a higher level of modernization did not enhance democracy's immunity to breakdown in Latin America in the 1960s and 1970s. In broader comparative perspective, this finding is interesting and distinctive.

There were only six classic democratic breakdowns (as opposed to erosions from democracy to semidemocracy) during this fifty-two-year period: Argentina 1976, Chile 1973, Guatemala 1954, Peru 1968, Uruguay 1973, and Venezuela 1948. This paucity of breakdowns is a testimony to how difficult it has been to build democracy in Latin America; with no democracy, there can be no breakdown. But it is encouraging to note that once they exist, democracies have not readily broken down.

In addition to the breakdowns, three regimes eroded to the point where they could no longer be considered democracies: Colombia, the Dominican Republic, and Peru. The distinction between democratic breakdown and democratic erosion in table 6 operationally depends on whether a democracy collapses to authoritarianism or to semidemocracy. Empirically, all of the breakdowns involved successful military coups that installed dictatorships. None of the democratic erosions involved coups, although the erosion in Peru was followed by Fujimori's 1992 coup.

Table 4 above showed that the likelihood of democracy was lower in the $1,800–$2,399 and $2,400–$3,199 categories than in the $1,200–$1,799 one. But table 6 shows that this is not because democracies were markedly more likely to break down at these higher income levels. The main reason for the high incidence of nondemocratic regimes in the $2,400–$3,199 income category in table 4 is rather that nondemocracies experienced economic growth that pushed them into this category. This is true for Argentina, which remained nondemocratic from 1930 to 1973 and reached the $2,400 level in 1946; Chile, which was authoritarian from 1973 to 1990 and reached $2,400 in 1981; Mexico, which reached this mark in 1980; and Uruguay, which was authoritarian from 1973 to 1985 and surpassed $2,400 per capita in 1980. Venezuela in 1948 was the only democracy that broke down when its per capita income was between $2,400 and $3,199.

In contrast to the regime-survival pattern for democracies, which oscillates randomly as per capita income increases, authoritarian regimes are more vulnerable to regime transitions as income increases. The transition rate of authoritarian regimes, i.e., the likelihood that they would switch to democratic or semidemocratic in a given year, increases in a nearly unilinear fashion as per capita income increases. Higher income semidemocracies are also substantially more likely to undergo regime transitions, though the increase is not as linear as it is for authoritarian regimes.

The reason democracy is more common at a higher income level in Latin America runs counter to the broader comparative pattern signaled by Przeworski and Limongi (1997). In Latin America, democracy is more prevalent at a higher income level not because it is less vulnerable—this is true only above $3,200 per capita in 1980 U.S. dollars—but rather principally because there is a greater likelihood of destabilizing nondemocracies, some of which are transformed into democracies. The greater stability of Latin American democracies above the $3,200 per capita threshold reinforces the correlation between higher per capita income and democracy, but this correlation exists mostly because nondemocracies are more likely to be transformed at higher income levels. The correlation between democracy and higher per capita income is weaker than it is globally because medium income democracies break down at a high rate until they reach the $3,200 threshold.

WHY MODERNIZATION FAVORED DEMOCRATIZATION SOMEWHAT

Two questions come to the fore on the basis of the previous discussion. The first is why countries with a higher per capita income have been somewhat more likely to be democracies. The second is why the correlation between democracy and per capita income has been modest in Latin America compared to the rest of the world.

As we have just seen, for Latin America, the answer to the first question hinges primarily on why nondemocratic regimes have higher transition rates at higher levels of development. Three factors, all discussed elsewhere in greater detail, help explain this conundrum (Diamond 1992; Lipset 1960; Rueschemeyer et al. 1992; Santos 1985). First, a higher level of development is associated with a more democratic political culture. More citizens have more information than in poorer countries. Education levels are higher, and more educated citizens make for more active citizens, capable of pushing for democracy. Table 7 shows a decreasing share of the illiterate for every country in Latin America between roughly 1950 and 1980. In most countries, the decreases are dramatic, for example, from 50.5% to 15.3% in Venezuela. It is not only rudimentary reading and writing skills that improved over the decades. A greater share of citizens attained high school and university degrees than ever before. This is not to claim that education levels became high in absolute terms in recent decades; only that they rose considerably.

Of course, some people have participated effectively in politics with

TABLE 7

Illiteracy Rates in Latin American Democracies
(Percentage of the population aged 15 and over)

	YEAR	ILLITERACY	YEAR	ILLITERACY
Argentina	1947	13.6a	1980	6.1
Bolivia	1950	67.9	1988	18.9
Brazil	1950	50.5	1980	25.5
Chile	1952	19.8	1980	8.9
Colombia	1951	37.7	1980	12.2b
Costa Rica	1950	20.6	1980	7.4
Dominican Rep.	1950	57.1	1980	31.4c
Ecuador	1950	44.3	1980	16.5
El Salvador	1950	60.6	1980	32.7d
Guatemala	1950	70.7	1980	44.2
Haiti	1950	89.5	1980	62.5
Honduras	1950	64.8	1985	40.5
Mexico	1950	43.2	1980	16.5
Nicaragua	1950	61.6	1980	13.0
Panama	1950	30.0	1980	12.9
Paraguay	1950	34.2	1980	12.3
Peru	1950	48.8f	1980	18.1
Uruguay	1960	9.5g	1980	5.0
Venezuela	1950	50.5	1980	15.3

a—Figure for those aged 14 and over
b—Figure for those 10 and over.
c—Figure for those aged 5 and over; excludes the indigenous population living in the jungle.
d—UNESCO estimate.
e—Figure for those from age 10 to 49.
f—Estimate (extrapolation from 1940 and 1961 figures)
g—No census held in Uruguay between 1908 and 1963.

Sources: ECLA, Statistical Yearbook for Latin America 1981, p. 97 for circa 1950; ECLA, Statistical Yearbook for Latin America 1990, p. 54 for circa 1980; Statistical Abstract of Latin America, vol. 26 (1988), p. 156, for Nicaragua 1980; Statistical Abstract of Latin America, vol. 29 (1992), p. 213, for Honduras 1985; Instituto Nacional de Estadistica, Peru: Compendio Estadistico, 1988, (1989), p. 99, for Peru circa 1950.

little formal education, and many educated people do not participate. In general, however, formal education paves the way for more effective participation. Survey data from Latin America have consistently shown that, as is true elsewhere, more-educated citizens are more likely to be interested in politics, more likely to participate, and more likely to express attitudes regarded as democratic.

Second, economic growth transformed the class structure in ways generally propitious to challenging authoritarianism. It led to the creation of a larger middle class. Although the middle sectors in Latin America have not uniformly supported democracy in most countries, they were important actors in transitions to democracy and have remained supporters of democracy. This argument is consistent with Lipset's (1960) view that an expanding middle class favors democracy.

Despite the capital intensive character of industrialization in Latin America, economic growth favored the expansion of organized labor (Rueschemeyer et al. 1992). Organized labor supported most transitions to democracy and fought military dictatorships. Labor usually supported democratic regimes, though it did not do so consistently (R. Collier forthcoming).

Growth also was associated with urbanization, which proceeded rapidly in every Latin American country between 1950 and 1980. For the region as a whole, the share of the population living in urban areas with at least 20,000 inhabitants virtually doubled during these three decades, from 25.7% to 47.3%. In some countries, the pace of urbanization was dramatic: for example, from 22% to 54% urban in Colombia, and from 11% to 41% in the Dominican Republic. In urban areas, the poor had more opportunities to participate in politics than in rural areas (Santos 1985). Poor people in cities joined neighborhood associations, social movements, and civic organizations. A larger share of the population living in urban areas also reduced the political impact of the countryside, where poor people had more often than not been subjected to personalistic and clientelistic domination.

Economic growth led to diversification. Manufacturing production expanded in virtually every Latin American country between 1950 and 1980, and the service sector grew everywhere as the share of agriculture in national economies declined. Modernization thereby weakened the grip of landlords over the political system, and landlords have frequently been authoritarian when they are the dominant actor in politics. Agriculture's comparative decline was especially discernible in its eroding share of exports. Between 1960 and 1980, agriculture's share in total exports fell from 50.7% to 29.3% for the region as a whole. In Mexico, agriculture's share of exports fell from 56.2% in 1965 to 11.1% fifteen years later; in Peru, during this same fifteen-year period, agriculture's share fell from 54.8% to 9.7% (ECLA 1984: 159). In Ecuador, agriculture's share declined from 96.5% in 1960 to 25.2% in 1980; in Brazil, from 88.4% to 46.8%.

These multifaceted economic and social transformations reduced the political clout of landowners. Over the long haul, economic growth promoted diversification of interests, creating new groups that counter-balanced the power of landowners. Rueschemeyer, Stephens, and Stephens (1992) have convincingly argued that in transitional societies, landowners are the most antidemocratic sector of the propertied classes.

Economic development helped fortify civil society, creating counterweights to the state and to the traditional elites and armed forces that dominated the state in so many Latin American countries. As Diamond (1992), Putnam (1993), Rueschemeyer et al. (1992), and Tocqueville (1969) have argued, a robust civil society is favorable to democracy because it creates organized groups that actively participate in civic life. This is not to suggest that all groups in civil society have fostered democracy, but many have.

Finally, economic growth integrated Latin America into a world system more tightly. It was strongly associated with growing imports and exports, which mean exposure to products, technology, and companies from other countries. It was also associated with expanding international communication and transportation and with expanding incomes that make it possible for people, interest groups, businesses, and governments to take advantage of those growing linkages.

Why then has the correlation between per capita income and democracy been weaker in Latin America than on a global basis? A definitive answer to this question awaits further research, but part of the answer is that, on a global level, the countries with the highest per capita incomes have been very likely to be democratic, while countries with very low per capita incomes have usually been authoritarian (Dahl 1971: 62–80; Przeworski et al. 1996). Most Latin American countries are in an intermediate category, precisely where one would expect the greatest uncertainty as to regime type. Notwithstanding important cross-national differences within Latin America, the range in per capita income is lower than it is for the entire universe of countries.

POLITICAL ATTITUDES AND DEMOCRATIC SURVIVAL

If economic transformations do not fully explain why Latin America became (and remained) mostly democratic, then we need to seek elsewhere to help explain this transformation. The second factor that has contributed to the greater survivability of Latin America's democracies revolves around changes in political attitudes, toward a greater valorization of democracy. This transformation was significant among several important actors and for most of the political spectrum.

Political attitudes do not inherently derive from a given level of development or cultural/historical background. It is more theoretically interesting to analyze changes in attitudes toward democracy and politics over time and across countries rather than positing an enduring set of values throughout Latin America as a whole. These attitudes can change significantly in a relatively short time. This approach differs from those that emphasize the long-established Catholic Iberian tradition, seen as inherently antidemocratic. The latter approach is too static and too homogeneous for the region as a whole, and it ignores important transformations within the Catholic Church (Levine 1992; Mainwaring 1986). If the Iberian Catholic tradition were intrinsically inimical to democracy, it would be hard to explain the persistence of democratic regimes in several countries for long periods. It would also be difficult to explain the demise of authoritarianism in the 1980s.

Attitudinal factors are related to but somewhat independent of structural factors. Democratic attitudes are more likely among urban than rural actors, among more educated than less educated populations, and in countries with a stronger rather than a weaker civil society. However, attitudes do not become more democratic in linear fashion as incomes increase, as societies become more urban, or as civil societies become stronger.

Changing attitudes toward politics and democracy have been studied in detail for individual actors in Latin America (e.g., specific political parties, intellectuals). Nevertheless, the profound consequences of these changes have not always been integrated into an understanding of the sea change away from authoritarianism (for exceptions, see Diamond 1996; Weffort 1985).

The greatest change in attitudes toward democracy in Latin America has come on the left. Never a numerically large force, the revolutionary left nonetheless had a major impact in many Latin American countries in the 1960s and 1970s. It was authoritarian in its practices and in its preferred political system, and it resorted to violence to accomplish its objectives (Gillespie 1982; Ollier 1998). It regarded liberal democracy as a bourgeois formalism, believed that violence was needed to "liberate" the working class, and advocated revolutionary socialism incompatible with democracy.

The left was never a serious contender for power in most countries, but it was seen as a threat by privileged elites, the militaries, and the U.S. In most Latin American countries, the right was authoritarian even before the youthful revolutionaries burst on the scene, but the far left spurred the right toward more violent positions. In the 1960s, conservative actors feared, not without foundation, that revolutionary change would lead to their destruction. They reacted intransigently, supporting authoritarian governments. In turn, right-wing authoritarianism led dissenting forces to believe that effecting political change through conventional channels was impossible.

By the mid-1980s, the revolutionary left had become a nonactor in most countries (Castañeda 1993), though Peru, El Salvador, Guatemala, and Nicaragua were still exceptions. In most countries, it was physically annihilated. It became obvious that its biggest effect was not to free "the people" but to spur the armed forces toward ruthless repression. In Brazil and the southern cone, most of the revolutionary left reassessed and rejected its earlier political convictions and practices (Ollier 1998). Having experienced life under brutal dictatorships, most survivors concluded that democracy was necessary and desirable. The Soviet Union and China increasingly appeared to the Latin American left as authoritarian models. The crisis of real socialism, culminating in the collapse of the Soviet Union, further diminished the appeal of authoritarian leftist ideologies.

By 1990, the left in most of South America had substantially changed its political views, but the Central American left (particularly in Nicaragua, El Salvador, and Guatemala) had not. The withering of the Sandinista regime in Nicaragua and its eventual defeat at the polls in 1990 initiated a process of critical reflection among Central American revolutionaries. The crushing defeat of Sendero Luminoso in Peru and the decimation of the FMLN in El Salvador further weakened support for revolution. By the mid-1990s, the revolutionary fervor was even weaker than it had been a decade before, and the civil wars in Central America came to a gradual halt. Most survivors of the FMLN in El Salvador joined the democratic process with the signing of the peace accord in 1992. The M-19 in Colombia became integrated into electoral politics. Most Sandinistas, previously ambivalent about or hostile to liberal democracy, gradually came to understand that there was no other way to go.

Intellectuals have historically had more political influence in Latin America than in the U.S., and this remains the case to this day. In the 1960s and 1970s, most politically influential Latin American intellectuals were on the left and were hostile to capitalism and were ambivalent (or worse) about liberal democracy. Dependency theory was in its heyday. Most intellectuals considered radical social change a more urgent priority than liberal democracy. Many doubted that "bourgeois" democracy was possible under conditions of dependent development.

In the post-1978 period, progressive intellectuals became more convinced of the importance of democracy (Lamounier 1979; Packenham 1986; Weffort 1985). By the late 1980s, dependency theory had lost its credibility (Packenham 1992); liberation theology was under attack; and the fascination with revolution had subsided. These changes occurred as part of an international trend; intellectuals in Europe, too, increasingly questioned the authoritarian left, renounced Marxism, and embraced liberal democracy. Nobody so epitomizes the dramatic transformation of Latin American intellectuals as Brazilian president Fernando Henrique Cardoso (1995–), who shifted from being one of the most prominent dependency theorists in the late 1960s and early 1970s to focusing principally on democracy and its intrinsic value in the late 1970s and 1980s, and finally to implementing market-oriented policies and state shrinking as president in the 1990s.

Change on the left was not limited to insurrectional groups and intellectuals; it extended to electorally significant parties. Committed to Leninist ideals and rhetorically favorable to a revolutionary uprising in the 1960s and 1970s, the Chilean Socialist Party became a stalwart of liberal democracy in the 1980s (Walker 1990). In 1972, the Central Committee of the Socialist Party criticized Salvador Allende's socialist government for respecting "bourgeois mechanisms that are precisely what impede us from accomplishing the changes that we need" and called for a dictatorship of the proletariat (Walker 1990: 159). By 1982, a mere decade later, the wing of the party that had most vigorously denounced bourgeois institutionality explicitly rejected real socialism, affirming that it had failed to "create mechanisms of democratic governance capable of resolving the conflicts that emerge in a modern society. For this reason, it does not constitute an inspiring model for Chilean socialism" (Walker 1990: 188). Having previously been ambivalent about liberal democracy, the Bolivian MNR (National Revolutionary Movement) embraced it in the 1980s. Notorious for its authoritarian past, the Peronist party in Argentina, of a predominantly center-left orientation until the 1980s, also largely accepted democracy by the 1980s. Before the 1973 breakdown, the Frente Amplio in Uruguay was dominated by semi-loyal and disloyal elements, in Linz's (1978) terms. By the early 1990s, most party leaders fully accepted democracy.

Change on the right was equally important though not as profound. Historically, the right was the greatest obstacle to democracy in Latin America. The oligarchy maintained unfettered power until sometime (varying by country) in the twentieth century, and it refused to accept democracy when doing so could threaten its core interests. As the revolutionary left became more significant in the aftermath of the Cuban revolution, the right became more disposed to undermine democracy (where it existed) to protect its interests, and less willing to contemplate democracy where it did not exist. Conservative political elites frequently conspired against democracy in Brazil between 1946 and 1964

(Benevides 1981) and in Argentina between 1930 and 1966 (Gibson 1996).

As the specter of communism faded, much of the right became willing to abide by democratic rules of the game, and the other sectors became less prone to support coups. The left's transformation in a more democratic direction fostered a similar trajectory on the right. One of the most dramatic transformations occurred with the right-wing party in El Salvador, Arena. Known for its close linkages to death squads and the oligarchy in the early 1980s, by the mid-1990s Arena had helped engineer the peace treaty that ended El Salvador's civil war and incorporated the former guerrillas into the political process (Wood forthcoming). The history of a violent, reactionary "despotic regime" (Baloyra 1983) would not have augured well for such a development. Business groups have not been at the forefront of democratization, but they have lived peacefully with it in most countries (see Payne 1994 on Brazil). It is questionable whether the right fully subscribes to democracy in most countries, but the mere fact that it accepts democracy marks a historic change.

Less can be said about the military's shifting attitudes because little research has been done on this subject. Past research has suggested that few coups are successful without the support of powerful civilian allies (Stepan 1971). Therefore, even if the armed forces have not undergone a significant change in values, the changing attitudes of other actors have prompted different military behavior in the political arena. It is likely that political values have changed in a more democratic direction at the mass level as well, but there are no reliable region-wide surveys from the earlier democratic period that would enable us to verify this proposition.

The changing attitudes toward democracy in Latin America were interactive, i.e., changes in one actor fostered change in others. The conversion of leftist groups to democratic politics, for example, reduced the fears of rightist actors that democracy could lead to their destruction. Similarly, the growing willingness of rightist groups and governments to abide by electoral politics signaled to the left that some positive change — minimally, the end to massive human rights violations — could occur through democracy.

The diffusion of democratic ideals was not uniform across or within countries. In the 1980s, the changing attitudes toward democracy advanced considerably in South America, with the sole exception of Peru. Central America, and more specifically Nicaragua, El Salvador, and Guatemala, remained outliers; the commitment to democracy lagged behind. But by the 1990s, most actors in these countries, with their histories of relentless, often brutal authoritarianism, had recognized the desirability of peace, and peace could be accomplished only with competitive elections. The transformation of political attitudes has also varied by region within countries. Democratic practice in less developed regions is often vitiated by traditional elites whose practice and rhetoric remain less than fully democratic (Hagopian 1996b; O'Donnell 1993).

Despite these limits, the changes in political attitudes in Latin America had profound implications. By the 1990s, politics was less polemical and less threatening. Gone is the sense that politics is an all-important zero sum game, a low-intensity warfare. Under these conditions, sustaining democracy is easier. Actors are willing to accept minor losses under democracy; earlier, they were not willing to play a game that might entail catastrophic losses. These changing attitudes about democracy and politics have offset some negatives that might well have conspired against democracy, especially poor economic and social performance. None of this is to suggest that attitudinal changes have made democracy in Latin America impregnable; the problems confronting democracy remain significant.

Paradoxically, these changing attitudes toward democracy, while salutary from the perspective of democratic survivability, have not been without their down side. Latin America has long been the region of the world with most pronounced inequalities, and these inequalities were exacerbated during the 1980s. With the weakening and transformation of the left in so many countries, fewer voices have called attention to the urgency of addressing inequalities and improving living standards. The price of democracy may have been, as Przeworski (1986) has suggested is generally the case, the inviolability of property relations.

INTERNATIONAL FACTORS

Until the 1990s, most work on democratization focused almost exclusively on domestic actors. Upon first reflection, this fact seems sensible; democracy is built within particular countries, and its construction usually rests primarily on domestic actors. Yet the international context and international actors are important influences in democratization. In the post-1978 period, they have helped sustain democracy in Latin America.

More generally, international influences and actors have significantly affected prospects for democracy around the world (Farer 1996; Pridham 1991; Whitehead 1986, 1991, 1996). In their careful study, Przeworski et al. (1996) found that an international diffusion effect outweighed all other factors in assessing the prospects that a democracy will survive. The international context holds weight partly because the international ideological context encourages or discourages democracy, and partly because external actors such as governments, multilateral organizations, churches, and other nongovernmental organizations can foster or debilitate democracies. In the extreme, democracy can initially be imposed by a foreign power, as occurred in Germany, Italy, and Japan after World War II (Stepan 1986). In a more proximate case, the European Community was a major influence in the regime consolidations in southern Europe after 1974 (Pridham 1991; Whitehead 1991).

The distinction between domestic and international actors and factors is not hard-and-fast. Domestic actors are often part of international networks, and international actors establish linkages to, and often financially support, domestic actors (Keck and Sikkink 1998). As Whitehead (1991) has observed, the international context shapes the calculations and behavior of domestic political actors. In Latin America, the impact of the international situation on the strategy of domestic actors was clear when coup-mongers in Paraguay (1996), Venezuela (1992), and Guatemala (1993) backed off when confronted with hostile international reactions and the likelihood of sanctions. In Guatemala, President Jorge Serrano suspended the constitution, dissolved congress, and dismissed the judiciary in May 1993, following the example of Peruvian president Alberto Fujimori's palace coup of April 1992. International reaction against Serrano, coupled with domestic mobilization, forced the president to resign within two weeks (Villagrán de León 1993). The OAS indicated that sanctions would be forthcoming, and the U.S. promptly suspended aid to Guatemala. In an earlier age, when the reactions would have been less adverse and the mechanisms for implementing sanctions less developed, the coup probably would have succeeded. Business leaders would have had less incentive to come to the support of democracy because they would not have faced crippling economic sanctions.

The International Ideological Context

The impact of the international ideological context is methodologically difficult to pinpoint, but it is nevertheless important. Domestic political actors do not operate in a vacuum sealed in by national borders. They act in a world of permeable borders and widely flowing information. Books and journals, television and radio, electronic communication, international conferences, and scholarly and political visits to other countries act as means of disseminating information.

Rather than constituting independent developments in Latin American countries, changing attitudes had powerful demonstration effects across borders—what Starr (1991) calls diffusion effects. Leftist groups in one country witnessed the futility of trying to win power through revolutionary means in neighboring countries. Intellectuals met at international conferences and exchanged ideas. Parties that were members of the Socialist International observed parallel transformations in Western Europe and Latin America.

These channels of communication are particularly significant for actors of proximate ideological persuasion. For example, on the left of the political spectrum, growing acceptance and valuing of democracy in Latin America was fueled by developments in Western Europe in the 1970s and by the withering of socialism in the 1980s. Many Latin American intellectuals and politicians who spearheaded the left's reevaluation of democracy had lived in Western or Eastern Europe in exile. In Western Europe, they were influenced by growing criticisms of extant socialist regimes.[13] Some Latin Americans living in Western Europe were influenced by progressive challenges to the old authoritarian left that came from new social movements (especially the women's, peace, and environmental movements) and green parties. Those on the left who did not go into exile were also influenced by the changing international climate.

The power of the international ideological context is suggested by different waves of regime transformation in the twentieth century. For example, fascism was broadly popular at a specific moment (the 1920s and 1930s), with dire consequences for democracy. In the third wave of democratization, with the partial exception of President Reagan's first couple of years in office, the international ideological context has been relatively favorable to democracy in Latin America. This favorable ideological context does not guarantee that specific countries will be democratic, but it enhances the likelihood of democracy. International factors only exceptionally *determine* regime transitions and processes, but they significantly alter the odds for or against democracy.

International Actors: The Catholic Church

The changing attitudes toward democracy in Latin America represent a paradigmatic case of the permeability between domestic and international influences. This is clear in the role of the Catholic Church, which is at once an international and a domestic actor.[14]

The Catholic Church has traditionally been an actor of some political import in most Latin American countries, and until the 1960s, it more frequently sided with authoritarians than with democrats. The church was a central protagonist in many coups against democratic or semidemocratic governments throughout the region. The revolutions in Mexico and Cuba were trenchantly anticlerical, and the church consistently opposed leftist movements and governments. The church applauded coups in Venezuela in 1948 (Levine 1973), Colombia in 1948, Brazil in 1964, and Argentina in 1976.

Since the 1970s, the Catholic Church has usually supported democratization (Huntington 1991: 74–85). Under the sway of the Second Vatican Council, the church came to accept and promote democracy in most of the region, though again with some exceptions. In Brazil, the church spearheaded the opposition to military rule in the 1970s and strongly advocated a return to democracy (Mainwaring 1986). Elsewhere, the church reached a peaceful *modus vivendi* with democratic governments (Levine 1981), notwithstanding conflict over issues such as abortion. In a few cases, such as Argentina and Guatemala, the church supported authoritarian rule in the 1970s and early 1980s but has not attempted to undermine democracy since its inception. In Chile, El Salvador, Nicaragua, and Peru, the church criticized authoritarian regimes and promoted transitions to democracy.

The U.S. Government and Governmental Agencies

Changes in international norms and practices, bolstered by U.S. diplomacy, created new pressures for democracy. This represents a change from most of the post-1945 period. Historically, the U.S. often supported coups against democratic governments (Brazil in 1964, Chile in 1973), occasionally (Guatemala in 1954) was a leading protagonist in coups, and rarely strongly promoted democracy in Latin America. During the cold war, the U.S. generally subordinated support of democracy to national security concerns (Packenham 1973). Given the ubiquitous nature of the Soviet/U.S. confrontation, the notion of national security interests became so expansive that the U.S. lent support for coups against reformist governments of different stripes. Franklin Delano Roosevelt purportedly said of Somoza, "He's a son of a bitch, but he's our son of a bitch." From the early twentieth century until Jimmy Carter's administration, this cozying up to friendly dictators was commonplace.

This practice started to change under President Carter, who publicly criticized human rights violations committed by authoritarian governments (Argentina, Brazil, Chile, and Uruguay) friendly to the U.S. Carter also supported democratic transitions in the Dominican Republic, Ecuador, and Peru. In the Dominican Republic in 1978, his initiatives blocked electoral fraud that would have extended authoritarian rule. By promoting an honest vote-count, Carter helped pave the road for the first democratic transition of Latin America's third wave. His policy also helped save lives and limit the use of torture in Latin America, and it started to change the public discourse in the United States regarding foreign policy.

During the 1980 presidential campaign, Ronald Reagan lambasted Carter's human rights policy. Early indications after Reagan's inauguration were that the new president would abandon a concern with democracy and human rights. He coddled the southern cone dictators until Argentina invaded the Falkland Islands in 1982, and he propped up sagging repressive regimes in El Salvador and Guatemala.

Surprisingly, and notwithstanding its visceral opposition to leftist governments, the Reagan administration's foreign policy efforts began to emphasize democracy during the president's second term (Carouthers 1991). The 1982 war in the south Atlantic between Britain and Argentina contributed to the administration's reorientation by unveiling the potential bellicosity and erratic behavior of authoritarian regimes. The administration supported Britain in the conflagration and thereafter never again coddled Argentina's generals.

In order to bolster the credibility of its much-criticized military offensive against the Sandinistas, the administration used prodemocracy rhetoric and ultimately criticized authoritarianism of the right (Arnson 1993; Whitehead 1991). Without a minimal effort to promote democracy elsewhere in Latin America, the crusade against the Sandinistas and support for the regimes in El Salvador and Guatemala would have encountered more congressional and public resistance than it already did.

Reagan's policies remained marked by gnawing tensions such as the effort to encourage democracy while simultaneously promoting a massive buildup of patently authoritarian militaries in Central America. In the isthmus, in order to combat communism, the administration sometimes allied with traditional authoritarian forces. The rhetorical commitment to democracy always outpaced the reality. In its Central American policy, the administration flouted mechanisms of democratic accountability by lying to and circumventing Congress. It supported blatantly authoritarian regimes in El Salvador and Guatemala and also helped arm the contras, many of whom were notorious for their authoritarian past. Anticommunism prevailed over democracy in Central America. Yet even in the isthmus, the administration did not wholly abandon the cause of democracy. As it pumped hundreds of millions of dollars into arming the Salvadoran military, the U.S. government also applied pressure to hold elections and attempted to prop up the centrist Christian Democrats over the right wing. In a context of massive human rights violations, the Salvadoran elections of the 1980s were very flawed, but outright fraud was kept to a minimum. Similar U.S. pressures pushed the Guatemalan military to hold elections in 1985, leading to the inauguration of civilian president Vinicio Cerezo in 1986. Although these governments were not democratic, they won office in competitive elections.

Elsewhere, free of the potential trade-off between anticommunism and democracy, the administration really attempted to promote democracy. Public and congressional pressures induced the administration to keep alive the rhetorical commitment to democracy. Surprisingly, in light of its unflinching criticisms of Carter's human rights policy, the Reagan administration declared its opposition to military uprisings in Argentina in 1987 and 1988, and it pressured for democratic change in Chile, Paraguay, Panama, and Haiti. The policy toward Chile changed in 1983 as the administration began to criticize human rights violations and call for a return to democracy. In Chile, Ambassador Harry Barnes, who was appointed in 1985, criticized authoritarian rule and human rights violations, supported opposition groups, and encouraged democratic elections. The administration also conditioned support for some multilateral loans to Chile on improvement in human rights and progress in democratization. Yet, all told, the administration did not contribute much to democratic change in Latin America, notwithstanding its fulsome rhetoric to the contrary,[15] but during Reagan's second term, it no longer coddled "friendly" rightist dictatorships. Reagan apologists claim credit for the fact that the Sandinistas held free and fair elections in 1990; in fact, it is not clear whether the war against the Sandinistas helped or hindered the cause of democracy.

Under President Bush, the U.S. generally supported democratic initiatives in Latin America. Supporting democratic governments was made easier by the collapse of the Soviet Union and the Sandinistas' setback at the polls in 1990. The U.S. no longer had the communist threat to contend with and anticommunism receded.

The Bush and Clinton administrations promoted democratization in Haiti, criticized authoritarian involutions in Peru (1992) and Guatemala (1993), and applied pressure against coup-mongers in Argentina (1987 and 1988), Peru (1989) Venezuela (1992), and Paraguay (1996). The 1989 invasion of Panama—although dubious from other perspectives—ousted dictator Manuel Noriega and led to the installation of a government that had been denied office through electoral fraud. The U.S. has used diplomatic pressure, public pronouncements, and economic sanctions to bolster democracy and hinder authoritarian regimes (Pastor 1989).

U.S. governmental agencies have also attempted to foster democracy in Latin America. In December 1980, the Agency for International Development (AID) began a "Human Rights and Democratic Initiatives" program under President Carter. This program funded human rights groups in Latin America, and it also helped fund the IFES (International Foundation for Electoral Systems), which in turn has helped promote fair elections. AID's Latin American and Caribbean Bureau began a democracy program for Latin America in 1984, funding a variety of initiatives intended to strengthen democracy. Although AID has worked in Latin America since the 1960s, its efforts at building democracy are more recent. The first time it provided ample technical assistance for an election was in 1982 in El Salvador. Subsequently, AID began programs designed to strengthen legislatures, judiciaries, local governments, and political parties. Even if these efforts are not always successful, they signal the U.S. desire to foster democracy.

In 1984, the U.S. government created the National Endowment for Democracy (NED), whose mission is to foster democracy around the world. NED is funded by Congress, but it is run by an independent bipartisan board. NED provides grants to groups in other countries that seek to promote democracy: civic organizations, human rights groups, etc. It supported the opposition to regimes as diverse as the Sandinistas' and Pinochet's. In some cases, NED provided funding for election monitoring and voter education. NED has supported democratic civic groups, judicial and legislative reforms, human rights groups, and legislatures in Latin America. Although some of NED's activities are of debatable merit, its existence also signals the U.S.'s greater willingness to promote democracy.

This is not to subscribe to an apologetic view of U.S. policy toward Latin America; the U.S. could have done more to bolster democracy in the hemisphere. But the contrast to the pre-1977 pattern of supporting coups and dictators is significant and helps account for greater democratic survivability in the third wave.

NGOs

Nongovernmental actors have also supported democracy in recent years. Human rights organizations such as Americas Watch, Amnesty International, the Washington Office on Latin America, and the Inter-American Dialogue monitor the situation of democracy and human rights in the region. The Socialist International and the German party foundations have poured resources into supporting Latin American democracies for years (Whitehead 1986: 25–31).

Multilateral organizations

Multilateral organizations have also defended democracy more vigorously than ever before. In recent years, the OAS and UN have become more vigorous agents on its behalf. In 1990, the UN and OAS had a major presence in the Nicaraguan elections in an effort to promote a fair process. This was the first time that the UN had monitored the election of a member nation. After that success, both organizations also monitored elections and promoted peace talks in El Salvador, Guatemala, and Haiti (McCoy, Garber, and Pastor 1991). In 1991, the OAS passed Resolution 1080, which created a new mechanism for the multilateral defense of democracy.

Signed by five Central American presidents in 1987, the Esquipulas Accord was an early step toward the effective multilateral promotion of democracy and peacemaking. This accord was also aimed at ending the Central American civil wars. The presidents collectively pledged to ensure that democracy and peace would prevail.

Democratic governments in Latin America have supported efforts to encourage democracy and to impose sanctions against authoritarian regimes. Collectively, NGOs, multilateral agencies, and the governments of Latin America, Western Europe, and North America have created a norm of disapproval for authoritarianism and support—ideological, if not material—for democracy.

Groups that monitor elections have enhanced the integrity of the electoral process. Such monitoring was important in Chile in the 1988 plebiscite and in Nicaragua in 1990. In both cases, massive foreign intervention promoted citizen expectations of fair elections and encouraged the incumbents to respect unfavorable results at the polls.

But it is not only that norms have changed; new institutional mechanisms to enforce these norms have emerged. In July 1996, the presidents of the Mercosur countries—Brazil, Argentina, Uruguay, Paraguay, Bolivia, and Chile—signed an agreement stating that any member nation would be expelled if democracy broke down. Pressure from neighboring Mercosur nations helped avert a coup in Paraguay in April 1996. In an age of growing international economic integration, authoritarian governments now faced the significant possibility of economic sanctions such as those that crippled the economies of Panama under Noriega and Haiti after the military deposed Aristide. The U.S., UN, and OAS have applied sanctions against patently authoritarian governments.

Never before in the Americas has there existed anything like the near universal ideological support for democracy that has been present since Reagan's second term. Even in this context, democratic breakdowns can occur, as in Peru in 1992. But they are less likely.

EXPLAINING DEMOCRATIC SURVIVABILITY: QUANTITATIVE ANALYSIS

Structural, ideological, and international factors have contributed to greater democratic survivability in the post-1978 period. Although the bulk of the explanation has rested on the comparative historical method, some statistical tests can help verify the arguments.

With a dichotomous categorical dependent variable, logistic regression provides a tool to assess whether the structural changes or an international contagion effect holds greater weight in explaining the vicissitudes of democratic survivability in Latin America. Because my measurement of the dependent variable (democracy) until 1972 is categorical with only three possible values (authoritarian, semidemocratic, and democratic), I dichotomized that variable and used logistic regression. I first ran the regression comparing the democratic cases with the semidemocratic and authoritarian ones and then comparing the democratic and semidemocratic with the authoritarian. Because there were no data for GDP per capita for some countries for 1940–44, the regression is restricted to 1945–96.

Table 8 shows the results of six models, three for each of the dependent variables. Models 1 and 4 specifically assess the relationship between per capita GDP and democratic survivability and confirm that the countries with a higher per capita income are more likely to be democratic. The only independent variable is per capita GDP. In this model, the probability of democracy increases from 11.5% at $133 per capita (the lowest of any country over the 52 years) to 27.7% at $1,309 per capita (the mean for the 19 countries over 52 years) to 95.2% at $5,597 per capita (the highest of any country during the 52 years).

Models 2 and 5 used two independent variables, a country's GDP per capita in a given year and the number of countries that were democratic that year excluding the country in question. The latter variable served as a proxy for an international democratic contagion effect. The variable could range from zero (none of the country's Latin American counterparts were democratic) to eighteen (all of the other countries were democratic). In both models, both independent variables are statistically significant at a very high level. Adding the second independent variable improved both the percentage of cases predicted correctly and the Nagelkerke R^2. At the mean per capita income of $1,309 for the 988 cases, the probability of democracy in model 2 increases from 21.7% if two other countries are democratic (the lowest figure during this time) to 27.4% with 5.28 other democracies (the mean), to 37.1% with ten other democracies (the high).

Models 3 and 6 include a dummy variable for democratic commit-

TABLE 8
Logistic Regression Models
(1945–1996)

INDEPENDENT VARIABLES	DEPENDENT VARIABLE					
	DEMOCRACY			DEMOCRACY AND SEMIDEM.		
	I	II	III	IV	V	VI
Per capita GDP[a]	.921**	.893**	.607**	.555**	.510**	.089
	(.084)	(.083)	(.110)	(.076)	(.076)	(.101)
Diffusion		.094*	.223**		.236**	.347**
		(.030)	(.040)		(.029)	(.034)
Commitment dummy[b]			4.279**			10.058
			(.292)			(6.499)
Constant	−2.163**	−2.639**	−3.967**	−.760**	−1.941**	−2.610**
	(.141)	(.213)	(.322)	(.115)	(.188)	(.231)
Predicted correct (%)						
Democracies	23.7	26.8	67.0	44.6	55.4	70.5
Nondemocracies	91.5	91.1	97.4	76.1	76.5	89.3
All regimes	71.6	72.2	88.5	60.7	66.2	80.1
Nagelkerke R^2	.205	.217	.601	.081	.169	.511
N	988	988	988	988	988	988

Logistic regression coefficients (standard errors)

a.—In thousand U.S. dollars (1980)

b.—Countries coded=1 were Argentina (1983–96), Brazil (1985–96), Chile (1945–70 and 1990–96), Colombia (1958–90), Costa Rica (1949–96), Uruguay (1945–71 and 1985–1996), and Venezuela (1963–92).

* Significant at .005 level

** Significant at. 0001 level

TABLE 9

Probability of Democracy by GDP per Capita
(Number of Democracies set at 5)

GDP PER CAPITA	PROBABILITY OF DEMOCRACY WITHOUT DEMOCRATIC COMMITMENT (%)	PROBABILITY OF DEMOCRACY WITH DEMOCRATIC COMMITMENT (%)
Lowest	133	5.9	82.1
Mean	1,309	11.3	90.4
Highest	5,597	63.3	99.2

Probability of Democracy by Number of other Democracies
(GDP per capita fixed at $1309)

NUMBER OF OTHER DEMOCRACIES	PROBABILITY OF DEMOCRACY WITHOUT DEMOCRATIC COMMITMENT (%)	PROBABILITY OF DEMOCRACY WITH DEMOCRATIC COMMITMENT (%)
Lowest	2.00	6.1	82.8
Mean	5.28	12.0	90.9
Highest	10.00	28.0	96.6

ment. An objective and continuous measure of democratic commitment would be preferable, but at this point in the development of the social sciences, such a task would be very difficult and enormously time-consuming. As a result, I coded countries on the basis of assessments found in the secondary literature. The criterion for coding was that the government and main opposition actors needed to be clearly committed to democracy in a given year. When in doubt, I did not include the country. The literature is relatively consistent in indicating that, with these criteria, Argentina (1983–98), Brazil (1985–98), Chile (1932–70, 1990–98), Colombia (1958–90), Costa Rica (1949–98), Uruguay (1942–71, 1985–98), and Venezuela (1963–92) stand out for strong commitments to democracy; hence they are coded as 1.

It is not certain whether this variable can be assessed independently of the dependent variable. By definition, only a democratic regime can be scored as having the commitment to democracy. Given the potential problems with this variable, I ran all the regressions both with and with-

TABLE 10

OLS models for Freedom House Scores
Standardized and Unstandardized
Regression Coefficients
(1972–1996)

INDEPENDENT VARIABLES	DEPENDENT VARIABLE		
	FREEDOM HOUSE SCORE[a]		
	I	II	III
Per capita GDP[b]	−.835*	−.879*	−.004
	(.129)	(.126)	(.120)
	−.286*	**−.301***	**−.014**
Diffusion		−.243*	−.191*
		(.049)	(.041)
		−.214*	**−.168***
Commitment dummy			−4.211*
			(.295)
			−.589*
Constant	8.390*	10.127*	9.435*
	(.241)	(.422)	(.356)
Adjusted R²	.080	.123	.387
N	475	475	475

OLS coefficients (standard errors) Bold font is for standardized coefficients (betas).
a—Measured as the sum of Freedom House scores on civil liberties and political rights (2=most democratic; 14=least democratic)
b—In thousand U.S. dollars (1980)
* Significant at .001 level

out it. Adding this variable further improves the percentage of cases predicted correctly and the Nagelkerke R^2. Table 9 shows how the democratic commitment variable affects the likelihood of democracy holding constant the number of other democracies and varying the income level, and then holding constant the income level and varying the number of other democracies.

Using the same independent variables, table 10 shows the results of a linear regression with Freedom House scores as the dependent variable for 1972–96. Model 1 uses only GDP per capita as an independent variable. Each increase of $1,000 in GDP per capita leads to an expected decline of .835 in Freedom House scores. Model 2 adds the number of other democracies as an independent variable. Both independent variables were statistically significant at the .001 level, strongly supporting the assertion that they have a significant impact on democratic survivability in Latin America. Both variables are also substantively quite significant, though neither had an overwhelming effect on Freedom House scores. Each increase of 1 in the number of other Latin American democracies produced a decline of .243 in expected Freedom House scores (Freedom House scores decline as conditions are more democratic). Thus an increase of 4.12 more democracies would lower the expected Freedom House score by 1.00. Each increase of $1,000 in GDP per capita accounted for a decrease of −.879 in expected Freedom House scores; thus, an increase of $1,138 per capita would generate a decrease of 1.00 in expected Freedom House scores. The model accounts for 12.3% of the variance in Freedom House scores. But this modest R^2 is to be expected given the indeterminate nature of politics. The two factors analyzed here significantly shape prospects for democracy, but political leadership, the specific nature of political conflicts in a country, and other factors related to political agency are also important. The very high statistical significance of both independent variables corroborates the argument that they help account for the increase in democratic survivability.

When a dummy variable for democratic commitment is added for 1972–96, GDP per capita lost its statistical significance, but the democratic contagion effect and commitment to democracy were highly significant. The democratic commitment variable has a powerful substantive impact. When a country is coded "1," meaning that the government leaders and main opposition actors were committed to democracy, expected Freedom House scores drop considerably, by 4.21. Given the measurement problems with the democratic commitment variable, the results of model 3 are not conclusive, but they suggest the surprising possibility that in Latin America, GDP per capita is significant because it masks differences in democratic commitment. As one would expect, commitment to democracy is more likely in wealthier countries.

If the argument is correct that changing political values and changes in the international system have bolstered democracy in the third wave, then we should also be able to detect a period effect. After roughly 1985, democracy should be more likely at most income categories than it was before 1978. Between 1978 and 1985, many authoritarian regimes installed during previous years were still intact, so the third-wave period effect would not necessarily be discernible. Table 11 shows the results, clearly confirming the hypothesis.

Democratic breakdown rates also show a period effect. The breakdown rate of democracies declined from 4.7% in 1945–77 (6 break-

TABLE 11

Likelihood of Democracy by Period, 1945–77 versus 1985–96

GDP/CAPITA (1980 U.S. DOLLARS)	1945–77		1985–96	
	REGIME-YEARS	PERCENT DEMOCRATIC	REGIME-YEARS	PERCENT DEMOCRATIC
0 to 399	39	0.0	12	0.0
400 to 799	271	6.6	47	34.0
800 to 1,199	133	15.0	35	40.0
1,200 to 1,799	87	57.5	56	55.4
1,800 to 2,399	35	45.7	35	60.0
2,400 to 3,199	27	3.7	18	61.1
3,200 or more	35	65.7	25	100.0
Total	627	20.4	228	51.8

downs of 128 cases) to 0.0% in 1985–96 (0 breakdowns of 118 cases). The lower incidence of breakdown cannot easily be attributed to a higher per capita income because, at most income levels, the number of democratic cases is similar for 1985–96 and 1945–77. If the lower breakdown rate of 1985–96 were primarily a result of modernization, one would expect a greater proportion of the democratic cases to be in higher income categories for this later period. However, as noted earlier, a new, pernicious phenemenon has also emerged in the third wave: the erosion of democracies into semidemocracies.

The transition rate of nondemocratic regimes increased substantially in the third wave. From 1945 to 1977, the transition rate of nondemocracies was 5.8% (29 transitions out of 499 cases). From 1985 to 1996, this rate increased to 10.0% (11 transitions out of 110 cases). This combination of fewer democratic breakdowns and more transitions of nondemocratic regimes (many to democracy) accounts for the greater prevalence of democracy in the 1990s.

CONCLUSIONS

In Latin America, during most of the last half-century, democracy was more likely to prosper in the more economically developed countries. In this sense, the conventional wisdom suggested by modernization theory is right—but with the many caveats discussed above.

The period since 1978 has shown that democracy can endure under adverse economic and social conditions if the main actors are committed to democratic rules of the game. Structural factors are important, but political actors develop values and behaviors that are far from reducible to the structural situation. In this sense, the analysis here is consistent with actor-oriented approaches to democratization (e.g., Levine 1973; Linz 1978; O'Donnell and Schmitter 1986). Still, the quality of democracy has generally been much better in the medium or wealthier countries of Latin America. This fact—and indeed the entire analysis here— suggests the importance of combining structural and actor-oriented approaches.

In the post-1978 period, Latin American democracies have survived despite dismal economic and social results. Given the previous record in Latin America, the resilience of democracy in this latest period is surprising. Although Latin America has achieved its most democratic period ever during a lengthy time of poor economic results, this is not to say that poor economic performance has not affected democracy. Presumably, growth would be propitious for democratic governments because it would foster higher legitimacy. The limited legitimacy of many new democratic governments in Latin America stems in part from lackluster economic results. Moreover, stronger economic growth would promote social transformations favorable to democracy.

Political science has not dealt particularly effectively with the role of ideas and attitudes in shaping political outcomes (for exceptions, see Goldstein and Keohane 1993; Hall 1989). Because the impact of ideas is difficult to measure, political scientists tend to prefer explanations that focus on structures. The Latin American evidence, however, suggests that changes in political attitudes have been important in sustaining democracy in the post-1980 period. Structural changes have been consequential, but they have been overshadowed by a new valuing of political democracy.

Until the 1990s, most works on democracy paid relatively little attention to international factors (for an exception, see Whitehead 1986). The dominant focus on domestic factors is easily comprehensible with macro quantitative studies designed to see what factors make some countries more likely to be democracies than others. Such approaches have not readily incorporated a dimension that can at best differentiate regions of the world (but not countries); the dissemination of international ideas argument does not explain why one country in a region is democratic while another is not. However, the international dimension is crucial for understanding why some periods have been much less favorable to democracy than others.

International factors have been important in sustaining democracy in Latin America since 1978. Three kinds of international factors have helped shape prospects for democracy: the dissemination of ideas (a diffusion effect), the actions of governments, and the actions of multilateral agencies and nongovernmental actors.

NOTES

Howard Handelman, Evelyne Huber, Aníbal Pérez-Liñán, Richard Snyder, and Kurt Weyland offered valuable criticisms. David Altman, Kalaya Chareony-ing, Charles Kenney, Marcelo Leiras, Aníbal Pérez-Liñán, and John Rieger provided helpful research assistance.

1. This definition is tailor-made for the Latin American cases, where presidentialism has reigned supreme. In a parliamentary system, only the parliament needs to be chosen in free and fair elections.

2. For similar definitions of democracy, see Diamond, Linz, and Lipset (1989: xvi–xvii); Gasiorowski 1993; Linz and Stepan 1996: 3–15. For purposes of this chapter, I do not distinguish between authoritarian and totalitarian regimes. There have been few if any totalitarian regimes in Latin America.

3. All economic data in this chapter come from various sources of the Economic Commission for Latin America and the Caribbean, which has not provided GDP data for Cuba in recent decades.

4. This series of democratic breakdowns generated a rich literature (Collier 1979; Linz and Stepan 1978; O'Donnell 1973; Santos 1986; Stepan 1971).

5. The third wave started with the coup that deposed the old authoritarian regime in Portugal in 1974, quickly leading to the establishment of democracy. Greece (1974) and Spain (1975) followed shortly thereafter. The first wave occurred between 1828 and the 1920s, and the second between the 1940s and 1962.

6. Coppedge and Reineke focus on four criteria: fairness of elections, freedom of organization, freedom of expression, and alternatives to official sources of power. Hadenius bases his measure on whether suffrage restrictions exist, whether elections were open and fair, and whether elected officials really held power; whether citizens and political organizations enjoyed organizational freedoms, freedom of opinion, and freedom from political violence and oppression.

7. A divergence occurred if a regime I coded as a democracy had a combined Freedom House score of 7 or more; if a regime I coded as a semidemocracy had a combined Freedom House score of less than 6 or greater than 8; or if a regime I coded as authoritarian had a Freedom House score of 8 or less.

8. It is entirely plausible that more specific differences in colonial background help account for contemporary regime differences.

9. Moreover, using data for 132 Third World countries in 1988, Hadenius (1992) argued that a high level of development had less impact on the

level of democracy than he expected on the basis of other studies. Although his dependent variable (level of democracy) differs from mine (democratic surviv-ability), his result suggests a need for some caution.

10. The association between a higher per capita income and democracy does not resolve the causal direction. It is conceivable that democracies pro-moted higher growth rates, hence ended up with higher per capita incomes. In this case, higher per capita income in the democracies would be a result of de-mocracy, rather than vice versa. This theoretical possibility is very unlikely in Latin America because the countries that fit the democratic, semidemocratic, and authoritarian regime types have shifted so much over time. Based on the entire set of countries in the world, Przeworski and Limongi (1993) found that authori-tarian and democratic regimes have similar growth rates. Further research is needed to definitively establish this result specifically for Latin America.

11. Linz and Stepan (1989, 1996) properly argue that democratic legiti-macy is not highly contingent on socioeconomic performance.

12. On the nonlinearity of the relationship between per capita income and democracy, see Dahl 1971: 62–80; Domínguez 1993; Hadenius 1992.

13. Among the Western European left, disenchantment with real socialism and Marxism became pervasive in the 1970s. Renowned scholars sympathetic to the left such as Claude Leffort, Felix Guattari, and Norberto Bobbio criti-cized the authoritarian nature of real socialism. Leaving behind the Leninist tra-dition and seeking inspiration in Antonio Gramsci, the Italian Communist Party adopted Eurocommunism and criticized authoritarian socialism. After the elec-tions of François Mitterand in France (1981) and Felipe González (1981) in Spain, the socialist parties of those countries governed in centrist fashion.

14. The literature on the church's transformation is ample, but it has not always been integrated into the analysis of democratic survivability in the region.

15. Huntington (1991: 91–98) emphasizes the role of the U.S. government in encouraging democracy in Latin America. Lowenthal (1991) and Whitehead (1986) are more skeptical.

REFERENCES

Arat, Zehra F. 1988. "Democracy and Economic Development: Modernization Theory Revisited." *Comparative Politics* 21, no. 1 (October): 21–36.

Arnson, Cynthia J. 1993. *Crossroads: Congress, the President, and Central America, 1976–1993*. University Park: Pennsylvania State University Press.

Baloyra, Enrique A. 1983. "Reactionary Despotism in El Salvador: An Impedi-ment to Democratic Transition." In Martin Diskin, ed., *Trouble in Our Backyard: Central America and the United States in the Eighties*, pp. 101–23. New York: Pantheon.

Benavides, Maria Victória de Mesquita. 1981. *A UDN e o Udenismo: Ambigüi-dades do Liberalismo Brasileiro (1945–1965)*. Rio de Janeiro: Paz e Terra.

Bollen, Kenneth A. 1980. "Issues in the Comparative Measurement of Political Democracy." *American Sociological Review* 45, no. 2 (June): 370–90.

Bollen, Kenneth A., and Robert W. Jackman. 1985. "Economic and Noneconomic Determinants of Political Democracy in the 1960s." *Research in Political Sociology* 1 : 27–48.

Carothers, Thomas. 1991. "The Reagan Years: The 1980s." In Abraham F. Lowenthal, ed., *Exporting Democracy: The United States and Latin America, Themes and Issues*, pp. 90–122. Baltimore: Johns Hopkins University Press.

Castañeda, Jorge G. 1993. *Utopia Unarmed: The Latin American Left After the Cold War.* New York: Alfred A. Knopf.

Collier, David. 1975. "Timing of Economic Growth and Regime Characteristics in Latin America." *Comparative Politics* 7 (April): 331–60.

———, ed. 1979. *The New Authoritarianism in Latin America.* Princeton: Princeton University Press.

Collier, Ruth. Forthcoming. *Paths Toward Democracy: Working Class and Elites in Western Europe and Latin America.* Cambridge: Cambridge University Press.

Collier, Ruth Berins, and David Collier. 1991. *Shaping the Political Arena.* Princeton: Princeton University Press.

Coppedge, Michael. 1997. "Modernization and Thresholds of Democracy: Evidence for a Common Path and Process." In Manus I. Midlarsky, ed., *Inequality, Democracy, and Economic Development*, pp. 177–201. Cambridge: Cambridge University Press.

Coppedge, Michael, and Wolfgang H. Reinicke. 1990. "Measuring Polyarchy." *Studies in Comparative International Development* 25, no. 1 (Spring): 51–72.

Coulter, Philip. 1975. *Social Mobilization and Liberal Democracy.* Lexington: D.C. Heath.

Dahl, Robert A. 1971. *Polyarchy: Participation and Opposition.* New Haven: Yale University Press.

Diamond, Larry. 1992. "Economic Development and Democracy Reconsidered." In Gary Marks and Larry Diamond, eds., *Reexamining Democracy: Essays in Honor of Seymour Martin Lipset*, pp. 93–139. Newbury Park: Sage.

———. 1996. "Democracy in Latin America: Degrees, Illusions, and Directions for Consolidation." In Tom Farer, ed. *Beyond Sovereignty: Collectively Defending Democracy in the Americas*, pp. 52–104. Baltimore: Johns Hopkins University Press.

Diamond, Larry, and Juan J. Linz. 1989. "Introduction: Politics, Society, and Democracy in Latin America." In Larry Diamond, Juan J. Linz, and Seymour Martin Lipset, eds., *Democracy in Developing Countries*, vol. 4, *Latin America*, pp. 1–58. Boulder: Lynne Rienner.

Diamond, Larry, Juan J. Linz, and Seymour Martin Lipset, eds. 1989. *Democracy in Developing Countries*, vol. 4, *Latin America*. Boulder: Lynne Rienner.

Domínguez, Jorge I. 1993. "The Caribbean Question: Why Has Liberal Democracy (Surprisingly) Flourished?" In Jorge I. Domínguez, Robert A. Pastor, and R. Delisle Worrell, eds., *Democracy in the Caribbean: Political, Economic, and Social Perspectives,* pp. 1–25. Baltimore: Johns Hopkins University Press.

Economic Commision for Latin America and the Caribbean (ECLA). 1984. *Statistical Yearbook for Latin America and the Caribbean, 1983.* Santiago: ECLA.

Farer, Tom, ed. 1996. *Beyond Sovereignty: Collectively Defending Democracy in the Americas.* Baltimore: Johns Hopkins University Press.

Gasiorowski, Mark J. 1993. "The Political Regime Change Dataset." Unpublished.

Gibson, Edward. 1996. *Class and Conservative Parties: Argentina in Comparative Perspective.* Baltimore: Johns Hopkins University Press.

Gillespie, Richard. 1982. *Soldiers of Peron: Argentina's Montoneros.* Oxford: Clarendon Press.

Goldstein, Judith, and Robert Keohane, eds. 1993. *Ideas and Foreign Policy: Beliefs, Institutions, and Policy Change.* Ithaca: Cornell University Press.

Hadenius, Axel. 1992. *Democracy and Development.* Cambridge: Cambridge University Press.

Hagopian, Frances. 1996a. *Traditional Politics and Regime Change in Brazil.* Cambridge: Cambridge University Press.

———. 1996b. "Traditional Power Structures and Democratic Governance in Latin America." In Jorge I. Domínguez and Abraham F. Lowenthal, eds., *Constructing Democratic Governance: Latin America and the Caribbean in the 1990s—Themes and Issues,* pp. 64–86. Baltimore: Johns Hopkins University Press.

Hall, Peter A., ed. 1989. *The Political Power of Economic Ideas: Keynesian Across Nations.* Princeton: Princeton University Press.

Hartlyn, Jonathan, and Arturo Valenzuela. 1994. "Democracy in Latin America since 1930." In Leslie Bethell, ed., *The Cambridge History of Latin America,* vol. 6, *Latin America since 1930: Economy, Society, and Politics,* part 2, *Politics and Society,* pp. 99–162. Cambridge: Cambridge University Press.

Horowitz, Donald L. 1985. *Ethnic Groups in Conflict.* Berkeley: University of California Press.

Huntington, Samuel P. 1991. *The Third Wave: Democratization in the Late Twentieth Century.* Norman: University of Oklahoma Press.

Karl, Terry Lynn. 1995. "The Hybrid Regimes of Central America." *Journal of Democracy* 6, no. 3 (July): 72–86.

Keck, Margaret E., and Kathryn Sikkink. 1998. *Activists Beyond Borders: Advocacy Networks in International Politics.* Ithaca: Cornell University Press.

Lamounier, Bolivar. 1979. "Representação Política: A Importância de Certos Formalismos." In Bolivar Lamounier, Francisco Weffort, and Maria Victória Benevides, eds., *Direito, Cidadania e Participação,* pp. 230–57. São Paulo: Tao.

Levine, Daniel H. 1973. *Conflict and Political Change in Venezuela.* Princeton: Princeton University Press.

——. 1981. *Religion and Politics in Latin America: The Catholic Church in Venezuela and Colombia.* Princeton: Princeton University Press.

——. 1992. *Popular Voices in Latin American Catholicism.* Princeton: Princeton University Press.

Lijphart, Arend. 1977. *Democracy in Plural Societies: A Comparative Exploration.* New Haven: Yale University Press.

Linz, Juan J. 1978. *The Breakdown of Democratic Regimes: Crisis, Breakdown, and Reequilibration.* Baltimore: Johns Hopkins University Press.

Linz, Juan J, and Alfred Stepan, eds. 1978. *The Breakdown of Democratic Regimes.* Baltimore: Johns Hopkins University Press.

——. 1989. "Political Crafting of Democratic Consolidation or Destruction: European and South American Comparisons." In Robert A. Pastor, ed., *Democracy in the Americas: Stopping the Pendulum,* pp. 41–61. New York: Holmes and Meier.

——. 1996. *Problems of Democratic Transition and Consolidation.* Baltimore: Johns Hopkins University Press.

Lipset, Seymour Martin. 1960. *Political Man: The Social Bases of Politics.* Garden City: Anchor.

Lipset, Seymour Martin, et al. 1993. "A Comparative Analysis of the Social Requisites of Democracy." *International Social Science Journal* 136 (May): 155–75.

Lowenthal, Abraham F. 1991. "The United States and Latin American Democracy: Learning from History." In Abraham F. Lowenthal, ed., *Exporting Democracy: The United States and Latin America, Themes and Issues,* pp. 243–65. Baltimore: Johns Hopkins University Press.

Mainwaring, Scott. 1986. *The Catholic Church and Politics in Brazil 1916–1985.* Stanford: Stanford University Press.

Mainwaring, Scott, and Timothy R. Scully. 1995. "Party Systems in Latin America." In Scott Mainwaring and Timothy R. Scully, eds., *Building Democratic Institutions: Party Systems in Latin America,* pp. 1–34. Stanford: Stanford University Press.

May, John D. 1973. "Of the Conditions and Measures of Democracy." Morristown: General Learning Press.

Mayorga, René Antonio. 1997. "Bolivia's Silent Revolution." *Journal of Democracy* 8, no. 1 (January): 142–56.

McCoy, Jennifer, Larry Garber, and Robert Pastor. 1991. "Pollwatching and Peacemaking." *The Journal of Democracy.* 2, no. 4, 102–14.

Moore Jr., Barrington. 1966. *Social Origins of Dictatorship and Democracy: Lord and Peasant in the Making of the Modern World.* Boston: Beacon Press.

O'Donnell, Guillermo A. 1973. *Modernization and Bureaucratic-Authoritarianism.* Berkeley: Institute of International Studies, University of California.

——. 1993. "On the State, Democratization and Some Conceptual Problems: A Latin American View with Glances at Some Postcommunist Countries." *World Development* 21, no. 8: 1355–69.

——. 1998. "Polyarchies and the (Un)Rule of Law in Latin America." In Juan

Méndez, Guillermo O'Donnell, and Paulo Sérgio Pinheiro, eds., *The (Un)Rule of Law and the Underprivileged in Latin America*. Notre Dame: University of Notre Dame Press.

O'Donnell, Guillermo, and Philippe Schmitter. 1986. "Tentative Conclusions about Uncertain Democracies." In Guillermo O'Donnell, Philippe Schmitter, and Laurence Whitehead, eds. 1986. *Transitions from Authoritarian Rule: Prospects for Democracy,* part 4. Baltimore: Johns Hopkins University Press.

O'Donnell, Guillermo, Philippe Schmitter, and Laurence Whitehead, eds. 1986. *Transitions from Authoritarian Rule: Prospects for Democracy.* Baltimore: Johns Hopkins University Press.

Ollier, María Matilde. 1998. "The Political Learning Process among the Argentine Revolutionary Left, 1966–1995." Ph.D. Dissertation, University of Notre Dame.

Packenham, Robert A. 1973. *Liberal America and the Third World: Political Development Ideas in Foreign Aid and Social Science.* Princeton: Princeton University Press.

———. 1986. "The Changing Political Discourse in Brazil." In Wayne Selcher, ed., *Political Liberalization in Brazil: Dynamics, Dilemmas, and Future Prospects,* pp. 135–73. Boulder: Westview Press.

———. 1992. *The Dependency Movement: Scholarship and Politics in Development Studies.* Cambridge: Harvard University Press.

Pastor, Robert A. 1989. "How to Reinforce Democracy in the Americas: Seven Proposals." In Robert A. Pastor, ed., *Democracy in the Americas: Stopping the Pendulum,* pp. 139–55. New York: Holmes and Meier.

Payne, Leigh A. 1994. *Brazilian Industrialists and Democratic Change.* Baltimore: Johns Hopkins University Press.

Power, Timothy J., and Mark J. Gasiorowski. 1997. "Institutional Design and Democratic Consolidation in the Third World." *Comparative Political Studies* 30, no. 2 (April): 123–55.

Pridham, Geoffrey, ed. 1991. *Encouraging Democracy: The International Context of Regime Transition in Southern Europe.* New York: St. Martin's Press.

Przeworski, Adam. 1986. "Problems in the Study of Transition to Democracy." In Guillermo O'Donnell, Philippe Schmitter, and Laurence Whitehead, eds., *Transitions from Authoritarian Rule: Prospects for Democracy,* part 3, pp. 47–63. Baltimore: Johns Hopkins University Press.

Przeworski, Adam, and Fernando Limongi. 1993. "Political Regimes and Economic Growth." *Journal of Economic Perspectives* 7, no. 3 (Summer): 51–69.

———. 1997. "Modernization: Theories and Facts." *World Politics* 49 (January): 155–83.

Przeworski, Adam, et al. 1996. "What Makes Democracies Endure?" *Journal of Democracy* 7, no. 1 (January): 39–55.

Putnam, Robert D. 1993. *Making Democracy Work: Civic Traditions in Modern Italy.* Princeton: Princeton University Press.

Remmer, Karen L. 1996. "The Sustainability of Political Democracy: Lessons from South America." *Comparative Political Studies* 29, no. 6 (December): 611–34.

Rueschemeyer, Dietrich, Evelyne Huber Stephens, and John D. Stephens. 1992. *Capitalist Development and Democracy.* Chicago: University of Chicago Press.

Santos, Wanderley Guilherme dos. 1985. "A Pós-'Revolução' Brasileira." In Hélio Jaguaribe et al., *Brasil, Sociedade Democrática,* pp. 223–335. Rio de Janeiro: José Olympio.

——. 1986. *Sessenta e Quatro: Anatomia da Crise.* São Paulo: Vértice.

Schmitter, Philippe C., and Terry Lynn Karl. 1993. "What Democracy Is . . . And Is Not." In Larry Diamond and Marc F. Plattner, eds., *The Global Resurgence of Democracy,* pp. 39–52. Baltimore: Johns Hopkins University Press.

Starr, Harvey. 1991. "Democratic Dominoes: Diffusion Approaches to the Spread of Democracy in the International System." *Journal of Conflict Resolution* 35, no. 2 (June): 356–81.

Stepan, Alfred. 1971. *The Military in Politics: Changing Patterns in Brazil.* Princeton: Princeton University Press.

——. 1986. "Paths toward Redemocratization: Theoretical and Comparative Considerations." In Guillermo O'Donnell, Philippe Schmitter, and Laurence Whitehead, eds., *Transitions from Authoritarian Rule: Prospects for Democracy,* part 3, pp. 64–84. Baltimore: Johns Hopkins University Press.

——. 1988. *Rethinking Military Politics: Brazil and the Southern Cone.* Princeton: Princeton University Press.

Tocqueville, Alexis de. 1969. *Democracy in America.* Garden City: Anchor Books.

Valenzuela, Arturo. 1978. *The Breakdown of Democratic Regimes: Chile.* Baltimore: Johns Hopkins University Press.

Vanhanen, Tatu. 1990. *The Process of Democratization: A Comparative Study of 147 States, 1980–88.* New York: Crane Russak.

Villagrán de León, Francisco. 1993. "Thwarting the Guatemalan Coup." *Journal of Democracy* 4, no. 4 (October): 117–24.

Walker, Ignacio. 1990. *Socialismo y democracia: Chile y Europa en perspectiva comparada.* Santiago: CIEPLAN/Hachette.

Weffort, Francisco C. 1985. *Por Que Democracia?* São Paulo: Brasiliense.

Weiner, Myron. 1987. "Empirical Democratic Theory." In Myron Weiner and Ergun Özbudun, eds., *Competitive Elections in Developing Countries,* pp. 3–34. Durham: Duke University Press/American Enterprise Institute.

Whitehead, Laurence. 1986. "International Aspects of Democratization." In Guillermo O'Donnell, Philippe Schmitter, and Laurence Whitehead, eds., *Transitions from Authoritarian Rule: Prospects for Democracy,* part 3, pp. 3–46. Baltimore: Johns Hopkins University Press.

——. 1991. "Democracy by Convergence and Southern Europe: A Comparative Politics Perspective." In Geoffrey Pridham, ed., *Encouraging Democ-*

racy: The International Context of Regime Transition in Southern Europe,
pp. 45–61. New York: St. Martin's Press.

——, ed. 1996. *The International Dimensions of Democratization: Europe and
the Americas.* Oxford: Oxford University Press.

Wiarda, Howard J. 1986. "Can Democracy Be Exported? The Quest for Democ-
racy in U.S.-Latin American Policy." In Kevin Middlebrook and Carlos
Rico, ed., *The United States and Latin America in the 1980s: Contending
Perspectives on a Decade of Crisis,* pp. 325–51. Pittsburgh: University of
Pittsburgh Press.

Wood, Elizabeth J. Forthcoming. "The Transformation of Elite Representation
in El Salvador." In Kevin Middlebrook, ed., *Conservative Parties, the
Right, and Democracy in Latin America.*

2

Hardliners and Softliners in the Middle East: Problems of Governance and the Prospects for Liberalization in Authoritarian Political Systems

Farhad Kazemi and Augustus Richard Norton

INTRODUCTION

AUTHORITARIANISM HAS BEEN AN enduring and common feature of most Middle Eastern political systems for some time. Despite the large variety of regime types that the Middle East has experienced, including monarchical, socialist, secular nationalist, Islamist, mobilizational, military junta, and others, authoritarian rule has persisted. Since authoritarianism depends largely on the use of tacit or explicit coercion to secure popular compliance, this also raises questions of political legitimacy and long-term stability.

Our basic argument is that political and economic reform is possible even in the authoritarian systems of the Middle East. Reform takes place when organized demands from within, united on a common goal, become strong enough to elicit a positive regime response. Further, once liberalization processes begin, the likelihood of reform continuation is enhanced, since it expands the constituencies for reform and increases pressures for regime accountability and responsiveness.

The possibility of reform reversal is also present. Reform is not necessarily a linear upward progression and its continued success cannot be assumed. It is rather an unstable process, where reversals are not uncommon. Middle Eastern regimes have access to a variety of strategies—enhanced repression, more efficient authoritarianism, controlled or staged elections—that can postpone or even defeat reform movements. On the other hand, various factors can help to ensure the continued success of reform movements. Among these are enlightened leadership, "defusing (but not necessarily disarming) the military" (O'Donnell and Schmitter 1986: 32), respect for private property, the extent of popular support, and the role of the bourgeoisie.

To examine these issues further, we shall organize this chapter around several broad themes relating to Middle Eastern authoritarianism. These are rentierism, reform and liberalization, and regime-opposition pacts. We shall initially define and consider the theoretical dimensions of these issues, and thereafter use selected examples to illustrate their practical implications for politics in the Middle East.

CONCEPTS AND DEFINITIONS

Authoritarian regimes, to rephrase Linz, are "political systems with limited, not responsible, political pluralism . . . in which a leader or occasionally a small group exercises power within formally ill-defined limits" (1975: 264; see also Linz 1975). Linz also includes "distinctive mentalities," the absence of "elaborate and guiding ideology," and the lack of "intensive political mobilization" among the features of these regimes. In a recent study, Linz and Stepan compare authoritarianism with other forms of rule and emphasize the different social bases of power for each type of nondemocratic regime (1996: 43–44).

A type of state that perpetuates authoritarianism, and which is common in the Middle East, is the rentier state. This is an allocation state in which a substantial portion of the government's revenue is derived from rents received from the outside world (Beblawi and Luciani, 1987). Rentierism can take the form of dependence on a single commodity, such as oil, or it can be based on security rents in the form of military and economic aid or remittances from citizens working abroad. As long as a major portion of the state's revenue is based on outside rents, the state takes the form of rentierism.[1]

The rentier state tends to become autonomous from society and increasingly unaccountable to its citizens. Since most revenue comes from sources exogenous to the economy and are not based on domestic economic activity and taxation, in contrast to the situation in the case of production states, the state can usually resist much of the pressure for reform and political accountability. The state's primary responsibility toward its citizens is the preservation of traditional entitlements, which means that it does not have to pay much attention to demands for political reform and liberalization. Rentierism, for this reason, helps to sustain autocratic regimes.

The key question for the Middle East, whatever the particular form of authoritarianism, is whether there is any space for reform and liberalization within its political systems. In this essay, we are using the term "reform" interchangeably with "liberalization." We are clearly not dealing with reform movements that are transparently retrogressive and help to entrench authoritarianism. Liberalization, as defined by O'Donnell and Schmitter, is "the process of making effective certain rights that protect both individuals and social groups from arbitrary or illegal acts committed by the state or third parties" (1986: 7). The principal concern here is the development, expansion, and sustainability of these rights, developments which are critical for transitions from authoritarianism. When such a process emerges and is sustained, with key allies in the ruling group as well as in society, a reform movement is born.

A principal feature of liberalization is the regime's eventual effort to incorporate nonviolent opposition into the system. Regime strategies can be either liberal or illiberal, although lines of demarcation between the two are not always clear. Illiberal strategies can take the form of buying off dissent through patronage and co-optation, various forms of corporatism, or controlled elections.

Alternatively, a regime can try to open up the system through a political pact, which involves an accord between the government and opposition in which the possibilities and limits of power-sharing are outlined. Such a pact is defined "as explicit, but not always publicly explicated or justified, agreement among a select set of actors which seeks to define (or better redefine) rules governing the exercise of power on the basis of mutual guarantees of 'vital interests' of those entering into it" (O'Donnell and Schmitter 1986: 37). Pacts do not necessarily bring a transition from authoritarianism (see Linz and Stepan, 1996: 56). As in reform, pacts can also be used to maintain autocratic systems, or key provisions may be ignored by the parties, especially on the government side. In spite of such potential problems, however, pacts that facilitate the inclusion of responsible opposition in the political system can serve as important breakthroughs for political liberalization.

THE MIDDLE EASTERN STATE AND ITS RESOURCES

Many of the problems and reasons for authoritarianism in the Middle East can be attributed to the state's behavior and its use of available resources for its own purposes. As Crystal has pointed out, the Arab state has used a variety of methods to ensure its control of society. These have included domination of the economy, manipulation of sociocultural diversity to fragment the opposition, repression, and the instrumental use of ideological formulas (1994: 262–89).

Moreover, some of the Gulf monarchies have the additional negative attribute of also being "sultanistic" (see note 1). Since sultanism depends on "unrestrained personal rulership," its operation limits the options for reform from within. In other words, it is much less likely, although not impossible, for political reform and liberalization to develop and endure in a sultanistic system than in other forms of authoritarian rule in the Middle East.

The Middle Eastern state extends well beyond the palaces of the rulers. Outside of agriculture, the state is almost always the leading employer. Middle Eastern states control their respective formal economies through a phalanx of public-sector companies or the flow of oil and other forms of rent that go directly to their coffers. Consequently, government expenditures often make up a larger share of the GNP than in other countries with comparable income levels. As al-Sayyid indicates, "in 1985, government spending made up 23 percent of GNP in middle income countries generally, while it amounted to 33 percent of GNP in the Yemen Arab Republic and in Morocco, 40 percent in Tunisia, and 48 percent in Egypt" (1991: 716).

The state's dominance of the formal economy and the continued exclusion of important segments of society have encouraged a sharp expansion of the informal sector. Not directly controlled by the state, this sector encompasses an array of craftspeople, physicians, lawyers, petty traders in legal and illicit goods, atelier operators, pieceworkers, criminals, and many others whose income is undocumented by the state. A World Bank estimate notes that the informal economy in Turkey is half the size of the formal economy (*Financial Times*, June 1995). In Egypt, the informal economy is commonly estimated to be comparable in size to the formal economy (Singerman 1995: 173–243).

In postrevolutionary Iran, the informal economy has mushroomed dramatically and is pointedly visible in a variety of crucial money-lending institutions and other arenas (Saffari 1996; see also Amuzegar 1993). A recent study concludes that the informal sector of the Iranian economy is both the exclusive source of income for a large number of people and an important second source for those who are gainfully employed in the formal sector. Moreover, a large portion of the foreign refugee population (primarily Afghans and to a lesser extent Iraqis) is employed in the informal sector. The study estimates that about half of all gainful employment in the urban areas is in the informal sector (Tabatabai and Mehran 1995: 212–13).

Although additional examples could readily be offered, the relevant point for this chapter is the unwillingness or inability of the state to incorporate large segments of the population into its economic activities. Even when the state attempts to regulate the informal sector, it is often unsuccessful. A prime example is the Syrian effort in the mid-1980s to control the informal sector, particularly the black market in Syrian currency smuggling from Lebanon, which "never came close" to success (Heydemann 1992: 26).

As a result of failures in the formal sector, the informal sector has grown steadily and become an important arena for undermining and quietly contesting the state's authority. Yet the informal sector's status, although not necessarily economically marginal, is often problematic. Those involved in it fear a loss of income and livelihood through arbitrary state action. Many see their particular form of entrepreneurial activity as a consequence of the state's failure to provide a place for them in the economic domains it controls.

OIL, RENTIERISM, THE BOURGEOISIE, AND REFORM

Although rentierism in the Middle East has provided many states with substantial resources and fiscal muscle, it has also had a detrimental effect on both economic development and political liberalization. Its economic impact can be seen in the state's dependence on rents, extracted primarily from oil, as the principal source of revenue. This has in turn discouraged the emergence of an independent bourgeoisie that can engage the state in economic give-and-take (see, e.g., Chaudhry 1994). In effect, the state has attempted to satisfy the population through provision of a host of services and economic activities paid for with income received from rents. As long as rent money from the outside world is available, the state will respond only to those concerns of the population which it finds necessary for maintaining its power and position.

Moreover, the rentier state's often extensive economic programs tend to engage the bourgeoisie fully and reward it economically in projects conceived and funded by the state. Hence, the bourgeoisie's fortunes come to center on the state and its defined economic goals. It becomes a dependent and fully co-opted bourgeoisie, unable and unwilling to engage the state in delineation of rights, responsibilities, and obligations.

The rentier state has the additional problem of becoming increasingly autonomous from the society. It can use its income from rent to enlist compliance and to pursue goals that are not necessarily in the best interests of society. Since most of the state's revenues are not extracted from the population, the corollary sense of responsiveness and obligation to society does not necessarily develop. Rentier states accordingly find themselves increasingly reluctant to liberalize their political systems. As Luciani indicates, the oil rent becomes "a factor perpetuating authoritarian government" (Luciani 1994: 131). This tendency stands in sharp contrast to what Luciani calls "production states," where income is acquired primarily "through taxation of domestic economic activity" (Luciani 1994: 131; Luciani, 1987; Vanderwalle, 1997). In Luciani's view, taxation and the widening of the state's fiscal base are essential inducements for democratization. He further posits that a state facing fiscal crisis and forced to resort to increased taxation will stimulate demands from within the society for accountability and democratic patterns of governance.

But taxation alone will not create a sense of obligation, responsibility, and accountability in a rentier regime. Aside from the differential impact of taxation by type—direct or indirect—in prompting political demands, any number of intervening variables may affect demands for accountability (Waterbury 1994: 30; see also Waterbury 1997). The fiscal crisis of the state may serve as one intervening variable. The leadership role of top political officials may serve as another. In addition, where direct taxes are imposed, tax collection has often proven incredibly inefficient. Rather than prompting demands for participation, direct taxation has often had the effect of promoting a shift to the informal economy, where income is characteristically undocumented and untaxed. Thus, it is difficult to see any direct relationship between rentierism and accountability when the essential features of rentierism remain intact. Political liberalization and reform are not the normal tendency of rentier states. Only when such states are forced to rethink the fundamental form of the state's relationship with society does reform appear as an option.

A valid distinction here is perhaps the difference between a rentier state such as Jordan and such rentier states as Saudi Arabia and the Gulf states. Wealthier rentier states like Saudi Arabia have far greater resources with which to accommodate fiscal crises and continue time-honored authoritarian structures. On the other hand, rentier economies with fewer and less reliable resources tend to respond more positively to fiscal crisis by allowing limited political and economic liberalization.

The link between fiscal crisis, reduction of rentier dependency, and political liberalization receives some support from the case of Jordan (Brand 1992: 184). From its inception, the Jordanian state has been dependent on foreign subsidy (external rent) for income and revenue. The extent, form, and continuity of this subsidy made rentierism the modal feature of the Jordanian state. Rentierism peaked in 1981 with important increases in "the two primary features of Jordan's rentier economy—workers' remittances and petro-dollar foreign aid" (Brynen 1992: 84; see also Satloff 1992: 130). Both of these sources of revenues declined as the price of oil dropped, however, and many unemployed expatriate workers returned from the Gulf to seek jobs at home. The resultant budgetary deficits were not rectified with increased taxation but through domestic borrowing.

As the economic crisis continued unabated, austerity measures were introduced. These included "freezing spending on development projects, banning the import of many luxury goods, and sharply raising fees for foreign worker permits, custom duties, and taxes on hotels and restaurants" (Satloff 1992: 136). These measures elicited widespread protest and public outcry against corruption and inequalities. As Brynen explains, "these calls for economic reform were soon taken in anonymous pamphlets, in appeals by East Bank community leaders in Karak, Salt, and elsewhere, and by the Amman-based (predominantly Palestinian) professional organizations, who added to them calls for greater political freedom and participation" (Brynen 1992: 90). In response, the Jordanian government began a process of incremental political liberalization which continues in some form to the present, although there is no mistaking the state's capacity to suspend or even roll back its concessions. In fact, some observers argue that, since 1997, at least some of Jordan's political liberalization programs have been reversed.

Jordan's transition from rentierism, fostered by an incipient fiscal crisis, ushered in a form of political liberalization that has allowed for a relatively free press, open parliamentary elections, and few restrictions on freedom of association. The role of individuals at the helm of power is a key factor in the decision to liberalize or repress. The decisive role of Jordan's King Hussein in promoting political liberalization and inclusionary politics is significant; many states facing a similar situation have resorted to repression instead. Rentier states confronted with fiscal crisis will not automatically select the path of political liberalization.

It is quite possible that some of the rentier Gulf states, given the degree of citizen involvement with the state, may also choose a path similar to that of Jordan's. In Gause's words,

as the role of the state in these countries has grown, it has begun to call forth new demands for representative institutions and responsible government from society. These demands spring from the very processes of state growth and expansion occasioned by the oil

boom. The recent upsurge in political activity in the Gulf monarchies is not only consistent with the realities of the rentier state and
its relationship to society, but is in fact generated by those realities.
(Gause 1994: 81)

Similarly, Salamé argues that in small Arab states, such as Kuwait
or even Lebanon, a different combination of factors may help to advance
nation-building and sustain incipient impulses for political liberalization.
These factors include a hostile regional environment, absence of regional
ambition, and the "fragility of the state entity" (1994: 85–111). For both
Lebanon and Kuwait the issue of an external hegemon is also relevant.
In Lebanon, the external hegemon (Syria) initially allowed some degree
of political reform but has since checked the options for increasing the
level of reform. In Kuwait, the experience of occupation by the external
hegemon (Iraq) and its subsequent defeat by the allied forces created an
opportunity to press for reform. Two other factors—the relative strength
of the Kuwaiti civil society as demonstrated during the occupation, and
the institutionalization of reformist opposition forces—also helped the
situation. Although initially reluctant, the emir of Kuwait had to accede
to the opposition's demands for relatively free parliamentary elections.
    The limited and parallel cases of Lebanon and Kuwait are not,
however, repeated in the Gulf monarchies where rentierism and the fiscal
crises so far have not transformed the basic relationship between the rulers and the ruled. In actual fact, these states have so far weathered their
fiscal crises and been able to contain demands for reform. This can be
explained at least partially by reiterating that in the Gulf monarchies citizen expectations from the government are not predicated on the principle of "taxation therefore representation," but rather on the continued
operation of efficient rentierism. As Gause says, "much as taxpayers want
responsible governments to spend their money, the beneficiaries of rentier
states want responsible governments to sign their checks" (1994: 81). Although this observation may be accurate, it leaves the basic issue intact,
since it makes the impulse for political liberalization dependent on the
rulers' whim and benevolence. This kind of environment is not conducive to the development of a system of rights, obligations, and entitle-
ment. Rulers who give can also take away.
    They would not be able to take away so easily if the rules of the
game were not subject to arbitrary changes. Some scholars have suggested that in these situations pacts agreed upon by both government and
opposition can be useful. In principle, pacts permit the rulers to maintain
control while ceding some political authority to their opponents. Since
these pacts specify the terms of reference for the opposition in return for

political concessions by the state, their violation by either side can be more easily documented (see Waterbury 1994; Leca 1994). In general, pacts tend to be conservative documents that preserve some degree of privilege and reassure those in power of the opposition's intent. More often than not, the more successful pacts ensure the preservation of basic military privileges and the sanctity of private property. In spite of their conservative thrust, however, pacts can be important for reform because they also set clear and agreed limits on arbitrary power.

In Algeria, arguably, the negotiation of a pact between the government and opposition forces may have mitigated some of the factors that were used to justify the army's seizure of power in January 1992. In practice, however, pacts have often had only limited success. In some cases, such as Jordan and Lebanon, pacts have held, whereas in other cases, such as Tunisia, the pact was only a tactical device to buy time. In Jordan, King Hussein oversaw the drafting of the National Pact of 1991, which opened the way for the legalization of political parties, widening the space for civil society, increasing the freedom of the press, and formally ending martial law (Brand 1995: 149). In Tunisia, Ben Ali shelved the pact negotiated in 1988, realizing that the Islamist al-Nahda party enjoyed a base of popular support (Anderson 1991: 244–60).

Other illustrations are provided by Kuwait, Yemen, Egypt, and Lebanon. The emir of Kuwait, who sought sanctuary in Saudi Arabia during Iraq's occupation of his country, agreed (in an oral pact) to the renewal of the Kuwaiti parliament and free elections but attempted unsuccessfully to renege on his promises once he was restored to the throne in 1992. Yemen's experiment with pact-making was overshadowed by the civil war that erupted in 1994. In Egypt, an attempt in the mid-1990s by the respected intellectual and activist Said al-Nagar to establish a pact on certain key principles also failed, largely because its power-sharing criteria and some of the liberal principles it championed were not accepted. In Lebanon, the Ta'if accord of 1989, which spelled out the terms for an end to the civil war, has often been observed, especially the provisions requiring Syrian cooperation.

The case of Syria gives another twist to the argument that economic crisis followed by relatively steady economic liberalization necessarily leads to political reform. As in some other authoritarian states, Syria has controlled the bargaining process associated with its economic liberalization program by confining it "to within a narrowly delimited arena that typically includes only a small set of privileged institutional or individual participants" (Heydemann 1993: 78).

Although there is an important political dimension to Syria's economic restructuring, the concern has been "to insulate the regime from

the political consequences of its economic mismanagement, to prevent
the economic crisis from provoking genuine democratization" (Heydemann 1993: 82). As Hinnebusch indicates, it is the regime's political interests that dominate the liberalization strategy. "These require a middle
way: while long-term durability requires fuller integration into the world
market, short-term stability requires that this be carefully managed, and
defending regime autonomy means preventing any one social force—
bourgeoisie or bureaucracy—from achieving dominance" (1997: 263;
see also Perthes 1995: 49–68). Moreover, the partially liberalized economy has kept the affected part of the private sector dependent on the
state. Consequently, demands for a "democratic pact" and a mutual
sense of dependency so far have not emerged on the Syrian political
scene.

The long-range impact, however, may not be all that dissimilar
from other cases of economic liberalization. As Hinnebusch observes,
"two segments of the bourgeoisie—industrial entrepreneurs and expatri-
ates—have particular potential to widen the civil society" (1995: 231).
Their concerns and views will have to be considered and eventually ac-
commodated by the regime. Moreover, those members of the business
community who have not benefited from economic reform will also be
making their access demands known to the regime, which can either suppress these demands or gradually open the political system. In either case,
there are important unintended consequences of economic liberalization
that will have to be dealt with. Economic liberalization unleashes forces
that will sooner or later make demands on the system for greater benefits
and shares. In contrast to political liberalization, it is more difficult for a
regime to reverse the process of economic liberalization after it has been
initiated. The Syrian experience will be an important future test case for
this proposition.

The examples of Iran and Turkey also shed some light on this issue.
In Iran, rentierism came to define the state in the 1970s. Its systematic
growth was conclusively evident after the oil boom of the post-1973
Arab-Israeli war. Supremely confident of its economic and political positions in domestic, regional, and international arenas, the state carried
out economic policies that resulted in two simultaneous developments.
It created a heavily dependent commercial and industrial modern bourgeoisie that benefited enormously from the state policies but remained
subservient to the state. The private sector's influence "was limited to
implementation. Being totally dependent on the state, Iran's rentier bourgeoisie had neither the incentive nor the means to 'capture the state'"
(Shambayati 1994: 321).

Growth of rentierism also made the state essentially oblivious to the concerns and priorities of civil society. The prerevolutionary Iranian state decided what was good for society and acted accordingly. The gap between the two increased as none of the normal checks and balances emerged or were allowed to operate. The state's "increasing independence from reliance on a tax base made it possible for various economic and social policies to be followed without much regard for social consent" (Najmabadi 1987: 215).

When the state was eventually challenged during the revolutionary years, it was the traditional bourgeoisie from the bazaar, which had preserved some of its autonomy from the state, that took the lead and in reality bankrolled the revolution. Using the well-established bazaar-mosque alliance networks, the opposition legitimized its attack on the Pahlavi state, utilizing the powerful Islamic ideology. The sharp lines of cleavage were defined in cultural and moral terms, much more so than economic ones, in order to mobilize support and to attack the state where it was most obviously vulnerable (see Ashraf 1988; Parsa 1989; Shambayati 1994). The bazaar furnished the funds, and the clerics provided the organizational structure and networks of mobilization. Their expression of opposition surfaced under a strong Shi'i-Islamic code with deep resonance in the society at large. This was once again an example of the pragmatic use of Islam to gain advantage in the political arena. The Iranian rentier state, alienated from significant segments of civil society and confronted with a major political challenge that was expressed in moral and cultural terms, proved incapable of sustaining itself. Political liberalization, granted under intense revolutionary pressures, came too late in the game to help preserve the regime.

The Turkish case advances a sharply different model, and different conclusions can be drawn from it about the role of the state in economic development. Although certain features of rentierism, such as remittances from workers abroad, were also present in Turkey, the state's income was based primarily on domestic sources, not external rent. Hence rentierism did not dominate the Turkish economy. To increase revenues in the 1970s, the state had to increase taxation and domestic production. A number of policies, including import substituting industrialization (ISI), were adopted to increase domestic production and reduce external dependence. Although these attempts did not help Turkey's negative trade balance and foreign exchange crisis, they prompted the state to engage in a serious give-and-take with the business community through chambers of commerce and industry (Shambayati 1994: 314). As Barkey points out, economic issues became politicized and those in the private sector who believed that they were not getting their fair share demanded compensation from the state (Barkey 1990: 26). The ensuing cleavages within the private sector led to the creation of several organizations devoted to the management of commerce and industry. The National Salvation Party (NSP) can be seen as an Islamist group that was established to protect the interests of the petite bourgeoisie against some of the more prominent organizations that were tied to the interests of larger industrial and commercial capitalists (Shambayati 1994: 316). The party "was successful in exploiting the perceived neglect of Anatolian business. Coupling an Islamic message with a strong emphasis on regional industrialization, the NSP was most successful in the East Central, Northeast and South Central regions of lesser development" (Barkey 1990: 158, 150–53).

Economic issues defined much of the political agenda of this Islamist party, as well as that of the industrialists, in interactions with the Turkish state. Arranged in a set of autonomous organizations, the private sector was a serious force in the society at large and in its relationship with the state. The private sector's concerns and demands could not be ignored by the state. As observed by Shambayati (1994: 327; see also Barkey 1990), the Turkish state responded in an essentially corporatist fashion to demands from within.

> In Turkey, however, corporatism was inclusionary. Associations were not merely instruments of government control; they also served as the channel through which civil society made claims upon the state. Furthermore, by the 1970s some sectors of society were financially and organizationally strong enough to make demands upon the state outside the corporatist structure. Since the Turkish state was financially dependent upon these groups, it could not afford to ignore their demands. In particular, the state had to be responsive to the demands of entrepreneurial classes. At the same time, since the state controlled scarce resources such as foreign exchange, the entrepreneurial classes had an incentive to institutionalize their ties with the state.

The precondition for such a scenario was the existence of an essentially liberal system in Turkey, which allowed for interest groups to function, develop, and make demands upon the state. The state's weakness contributed to the private sector's freedom to engage the state in a serious exchange on issues of economic policy before the military takeover of 1980. Barkey, however, argues that the absence of state autonomy in this period was responsible for some of the ISI's subsequent problems. He maintains that "the military interventions, which followed ISI-induced crises, have to be viewed in light of the fragmentation of the state apparatus and the need to impose a dominating vision on the unruly segments of the private sector" (Barkey 1990: 34).

From the perspective of this analysis, the real issue is not so much the state's weakness or strength as the degree of freedom allowed to economic and political interests to organize and articulate their concerns. Although the weakness of the Turkish state in the 1970s may have been responsible for the ISI crisis, it also allowed greater freedom for interest aggregation and articulation. This inclusionary posture contributed to the prospects for political reform in the long run. In short, the absence of dominant rentierism, increasing domestic taxation and extraction, the foreign exchange crisis, and the willingness to engage opposition from within the society in an inclusionary way, all combined to increase prospects for political reform in Turkey. This pattern stands in sharp contrast to the Iranian case in the prerevolutionary decade, during which rentierism and exclusionary politics were the dominant norms. Similar observations can be made about rentier Arab states and their aversion to inclusionary politics and power-sharing policies.

To sum up, then, it is clear that prospects for reform are particularly constrained in rentier states. Reform, however, is possible (especially in rentier economies as opposed to rentier states) under certain circumstances and in response to certain pressures. These include the role of the bourgeoisie and the degree of its dependence on the state, the form and type of fiscal crisis facing the state, the place of regime-opposition pacts, and the strength of the reformists inside and outside of the government. A real long-term problem, antithetical to reform, is the ability of regimes to adopt "survival strategies" which allow them "to minimally respond to the pressures for economic and political change without engaging in the risky business of power sharing" (Brumberg 1995: 229; see also Barkey 1992).

ELECTIONS AND POLITICAL REFORM

Elections are relatively unimportant as measures of political freedom in the Middle East. In fact, several elections in recent years have actually had a corrosive effect upon political liberalization and incipient democratization. The cases of Algeria and Yemen are obvious examples. In Algeria, a poorly designed electoral process in operation from 1989 until 1992 was aborted by a coup (see Entelis 1996: 45–86). In Yemen, the 1993 elections destabilized a tentatively successful power-sharing arrangement and curtailed liberalization efforts. Elections that serve the cause of autocracy are problematic, but those that curtail incipient political reform are profoundly counterproductive.

Yet there are important exceptions to this general pattern, not only in Israel but also in recent elections in Turkey and in the 1996 inaugural elections in the Palestinian entity, where participation was remarkably high (over 90 percent in Gaza). There is no guarantee that these exceptions will become the norm for the rest of the region. Electoral reform, however, remains one of the most important arenas, in both real and symbolic terms, for opening up the political system and promoting institutionalized inclusionary politics.

Examining electoral laws across the region, there is a pattern of modest liberalization and nominally competitive elections that have occurred in Egypt (1979, 1984, 1987, 1990, 1996), Iran (1980, 1984, 1988, 1992, 1996), Kuwait (1992, 1996), Lebanon (1992, 1996), Yemen (1993), Morocco (1993), and Jordan (1989, 1993). Nonetheless, even if the pattern of blatant manipulation has been softened somewhat, the rules are still heavily skewed in favor of governments and to the disadvantage of the opposition.

In general, elections continue to be carefully choreographed affairs, in which the results do not include upsets or surprises. In the Islamic Republic of Iran, for example, the government has routinely used the appointed Guardians Council, as well as a host of other extralegal methods, to prevent opposition candidates from standing for elections (Kazemi 1996b: 139–40). In the 1995 parliamentary elections in Egypt, opposition participation was restricted. As a result, 95 percent of the seats went to the ruling National Democratic Party, with only thirteen seats secured by the four opposition parties. Only one avowedly Islamist candidate, running as independent, was elected. The Labor Party, a convenient vehicle for moderate Islamists who are barred from creating a party of their own, did not win a single seat. This was a marked contrast to the 1984 and 1987 elections, in which dozens of Islamists won parliamentary seats. In the December 1995 elections, some of the Egyptian government's ballot-box stuffers were so overzealous that they completed more ballots than they could fit in the boxes. The extras were dumped as trash in alleys adjoining the polling stations (*Mideast Mirror,* 1996).

In a few cases, elections have improved governmental accountability, if not performance, and balloting has sometimes allowed for the expression of public demands for better and more responsive government. Portions of the electorate in places such as Kuwait, Lebanon, and Palestine have been able to vent their demands and even to send a rebuke to the ruling autocrats. These examples are not to be dismissed. Yet, in all these cases, significant segments of the population were unrepresented in the electoral process.

Electoral politics in the Middle East, then, is not the most common place to search for political reform. Nevertheless, it remains an important and highly visible arena where government accountability, or its absence, can be relatively easily observed and measured. As part of a larger reform movement, elections can serve an important role in sustaining reform and liberalization (see Drake and Silva 1986, for Latin America). Electoral politics matters when it gives ordinary citizens a sense of efficacy. The electorate votes readily when it believes that voting counts. This explains why voters in Turkey are so heavily involved in elections and why Egyptians vote enthusiastically in voluntary associations and sporting-club elections but not in general elections. In fact, the level of voter participation in national elections in Egypt, in contrast to the West, is inversely associated with education and socioeconomic status (see Kazemi and Norton, 1996: 110–11).

THE JUDICIARY AND THE PRESS AS AGENTS OF REFORM

Two important institutions in the Middle East—the judiciary and the press—can play a potentially positive role in loosening the reigns of authoritarianism. The judiciary is important because of the traditional emphasis in Islam on law, legal traditions, and the role of the judges. What Max Weber called "qadi justice" in his famous book *Economy and Society* is in some ways an affirmation of the Muslim judges' autonomy in also considering ethical and moral issues in the rendering of legal decisions.

There is, therefore, a certain quality attached to the judicial institutions that helps to protect them from undue influence by the government or the powerful. Although this autonomy and independence can be (and has been) violated, regimes have to avoid going too far in this area. In Egypt, in particular, considerable judicial activism has marked the legal system. As Brown indicates, "this has made possible a fair degree of judicial independence as well as official observance of legality in the bulk of governmental affairs. On matters deemed too critical to leave to a strict legal framework, rulers have generally escaped constitutional and legal restrictions less by attacking them than by avoiding the judicial structure" (Brown 1997: 157).

The Egyptian judiciary has succeeded on several occasions in restraining the government from imposing its own will on the accused. This is especially applicable to some of the Islamist opponents of the regime whose detention and treatment by the police were extralegal. As a result of the judiciary's emphasis on the necessity of a fair trial for the accused, as well as the willingness of the Supreme Constitutional Court of Egypt to declare certain statutes unconstitutional, judicial institutions appear to be an important protector of the rule of law (see Sherif 1996). Further strengthening of the judiciary, and greater independence from the regime, can thus help to sustain political and legal reform and limit arbitrary state behavior.

Unfortunately, the Egyptian experience cannot be easily exported to other Middle Eastern countries. For example, as Brown points out, Kuwait and Qatar have had different experiences with the rule of law (1997: 157–86). But even in these two cases, and particularly with regard to Kuwait, the legal arena has become an important avenue for reform and liberalization. Giving further credence to this claim is the experience of Iran, where the initial excesses of the regime's new criminal code have been moderated over time.

The issue of the press is somewhat more complicated. A free press is a thorn in the side of authoritarian regimes. It can expose a regime or individuals in positions of power and highlight corruption and other abuses. The press can also act as an influential force in the transition process. Customarily, Middle Eastern regimes have used a variety of means to control all media, but especially the print media. These include outright ownership, coercion, violence, trial, suspension, imprisonment, financial pressures, and censorship. As one observer notes, the press is "the most vulnerable actor" in the transition process away from autocracy (Garon 1995: 150).

In spite of all the obstacles, the press remains an important agent of reform. There have been examples in the Middle East where the press has been able to push for reform and support those who clamor for liberalization. The most dramatic recent case involves the Press Law 93, which was promulgated by the Egyptian parliament in 1995 at the behest of the hard-liners. The law, which was passed by parliament with almost no debate, had many troublesome features, including the preventive detention of journalists. It took away many of the hard-won rights of journalists, essentially giving the government a free hand to muzzle the press at will and punish journalists who do not follow the regime's policy line (for details, see al-Naqqash 1996 and various issues of *al-Ahram*).

This is not the place for a detailed analysis of the long struggle that the Egyptian press syndicate undertook against this law. The syndicates' membership and leadership group, which included some avowedly proregime individuals, presented a united front, and after a long and elaborate process, all within the system, the law was abrogated in 1996. The new law, Press Law 94, returned the privileges and rights of journalists to the pre-1995 situation. This was a victory for the reformists, who, in cooperation with individual soft-liners in the government, were able to reverse an authoritarian trend. Although it is difficult to claim that this is a harbinger of future reform, it was an important reformist victory and, potentially, can serve as a model for future reformist movements.

CONCLUSION

Our purpose in this chapter has been to highlight the problems of reform in the Middle East, given the long history of authoritarianism in the region. We have argued that even though Middle Eastern politics is embedded in authoritarianism, there are possibilities for reform and liberalization. These possibilities include situations where rentier states confront fiscal crises, where partially independent bourgeoisies emerge, or where pacts between the regime and the opposition are negotiated. We have also assessed the role of electoral politics as an avenue that may encourage political reform. Finally, we have investigated the role of the judiciary and the press in the liberalization process.

Long-term political stability in the Middle East ultimately depends on the existence of regimes that are judged by the people to be legitimate. Although legitimacy is a difficult analytical tool to measure precisely, it remains as relevant to politics in the Middle East as elsewhere. Political legitimacy will be enhanced when a regime makes a genuine effort to respond to the populace's demands and pursues policies that promote economic and political inclusion. When authoritarianism is efficient, the silent majority will probably support it for a time. But there is a breaking point even for efficient authoritarianism. Given the changing domestic circumstances in the Middle East—with dramatic increases in population, urbanization, literacy, and other socioeconomic trends that increase demands on the political system—even efficient authoritarian regimes will be sooner or later called to task.

NOTES

1. An important category of nondemocratic regimes with some relevance to the Middle East, is what Linz and Stepan call sultanistic. The origin of this term goes back to Max Weber's discussion of patrimonialism in his classic work,

Economy and Society, where he elaborates on those traditional forms of rule that develop "an administration and a military force which are purely personal instruments of the master" (in Linz and Stepan, 1996: 51). Sultanism is a more extreme form of authoritarianism where, at least in its pure version, "there is no rule of law, no space for semiopposition, no space for regime moderates who might negotiate with democratic moderates, and no sphere of the economy or civil society that is not subject to the despotic exercise of the sultan's will" (Linz and Stepan 1996: 53). Of course not all personalistic rules are necessarily sultanistic as, for example, the case of Oman.

References

Amuzegar, Jahangir. 1993. *Iran's Economy under the Islamic Republic.* London: I. B. Tauris.

Anderson, Lisa. 1991. "The Tunisian National Pact of 1988." *Government and Opposition,* 26 (2): 244–60.

———. 1995. "The Prospects for Democracy in the Arab World." In Martin Kramer, ed., *Middle Eastern Lectures.* Tel Aviv: Dayan Center for Middle Eastern and African Studies, Tel Aviv University.

Ashraf, Ahmad. 1988. "Bazaar-Mosque Alliance: The Social Bases of Revolts and Revolutions." *Politics, Culture, and Society,* 1 (4): 538–67.

Barkey, Henri. 1990. *The State and the Industrialization Crisis in Turkey.* Boulder: Westview.

———, ed. 1992. *The Politics of Economic Reform in the Middle East.* New York: St. Martin's.

Beblawi, Hazem, and Giacomo Luciani, eds. 1987. *The Rentier State.* London: Croom Helm.

Brand, Laurie. 1992. "Economic and Political Liberalization in a Rentier Economy: The Case of the Hashemite Kingdom of Jordan." In Iliya Harik and Denis Sullivan, eds., *Privatization and Liberalization in the Middle East.* Bloomington: Indiana University Press.

———. 1995. "'In the Beginning Was the State . . . ' The Quest for Civil Society in Jordan." In Augutus Richard Norton, ed., *Civil Society in the Middle East,* vol. 1. Leiden: Brill.

Brown, Nathan. 1997. *The Rule of Law in the Arab World: Courts in Egypt and the Gulf.* Cambridge: Cambridge University Press.

Brumberg, Daniel, 1992. "Survival Strategies vs. Democratic Bargains: The Politics of Economic Reform in Contemporary Egypt." In Henri Barkey, ed., *The Politics of Economic Reform.*

———. 1995. "Authoritarian Legacies and Reform Strategies in the Arab World." In Rex Brynen, Bahgat Korany, and Paul Noble, eds., *Political Liberalization in the Arab World,* vol. 1, *Theoretical Perspectives.* Boulder: Lynne Rienner.

Brynen, Rex. 1992. "Economic Crisis and Post-Rentier Democratization in the Arab Word: The Case of Jordan." *Canadian Journal of Political Science,* 15 (1): 69–97.

Chaudhry, Kiren. 1994. "Economic Liberalization and the Lineages of the Rentier State." *Comparative Politics,* 27 (1): 1:25.

———. 1997. *The Price of Wealth: Economies and Institutions in the Middle East.* Ithaca: Cornell University Press.

Crystal, Jill. 1994. "Authoritarianism and Its Adversaries in the Arab World." *World Politics,* 46 (2): 262–89.

Drake, Paul, and Eduardo Silva, eds., 1986. *Elections and Democratization in Latin America, 1980–85.* San Diego: Center for Iberian and Latin American Studies, University of California.

Entelis, John. 1996. "Civil Society and the Authoritarian Temptation in Algerian Politics: Islamic Democracy vs. the Centralized State." In Augustus Richard Norton, ed., *Civil Society in the Middle East,* vol. 2. Leiden: Brill.

Garon, Lisa. 1995. "The Press and Democratic Transition in Arab Societies: The Algerian Case." In Rex Brynen, Bahgat Korany, and Paul Noble, eds., *Political Liberalization in the Arab World.*

Gause, F. Gregory. 1994. *Oil Monarchies: Domestic and Security Challenges in the Arab Gulf States.* New York: Council on Foreign Relations.

Heydemann, Steven. 1992. "The Political Logic of Economic Rationality: Selective Stabilization in Syria." In Henri Barkey, ed., *The Politics of Economic Reform.*

———. 1993. "Taxation without Representation: Authoritarianism and Economic Liberalization in Syria." In Ellis Goldberg, Resat Kesaba, and Joel Migdal, eds., *Rules and Rights in the Middle East: Democracy, Law, and Society.* Seattle: University of Washington Press.

Hinnebush, Raymond. 1995. "State, Civil Society, and Political Change in Syria." In Augustus Richard Norton, ed., *Civil Society in the Middle East,* vol. 1.

———. 1997. "Syria: The Politics of Economic Liberalisation." *Third World Quarterly,* 18 (2), June: 249–65.

Kazemi, Farhad. 1996a. "Civil Society and Iranian Politics." In Augustus Richard Norton, ed., *Civil Society in the Middle East,* vol. 2.

———. 1996b. "The Inclusion Imperative." *Middle East Studies Association Bulletin,* 30 (2): 147–53.

Kazemi, Farhad, and Augustus Richard Norton. 1996. "Civil Society, Political Reform, and Authoritarianism in the Middle East: A Response." *Contention,* 5 (2): 107–19.

Leca, Jean. 1994. "Democratization in the Arab World: Uncertainty, Vulnerability and Legitimacy; A Tentative Conceptualization and Some Hypotheses." In Ghassan Salamé, ed., *Democracy Without Democrats?* London: I. B. Tauris.

Linz, Juan. 1975. "Totalitarian and Authoritarian Regimes." In Fred Greeenstein and Neslon Polsby, eds., *Handbook of Political Science,* vol. 3. "Macropolitical Theory." Reading: Addison-Wesley.

Linz, Juan, and Alfred Stepan. 1996. *Problems of Democratic Transition and Consolidation: Southern Europe, South America, and Post-Communist Europe.* Baltimore: Johns Hopkins University Press.

Luciani, Giacomo. 1987. "Allocation vs. Production States: A Theoretical Framework." In Hazem Beblawi and Giacomo Luciani, eds., *The Rentier State.* London: Croom Helm.

———. 1994. "The Oil Rent, The Fiscal Crisis of the State and Democratization." In Ghassan Salamé, ed., *Democracy Without Democrats?*

———. 1995. "Resources, Revenues, and Authoritarianism in the Arab World: Beyond the Rentier State?" In Rex Brynen, Bahgat Korany, and Paul Noble, eds., *Political Liberalization in the Arab World.*

Najmabadi, Afsaneh. 1987. "Depoliticization of a Rentier State: The Case of Pahlavi Iran." In Hazem Beblawi and Giacomo Luciani, eds., *The Rentier State.*

Naqqash-al, Aminah. 1996. "Al-Sahafiyun wa Ma'raka: Sa'ud wa Suqut al-Qanun." *al-Yasar*, 77: 6–13.

O'Donnell, Guillermo, and Philippe Schmitter. 1986. *Transitions from Authoritarian Rule: Tentative Conclusions about Uncertain Democracies.* Baltimore: Johns Hopkins University Press.

O'Donnell, Guillermo, Philip Schmitter, and Laurence Whitehead. 1986. *Transitions from Authoritarian Rule: Comparative Perspectives.* Baltimore: Johns Hopkins University Press.

Parsa, Misagh. 1989. *Social Origins of the Iranian Revolution.* New Brunswick: Rutgers University Press.

Perthes, Volker. 1995. *The Political Economy of Syria under Asad.* London: I. B. Tauris.

Przeworski, Adam. 1991. *Democracy and the Market: Political and Economic Reforms in Eastern Europe and Latin America.* Cambridge: Cambridge University Press.

Saffari, Said. 1996. "The Islamic Financial Sector in Iran: Locating the Informal-Organized Qarz al-Hasseneh." Paper presented at the conference on "State and Informal Economies," Harvard University.

Salamé, Ghassan. 1994. "Small Is Pluralistic: Democracy as an Instrument of Civil Peace." In Ghassan Salamé, ed., *Democracy Without Democrats?*

Satloff, Robert. 1992. "Jordan's Great Gamble: Economic Crisis and Political Reform." In Henri Barkey, ed., *The Politics of Economic Reform.*

al-Sayyid, Mustapha Kamil. 1991. "Slow Thaw in the Arab World." *World Policy Journal*, (fall): 711–38.

Shambayati, Hootan. 1994. "The Rentier State, Interest Groups, and the Paradox of Autonomy." *Comparative Politics*, 26 (3): 307–31.

Sherif, Abdel Omar. 1996. "The Supreme Constitutional Court of Egypt and Vicarious Criminal Liability." Paper presented at the conference on "The Role of Judiciary in the Protection of Human Rights." Cairo, Egypt.

Singerman, Diane. 1995. *Avenues of Participation: Family, Politics, and Networks in Urban Quarters of Cairo.* Princeton: Princeton University Press.

Tabatabai, Hamid, and Farhad Mehran. 1995. "Jami'yyat, Kar, va Mas'aleh-ye Eshteghal." *Iran Nameh*, 13 (1–2): 209–28.

Vanderwalle, Dirk. 1997. "The Distributive State: Oil, State-Building and Politics in Libya, 1951–1996". Unpublished ms.

Waterbury, John. 1994. "Democracy Without Democrats?: The Potential for Political Liberalization in the Middle East." In Ghassan Salamé, ed., *Democracy Without Democrats?*

———. 1997. "From Social Contracts to Extraction Contracts: The Political Economy of Authoritarianism and Democracy." In John Entelis, ed., *Islam, Democracy and the State in North Africa*. Bloomington: Indiana University Press.

3

Institution Building and Democratization in China

Joseph Fewsmith

IN RECENT YEARS, some of the bloom has faded from the euphoria generated by the "third wave" of democratization, particularly by the collapse of socialism in Eastern Europe and the Soviet Union. It has been seen that democratic transition does not lead automatically to sustainable democratic governance ("consolidation") and that the outcomes of democratic transition depend on both the legacies, cultural and institutional, of the preceding regimes as well as the modalities of the transition itself (Mandelbaum 1996). The gap in democratic governance between those countries of the former socialist world that are geographically (and culturally) closer to Europe and those farther east has been noted. Yet hopes remain high for a "fourth wave" of democratic transition, and China looms large in these projections. As Larry Diamond puts it, "half of these 2.2 billion people [who continue to live under authoritarian rule] live in one country: mainland China." For Diamond, the prospects for the future of world democratization—both the absence of a reversal of the recent wave of democratizations and the development of a new wave of democratization—"hinge primarily on events in one country: China" (Diamond 1997: xliii).

This is a heavy burden to place on any given country, and perhaps gives too much weight to the potential influence of any Chinese model. Yet the attention that Diamond and others have focused on China make it important to assess realistically where China is, politically, at the present time, whether liberalization and perhaps democratization are realistic options, and, most important, under what conditions China is most likely to democratize successfully. A democratic transition that leads not to sustainable democratic governance but to the collapse of political authority, with all the potential for civil violence, famine, and exodus of refugees that that would entail, would hardly advance the cause of either human rights or global democratization. Yet the downside risk of political change in China is rarely considered. This is no doubt in part because worries about chaos can and have been used by the political authorities in Beijing to justify repressive measures. Nevertheless, such a liberal observer of contemporary China as Ding Xueliang worries openly about the impact of political implosion. "If an anarchic situation appears in China," he warns, "the violence that Chinese will inflict on each other will far exceed the barbarism inflicted by the Japanese army when it invaded in the 1930s." (Ding 1994: xxii).

The question that must be addressed, therefore, is whether China has or is developing the political, institutional, and social conditions that would allow not only for democratic transition but, more important, for democratic consolidation. Knowledgeable observers of China can and do assess these factors quite differently. Optimists point to the vast improvements in China over the past decade and more, and assume that the future will see similar improvements. They also generally assume that the more China develops economically and the more it enters the international arena, the more it will develop a middle class and the more likely it will be to democratize. The "East Asia development model" plays an important role in many people's thinking—both inside and outside of China—even if specifying precisely what such a model is or the dynamic development of any such model is not as easy or straightforward as sometimes assumed (Overholt 1993). In contrast, pessimists view China's human rights record, the government's penchant for rejecting even modest movement in the direction of democratization, efforts to modernize the military, and the growth of nationalism as indications that China will develop into a strong, menacing presence in the Asia-Pacific region. In addition, there have been suggestions from time to time that China may break up, which could be an optimistic or pessimistic prediction depending on the person making it (Miles 1996; and Friedman 1995. For an overview of prospects and possibilities, see Baum 1996).

In recent years, Juan Linz, Alfred Stepan, and others have called attention to the importance of institutions (a "usable bureaucracy"), a state effectively subjected to the rule of law (a *Rechsstaat*), institutionalized economic society, a "free and lively" civil society, and a "relatively autonomous" political society or successful transition to democratic governance (Linz and Stepan 1996; and Linz and Stepan 1997). Even to list such factors suggests the gap between China's current reality and effective democratic governance. The question then is whether China is moving in a direction that will at least narrow this gap.

Much has been said about China's economic reforms, which have propelled China to a nearly 10 percent per annum growth rate over the last decade, an unprecedented achievement for such a large country. The impact of economic reform on China's political system, however, has achieved considerably less attention. While it is widely noted that the economic reforms have shredded faith in Marxism-Leninism, thus undermining the legitimacy of the regime, fewer questions have been asked about the degree to which China's economic reforms have supported the creation of new political institutions that might sustain the polity in the course of democratic transition.

The purpose of this chapter is to sort through a number of different pressures facing Chinese society and government, look at some of the ways China is dealing with them, and try to assess whether China is institutionalizing or deinstitutionalizing. The basic conclusion of this chapter is that the pressures on the contemporary polity are forcing institution-building changes which are necessary and healthy over the long run. This conclusion is advanced cautiously because it is also apparent that there is a long way to go and that important obstacles remain in the way of building sound economic and political institutions, much less the construction of a democratic polity.

Where do institutions come from? In his monumental comparative study of the development of bureaucracy in four polities, Bernard Silberman argued that bureaucracies (as well as important characteristics of their relations with the political system) emerge and are shaped as solutions to political problems (Silberman 1993). Under certain circumstances, there is a perceived political need to shift contentious issues from the political arena to the "neutral" zone of administration. In this perspective, there is much reason for pessimism in the Chinese case. Relations between the Chinese Communist Party (CCP) and the state bureaucracy have always been an issue of contention, and each time there has been some movement in the direction of the establishment of a separate and institutionally autonomous state bureaucracy, the party has, for one reason or another, reintervened to curtail that process (Zheng 1997). Yet the past need not be prologue. There is reason to believe that the process of economic reform has set in motion forces that may lead to the separation of party and state, between the state and the economy, and thereby to a substantial reordering of state-society relations. The basic argument of this chapter is that economic reform, diminished ideological legitimacy, generational succession, and even political conflict are generating pressures for the separation of politics and the economy, for institutionalization of the state (creating a "usable bureaucracy"), and the application of rule-based solutions to resolve political conflict. This process has been uneven at best, but it has been present and it may provide a window of opportunity through which China may emerge successfully from its difficult transition.

THE DYNAMIC OF REFORM

Beginning in 1978, the Chinese government undertook a program of economic reform largely because it had no other choice. Politically, the cultural revolution had undermined Maoist ideology by driving it to extremes; economically, the country was on the the brink of collapse. A massive oil-exploration program in 1978–79, which might have supported a program of economic development without significant marketization, turned up little but dry holes (Naughton 1995: 69–74). Political stability in the face of economic stagnation could not be taken for granted. In an important report to the State Council in July 1978, Hu Qiaomu, Mao's former secretary and the party's foremost ideological authority, declared, "The basic purpose of all communists is to work for the interests of the majority of people. If communists fail to work for the interest of the majority of people, then why do the masses need the Communist Party and why should they support it?" (Hu 1978: E11). Senior party leader and economic specialist Chen Yun was even blunter, warning the central work conference that met in the fall of 1978 that if the livelihood of the peasants did not improve, party secretaries would lead the peasants into the cities to demand food (Chen 1986: 226–31). This recognition that political stability and the party's continued rule required improving the livelihood of the people found concrete expression in the decision to raise the procurement price of grain by 50 percent and to increase the wages of urban workers by 20 percent in 1979. In short, it was the decline of regime legitimacy that prompted the party to switch from ideological legitimacy to performance legitimacy.

This shift set off a logic that remains in place today, one that demands that living standards increase continuously and hence that economic reform continue apace. Once reform was inaugurated, it was impossible to set the clock back. The closest the party came to attempting to do so, prior to Tiananmen, was in the 1980–81 period when inflation and other imbalances emerged from an initial round of reform. Planners inaugurated a period of economic retrenchment, but reductions in procurements through the plan created new and important incentives for enterprises to seek new outlets for their products. Once the window of markets was opened, efforts to tighten control through the plan could only create incentives to increase marketization (Fewsmith 1994: 87–122; and Naughton 1995: 119–27). Indeed, the increased marketization in this period helped keep the economy going in a period of retrenchment and laid a foundation for the next wave of economic reform that began in 1984.

The economic growth that has occurred since then and the structural changes that have been brought about have been largely, though not exclusively, due to the emergence of township and village enterprises (TVEs). Although the enterprises existing at what were then the commune and brigade levels predate the inauguration of reform, such enterprises were extremely backward and, surprisingly, capital-intensive. With the inauguration of reform and the subsequent transformation of agricultural organization (that is, the implementation of household farming, the dissolution of communes and brigades in favor of townships and villages, and the emergence of rural markets), labor flowed into newly created TVEs. Such industries, taking advantage of the shortage of consumer products in the economy and the high prices such products garnered under China's distorted price structure, grew quickly and under conditions of market competition. Not controlled by China's planned economy, TVEs purchased their raw materials and sold their produce at market prices.

The emergence of the township and village enterprises, which played to China's comparative advantage of a nearly inexhaustible supply of inexpensive labor, not only imparted a new dynamism to China's economy (in 1996 the TVE sector accounted for about 60 percent of China's industrial output) but also eroded the plan and spearheaded the emergence of a market economy. By the mid-1990s, less than 10 percent of consumer goods and only about 15 percent of capital goods were still being sold at state-determined prices under the old plan (Shang 1995). Reforms of state-owned enterprises, the bulwark of the planned economy, took place slowly and under pressure from the competition provided by the TVEs and then from foreign products entering the market.

Reform not only set in train a series of economic pressures that have led to tremendous economic growth, it also generated pressures to reform in important ways China's political and administrative systems. The increasing marketization of the economy has done much to force the government to develop the tools to begin to manage the economy through economic means. It has diminished and transformed the role of the State Planning Commission, the nerve center of the old planned economy, it has strengthened new economic organs, especially the Economic and Trade Commission, and it has increased the still very incomplete role of the central bank, the People's Bank of China.

Perhaps more important, the demand for economic development and the politics of reform put a premium on economic expertise. As Hu Qiaomu put it in the report cited above, "Economics is a science for studying economic laws. To be able to act according to economic laws, we must step up the popularization of the study of economics and raise its level. . . . This calls for vastly expanding our country's economics-study contingent, because we must study many economic problems, many of which require meticulous and quantitative study" (Hu 1978: E19). Economic reform has produced vast growth in the number of professional economists and a growing acceptance of their role in the polity. Just as the implementation of reform in late nineteenth- and early twentieth-century Europe created a demand for the services of the growing number of social scientists, so reform in China created a new demand for expertise (Rabinbach 1996; Wittrock and Wagner 1996). The expansion of expertise and the growth of economic organs has meant that information acquisition is better, and that it is better utilized in the decision-making process.

Reform also created an unprecedented demand for regularizing retirement. The need to develop a retirement system was in part a by-product of one of the peculiarities of reform, namely, that reform was inaugurated by a group of aging revolutionaries who had been purged during the cultural revolution and returned to power late in life. Many were quite old—Deng Xiaoping was seventy-three in 1978—and most had lived difficult lives. Moreover, political conflict deepened the need to develop a retirement system. Many of those who came back into power at the end of the cultural revolution, however much they had opposed it, had neither the desire nor the ability to lead reform. They were generally reluctant to implement even modest change, much less the rapid marketizing reforms Deng had in mind. Thus, both the age structure of China's political leadership and political need to "ease out" those opposed to reform converged to form a new norm in favor of retirement. Such a shift was incremental; it was eased in at the highest level by providing a variety of perks, including membership in the newly created Central Advisory Commission that would allow retired officials to continue to participate in China's political affairs (sometimes with very detrimental results). Initially, many exceptions to the retirement age were allowed. Nevertheless, the Central Advisory Commission was ended in 1992, a decade after it had been established, and over time fewer exceptions to the age of retirement were allowed (Manion 1993). Although it is difficult to say that a firm commitment has been made to complete retirement at all levels, the results of the Fifteenth Party Congress in 1997 and the National People's Congress in March 1998 suggest considerable movement in this direction.

At the same time, economic reform and the implementation of retirement policies required the recruitment of a new generation of bureaucrats. This need was all the more imperative because so many careers had been sidetracked during the cultural revolution. In the course of the party rectification of 1983–86 and in successive party conclaves in 1985, 1987, 1992, and 1997, those too old or unqualified for high office were weeded out or passed over, while those better qualified were promoted. Although the official slogan for the recruitment and promotion of younger officials was to promote those who were "more revolutionary, better educated, more professionally competent, and younger," in practice the term "more revolutionary" was difficult to define and highly contentious. The result has been to rely on more objective criteria, particularly education and age, for selecting the party elite and state cadres. Because the social sciences were highly suspect in the early part of the PRC, and even remain so today, there has been a very strong tendency to recruit those who have had technical training, particularly engineering, thus giving China's political elite a very technocratic cast. An issue that is highly contentious—who to recruit—has been delimited if not resolved by falling back on "objective" indicators such as age and education (Lee 1991).

Obviously these new criteria have not resolved all problems of recruitment and bureaucratic building. Often there are several individuals who satisfy the "objective" criteria, leaving promotion decisions up to political and other considerations. China has been slow to develop a civil service system, although there has been movement in that direction in recent years (Tang 1995; Huang 1996). But even in the absence of an effective civil service system, there are some indications that more objective criteria are being applied to promotion. Prior to an official being promoted, the views of subordinates, peers, and superiors are solicited in an effort to weed out objectionable people. Such a process hardly eliminates personalism, but perhaps it limits its worst abuses.

Although reform generated a variety of positive pressures, as suggested above, it also produced negative effects and conflict, both within the state, and between state and society. One of the central consequences of reform was to undermine the legitimacy of the socialist system. The divergence between ideological understandings of socialism and the reality of what was happening stretched credulity and generated cynicism. The problems of partial reform were everywhere, straining the relations between those who insisted that problems could be resolved only through more reform and those who insisted the problems were caused by reform itself. "Hard-liners" wanted to reemphasize socialist ideology in order to rein in the consequences of reform, while "moderates" wanted to push ahead. It did not help that moderates ("reformers") were themselves badly divided, as followers of Hu Yaobang (the general secretary ousted in January 1987 for his supposed "laxness" in the face of "bourgeois liberalization") often engaged in acrimonious disputes with those who looked to premier, then general secretary, Zhao Ziyang for leadership. (This was particularly visible in the debate over the so-called "new authoritarianism." See Rosen and Zou 1990–91.) But such disputes reflected the real problems involved in deciding how to move forward in the face of both economic difficulties and political opposition.

At the same time, there was an ever-widening gulf developing between state and society, particularly with the younger generation that had grown up not knowing the Maoist period and were thus frustrated with the distance that remained between the reality they did know and their expectations for the future. Anger was increasingly focused on corruption and bureaucratic privilege. The example of the West, both presumed and real, help fuel expectations, while Gorbachev in the Soviet Union and popular efforts to bring about democracy in the Philippines and South Korea suggested what might be done to realize those expectations.

Tensions at the highest political level and the growing estrangement between state and society created a tinderbox that exploded in the spring of 1989. The tragedy that ensued dashed hopes for an easy and rapid transition. For a while, it seemed that the possibility of resuming market-oriented economic reform, much less political reform, was small, but the evolution of events has confounded the expectations of domestic and foreign observers alike and opened up possibilities not only of continued economic reform but also, eventually, of political change.

THE IMPACT OF TIANANMEN

This is not the place to analyze the dynamics of Tiananmen; that has been done elsewhere (Tsou 1991). It is important to point out, however, that the suddenness with which the demonstrations arose and the ferocity with which they were then suppressed ensured that China would not follow the path of the "classic" four-actor model said to characterize the most successful transitions to democracy (Pzreworski 1991). Within the regime there was a division between the "hard-liners" and "moderates," but the unique role of Deng Xiaoping as the supreme leader meant that this division could never really develop as two separate, roughly evenly balanced wings of the party. Deng hesitated a long while during the Tiananmen crisis, as various political forces played themselves out, but then threw his full weight behind the hard-liners. Within the student movement there was a similar tendency for the leadership to divide between "moderates" and "radicals" but the dynamic of the movement continuously pushed it in a more radical direction. Moderate student leaders never had a chance to emerge as a separate and viable political force. In any event, the whole movement was over in six weeks. There was a chance, but only a brief chance, for moderates within the leadership to work with moderates within the student movement. It was a chance that was not seized, and the possibility of a "pacted" transition of some sort quickly passed from the scene.

The crushing of the student movement appeared to end any chance that China could embark on a period of gradual transition. It seemed that hard-liners were in total control and there were fears, not altogether unfounded, that they would use their power to roll back the reforms. However, there were a number of factors, both particular and structural, that prevented this from happening. One, of course, was the role that Deng Xiaoping played. Deng threw his support behind the hard-liners and ordered the military to end the demonstrations, but he also denied the fruits of victory to the hard-liners. Talking to hard-liners Li Peng and Yao Yilin, who no doubt expected to gain from the demise of Zhao Ziyang, Deng explained the choice of Jiang Zemin as the new general secretary. Almost contemptuously he said, "The people see reality. If we put up a front so that people feel that it is an ossified leadership, a conservative leadership, or if the people believe that it is a mediocre leadership that cannot reflect the future of China, then there will be constant trouble and there will never be a peaceful day" (Deng 1993a: 296–301). At the same time, Deng insisted that economic reform and opening up be continued. His position was much weakened in the aftermath of Tiananmen and his policy preferences hardly prevailed. But his power was sufficient to prevent hard-liners from consolidating their position and finally, in 1992, Deng struck back; by the end of the year he was once again able to dominate China's policy agenda (Fewsmith 1997).

Deng's role in the post-Tiananmen period was thus primarily as a stabilizer, preventing the Chinese political system from lurching out of control, and then as the promoter of a new round of reform. In this sense, Deng's role was unique and critical. But there were also other forces at work that contributed not only to the revival of reform but more importantly to greater, albeit still nascent, institutionalization.

The first factor was the further disintegration of the role of ideology. This was one of the most contentious issues in the post-Tiananmen period, with conservative ideologues arguing that it had been precisely the implementation of marketizing reforms that had eroded the legiti-

macy of ideology and thus weakened the party. This argument intensified as socialism collapsed in Eastern Europe as the Soviet Union disinte-
grated. Deng opposed the arguments of hard-liners by turning their logic
upside down. He argued that economic reform was not the cause of the
Tiananmen crisis but had, on the contrary, provided the Chinese system
with the resilience to survive that upheaval. By way of contrast, Eastern
Europe and the Soviet Union had not carried out economic reform successfully and were therefore more vulnerable. In making this argument,
however, Deng was pushing performance legitimacy to a new level. In
effect, he was arguing that Marxism-Leninism had lost all effectiveness
in ensuring the regime's legitimacy; the only way the regime could "buy"
the acquiescence of the people was to improve their livelihood through
developing the economy. In his critical tour of Shenzhen in early 1992,
Deng defined socialism in terms of the so-called "three advantages." Reforms were to be judged by three criteria: Whether they were advanta-
geous to the development of socialist productive forces, whether they
increased the comprehensive strength of a socialist nation, and whether
they raised the people's standard of living (Deng 1993b: 372). Clearly,
Tiananmen had shattered whatever legitimacy remained in Marxism-
Leninism, forcing the regime to base its continued existence ever more
firmly on its ability to "deliver the goods."

A second critical factor has been that of leadership succession, both
personal and generational. Jiang Zemin, born in 1926, was seventy-one
years old when the Fifteenth Party Congress convened in September
1997. Whatever his abilities, Jiang clearly does not carry the political
authority of a Mao Zedong or a Deng Xiaoping (and Deng's authority
was certainly less than Mao's). There was considerable doubt whether
senior political leaders, including his own age cohorts who might regard themselves as being as well qualified as Jiang to hold the top position, would be willing to accept his authority. No doubt party norms
give a considerable advantage to incumbency; to be seen as "splitting"
the party is a serious offense, making challenges to the top leadership
difficult and hazardous. Still, there are ways of challenging the scope of
the leader's authority without directly challenging his position, and it
was widely expected that a number of top leaders might undermine
Jiang's authority directly or indirectly.

To an important extent such challenges are extra-institutional
in that there is no defined forum in which conflicts are mediated or
to which decisions can be referred. In other words, politics at the top
remains uninstitutionalized, and outcomes are based on who has more
power. In the Mao period, there was little doubt about who had the most
power. In the Dengist period, Deng remained preeminent and was will-

ing to exercise the prerogatives that came with that position from time to time; but he was also more willing to accede to, and even encourage, the emergence of norms that curtailed the arbitrary exercise of power— at least to some extent (Fewsmith, forthcoming). With less personal authority and unable to appeal to historical contributions in the revolution (he was only a student organizer in Shanghai in the late 1940s), Jiang Zemin has tried to respond to challenges to his position and authority by invoking rules. One can take the invocation of rules as a shallow exercise in formalism, and it may turn out that way, but it is also possible that the invocation of rules will prove binding, setting the political system on a course of institutionalization.

In personal terms, there have been three major challenges to Jiang's authority so far (Fewsmith 1997). The first came in 1992 when in response to Deng Xiaoping's trip to the south and his implicit criticism of Jiang's tolerance of the "left," Yang Shangkun, then permanent vice chairman of the Central Military Commission, and Qiao Shi, then head of the National People's Congress, apparently joined forces in an effort to oust Jiang. What precisely happened is in doubt and many different versions have swirled through the rumor mill, but it appears that there was a significant challenge to Jiang's authority. This was the sort of challenge that Jiang could hardly meet on his own, given Yang's seniority in the political system and position in the military. Whatever the details, Jiang eventually was able to win Deng Xiaoping's support, and in the presumed interest of maintaining long-term stability in the political system, Deng turned against his longtime friend, removing Yang's younger half brother from his critical position in the Central Military Commission and effectively depriving Yang Shangkun of much of his influence. This move allowed Jiang to shake up the military structure and to begin to promote officers who at least appeared to be loyal to him.

In important ways, this shake-up was an old-fashioned political struggle. Conflict revolved around generational differences, personalities, and professionalization. In getting rid of the Yang brothers and their supporters, Jiang was able to promote a number of younger military officers, many of whom had been promoted on the basis of their military professionalism. In order to develop a younger and more professional officer corps, Jiang invoked long-standing rules about factionalism in the military as well as rules regarding the military's obedience to the party. None of this ensures the loyalty of the military to Jiang or to the civilian party leadership in general, but it *could* pave the way for greater professionalization and regularization of civilian-military relations, trends that have been under way for some time in any event (Godwin, forthcoming).

The second challenge to Jiang's authority came from Beijing party secretary and politburo member Chen Xitong. The extent to which Chen posed a threat to Jiang or merely resisted his authority is not clear, but it does seem clear that Chen felt his own connections to top-level leaders, including Deng Xiaoping, would protect him and permit him to defy the party general secretary. As later events demonstrated, there was also enormous corruption involved—Chen apparently had amassed a fortune of some 18 billion *yuan* (over $2 billion). This conflict also came at a time when Jiang was concerned with being able to assert his authority over China's provincial leaders, some of whom were increasingly resisting Beijing's demands. Thus, Chen Xitong's case cut across a number of issues, and Jiang no doubt considered the impact of ousting Chen for increasing Jiang's authority in a number of these areas.

It appears that Jiang waited until Deng was seriously ill before acting to oust Chen, and apparently he did so only after cutting a number of deals with other members of the Politburo Standing Committee. As with the Yang Baibing/Yang Shangkun case, Jiang's conflict with Chen Xitong contained significant elements of a power struggle. But Jiang handled it by referring the case to the party's Central Discipline Inspection Commission (which, in turn, eventually referred it to the court system, which five years later finally sentenced Chen to sixteen years in prison), and used Chen's dismissal to raise the profile of Jiang's struggle against corruption. That strategy raised Jiang's profile both as protector of the common interest and as advocate of a law-based society. Apparently, Chen's corruption was of such a degree that when Jiang made an issue of it, Chen could hardly rally support to his cause (Yang 1996: 307–16).

Chen's dismissal on corruption charges, as Melanie Manion notes, was part of a broader *campaign* against corruption rather than part of an institutionalized enforcement of anti-corruption laws (Manion 1997). Yet the seriousness of corruption in contemporary China, and Jiang's apparent desire to avoid being tagged with charges of pursuing a personal power struggle, could lay the foundation for a more routinized effort to deal with that issue. The problem is so large and complex, involving so many vested interests, however, that it will be some time before it becomes clear if China can deal with corruption on more than an episodic basis. In any case, Jiang's ouster of Chen for specific cause—rather than on the grounds of loosely defined ideological criteria such as being lax against "bourgeois liberalization"—and especially the decision to refer Chen's case to the legal authorities (rather than define it simply as a matter of party discipline) lays a foundation for bureaucratization of anti-corruption efforts, if such efforts can continue to be followed up regularly.

Perhaps the most intriguing case has been that of Qiao Shi, the third-ranking member of the Politburo Standing Committee and head of the National People's Congress who was not reelected to the Central Committee, much less the politburo, at the Fifteenth Party Congress in September 1997. Qiao's dismissal has occasioned a great deal of public comment since he seemed to represent the "liberal" wing of the party, calling more explicitly and continuously than any other party leader for institutionalizing the rule of law and strengthening the role of the National People's Congress. Qiao certainly did champion the rule of law in his many public statements, but it had become increasingly apparent that, whatever might be his feelings about law per se, he was using the issue to distinguish himself publicly from Jiang Zemin, who continuously emphasized democratic centralism and obedience to the "core" (himself) (Fewsmith 1995). In short, there was a personal power struggle going on as well as a difference in political emphasis.

According to the various rumors circulating since the Fifteenth Party Congress, Jiang apparently invoked the age criterion to force Qiao's ouster (Xia 1997). As noted above, retirement norms have been increasingly institutionalized over the past two decades, but they had remained loose at best at the highest level. This time, Jiang apparently invoked age as a reason to retire both the eighty-three-year-old Liu Huaqing (the military's representative on the Politburo Standing Committee) and the seventy-two-year-old Qiao Shi. Qiao is only one year older than Jiang, and both men were slightly above the officially mandated retirement age of seventy that was invoked to force Qiao out. So it appears a bit disingenuous to say that Qiao was ousted on grounds of age. Nevertheless, Jiang's invocation of an "objective" criterion now makes it more difficult for others to stay on the Politburo Standing Committee past the age of seventy; accordingly, it is widely expected that Jiang will retire after serving his current five-year term in office. If he does indeed retire, it could pave the way for a more orderly succession process than China has been blessed with in the past.

While Jiang has tended to invoke "objective" rules and standards (factionalism, corruption, age) in order to thwart personal challenges to his power, the more interesting trend has been the invocation of such decision-making rules to ensure large-scale change in the Central Committee. The transition from Deng's generation of aging revolutionaries to Jiang's generation of party bureaucrats has evoked the most discussion, but it is the rejuvenation and promotion of better-educated cadres to the Central Committee that is more important in institutional terms. This is a change that has been taking place for some time. A special "party representatives" meeting in 1985 saw a large-scale turnover in the membership of the Central Committee as many younger and better-educated cadres were promoted. This trend continued in the Party congresses of 1987 and 1992. At the Fifteenth Party Congress in September 1997, almost 60 percent of the Central Committee was replaced, ensuring the promotion of younger and better educated cadres, particularly in the provinces. Such trends are important in terms of both formal and informal authority. In terms of the formal structure, norms concerning retirement and educational criteria are increasingly institutionalized—only three of the 193 members of the newly elected Central Committee came to prominence as "model workers." Moreover, all three have long since demonstrated administrative competence in a variety of important positions, showing that they have qualifications beyond just being "model workers." In terms of the informal power structure, it is simply much more likely that Jiang will be able to gain compliance from those who are clearly his juniors and, moreover, owe their promotion at least in part to him.

The third major pressure for rationalization (in a Weberian sense) comes from the economic realm. As noted above, the growth of the TVE sector spurred economic growth, marketization, and important structural changes in industry (including the rapid growth of a consumer goods sector and the development of horizontal linkages among industries). It also brought competitive pressures to bear on the state-owned sector, which had previously enjoyed large economic rents. Over time, the profits of state-owned enterprises (SOEs) eroded, and subsidies to those enterprises increased. The pressures facing SOEs provoked one of the most critical political debates in the late 1980s. When conservatives had a free hand to try to revive aspects of the planned economy in the wake of Tiananmen, they attempted to shore up the role of SOEs. These efforts, however, were mishandled, not to mention misconceived, and profitability declined sharply and inter-enterprise debt (so-called "triangular debt") exploded.

By the mid-1990s, the problems of SOEs were threatening state solvency and the entire fiscal system. Whereas approximately 20 percent of China's SOEs perennially ran deficits in the 1980s, the figure rose to more than 30 percent by the early 1990s. By 1995, it was close to 40 percent, and it reached 43.7 percent the following year (Yang 1997: 3). Meanwhile, the volume of losses surged almost 30 percent to 61.6 billion *yuan* ($7.4 billion). These losses were particularly disturbing because they were beginning to exceed the surplus generated by the SOEs that were profitable. In the first four months of 1996, China's SOEs ran a net loss. Although the situation improved somewhat in later months, it remained very serious: In the first nine months of the year, net profits were only 20.2 billion *yuan* ($2.43 billion), a decline of 62.1 percent from the

previous year. Even in the prosperous coastal areas of Shanghai and
Guangdong losses were up and profits were down (Wu 1996: 3).

Because taxes from SOEs continue to account for more than 60
percent of central government revenues, such figures mean that the fiscal
situation facing the government, already tight for many years, will remain precarious. It also means that so-called "triangular debts" (the
money enterprises owe each other) are increasing. Such debts rose from
300 billion *yuan* ($36.1 billion) in the early 1990s to 700 billion *yuan*
($84.3 billion) in 1994 and 800 billion *yuan* ($84.3 billion) in 1995
(Yang 1997: 4). These developments cannot be good news for China's
banking system, in which at least one-third of outstanding loans are said
to be nonperforming (Lardy 1996).

Such figures suggest the economic and fiscal pressures behind continued economic reform in the 1990s and the Fifteenth Party Congress'
endorsement of restructuring, reorganizing, and selling off SOEs. A major feature of these reforms is the effort to clarify property rights. Although there remain sharp debates within China over how to clarify
those rights (Cui 1998), the very effort to do so reflects an important
turning point in China's economic reform. It can be argued that economic reform progressed as rapidly as it did in the 1980s because China
sidestepped the complicated and contentious issues of property rights.
The deepening of reform, the plight of state-owned industries, and the
emergence of financial markets, however, are creating new and intense
pressures to clarify them. This is a difficult and politically contentious
issue that will not be solved quickly. Nevertheless, a large number of
smaller SOEs are likely to be privatized, while a smaller number of large
SOEs will implement some form of a shareholding system—a step that
requires the evaluation of assets and the assignment of ownership. To the
extent that property rights are clarified, there will be a greater separation
between the political sphere and the economic, again with the caveat that
there is a long way to go.

One sees the same pressures in the fiscal area. The structure of
China's planned economy and SOEs were established in large measure to direct fiscal resources to the state (Naughton 1995: 26–33), and
even in the reform era, as the role of SOEs has diminished, the central
state has relied disproportionately on those enterprises for its fiscal revenues. The role and financial health of SOEs have declined in part because
of the rapid growth of TVEs. These township and village enterprises
have grown rapidly not only because they supplied consumer goods,
which had been neglected under the planned economy, but also because
they have been supported by local governments, which have benefited
from the increased tax revenues TVEs provide (Oi 1999). At the same

time, as TVEs have grown, they have cut into the monopoly rents once enjoyed by the SOEs, causing the revenues available to the central government to decline (relatively) as those taken in by local governments have grown rapidly. Central government revenues as a share of GDP have declined from 35 percent in 1978 to only 12 percent in 1994. This rapid decline in fiscal resources to a point considered quite low in comparative terms, and which leading Chinese and U.S.-based scholars such as Hu Angang and Wang Shaoguang fear could lead to the physical breakup of China, prompted a major reform of the tax system in 1994 (Hu and Wang 1993). That reform constituted an important effort to diversify the sources of central government revenue so as to reflect the changing composition of the economy and, most important, to establish a genuinely independent, central tax system. Previously taxes had been collected at the local level and remitted to the center, an arrangement that exists in no other modern state. Fears that continued fiscal decentralization would undermine the ability of the state to carry out its functions—from welfare to national defense—and to exercise macro-economic control prompted rationalizing reforms. Although such reforms are far from complete, they mark an important step toward institution-building.

This pressure to separate the political realm from the economic and to rationalize the administrative system took a major step forward in the spring of 1998 when the first session of the Ninth National People's Congress announced a major reorganization of the government to reduce the number of ministries and commissions under the State Council from forty to twenty-nine and to cut government personnel by 50 percent. Perhaps the most important feature of this government reorganization, assuming it proceeds more or less as intended, is that it separates the ministries from direct control of enterprises. This change strikes at the very heart of the old planned economy, and appears to be a serious effort to address the institutional basis of much corruption, namely, the control that government bureaucrats exercise over scarce resources (Fewsmith 1998).

If one of the distinctions between authoritarian and totalitarian political systems is the general separation of the political and economic spheres and the recognition of property rights in the former and the conflation of politics and economics and the nonexistence of property rights in the latter, then China has moved quite far in the authoritarian direction over the past two decades. Authoritarianism does not necessarily lead to a successful transition to democracy, but if space is provided for the growth of institutions, the prospect for democratization appears better than for a more totalitarian regime.

PROBLEMS OF PARTIAL REFORM

This chapter has argued that important political and economic pressures are pushing China toward the creation of effective institutions. These are noteworthy trends because the nation's tumultuous history over the past century has not allowed state-building to take place, and as Linz and Stepan have argued, one cannot have a democratic state unless one has a *state* (Linz and Stepan 1997: 16–33). Although a variety of caveats have been registered above, it is nevertheless necessary to emphasize that the trends outlined remain nascent and are offset to a considerable degree by countervailing developments that could overwhelm the progress made.

One such tendency is that the conflation of public and private continues to grow, even as there are simultaneous pulls in the opposite direction. This conflation takes place on two levels, one local, the other higher. At the local (county) level, reform and the development of TVEs have strengthened the role of government, while party secretaries act more like CEOs of holding companies than government officials. Local party and government officials are deeply involved in the economy, often deciding how to allocate resources among competing demands and deciding on local development strategies (Oi 1992). Although the government has encouraged and fostered private entrepreneurship in some areas, the more prevalent pattern is for the government itself to be entrepreneurial. To the extent that such patterns become entrenched, and that appears to be considerable, there is a lack of separation between economic and political society and a corresponding conflation of state and society (He 1998).

At other levels, there is similarly a widespread tendency for the political and economic arenas to overlap. Government officials can frequently collect "rents" on their control over everything from scarce resources to permits. Similarly, leaders in large SOEs are frequently able to siphon off state-owned resources to set up enterprises controlled by their families or friends. An important part of enterprise reform allows SOEs to buy and sell capital goods as their businesses require, but opening up such capital goods markets, where state-owned assets are often not valued fairly, creates enormous opportunities for corruption. Although such "stripping" (*liushi*) of state assets is difficult to define or quantify, one recent estimate states that in the decade between 1982 and 1992, some 500 billion *yuan* (approximately $60 billion)—nearly a fifth of all state-owned assets—were drained legally or illegally into private accounts (He 1996; He 1998: 106–16). Another estimate claims that, in the 1980s, some 50 billion *yuan* ($5.8 billion) worth of state assets were being stripped per year, and that that figure has almost doubled to 80–100 billion *yuan* ($9.5–11.8 billion) in the 1990s (Chen 1998: 1). Although such trends could lead to de facto privatization of a significant portion of the Chinese economy (a process referred to ironically as "primitive socialist accumulation"), in the short run there is a very substantial overlap between the public and private economies.

In part as a result of this stripping or direct corruption, income inequality has increased rapidly in recent years. Between 1981 and 1996, urban residents having the lowest 20 percent of income increased their income only 1.6 times, whereas the highest 20 percent increased their incomes by 12.7 times (Yan 1997: 14). According to one report, income inequality in China now parallels that in the United States and is worse than in Japan (Fei 1996). Another report states that the wealthiest 7 percent of China's urban residents possess over 30 percent of urban wealth (He 1996: 153; see also Li 1995).

If there has been a concentration of wealth at the top of the system, there has also been suffering at the lower end of the spectrum. Increasingly Chinese workers are "furloughed" (*xiagang*) from state-owned enterprises that are trying to cut losses. In 1996, it was authoritatively estimated that over 8 percent of urban workers had had their wages reduced or stopped, and that some 15 million urban residents had been affected by the loss and reduction of wages (Wu 1996). As a result, labor discontent has grown. According to Vice Premier Wu Bangguo, between January and August 1996 there were a total of 4,032 strike actions, over half of which were caused by disputes over delayed payment of wages. Some were reported to have signs of organization and planning (Wu 1996).

Thus, the conflation of economic and political societies is directly related to volatile social issues such as income inequality and corruption. In its survey of fifty-four countries, Transparency International has reported that China is the fifth most corrupt country, trailing only Bangladesh, Kenya, Pakistan, and Nigeria. Moreover, as Melanie Manion has recently observed, repeated efforts to tighten controls against corruption have yet to reveal visible results. Corruption was one of the focal points of the 1989 Tiananmen demonstrations, and it remains one of the most volatile issues in China's public life. A survey of urban workers in 1996 found that corruption was at or near the top of most workers' concerns (Manion 1997).

Another particularly difficult issue is the continued conflation of party and state. In the 1980s, reformers pressed concerns about separation of party and state, and after the Thirteenth Party Congress in 1987 party groups (*dangzu*) were removed from most ministries of the State Council and efforts were made to create a professional civil service. Following the upheaval of 1989, these trends were reversed and party groups were reestablished. Then in 1992, the Fourteenth Party Congress increased the overlap between party and state by making the top four members of the Politburo Standing Committee simultaneously the heads of the major state organs (Jiang Zemin as president, Li Peng as premier, Qiao Shi as head of the NPC, and Li Ruihuan as head of the Chinese People's Political Consultative Conference), a trend that was continued at the Fifteenth Party Congress in 1997 (although Zhu Rongji replaced Li Peng as premier, and Li Peng replaced Qiao Shi as head of the NPC). The same trend of strengthening the party at the expense of the state has been apparent in recent years as Jiang Zemin has tried to consolidate his power. Although there have been trends to rationalize and regularize politics at the highest level, as pointed out above, the rallying cry Jiang used to reinforce his own power was that of strengthening democratic centralism, a Leninist norm rather than a statist norm. Nevertheless, at the Fifteenth Party Congress in September 1997, Jiang made a strong pitch for rule by law (Jiang 1998). How the tension between the different norms of democratic centralism and law will be worked out remains one of the critical issues of the coming years.

To the extent that the economic and public spheres and the realms of party and state are conflated, it is difficult at best for either a vital civil society to emerge or for law to become more than an adjunct to administration. These are important weaknesses when we look at China today. The state has retreated significantly from society, giving individuals greater freedom than ever before in Chinese history, but studies of "civil society" point to a high degree of intermingling of public and private and of dependence on the state (Unger and Chan 1996; Wank 1995; and Nevitt 1996). Similarly, law has become increasingly important in the course of economic reform, but it has yet to emerge as really independent from the state. Rule *by* law remains far stronger than rule *of* law (*The China Quarterly,* 1995). The possibility of a Chinese *Rechsstaat* remains a distant hope.

CONCLUSION

Discussions on democratic prospects in China have generally revolved around whether or not there is widespread public support for democracy, the activity of political dissidents, whether or not there is an emergent civil society or pressures for democracy from below, and the presence or absence of democratic traditions in Chinese history (for instance, Des Forges et al. 1993). Generally speaking, these discussions have focused on the possibility of democratic transition in China. The experience of other countries and the burgeoning literature on the difficulties many countries have had following democratic transitions, however, have focused greater attention on the social, economic, and political requisites of successful transitions as well as the modalities of the transitions themselves (Shain and Linz 1995). Such literature should force those who study China as well as those who are concerned about the country's democratization to rethink the categories and modes of analysis they use. Accordingly, this chapter has tried to look realistically at the "state of the state" in China and at the political and economic dynamics of the post-Tiananmen period to assess not just the possibility of democratic transition in China but, more important, the probability of sustainable democratic governance in the future.

Accordingly the emphasis in this chapter has been on the development of institutions. Institutions can be both formal, as in the development of a "usable bureaucracy," and informal, as in regular behavior patterns. Formal institutions and informal patterns of behavior can be mutually reinforcing, but it is difficult to develop formal institutions if informal behavior is destructive of stable expectations. In general, twentieth-century Chinese politics have witnessed a continual clash between informal patterns of behavior and emergent institutions, to the detriment of political stability and state building (Tsou 1986: 241).

China has now been undergoing a reform process for nearly two decades. With the notable exceptions of the 1979 border war with Vietnam and the violent suppression of demonstrators in 1989, these two decades have been the longest period of sustained domestic and international peace and economic development since the Opium War. Given the violence of China's political history over the past century and a half, it is not surprising that the country has not been able to develop formal institutions and informal patterns of behavior that are mutually supportive. The question that China's reform process raises is whether such a mutually supportive pattern is taking shape. This chapter has offered a cautiously optimistic assessment of this possibility. It has been noted that there were both positive and negative trends in the 1980s, followed by the perhaps unexpected reemergence of positive trends in the 1990s. The dynamics of economic reform, political conflict, and generational succession have generated pressures to separate political and economic society, to build more competent and "rational" bureaucratic structures, to regularize political promotion and change through the use of more objective criteria for promotion and by enforcing norms for retirement.

It has also been noted that this process remains tentative, ambiguous, and fragile. China faces a number of enormous challenges, including reform of the SOEs, the pressures from those to be thrown out of work and those coming on to the job market (at a rate of about 10 million per year), the building of a viable system of social security, the need to address growing regional and income inequalities, the reform of the health care system, addressing deteriorating environmental conditions, and so forth. These or other issues could provoke large-scale protests of various sorts that could once again cause political upheavals that would set back the progress made in recent years.

If such challenges are to be addressed adequately and tensions between state and society and within the political system ameliorated, China will have to develop more effective institutions, particularly at the central state level. Building a stronger, more bureaucratic state is not necessarily incompatible with greater democratization. In a narrow, limited sense, bureaucratization means professionalization, which, in turn, implies a widening of the consultative process as professional competence spreads through the policy community, encompassing both state bureaucrats and the broader intellectual community. In a broader sense, it seems likely that the central-state will have to grant greater political participation to local governments if it wants to convince the latter to yield control over revenue sources (Wang 1996: 32–36). Neither the development of broad policy communities nor the participation of local levels of government in decision-making necessarily implies voting and democratization. But it does imply the development of institutions and the sort of "soft authoritarianism" that prefaced the successful transition to democracy in Taiwan and elsewhere. Perhaps China can follow in this path.

NOTES

The author would like to thank Boston University and the Smith Richardson Foundation for providing support for the research that went into this article.

REFERENCES

Baum, Richard. 1996. "China After Deng: Ten Scenarios in Search of Reality," *The China Quarterly* 145 (March): 153–75.
Chen Jian. 1998. *Liushi de Zhongguo* (Loss of Chinese property). Beijing: Zhongguo chengshi chubanshe.
Chen Yun. 1986. "Jianchi an bili yuanze tiaozheng guomin jingji" (Readjust the

national economy in accordance with the principle of proportionality), in Chen Yun, *Chen Yun wenxuan (1956–1985)* (Selected works of Chen Yun, 1956–1985). Beijing: Renmin chubanshe: 226–31.

The China Quarterly. 1995. Special issue on law.

Cui, Zhiyuan. 1998. "Whither China: The Discourse on Property Rights in the Chinese Reform Context." In *Social Text*, special issue on "The Intellectual Politics in Post-Tiananmen China."

Deng Xiaoping. 1993a. "Zucheng yige shixing gaige de you xiwang de lingdao jiti" (Organizing a reformist, hopeful leadership collective), in *Deng Xiaoping wenxuan*, (Selected Works of Deng Xiaoping), vol. 3. Beijing: Renmin chubanshe: 296–301.

———. 1993b. "Zai Wuchang, Shenzhen, Zhuhai dengdi de tanhua yaodian" (Essential points from talks in Wuchang, Shenzhen, Zhuhai), in *Deng Xiaoping wenxuan* (Selected Works of Deng Xiaoping), vol. 3. Beijing: Renmin chubanshe 370–83.

Des Forges, Roger V., Luo Ning, and Wu Yen-bo, eds. 1993. *Chinese Democracy and the Crisis of 1989: Chinese and American Reflections.* Albany: State University of New York Press.

Diamond, Larry. 1997. "Introduction: In Search of Consolidation." In Larry Diamond, Marc F. Plattner, Yun-han Chu, and Hung-mao Tien, eds. *Consolidating the Third Wave Democracies: Themes and Perspectives.* Baltimore: Johns Hopkins University Press, pp. xiii–xlvii.

Ding Xueliang. 1994. *Gongchanzhuyihou yu Zhongguo* (Post-communism and China). Hong Kong: Oxford University Press.

Fei Yuanxiu. 1996. "Dangqian woguo de geren shouru fenpei wenti" (The question of individual income distribution in contemporary China), *Dangdai sichao,* no. 3 (June 20), pp. 42–47.

Fewsmith, Joseph. 1994. *Dilemmas of Reform in China: Political Conflict and Economic Debate.* Armonk: M. E. Sharpe.

———. 1995. "Jockeying for Position in the Post-Deng Era," *Current History,* 94, no. 593 (September): 252–58.

———. 1997. "Reaction, Resurgence, and Succession: Chinese Politics since Tiananmen." In Roderick MacFarquhar, ed., *The Politics of China: The Eras of Mao and Deng.* New York: Cambridge University Press, 1997, pp. 472–531.

———. 1998. "Jiang Zemin Takes Command," *Current History* (September): 250–56.

———. Forthcoming. "The Impact of Reform on Elite Politics." In Merle Goldman and Roderick MacFarquhar, eds., *The Paradoxes of Reform.* Cambridge: Harvard University Press.

Friedman, Edward. 1995. *National Identity and Democratic Prospects in Socialist China.* Armonk: M. E. Sharpe.

Godwin, Paul H. B. Forthcoming. "Economic Reform and Party-Military Relations in China: The Evolution of a Political Dilemma." In Merle Goldman and Roderick MacFarquhar, eds., *The Paradoxes of Reform.* Cambridge: Harvard University Press.

He Qinglian. 1996. "Dangdai Zhongguo de zeben yuanshi jilei" (Primitive capital accumulation in contemporary China), *Ershiyi shiji*, April 1996, pp. 150–57.

——. 1998. *Xiandaihua de xianjing* (The pitfall of modernization). Beijing: Jinri chubanshe.

Hu Angang and Wang Shaoguang. 1993. *Jiaqiang zhongyang zhengfu zai shichang jingji zhuanxing zhong de zhudao zuoyong* (Strengthening the central government's leading role in the transition to a market economy). Shenyang: Liaoning renmin chubanshe.

Huang Haixia. 1996. "Two Adjustments Shall Be Implemented in Personnel-Related Work," in *Liaowang*, no. 7 (February 12):10–11, trans. Foreign Broadcast Information Service, *Daily Report*, no. FBIS-CHI-96-059.

Hu Qiaomu. 1978. "Act in Accordance with Economic Laws: Step up the Four Modernizations," Xinhua (New China News Agency), October 5, 1978, trans. Foreign Broadcast Information Service, *Daily Report: China*, October 11, 1978, pp. E1-E22.

Jiang Zemin. 1998. "Political Report." Beijing Central Television, September 12, trans. Foreign Broadcast Information Service, *Daily Report*, no. FBIS-CHI-97-255.

Lardy, Nicholas. 1996. "Testimony: Statement Before the Committee on Banking and Financial Services, U.S. House of Representatives," March 20.

Lee, Hong-yung. 1991. *From Revolutionary Cadres to Party Technocrats in Socialist China*. Berkeley: University of California Press.

Li Qiang. 1995. "Zhongguo jumin shuoru chaju wenti baogao" (Report on income differences among Chinese citizens). In Li Peilin, ed., *Zhongguo xin shiqi jieji jieceng baogao*. Shenyang: Liaoning renmin chubanshe, pp. 334–49.

Linz, Juan J., and Alfred Stepan. 1996. *Problems of Democratic Transition and Consolidation: Southern Europe, South America, and Post-Communist Europe*. Baltimore: Johns Hopkins University Press.

——. 1997. "Toward Consolidated Democracies." In Diamond, et al., eds., *Consolidating the Third Wave Democracies: Themes and Perspectives*. Baltimore: Johns Hopkins University Press, pp. 14–33.

Mandelbaum, Michael, ed. 1996. *Post-Communism: Four Perspectives*. New York: Council on Foreign Relations.

Manion, Melanie. 1993. *Retirement of Revolutionaries in China: Public Policies, Social Norms, Private Interests*. Princeton: Princeton University Press.

——. 1997. "Corruption and Corruption Control: More of the Same in 1996." In Maurice Brosseau, Kuan Hsin-chi, and Y. Y. Kueh, eds., *China Review, 1997*, pp. 33–56.

Miles, James. 1996. *The Legacy of Tiananmen: China in Disarray*. Ann Arbor: University of Michigan Press.

Naughton, Barry. 1995. *Growing Out of the Plan: Chinese Economic Reform, 1978–1993*. Cambridge: Cambridge University Press.

Nevitt, Christopher Earle. 1996. "Private Business Associations in China: Evidence of Civil Society or Local State Power?" *The China Journal* 36 (July): 26–45.

Oi, Jean. 1992. "Fiscal Reform and the Economic Foundations of Local State Corporatism in China," *World Politics* 45, no. 1: 99–126.

———. 1999. *The Institutional Foundations of Economic Reform.* Berkeley: University of California Press.

Overholt, William H. 1993. *The Rise of China.* New York: W. W. Norton.

Pzreworski, Adam. 1991. *Democracy and the Market: Political and Economic Reforms in Eastern Europe and Latin America.* New York: Cambridge University Press.

Rabinbach, Anson. 1996. "Social Knowledge, Social Risk, and the Politics of Industrial Accidents in Germany and France." In Dietrich Rueschemeyer and Theda Skocpol, eds., *States, Social Knowledge, and the Origins of Modern Social Policies.* Princeton: Princeton University Press, pp. 48–89.

Rosen, Stanley, and Gary Zou, eds. 1990–1991. "The Chinese Debate on the New Authoritarianism (I), (II), (III), (IV)," *Chinese Sociology and Anthropology* (Winter 1990, Spring 1991, Summer 1991, and Fall 1991).

Shain, Yossi, and Juan Linz. 1995. *Between States: Interim Governments and Democratic Transitions.* New York: Cambridge University Press.

Shang Xiuyun. 1995. "Spurring Economic Growth and Making Life Easier; China Scores Marked Achievements in Reform of Circulation Structure." In *Renmin Ribao,* overseas edition, October, 4, p. 2, trans. Foreign Broadcast Information Service, *Daily Report,* no. FBIS-CHI-95-229.

Silberman, Bernard S. 1993. *Cages of Reason: The Rise of the Rational State in France, Japan, the United States, and Great Britain.* Chicago: The University of Chicago Press.

Tang Hua. 1995. "New Trends in Personnel and Institutional Reforms," in *Liaowang,* no. 11 (March 13):12–13, trans., Foreign Broadcast Information Service, *Daily Report,* no. FBIS-CHI-95-062.

Tsou, Tang. 1991. "The Tiananmen Tragedy: The State-Society Relationship, Choices, and Mechanisms in Historical Perspective." In Brantley Womack, ed., *Contemporary Chinese Politics in Historical Perspective.* Cambridge: Cambridge University Press, 1991, pp. 265–327.

———. 1986. "Political Change and Reform: The Middle Course." In Tang Tsou, *The Cultural Revolution and Post-Mao Reforms.* Chicago: The University of Chicago Press, pp. 219–58.

Unger, Jonathan, and Anita Chan. 1996. "Corporatism in China: A Developmental State in an East Asian Context." In Barrett L. McCormick and Jonathan Unger, eds., *China After Socialism: In the Footsteps of Eastern Europe or East Asia?* Armonk: M. E. Sharpe, pp. 95–129.

Wang Shaoguang. 1996. "Gonggongcaizheng yu minzhu zhengzhi" [Public finance and democratic politics], *Zhanlue yu guanli* [Strategy and Management], no. 2, pp. 32–36.

Wank, David. 1995. "Bureaucratic Patronage and Private Business: Changing Networks of Power in Urban China." In Andrew G. Walder, *The Waning of the Communist State: Economic Origins of Political Decline in China and Hungary.* Berkeley and Los Angeles: University of California Press, pp. 153–83.

Wittrock, Bjorn, and Peter Wagner. 1996. "Social Science and the Building of the Early Welfare State: Toward a Comparison of Statist and Non-Statist Western Societies." In Dietrich Rueschemeyer and Theda Skocpol, eds., *States, Social Knowledge, and the Origins of Modern Social Policies.* Princeton: Princeton University Press, pp. 90–109.

Wu Bangguo. 1996. "Guanyu guoyou qiye gaige yu fazhan de jige wenti" (Some issues concerning the reform and development of state-owned enterprises), *Zhongyang dangxiao baogaoxuan,* no. 18, pp. 2–14.

Xia Wensi. 1997. "Qiao Shi xiatai neimu" (The inside story of Qiao Shi's stepping down), *Kaifang,* 10 (October), pp. 14–17.

Yan Wen. 1997. "Chengzhen jumin shouru chaju zheng guoda" (The increasing gap in income of urban residents), *Gaige neican,* no. 10 (May 20), pp. 14–16.

Yang Qixian. 1997. "Guanyu guoyou qiye gaige de lixing sikao" (Thinking rationally about reform of state-owned enterprises), *Jingji yanjiu cankao,* no. 13 (February 7), pp. 2–18.

Yang Zhongmei. 1996. *Jiang Zemin zhuan* (Biography of Jiang Zemin). Taipei: Shibao wenhua, 1996, pp. 307–16.

Zheng, Shiping. 1997. *Party vs. State in Post-1949 China.* New York: Cambridge University Press.

4

Patronage Politics as an Obstacle to Democracy in South Korea: Regional Networks and Democratic Consolidation

Sunhyuk Kim

OVER A DECADE HAS elapsed since the most recent—and still ongoing—"Korean experiment" with democracy (Han 1991) started in earnest.[1] On June 29, 1987, Roh Tae Woo, then the chairman of the ruling Democratic Justice Party of South Korea, announced his eight-point democratization package. It included, inter alia, a constitutional revision introducing direct presidential elections, fair election management, restoration of civil rights for Kim Dae Jung (then a leading opposition politician and now, following his fourth try, president of South Korea), freeing political prisoners, human rights guarantees, lifting of press restrictions, encouragement of local autonomy and university independence, and promotion of political parties. The June 29 announcement brought to an end the authoritarian era in which the military-dominated regime had tenaciously resisted and harshly suppressed popular demands for democratic transition. It thereby also provided a long-overdue reward for the prodemocracy movement dating to the early 1960s.

Since 1987, there have been several positive changes in South Korean politics. First, political contestation became fairer and more extensive.[2] There were two "founding elections" (O'Donnell and Schmitter 1986: 61–64) during the democratic transition—the presidential elections in 1987 and the National Assembly elections in 1988. The direct presidential elections in 1987, despite allegations of election-rigging from the defeated candidates, sharply contrasted with the so-called "gymnasium elections" (*Ch'eyukkwan son'go*) held during the previous authoritarian period. That is, under Park Chung Hee's *Yusin* (Revitaliz-

ing Reforms, 1972–79) and the Chun Doo Hwan (1980–88) dictatorships, the president was elected indirectly by members of the national
"electoral college" who gathered in a large athletic gymnasium and
voted nearly unanimously for the designated authoritarian ruler.

Since 1993, the Law on Political Funds and other legal reforms have
also substantially improved opposition party candidates' chances of getting elected (Lee and Sohn 1995: 30–31). At the same time, local autonomy has been restored. For some three decades the various authoritarian regimes had postponed local autonomy indefinitely, arguing that
centralized leadership was essential for confronting the North Korean
threat to national security. In March 1994, however, local autonomy
laws were enacted, making all local executives and representatives popu-
larly elected. And, on December 18, 1997, longtime opposition leader
Kim Dae Jung was elected to the presidency on his fourth try (he took
office three months later). As the first true outsider elected to South
Korea's presidency, Kim may introduce importance changes in the country's system of patronage politics, though at this time it is hard to know
whether change will prevail.

Second, important strides have been taken toward expanding civil
liberties.[3] For example, the Basic Press Law, a sophisticated and comprehensive system of press censorship enacted in 1980 by the Legislative
Council for National Security (*Kukpowi*), was abolished. A number of
labor laws, which had greatly restricted the exercise of labor rights, were
overhauled as well. The National Security Planning Agency (NSPA, formerly the Korean Central Intelligence Agency), which had served the previous authoritarian regimes by monitoring opposition politicians and
suppressing dissident movements, pledged to terminate domestic surveillance and shift its focus to intelligence operations related to counterter-
rorism and foreign criminals.[4]

Third, civilian control over the military has been significantly aug-
mented. Given that democratic "elected officials must be able to exercise
their constitutional powers without being subjected to overriding opposition from unelected officials" (Schmitter and Karl 1991: 81), such civilian control over the military is integral to the practice of democracy.
President Kim Young Sam (1993–98) designed and implemented sweeping reforms to restructure civil-military relations. He chose an army chief
of staff who was known to be without political aspirations and was not
from the elite *Hanahoe* faction of the Korean Military Academy, whose
members had intruded on politics under earlier authoritarian regimes.
Kim also enacted measures to downgrade the influence of the military's
intelligence division, banning civilian surveillance and appointing a relatively low-ranking officer to head the division. He also discharged dozens

of navy admirals and air force generals for accepting bribes for the promotion of junior officers (Cha 1993: 855–56).

Despite these democratic reforms, however, many South Koreans—scholars, democratic activists, and politicians—remain generally dissatisfied with the democratic progress in their country. Underlying that dissatisfaction with past democratic progress and future prospects is a persistent, if not permanent, debate regarding two different "visions" of South Korean democracy. One vision focuses on "procedural" or "formal" democracy; the other on "substantive" democracy.

For those who advocate "procedural" democracy ("proceduralists"), the political transformations that occurred from 1985 to 1987 are sufficient to warrant fundamental rethinking about what stage South Korean democracy is currently in. Both the Roh Tae Woo regime and the Kim Young Sam regime, despite their limitations and shortcomings, were basically democratic regimes, clearly differentiated from earlier authoritarian regimes. In contrast, for those who demand "substantive" democracy ("substantivists"), South Korean democracy is still in the midst of its democratic transition and will likely remain so for a considerably long time into the future. They insist that it is gravely mistaken and misleading to claim that South Korea is in a stage of "democratic consolidation." These substantivists argue that, to be genuine, South Korean democracy must transcend "procedural" democracy, which stresses constitutional structures, elections, and other formal political institutions. Instead, they maintain, the ultimate goal of South Korean democracy should be to achieve a form of democracy capable of addressing fundamental socioeconomic injustices and significantly reduce, inter alia, class, gender, and regional inequalities.[5] In short, the central issue in this debate over conflicting visions of South Korean democracy is whether the process of democratization is principally characterized by *continuity* or *discontinuity* with the previous authoritarian regimes. The proceduralists emphasize discontinuity while the substantivists stress continuity.

As far as the critics of South Korean democracy are concerned, the most crucial hurdle to clear in order to attain the goal of substantive democracy is the continued prevalence of patronage politics. Based on kinship, friendship, school ties, and common regional or village roots and composed of patron-client relations, i.e., "an alliance between two persons of unequal status, power, or resources each of whom finds it useful to have as an ally someone superior or inferior to himself" (Landé 1977: xx), patronage politics has been considered one of the most prominent continuities between the "democratic" regimes and the previous authoritarian regimes.

With more than ten years of experience, students of South Korean politics now can and should reassess the true significance of that country's democratization since 1987. Were there (m)any fundamental changes? What has really changed? What changes can be considered fundamental and substantive? Has the process of South Korean democratization been characterized by *continuity* or by *rupture* with the past? This chapter, focusing on the persistence and procedures of patronage politics based on shared regional roots through the administration of Kim Young Sam, highlights some of the limitations and future tasks of Korean democratization. In an epilogue, I will speculate as to the potential role the incoming Kim Dae Jung administration may play in reforming patronage and consolidating democracy.

REGIONAL PATRONAGE POLITICS IN SOUTH KOREA— HISTORICAL BACKGROUND

In contemporary South Korean politics, two regional patronage networks are particularly salient: the TK (Taegu-Kyŏngsangbukto) network and the PK (Pusan-Kyŏngsangnamdo) network. Taegu is the capital of North Kyŏngsang province (Kyŏngsangbukto or Kyŏngbuk) and Pusan, South Korea's second largest city and its largest port, is the biggest city in South Kyŏngsang province (Kyŏngsangnamdo or Kyŏngnam). Both networks are based in the southeastern part of the Korean peninsula. During the past authoritarian regimes, owing to the influence of the rulers from the Taegu area, the TK network dominated the most powerful political positions. For example, presidents Park Chung Hee (1961–79), Chun Doo Hwan (1980–88), and Roh Tae Woo (1988–93) were all from the Taegu-Kyongbuk region. In recent years, the dominance of that network has been rapidly eroded in the face of the PK network's vigorous expansion, helped by recent president Kim Young Sam, who was from the PK region.

Regional rivalry has a long history in Korea. Between 57 B.C. and 676 A.D., the Korean peninsula was divided into three kingdoms: Kokuryo, Paekche, and Silla. Kokuryo was located in the northern part of the peninsula which is now North Korea; Paekche was in the southwestern region; and Silla was in the southeastern area. The three kingdoms had distinct dialects, though they were somewhat mutually intelligible. Their respective cultural, political, and social systems differed as well. After extensive competition and rivalry between the three kingdoms, Silla, now the base for South Korea's two dominant regional patronage networks, unified the entire Korean peninsula with China's help.

Regional rivalries continued, however, even after unification. During the Koryo kingdom (918–1392), for example, there were numerous regional revolts and uprisings aimed at independence and led by leaders of the three former kingdoms. Subsequently, the Choson dynasty (1392–1910) was controlled by competing political elites with different regional backgrounds. High-ranking government officials were recruited from a group of prestigious families. Sometimes bypassing or overriding the power of the kings, these powerful aristocratic families became de facto rulers of Choson kingdom.

At the same time, competing cultural and religious elements in Korean society contributed to the development of regional patronage political networks. Confucianism, strictly speaking, is not a religion, as it has neither an absolute God nor a systematic *Weltanschauung*. Nevertheless, Korean Confucianism has always provided a set of powerful moral injunctions with a significant degree of binding force. Its teachings stress the significance of human relations in general and, more particularly, the importance of relations with elders and friends from one's hometown. In the Confucian tradition, having courteous, friendly, and mutually beneficial relations with hometown colleagues is considered a critical virtue of a man of character. At the same time, Buddhism, the state religion of Koryo kingdom (918–1392) and a very powerful influence in contemporary Korea, emphasizes the fateful and predestined nature of encountering and relating with various people throughout one's life. For example, casually bumping into a stranger on the street, Buddhism maintains, is not a matter of sheer chance but rather results from the workings of mysterious and wondrous forces of fate and predestination. If coming across a total stranger receives that much importance, relations with elders and friends in one's local community obviously deserve far greater appreciation and attention. That two people are from the same hometown almost instantaneously provides an effective rallying point around which a patronage network can be formed and nurtured.

These historical and cultural factors notwithstanding, it was not until the authoritarian regime of former general Park Chung Hee that regional patronage networks took on an institutionalized character. In this respect, South Korea's regionalism is not as primordial as it is modern. During the first and second republics between 1948 and 1961, regional patronage networks and connections did not pose a serious problem to the workings of South Korean democracy. It was Park who, after leading a military coup in 1961, extensively developed and maintained regional patronage networks in various parts of the political arena. These networks, based on regional roots, became particularly salient after the 1971 presidential election. In that contest, Park, who came from the TK region, narrowly defeated Kim Dae Jung, who was from South

Chŏlla province. The bitter electoral rivalry between the two had a lasting impact on the subsequent unfolding of South Korean politics. As president, Park Chung Hee became increasingly dependent on the TK patronage network. During his tenure, 130 of 432 high-ranking government officials (30.1 percent)—including ministers, vice ministers, and directors of state offices—came from either North or South Kyŏngsang provinces, whereas only 57 (13.2 percent) came from the two Chŏlla provinces (Mun 1989: 76).

Regional preference was not limited to the recruitment of high-ranking government officials. Park's industrialization policy also located most of its principal projects in North and South Kyŏngsang provinces. For example, many of the major textile, electronics, steel, machinery, automobile, shipbuilding, and petrochemical plants during the "economic miracle" of the 1960s and 1970s were established there, including Taegu, Pusan, Kumi, Masan, Ch'angwŏn, Ulsan, and P'ohang. The nation's major infrastructures as well—notably highways and railways—were built to connect the capital, Seoul, with the industrial cities of the Kyŏngsang provinces. While other parts of the country, particularly the southwestern provinces of North and South Chŏlla, remained largely agrarian and underdeveloped, cities in Kyŏngsang were rapidly transformed into major industrial centers featuring steel mills, automobile factories, and shipbuilding yards.

Preferential policy toward the Kyŏngsang provinces and the extensive use of regional patronage political networks increased during the tenure of another general turned president, Chun Doo Hwan. Chun, who was also from the TK region, widely recruited and mobilized his "hometown buddies." Thus, during his tenure, 67 of 156 high-ranking government officials (43.6 percent) were from North and South Kyŏngsang provinces whereas only 15 (9.6 percent) were from the Chŏlla provinces (Mun 1989: 76).

REGIONAL PATRONAGE NETWORKS AND DEMOCRATIC CONSOLIDATION

It is these regional political patronage networks—formed, developed, and bequeathed by the earlier authoritarian regimes—that are currently bedeviling South Korea's democratic consolidation. Thus, the birth of Kim Young Sam's administration (1993–98) was greatly helped by the cooperation of the old TK patronage network. The direct reason for Kim's victory in the 1992 presidential elections was a grand party merger. In 1990, the ruling Democratic Justice Party of Roh Tae Woo decided to merge with two opposition parties—the Reunification Democratic Party led by Kim Young Sam and the New Democratic Republican Party led by Kim Jong Pil. This closely paralleled Italy's *trasformismo* (transformism) in 1876, when Agostino de Pretis, the new prime minister, invited the opposition Destra Party to shift to the government majority in exchange for personal benefits, access to state patronage, and the right to local rule (Hagopian 1992: 282; Choi 1995: 187–99). The opposition, finding itself marginalized from power and state spoils, agreed and "transformed" itself from the opposition into an integral part of the governing majority. In the process of Korea's own *transformismo,* the mobilization and cooperation of the TK network were extremely crucial to Kim Young Sam's election and thus the birth of a new democratic regime.

To the surprise of many Koreans, however, immediately after the election, Kim Young Sam turned his back on the TK network, purging and prosecuting its major leaders on charges ranging from corruption to insurrection. That early attack, however, did not develop into a genuine campaign against regional patronage networks per se. Instead, Kim developed his own networks. Specifically, following his inauguration he turned to another regional patronage network, called the PK network, which soon dominated and eventually replaced the existing TK network.

The PK network's dominance was manifested in the background of high-ranking officials in government. For example, from the time of Kim Young Sam's inauguration in March 1993 through September 1995, that network accounted for 23.3 percent of his government's 60 ministers and 20.9 percent of his 62 vice ministers (*Han'gyore 21*). According to calculations by an opposition legislator, the PK network provided 41 of 201 high-ranking government officials, while the TK group provided 38. The combined total of officials from the new PK and the previously existing TK networks was 2.5 times the number from both Chŏlla provinces and 3.5 times that of Ch'ungch'ŏng province (*Chungang ilbo* [Chungang Daily], October 5, 1995). Most significantly, as of September 1995, of the "big five" most powerful government posts—the director of the National Security Planning Agency, the public prosecutor-general, the director of the Office of National Police, the director of the Office of National Tax Administration, and the army chief of staff—four were from the PK network.

The PK network has also dominated the police and the Public Prosecutor's Office, which retain considerable influence in South Korean politics. For example, at one point in the Kim Young Sam administration, the public prosecutor-general, the minister of justice, and the director of the Office of National Police were all active members of that network. The PK network has been prominent in government posts that deal with business and economy as well. One of President Kim Young Sam's leading economic advisors was a network leader. At the same time, two of the former president's three most important officials in the Ministry of Budget and Economy (heading the Office of Financial Policy and the Office of Taxation) were also PK network members (*Han'gyore 21*).

Finally, within the top military command, the army chief of staff, the air force chief of staff, and the marine corps commander in the mid-1990s were all from that network. So, too, was the head of the powerful Military Intelligence Agency. In all, 22 percent of the 470 generals and admirals in the army, air force, navy, and marine corps were linked to that group. In fact, in the army that percentage rose to 36.2 percent, double the proportion that the TK network had held when it had dominated the military leadership under the authoritarian regimes of presidents Park, Chun, and Roh (*Han'gyore 21*). Considering this, the widely acclaimed military reforms by the Kim regime are in essence no more than the replacement of the existing TK network by the new PK network.

All of this indicates that democratic reforms under the Kim Young Sam administration failed to remove or even decrease the influence of the regional political patronage networks. Instead, Kim's tenure (1993–98) merely replaced the old TK network with another one.

In several important ways, the continued influence of these networks has negatively affected South Korea's democratic consolidation. Such consolidation has been defined as the "process in which democracy becomes so broadly and profoundly legitimate among its citizens that it is very unlikely to break down" (Diamond 1994: 15).[6] That clearly indicates that legitimacy is central to the consolidation process. Legitimation requires not merely a commitment to democracy in the abstract; it must also involve a shared normative and behavioral commitment to the specific rules and practices of the country's constitutional system. To expand and deepen legitimacy, a democratic regime must meet certain challenges including, but not limited to, greater executive and military accountability to the law and to the public; increased political mobilization of and participation by previously marginalized groups; and greater reassurance to the citizenry that electoral competition will be fair and circumscribed by a predictable range of outcomes (Diamond 1996: 33–34; Schmitter 1997: 240–41). The continued prevalence of political patronage networks such as the TK and PK undermines and compromises the democratic regime's efforts to meet these important challenges in several ways.

First, the prevalence of these kinds of networks impedes any efforts to increase executive and military accountability to the law or to the public. High-ranking government and military officials have routinely been selected because of their geographic origin and patronage connections, rather than their merit or experience. Public officials chosen in this way are naturally more responsive to the leaders of their patronage network than to the law or the general public. They also tend to favor their own factional interests over national ones.

Second, the continued prevalence of influential patronage networks perpetuates and reinforces the exclusion of marginalized groups in the polity. These networks of political elites are by definition exclusive. Their reliance on common identities and experiences excludes those who do not share that background, thereby creating various forms of social exclusion. For example, North and South Chŏlla provinces consistently suffered discrimination in terms of government appointments from the time of the authoritarian regime of Park Chung Hee. The preservation and expansion of the existing patronage networks strengthens the position of the privileged and weakens the status of these marginalized regions or groups.

Third, the existence of influential patronage networks has generated a considerable degree of political cynicism and frustration. At least until the inauguration of reformist President Kim Dae Jung in early 1998, South Koreans often sarcastically commented that their country was no longer "the Republic of Korea" but a "Republic of the PK Network." Similarly, they observed that "Hometown is above merit; PK is above TK." This frustration and cynicism greatly impedes the growth of public behavioral and attitudinal commitment to democratic norms and blocks the development of democratic rules, thereby making democratic consolidation almost unattainable (Linz and Stepan 1996: 3–7). With the continued dominance of elite political networks, South Koreans have remained unsure and suspicious of their political system's fairness, thereby ultimately undermining their commitment to democracy.

The foregoing analysis demonstrates that eliminating the negative effects of patronage politics in South Korea is extremely important both for attaining "substantive" democracy *and* for consolidating "procedural" democracy. Consequently, it is somewhat misleading to connect the issue of patronage politics narrowly to substantive democracy alone, as some South Korean "substantivists" currently do. "Procedural" democracy is equally subject to regional patronage politics, as evidenced by recent presidential and National Assembly elections in South Korea in which candidates effectively politicized and widely mobilized regional networks to win elections. Combatting patronage politics, therefore, should be a unifying theme for both "proceduralists" and "substantivists" hoping to consolidate South Korean democracy.

SUMMARY AND CONCLUSION

In this chapter, I have examined the persistent limitations that regional political patronage networks impose on South Korean democratization. I first introduced two different visions of South Korean democracy, one "procedural" and the other "substantive," to highlight the salience of the problem. After briefly reviewing the historical, cultural, and institutional origins of these regional networks, I analyzed their workings and effects, focusing on President Kim Young Sam's recently completed administration. Kim's election was made possible by a form of *transformismo,* a political party merger in which the then-ruling party mobilized its patronage networks to co-opt and incorporate opposition parties. After taking office, Kim Young Sam significantly weakened the power of the existing patronage network, but created and expanded his own regional network, the PK network, in its stead. That new network was prominent in both the government and the military during his presidency. Until now, the dominance of patronage networks has constricted South Korean democracy, making it difficult for the government to meet the challenges of democratic consolidation. For further consolidation of South Korean democracy to take place, in both "procedural" and "substantive" terms, the political system must eliminate, or at least greatly reduce, its excessive reliance on these networks.

This can be accomplished only if the politics of democratization is recovered from the hands of a few elite politicians and returned to civil society. Put in comparative perspective, what sets South Korean democratization apart from most of the "classic" cases belonging to "the third wave" of global democratization (Huntington 1991) is the critical role played by groups in civil society—student movements, labor unions, and religious organizations in particular—in the country's authoritarian breakdown and the democratic transition. Unlike many countries in Southern Europe and Latin America, South Korea's civil society was not merely "resurrected" through an initial opening in its authoritarian regime brought about by a fateful split between regime hard-liners (*duros*) and soft-liners (*blandos*) (O'Donnell and Schmitter 1986: 15–56). Rather, it was Korean civil society itself—"the realm of organized social life that is voluntary, self-generating, (largely) self-supporting,

[and] autonomous from the state" (Diamond 1994: 5)—that significantly facilitated, if not directly caused, the democratization process.

During the prodemocracy struggle through the authoritarian breakdown in June 1987, groups in civil society had almost always been the central force behind political change. In particular, the resurrection, reactivation, and remobilization of the groups in the people's movement played a leading role in facilitating the authoritarian breakdown. Those groups formed a formidable prodemocracy alliance and challenged the authority and legitimacy of the regime. They also took the initiative in forging and developing a grand democratic coalition with the major opposition party. In short, civil society had largely exercised a hegemony over political parties. However, after the authoritarian regime agreed to carry out a series of democratic reforms, including direct presidential election, that hegemony started to unravel. Transitional politics focused on the founding elections—the presidential elections in December 1987 and the National Assembly elections in April 1988. As these elections approached, South Korean politics revolved more and more around party politics and electoral competitions in political society. The people's movement in civil society became incrementally marginalized. Transitional politics was "delegated" to political parties and eventually it fell victim to a serious regional and personal split that erupted between Kim Young Sam and Kim Dae Jung, helping the ruling bloc consolidate power.

It was this "premature delegation" in 1987 that ultimately emboldened South Korea's political elite to launch an historically unprecedented transformative project in 1990 and later to expand political patronage networks. Consequently, South Korea's democratic consolidation can overcome the legacy of patronage politics only if civil society is reactivated and remobilized to initiate a massive and united movement against the long-standing patronage system. That is, just as it was the key to the country's democratic transition, civil society must also be central to the politics of democratic consolidation. Without civil society's organized efforts to put an end to regional patronage politics, South Korean democracy—both procedural and substantive versions—will remain fragile and shallow.

EPILOGUE

On December 18, 1997, Kim Dae Jung was elected South Korea's new president. Kim had been an internationally renowned opposition leader and had run for presidency three times before his eventual victory. His election marks a historic moment for South Korea in two respects. For the first time, there has been a horizontal alternation of power from the governing party to the opposition. There was a somewhat similar power transition in 1960, but the preceding government of Syngman Rhee was not peacefully voted out of office at that time. Rather it was overthrown by a student rebellion. Second, Kim Dae Jung is from South Chŏlla province and consequently has been one of the prominent victims of the exclusive patronage politics long-dominated by the ruling TK and PK regional networks.

What will be the impact of his election on patronage politics in South Korea? First compared to Kim Young Sam, his predecessor, Kim Dae Jung seems more able and willing to reduce the influence of patronage. Indeed, he has already shown himself to be more geographically balanced in recruiting his advisors. Thus, a number of his top advisors are not from the two Chŏlla provinces. He also has pledged that he will make the recruitment of high-ranking officials more transparent and more merit-based. Second, he has maintained more extensive and cooperative relations with a variety of groups in civil society. Support from some of these social groups was critical for his election. By continuing close cooperation with these groups which, as pointed out in my analysis, has been relatively free from patronage politics, Kim Dae Jung may be able to avoid excessive reliance on his own patronage networks for information and personnel. Third, immediately after his election victory, Kim publicly promised that he would not pursue a politics of vindication. Although he and other political representatives from the Chŏlla provinces suffered systematic discrimination under past regimes, he announced that he would neither seek nor endorse another form of regional favoritism and would instead pursue a politics of grand reconciliation and unity.

At the same time, however, Kim Dae Jung is faced with challenges similar to those that confronted his predecessor. After all, he has undeniably been one of the beneficiaries, if not advocates, of regional patronage politics. Against the dominance of TK and PK networks in power, he successfully managed and mobilized his own regional patronage networks based in Chŏlla provinces. Support from the Chŏlla provinces for Kim Dae Jung in recent elections has been impressive, ranging from 80 to 90 percent of the vote. This is why he was often called Chŏlla's president, more so than Korea's president.

Second, one of the critical factors behind Kim's triumph in the 1997 presidential election was his alignment with Kim Jong P'il. Kim Jong P'il, an ultraconservative and staunch anticommunist, had served as a prime minister under Park Chung Hee and had created the powerful Korean Central Intelligence Agency. Kim Dae Jung's affiliation with him, a marriage of convenience between two ideologically antithetical politicians, was quite instrumental in Kim Dae Jung's election, because Kim Jong P'il helped him garner substantial support from the two Ch'ungch'ŏng provinces which had been the former's sphere of influence. Kim Jong P'il, a practitioner and champion of traditional patronage politics, is very likely to prefer the status quo, retarding and sabotaging any effort by Kim Dae Jung to reform the system.

Compared to the 1990 grand party merger, Kim Dae Jung's alliance with Kim Jong P'il is much less secretive, much less dramatic, and much less antidemocratic. However, just as the *transformismo* at that time later haunted Kim Young Sam by tarnishing his democratic image and tainting his democratic reforms, this alignment with Kim Jong P'il could similarly haunt Kim Dae Jung's government, fettering efforts to reduce patronage politics and, thus, hampering democratic consolidation. Finally, resistance to reform from existing patronage networks will be quite substantial, if not insurmountable. Those networks will try everything to characterize Kim Dae Jung as a promise-breaker and discredit his efforts to reform patronage politics, by labeling any significant challenge to the status quo as the politics of revenge that Kim Dae Jung promised not to pursue. In conclusion, there are both positive and negative forces affecting Kim Dae Jung's ability to reform patronage politics and consolidate South Korean democracy. Which of those two forces will prevail remains to be seen.

NOTES

1. For a comparative analysis of different democratic "cuts" in the history of South Korea, see Sunhyuk Kim (1996).

2. Holding relatively free, fair, and regular elections is a central element found in diverse definitions of democracy (Dahl 1971: 3; Huntington 1991: 7; Diamond, Linz, and Lipset 1995: 6). For a definition of democracy which emphasizes civil liberties in particular, see Diamond, Linz, and Lipset (1995: 7).

3. However, the passage of several controversial laws in the National Assembly in December 1996, which, if implemented, would weaken labor and considerably strengthen the intelligence agency, clearly demonstrates that these reforms for greater democratic freedoms are not completely irrevocable.

4. In this respect, "substantive democracy" is similar to what O'Donnell and Schmitter (1986: 12) call "socialization," which involves both "social democracy" and "economic democracy." "Substantive democracy" is also similar to what Linz and Stepan (1996: 457) call "deepening of democracy," which en-

compasses gender equality, access to critical social services, inclusive citizenship, etc.

5. For more elaborate definitions, see Linz and Stepan (1996: 3–15); Valenzuela (1992: 69).

References

Cha, Victor D. 1993. "Politics and Democracy Under the Kim Young Sam Government: Something Old, Something New." *Asian Survey* 33, 9: 849–63.

Choi, Jang Jip. 1995. "'Pyonhyongjuǔi'wa han'gukǔi minjujuǔi" ("Transformism" and South Korean Democracy). *Sahoe pip'yong* (Social Critique) 13: 183–221.

Dahl, Robert A. 1971. *Polyarchy: Participation and Opposition.* New Haven: Yale University Press.

Diamond, Larry. 1994. "Rethinking Civil Society: Toward Democratic Consolidation." *Journal of Democracy* 5, 3: 4–17.

———. 1996. "Is the Third Wave Over?" *Journal of Democracy* 7, 3: 20–37.

Diamond, Larry, Juan J. Linz, and Seymour M. Lipset, eds., 1995. *Democracy in Developing Countries: Comparing Experiences with Democracy,* 2d ed. Boulder: Lynne Rienner.

Hagopian, Frances. 1992. "The Compromised Consolidation: The Political Class in the Brazilian Transition." In Scott Mainwaring, Guillermo O'Donnell, and J. Samuel Valenzuela, eds., *Issues in Democratic Consolidation: The New South American Democracies in Comparative Perspective.* Notre Dame: University of Notre Dame Press.

Han, Sung-joo. 1991. "The Korean Experiment." *Journal of Democracy* 2, 2: 92–104.

Han'gyore 21 (Han'gyore Weekly), September 28, 1995.

Huntington, Samuel P. 1991. *The Third Wave: Democratization in the Late Twentieth Century.* Norman: University of Oklahoma Press.

Kim, Sunhyuk. 1996. "Civil Society in South Korea: From Grand Democracy Movements to Petty Interest Groups?" *Journal of Northeast Asian Studies* 15, 2: 81–97.

Landé, Carl H. 1977. "The Dyadic Basis of Clientelism." In Steffen W. Schmidt, Laura Guasti, Carl H. Landé, and James C. Scott, eds., *Friends, Followers, and Factions: A Reader in Political Clientelism.* Berkeley: University of California Press.

Lee, Chong-sik, and Hyuk-Sang Sohn. 1995. "South Korea in 1994." *Asian Survey* 35, 1: 28–36.

Linz, Juan J., and Alfred Stepan. 1996. *Problems of Democratic Transition and Consolidation: Southern Europe, South America, and Post-Communist Europe.* Baltimore: Johns Hopkins University Press.

Mun, Sok Nam. 1989. "Chiyok kamjongǔi wonin'gwa haeso pangan" (Causes and Resolutions of the Regional Sentiment). In IFES (Institute for Far

Eastern Studies), ed., *Han'gukŭi minjuhwa: kwajewa chonmang* (South Korean Democratization: Tasks and Prospects), Seoul: IFES, Kyongnam University.

O'Donnell, Guillermo, and Philippe Schmitter. 1986. *Transitions from Authoritarian Rule: Tentative Conclusions about Uncertain Democracies.* Baltimore: Johns Hopkins University Press.

Schmitter, Philippe C. 1997. "Civil Society East and West." In Larry Diamond, Marc F. Plattner, Yun-han Chu, and Hung-mao Tien, eds., *Consolidating the Third Wave Democracies: Themes and Perspectives.* Baltimore: Johns Hopkins University Press.

Schmitter, Philippe C., and Terry Lynn Karl. 1991. "What Democracy Is . . . and Is Not." *Journal of Democracy* 2, 3: 75–87.

Valenzuela, J. Samuel. 1992. "Democratic Consolidation in Post-Transitional Settings: Notion, Process, and Facilitating Conditions." In Scott Mainwaring, Guillermo O'Donnell, and J. Samuel Valenzuela, eds., *Issues in Democratic Consolidation: The New South American Democracies in Comparative Perspective.* Notre Dame: University of Notre Dame Press.

5

Institutions and Democracy in Brazil

Barry Ames

Introduction

BRAZIL'S DEMOCRATIC REGIME HAS now endured for more than fourteen years, but it has surely been a rocky fourteen years. One president suffered impeachment; an enormous corruption scandal shook the Congress; social services sank to new lows, and the economy, though stabilized, still faces serious problems. The current president, renowned sociologist Fernando Henrique Cardoso, came to office with enormous advantages. He is credited with authorship of Brazil's successful macroeconomic stabilization program; the political parties backing him claim a solid congressional majority; and his political skills are substantial; left opposition is in a chaotic state. So far, however, Cardoso's record is quite mixed. Measures opening the economy sailed through the Congress, but crucial reforms of the administrative structure and the welfare system were delayed for years and passed only with important concessions, while reform of the tax system has not begun. Cardoso persuaded the Congress to approve a constitutional revision allowing his reelection, but the amendment passed only after the distribution of liberal doses of patronage. If Fernando Henrique Cardoso, playing such favorable cards, has this much trouble advancing a legislative agenda, imagine the situation of a "typical" president. Brazil's chief executives usually lack even nominal congressional majorities. They depend on deputies mainly interested in their own fortunes, in local pork barrel, or in the defense of narrow interests. They face a public dramatically dissatisfied with governmental performance at all levels. In sum, Brazil faces a permanent governability crisis, devastating in normal times, debilitating even for seemingly powerful presidents like Cardoso.

This chapter argues that failures in institutional design lie at the

130

heart of Brazil's governability problem. What does it mean to claim that a nation's political institutions work badly? Do they serve only the rich, the economic elite? Remember, the people who design political institutions belong to the elite, and we can hardly fault institutions for serving their creators. The problem of the Brazilian state is not that the system benefits elites. The problem is that the system primarily benefits itself, that is, the politicians and civil servants who operate within it. Brazil's policy makers, at least since 1990, have been able to adopt macroeconomic policies facilitating the nation's integration into the global economy. But these same policy makers have been unable to reform the state apparatus or to implement social programs providing services commensurate with Brazil's wealth.

This argument, that a state apparatus can benefit mainly those occupying places within it, does not imply—contrary to the rhetoric of antigovernment conservatives—that politicians are intrinsically thieves. To the contrary, many Brazilian politicians and civil servants sacrifice personal gain to serve the public good. Rather, the argument begins with the notion that political institutions create *incentives* for politicians. These incentives, which differ from system to system, motivate politicians to act in ways that either facilitate or hinder the adoption of public policies likely to improve life for the average citizen. In the Brazilian case, the nation's political institutions generate incentives that weaken parties and encourage politicians to enrich themselves or to concentrate on delivering pork-barrel programs to narrow groups of constituents and political benefactors. Some politicians, resisting these incentives, struggle to legislate on national issues, but they face an uphill and usually unsuccessful battle.

What is the basis of the claim that Brazil's political institutions function poorly? In terms of formal powers, the country's presidents rank among Latin America's most powerful. What they need most, however, is support from a political party commanding a congressional majority, and only rarely do Brazil's chief executives enjoy such support. Instead, presidential authority—even, at times, presidential survival itself—depends on the distribution of construction projects and political jobs to crucial governors, mayors, deputies, and senators. Presidents begin their terms with high-minded pieties about avoiding the *troca de favores,* the exchange of favors, their predecessors so scandalously pursued. But political necessity soon rears its head. Unfortunately, even after liberally spreading the "pork," the most the president can expect from the Congress is a limited acquiescence rather than active participation in the legislative process.

Because the legislature cannot respond nimbly to presidential initiatives, recent Brazilian presidents have frequently resorted to emergency decrees, the so-called *medidas provisórias*. Since 1988, over a thousand emergency decrees have been sent to the Congress. These decrees take immediate effect, but after thirty days they lapse unless approved by Congress. Since the presidency has no monopoly on either wisdom or virtue, the light of day quickly reveals serious legal or substantive flaws in many emergency decrees, and by mutual agreement they are allowed to die. In many other cases, the Congress fails to act, and the president simply reissues the decree. Some emergency measures do become permanent laws, but rarely do they survive their legislative voyage unscathed. Final versions of these bills often include major compromises reflecting the pork-barrel or interest-group demands of particular legislators or parties. Overall, emergency decrees circumvent congressional obstructionism, but they also put up one more roadblock keeping the Congress from meaningful participation in policy making.

On its own, the Congress has been too weak, either in the current democratic experiment (post-1985) or in its earlier incarnation (1947–64), to legislate on issues of national concern.[1] The legislature's weakness was especially painful in 1988, when the Senate and the Chamber of Deputies joined together as a Constituent Assembly. The Assembly produced a 160-page constitution. It granted life tenure to bureaucrats and capped interest rates, but it left major issues in health and education for resolution by future legislatures. These subsequent legislatures, to no one's surprise, resolved nothing, doing little more than reacting to the many emergency decrees of Presidents Collor de Mello, Franco, and Cardoso. Indeed, though Brazil's social services may be the worst of any large Latin American country, the Congress has not passed, on its own initiative, a single bill affecting education, health, or housing since the constitution went into effect in 1988.

Without question, macroeconomic stabilization has been the dominant economic problem in Latin America during the early 1990s. Brazil was the last Latin nation to adopt and stick to a workable stabilization program. It was long understood that inflation discouraged productive enterprise and foreign investment, but even when it became clear that inflation hurt the poor most, Brazilian politicians found it impossible to reach an accord. In 1994, when the alternative was a victory by a truly leftist candidate, conservative and moderate legislators finally accepted Cardoso's program (Dimenstein and De Souza 1994). Even then, rural politicians in the Chamber of Deputies extracted major concessions in exchange for their votes. These concessions, worth billions of dollars, represented not policy compromises but personal financial benefits.

Why are Brazil's political institutions so ineffectual? Consider the party system and the legislature. Major electorally sucessful parties fall all across the ideological spectrum. Some parties embrace distant, hostile points of view; others shelter deputies sharing no ideas at all. Party leaders have little control over their members, and many, perhaps most, deputies spend the bulk of their time arranging jobs and pork-barrel projects for their constituents. Parties in Brazil rarely organize around national-level questions. The Congress, as a result, seldom grapples with serious social and economic issues.

Brazil's presidents benefit little from the policy-making weakness of the Congress. With little chance of stable legislative support, the executive faces politically independent governors, a crowded electoral calendar, municipalities depending for their very survival on federal largesse, and a substantial core of deputies caring about their personal incomes first, reelection second, and public policy a distant third. Because inflation has been the overriding problem since the end of military rule, new presidents often take office with elaborate macroeconomic plans, but rarely do their programs go further. And because congressional support must be built upon a wide, multiparty base, cabinets include ministers whose loyalties are tied more to their own political careers than the president's program.

What causes these political failures? How can we understand Brazilian politics? This chapter begins with a brief discussion of recent Brazilian political history, emphasizing the pluralist regime that lasted from 1946 until 1964 and the military regime that held power from 1964 until 1985. I then discuss Brazil's core political institutions—the electoral system, the legislature, and the presidency—and show how they contribute to the problem of governability. In the conclusion, I consider proposals for reform.

PART I. RECENT BRAZILIAN HISTORY

A Shaky Democracy: 1946–64

By the end of World War II, President Getúlio Vargas had ruled Brazil for fifteen years. As the war wound down, traditionally anti-Vargas elements in the economic elite and the middle class—mindful of the incongruity between Brazil's military involvement against fascism and its own dictatorship—intensified their pressure for democratic elections (Skidmore 1967).

Recognizing the inevitability of democratic politics, Vargas moved to ensure his political survival by creating not one but two political parties. The Partido Social Democrático, or PSD, found its supporters among three groups: local and state politicians linked to the New State, businessmen benefiting from the protection afforded by import-substitution industrialization, and landowners. The Partido Trabalhista Brasileiro, or PTB, included union leaders and labor bureaucrats who had gained importance as Vargas nurtured the corporatist structure of labor controls. The opposition coalesced into the União Democrática Nacional, or UDN, a mix of urban and rural conservatives plus longtime opponents of the Vargas machine.

The PSD held absolute majorities of seats in both the Senate and Chamber of Deputies between 1945 and 1950, but in no later legislature did a single party hold a majority in both chambers. Over the course of the 1946–64 democracy, the PSD steadily gave ground to the PTB as the dual forces of urbanization and industrialization increased the size of labor's natural constituency and shrank the pool of rural peasants that the PSD's clientelistic politics helped dominate.

Party fragmentation, first manifesting itself in 1950, was also related to populism. As Latin American cities swelled with the influx of millions of rural immigrants, political entrepreneurs sought ways to compete for these new masses with the Socialists and Communists, the traditional working-class parties. "Populists" emphasized social-welfare programs and immediate benefits, including government jobs. They bypassed intermediate political organizations like class-based parties. Instead, they forged direct links between themselves and their followers. Economic nationalism helped create, at least temporarily, coalitions with domestic industrialists. Populist politicians such as Vargas and Argentina's Juan Perón maintained their popularity—and the support of many domestic business executives—as long as their economies grew. When the economic pie stopped expanding, the inflationary bias of their "no losers" politics revealed the fragility of the populist coalition.

In the 1950 election, Vargas regained the presidency democratically. Less than four years later, however, facing a likely military takeover, he committed suicide. By that point a combination of Vargas's left-nationalism rhetoric, growing budget and trade deficits, and, finally, a botched assassination attempt by a presidential lieutenant had polarized the political system.

After a brief military interregnum, the PSD-PTB coalition managed in 1956 to elect Juscelino Kubitschek. The Kubitschek administration constituted the high point of ISI. Per capita income expanded by 27 percent. To help motivate new industrial sectors the government created "executive groups" of well-trained technocrats. The *técnicos* bypassed the regular bureaucracy, thought to be crippled by patronage and inefficiency, and made the government a more agile policy maker. At the same time, however, constructing a new capital city, Brasília, required substantial payoffs to politicians and construction companies along with enormous financial outlays that resulted in government deficits and inflation. Thus, by the time Kubitschek left office his developmentalist-populist model was showing fatigue.

In 1960 the UDN finally won a presidential election. Right-wing populist Jânio Quadros, a party outsider, easily defeated the PSD-PTB candidate, but the vice-presidency went to João Goulart, Vargas's labor minister and Kubitschek's vice-president. Quadros began his term with an orthodox stabilization program and a vigorous attack on the financial profligacy and corruption of the Kubitschek era. But after seven months of highly unpredictable governance, Quadros suddenly resigned. As a result, the historic enemy of the UDN, in the person of Vice-President João Goulart, assumed the presidency. Goulart was also anathema to much of the military and major economic actors. His administration lasted until April of 1964, when a military coup ended Brazil's democratic experiment.

What caused the military coup? The opposition of business leaders and the U.S. government to Goulart's economic nationalism and political radicalism certainly counted. Falling growth rates and rising inflation (up to 70 percent annually) further weakened the president. Still, a coup represents a military response to a political deadlock. The key to the coup of 1964, as we shall see, lies in the politically deadlocked legislature and in the breakdown of bargaining between moderates on both the left and the right.

João Goulart was an incompetent leader. He vastly overestimated the strength of his support in the trade unions and the military, and he could never decide whether to cast his lot with left moderates or left extremists. The president polarized opinion more than he intended and encouraged his opposition. But forces beyond the president's control victimized him as well. Extremists on both left and right furthered the polarization of opinion. And the continuous tendency toward party fragmentation increased the strength of minor parties.

Continued pressure from his left flank (most notably, from Goulart's brother-in-law, Leonel Brizola, a congressman and former governor) pulled the president leftward. But, as it turned out, the left had no teeth: there was hardly any reaction when the military deposed Goulart in April of 1964.

Why were democratic moderates on the left and right unable to unite to prevent a coup that brought precisely the outcome both sought to avoid? Youssef Cohen (1994) argues that moderates on both sides found themselves in a classic "prisoner's dilemma." Moderate leaders in the PTB, PSD, and UDN could have agreed on a program of reforms, but only if they disavowed the extremists in their own camps. On the left, the PSD and PTB moderates had to separate themselves from the extreme left of the PTB. On the right, the PSD and the more progressive elements of the UDN had to keep their distance from far-right elements among the military, industrialists, and landowners. But neither group of moderates disavowed its extremist allies, because each side feared the other would retain its links to its own extreme wing. The moderate right thought that Goulart really intended to rule as a dictator. Goulart himself believed the moderates in the PSD were plotting with right-wing military and pro-coup businessmen to block any serious reforms and overthrow him. Thus moderates on both sides thought that if they jettisoned their radical allies, the other side—moderates plus extremists—would overwhelm them and produce an unacceptable outcome. So each side stuck with its own extremists. Since no one wanted the stalemate and the military coup of 1964, both sides ended up worse off than they would have been if they had cooperated.

The Military in Power: 1964–85

Like other politically experienced militaries, Brazil's officer corps is far from monolithic. General Humberto Castelo Branco, the first president of the military regime, represented its more liberal wing. Although the junta quickly exiled radical nationalist politicians like Brizola, it did not initially engage in mass repression at the level of the post-1973 Chilean coup. Castelo Branco's main task was economic stabilization. His economic team applied standard orthodox measures, and the military utilized the corporatist system of labor controls to remove dissident union leaders and prevent labor from fighting wage-reduction measures. With the elimination of any oposition to orthodox stabilization, Castelo Branco's technocrats successfully reduced inflation to 31 percent in 1967. But workers paid the bill: by that year the average industrial wage had fallen nearly 20 percent. The technocrats were less successful in restoring growth, which averaged only 4.4 percent under Castelo Branco, barely better than in the Quadros-Goulart years. In 1967 a new military president, Artur da Costa e Silva, took over with a much more aggressive and growth-oriented economic team which expanded cheap credit to the private sector and ended the fall in wages. The result was rapid growth and moderate inflation. GDP increased by more than 10 percent per year, while inflation stabilized at just over 20 percent. The 1968–73 period became known as the "Brazilian miracle."

What kind of political system did the military want? This question has long bedeviled observers. Military rhetoric stressed the need to restore a "purified" democracy; indeed, the generals often portrayed themselves as democracy's "saviors." Still, their idea of democracy was profoundly ambivalent. In 1965 the regime allowed scheduled gubernatorial elections to proceed. When opponents of the military won key governorships, military hard-liners forced Castelo Branco to issue a new "Institutional Act." This decree eliminated all political parties, made the 1966 presidential elections indirect, allowed the president to fire elected officials, and gave the president the right to suspend any citizen's political rights. The regime then established an official proregime party, the National Renovating Alliance, or ARENA, and an official opposition, the Brazilian Democratic Movement, or MDB. ARENistas were mostly right-wing PSD and UDN politicians; MDBistas were the traditional centrists. The left was simply banned (Stepan 1973).

Costa e Silva and his successor, General Garrastazú Médici, initiated not merely a growth-oriented economic policy but a period of brutal repression as well. At the time of the coup, terrorism and other violent political activities were absent from Brazil. By 1967, when the hard-liners took over, civilian politicians and students had stepped up their demands for a return to open politics, and two big strikes had occurred in the industrial heartland. The military reaction was swift and crushing. Its central weapon was a decree allowing the president to suspend civil liberties and close all legislatures. Under the legal cover of this decree, military "intelligence" units tortured and killed thousands, only a small number of whom were involved in acts of terrorism. The regime prevented criticism by ruthless media censorship. When the federal Congress reopened in 1971, it had been purged of serious opposition and emasculated of legislative powers.

By 1973 the regime could claim substantial successes. The nation had enjoyed six years of extraordinary economic expansion. The army had wiped out the guerrillas and eliminated terrorism. And yet, just at this moment of success, the regime began to liberalize, easing its repression and accepting competitive politics. The political opening took fifteen years to complete, and there were many backward steps, but the movement toward political liberalization was inexorable.

With hindsight, the causes of liberalization are clear. In 1973 the military regime had selected General Ernesto Geisel as its new president. Like Castelo Branco, Geisel represented the liberal wing of the armed forces, the wing that had always wanted a return to competitive politics. The end of guerrilla and terrorist opposition eliminated one of the regime's chief reasons for existence. It was hard to ignore the clamor for liberalization coming from society, especially from upper-status groups like lawyers and clerics. And finally, the regime's technocrats recognized that economic growth could not continue at the pace of 1968–73. The excess capacity that had allowed low-inflation growth was no longer available. Savings rates were too low, and the 1973 oil shock dramatically worsened Brazil's balance of payments. High growth-rates could distract attention from repressive authoritarianism, but low growth would inevitably fuel criticism.

In a broader sense, the regime's movement toward liberalization was a recognition that authoritarianism had failed to institutionalize itself. Juan Linz had argued that the Brazilian case represented an authoritarian "situation" rather than an authoritarian regime (1973: 235). As an idea, as a symbol, authoritarianism could never match democracy's popular acceptance. Legitimation of the military regime around a charismatic leader was impossible, because the military feared charismatic leaders of the Vargas type. Legitimation around a full-blown corporatism, à la Mussolini, was simply alien to Brazilian reality, especially given the organization of civilian politics along federal and regional lines. And while the regime's leaders knew the United States government supported its doctrines of anticommunism and national security, they also knew Brazil would not get the respect it deserved until it returned to liberal-democratic institutions.

If a political opening was inevitable, smooth progress was not. Geisel gradually brought the repressive apparatus under control, but sporadic human rights violations continued until the end of the 1970s. The media, especially newspapers, gradually recovered the freedom to criticize the regime and to discuss substantive issues. In 1974 the regime allowed relatively free legislative elections, because the high command believed the electorate would be grateful for the success of the "miracle." Instead, the election delivered a stunning rebuke to the regime: the opposition MDB nearly doubled its seats in the Chamber of Deputies and quadrupled its seats in the Senate. ARENA suffered its most severe losses in the industrialized states of the south and southeast. The regime respected the results of that contest, but it tried to rig future elections to strengthen ARENA. Knowing, for example, that the MDB's candidates were younger and more attractive, the regime restricted television ads to still photographs. In spite of such rules, the opposition gradually gained strength in the Congress and in state assemblies.

As the military regime withdrew from power, it tried to implement a survival strategy; that is, it sought to create conditions maximizing its support post-departure. The strategy centered on attempts to increase backing in potentially supportive regions and to reduce the strength of traditional opponents. Fusing the states of Guanabara and Rio de Janeiro eliminated three senators from an opposition stronghold. The formation of new states in the north and center-west created seats for new, mostly conservative deputies and senators. Encouraging industrial growth away from the Rio-São Paulo area meant more jobs in the northeast. New housing programs outside the traditional urban centers created progovernment voters. Spending in education shifted a bit toward lower-level schools. A frankly redistributive wage policy was adopted in 1979, and rural credit programs were aimed at lower-income groups.

Economic reality caught up to the regime, and by the beginning of the last military presidency, that of General Figueiredo, the regime lost its ability to keep the lid on. The economy had substantially declined, and the political opening enabled a wide variety of interests to pressure the government. When the oil shock and rising interest rates on the external debt induced the regime to launch a strong anti-inflation program, a popular outcry resulted. President Figueiredo first gave in to demands for a growth-oriented strategy but then switched to differing policies. By 1982, the first of many agreements with the International Monetary Fund sharply reduced Figueiredo's (and the regime's) popularity and paved the way further for a transition to civilian government.

History's Legacy

This chapter stresses the relationship between institutions and democratic consolidation. In the historical summary above, we can see how social, economic, and demographic factors affect institutions: by encouraging the creation of one set of institutions rather than another and by influencing the ongoing operation of the institutions ultimately adopted. The strength of traditional regional forces, the early power of landowning wealth, the extreme poverty and backwardness found in regions like the northeast: these factors encouraged the development of federal institutions. Federalism weakens the accountability of governments to the population and creates multiple petitioners for government largesse. A second factor is Brazil's traditional clientelism. Clientelism politicizes policy making. The state must absorb thousands of political appointees, and policy focuses on delivering pork to local bosses. Finally, state intervention in the economy has been a hallmark of the twentieth century. The state initiated and directed the policy of import-substitution industrialization. ISI made Brazil a major industrial power, but it also brought pervasive inefficiency and corruption. Together, these enduring structural factors—federalism, clientelism, and state intervention—led to the creation of an "accommodationist" state. Political leaders and high-level bureaucrats paid off opponents and avoided trespassing on the vital interests of any group possessing political resources.

Part II. Political Institutions and Governability

This section examines the electoral system, the federal Congress, and the presidency. The legal framework of these institutions is found in the Constitution of 1988, a document written by a constitutional assembly composed of the senators and deputies elected in 1986. To the surprise of few, they preserved the electoral system that had elected them, the scheme of open-list proportional representation Brazil had utilized since 1946.

The discussion begins with a basic description of Brazil's electoral rules. We shall see that deputies have enormous flexibility in constructing coalitions of voters. In effect, the system is hyper-democratic; i.e., it makes no presuppositions about the kinds of societal cleavages that ought to be the basis of election. Unlike single-member systems, which clearly favor locality as their dominant cleavage, or closed-list proportional representation, which favors social class, open-list PR (given districts of high magnitude) allows the campaign itself to determine which cohorts of voters get representation.

Brazil's openness and flexibility come at the cost of weak parties and personalized politics. After describing the system, I examine some of its implications for the process of democratic consolidation.[2] These include disproportionality, corruption, the nature of representation and accountability, and party building.

How Brazilian Open-List PR Works

Brazil's voters face a choice: they may vote for the party label or they may cast their ballot directly for an individual candidate. Most—about 90 percent—vote for an individual. After the election, the votes won by all the candidates of each party (plus the few votes for the party label) are added together. A formula determines how many seats each party gets, and each party's candidates are ranked according to their individual vote totals. If the party is entitled to ten seats, its ten top vote-getters are elected.

All open-list systems shift power from party leaders to individual candidates, but the Brazilian system magnifies this tendency. Actual ballots, for example, do not include candidates' names (voters must know the name or code number of their candidate), so the party cannot list its preferred order. The rules allow unlimited reelection, and parties are obligated to renominate incumbents desiring reelection, no matter how they voted in the previous legislature. Together, these details remove important means of disciplining deputies from party leaders.

Other nations, including Finland and pre-1973 Chile, adopted open-list proportional representation, but Brazil's version differs significantly. In elections for the Chamber of Deputies, each state is an at-large, multimember district. The number of seats per state ranges from 8 to 70. Lightly populated states, mostly in the north and center-west, are over-represented; heavily populated states, principally São Paulo, have too few seats. State parties, not national parties, select legislative candidates, and the states are important political arenas in their own right.[3] Some states have powerful governors controlling nominations and dominating campaigns. In other states local leaders deliver blocs of votes to deal-making candidates; in still others neither governors nor local bosses have much influence over individual voters.

Brazilian campaign regulations are both restrictive and permissive. Candidates cannot buy ads on radio or television, but parties receive TV time free. Parties dole out TV time in proportion to the importance of each race, so the hundreds of congressional candidates get only a few seconds each week. Practically everyone advertises in newspapers, but print ads have little impact (Straubhaar et al. 1993). Candidates erect billboards and paint signs on walls, but they generally do so in conjunction with other campaign efforts, such as participation in rallies or delivery of public works to local leaders.

Permissive spending laws allow candidates for the federal legislature to finance state assembly campaigns. Because state assembly districts are also whole states, with all candidates elected at large, politicians engage in *dobradinhas,* or double-ups, in which federal legislative candidates pay for the campaign literature of assembly candidates whose bases of support lie far away. The assembly candidates reciprocate by instructing supporters to vote for their benefactor for the national legislature. Such deals add little, of course, to linkages between representatives and their constituents.

A Taxonomy of Spatial Patterns

Legally, candidates seek votes everywhere in their states, but in reality most limit their campaigns geographically. The spatial patterns that result have two dimensions, each based on *municipal* performance. Suppose, for every candidate in each municipality, we calculate V_{ix}, candidate i's share of all the votes cast in municipality x. We define each candidate's *municipal dominance* as the candidate's share of the total votes cast for members of all parties. These shares represent the candidate's dominance at the municipal level.[4] Now suppose we use V_{ix} to calculate D_i, the average dominance for each candidate across all the state's municipalities, *weighted by the percentage of the candidate's total vote each municipality contributes*. Candidates with higher-weighted averages tend to "dominate" their key municipalities; those with lower-weighted averages "share" their key municipalities with other candidates. Thus "dominance-sharedness" is the first dimension of spatial support.

The second dimension also begins with V_{ix}, candidate i's share of the total vote cast in each municipality, but this dimension utilizes a statistical measure called Moran's I to assess the *spatial* distribution of those municipalities where the candidate does well.[5] These municipalities can be concentrated, as close or contiguous neighbors, or they can be scattered. Combining the two dimensions yields four spatial patterns:

Concentrated-dominated municipalities. In the classic Brazilian *reduto* (literally, "electoral fortress"), a deputy dominates a group of contiguous municipalities. Candidates' families may have traditional economic or political dominance in a particular region; they might climb the ladder of politics from local jobs; they may strike deals with local bosses. Figure 1, mapping the 1990 vote of Deputy Laire Rosado Maia, illustrates extreme concentration.[6] Rosado Maia received nearly all his votes in the "elephant's trunk," the western section of Rio Grande do Norte. Maias have long controlled this area—one county even carries the family name. Note that where Rosado Maia received votes, he averaged at least 50 percent of all votes cast. So not only does Rosado Maia get all his votes in this region, other candidates rarely dare to compete in his impermeable *reduto*.[7]

Concentrated-shared municipalities. In large metropolitan areas, particular blocs of voters may be able to elect many deputies by themselves. In the state of São Paulo, for example, working-class candidates often get three-fourths of their total state-wide vote from one municipality, the city of São Paulo. Because they share these municipalities with many other candidates, they may never receive more than 5 percent of the votes cast in the city or in any other single county. Figure 2 illustrates this possibility: *PTista* Eduardo Jorge got most of his votes in São Paulo and its

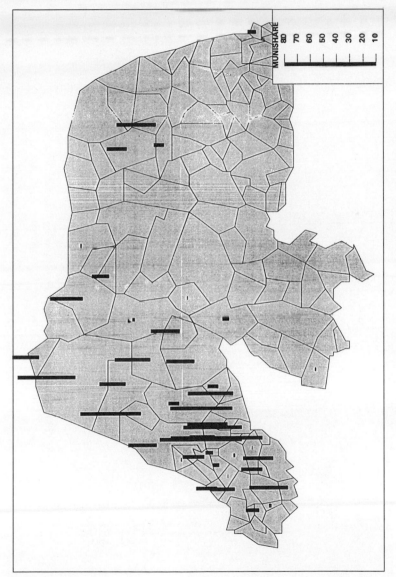

FIGURE 1. *Vote Distribution For a Traditional Regional Politician*
Municipal Vote Share of Laire Rosado Maia, PMDB-RN

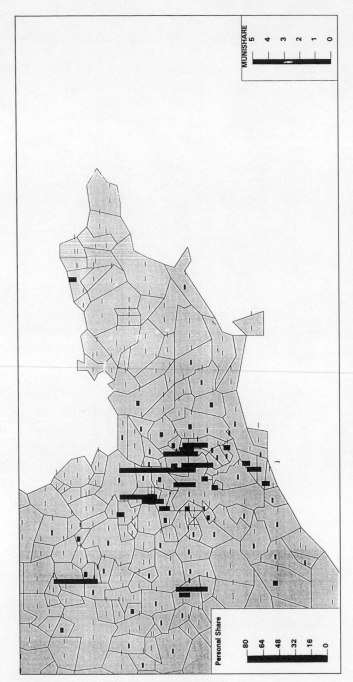

FIGURE 2. *Vote Distribution For a Working-Class Candidate*
Eduardo Jorge, PT-São Paulo

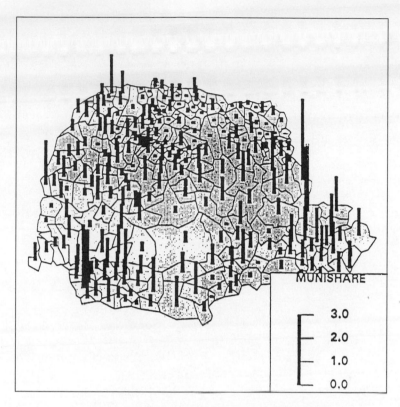

FIGURE 3. *The Scattered-Shared Vote of an Evangelical*
Municipal Vote Share of Matheus Iensen, PTB-Parana

industrial suburbs, but he shared these municipalities with dozens of other candidates, including many others from the PT.

Scattered-shared **municipalities.** Some candidates appeal to voter cohorts that are small fractions of any single municipality. Two common examples are Japanese-Brazilians and *evangélicos,* the latter being Protestants who typically vote for evangelical candidates. These cohorts are cohesive and loyal but small, so candidates relying on them construct coalitions composed of small slices of many municipalities. The vote of Matheus Iensen, a Protestant minister from Paraná, is displayed in figure 3. Candidates occupying ideological niches also fall into the scattered-shared category. Cunha Bueno, a *paulista* conservative, is famed for his campaign to restore the monarchy. A return to the monarchy was rejected seven to one in a nationwide plebiscite, but Cunha Bueno finds enough support across the state of São Paulo to win a Chamber seat.

Scattered-dominant municipalities. This pattern fits candidates who make deals with local leaders—a theme examined further below—as well as those who once held such state-level bureaucratic posts as secretary of education, that is, jobs with substantial pork-barrel potential. To save space, the graphic illustration of this pattern is found in the section on corruption (see figure 4 on page 151).

Although many deputies combine elements of different distribution patterns, most deputies' electoral maps are classifiable as a single type. With each type is associated a distinctive modal campaign and legislative behavior. As we turn to the consequences of open-list PR, we will see how these strategic adaptations of candidates interact with the overall rules of the system.

Disproportionality

Like the U.S. Congress, Brazil's legislature is bicameral, but in Brazil the allocation of seats favors small states in both houses. In the Chamber of Deputies, seats are allocated by population, but with a minimum of 8 and a maximum of 70 the number of voters per deputy varies enormously (see table 1). The big loser, obviously, is São Paulo; the big winners are the lightly populated frontier states of the north and center-west.

Does disproportionality matter? Most observers believe that disproportionality weakens "progressive" forces. With more seats, São Paulo would elect more deputies who would be more likely to represent the working class. The frontier states, which have few industrial workers and which are invaded by free-spending business types, would elect fewer deputies. Without question, Brazilian politicians have acted as if they believed disproportionality favored the right. In the Constitutional Convention of 1946, conservative delegates from São Paulo supported allocation rules that penalized their state (Fausto 1970). The military regime (1964–85) followed the same reasoning when it added one senator to each state, divided certain states to increase their representation, and joined two states in order to minimize opposition from the former capital.[8] Like the *paulista* conservatives, military strategists based their tactics on an estimate of the inclinations of São Paulo and frontier delegates.

Can we estimate the legislative effects of disproportionality? After any election, it is possible to determine which candidates would have won or lost seats if a state's allocation were smaller or larger. We know,

TABLE 1

*State Representation in the Chamber of Deputies According
to the Sainte-Lague Formula (Electorate of 1989)*

STATE	ELECTORATE	CURRENT SEATS	"CORRECTED" SEATS	DIFFERENCE
Roraima	73,011	8	0	-8
Amapá	118,144	8	1	-7
Acre	182,797	8	1	-7
Tocantins	485,048	8	3	-5
Rondônia	557,781	8	3	-5
Sergipe	776,071	8	5	-3
Amazonas	842,083	8	5	-3
Distrito Federal	857,330	8	5	-3
Mato Grosso do Sul	1,002,232	8	6	-2
Mato Grosso	1,027,972	8	6	-2
Alagoas	1,210,797	9	7	-2
Rio Grande do Norte	1,298,088	8	8	0
Piauí	1,334,282	10	8	-2
Espirito Santo	1,407,759	10	9	-1
Paraíba	1,756,417	12	11	-1
Maranhão	2,144,352	18	13	-5
Goiás	2,178,977	17	13	-4
Pará	2,186,852	17	13	-4
Santa Catarina	2,729,916	16	17	+1
Ceará	3,351,606	22	21	-1
Pernambuco	3,764,143	25	23	-2
Paraná	5,045,626	30	31	+1
Rio Grande do Sul	5,700,461	31	35	+4
Bahia	5,893,861	39	36	-3
Rio de Janeiro	8,166,547	46	51	+5
Minas Gerais	9,432,524	53	58	+5
São Paulo	18,500,980	60	114	+54
Total	82,025,647	503	503	0

of course, how the excluded deputies voted. Suppose we assume that the
deputies added to a slate by new proportionality rules will vote according to the mean of their parties' current votes. In other words, we know
which candidates will be added to state delegations, and we know which
parties they represent. If we know that the *paulista* PMDB delegation

will expand 25 percent, then we weight each current vote by 1.25; if the PFL delegation expands 10 percent, then we weight each current PFL vote by 1.10. Thus we simply assume that the *paulista* delegation will cast its votes in the same proportion as it does currently, by party, except that it will cast 54 more votes. Let us call this technique the "party ratio" method. The key to this method is that we actually know which deputies, from which parties, will be added to the delegation.

The above reallocation assumed that preelection slates (all the people running for office) would be the same if a state's politicians knew they had one seat rather than eight, or 114 rather than 60. This assumption is frequently wrong: leaders often fill out their slates with candidates who bring in a few votes but whom no one expects to win. In states losing the bulk of their representation, the winner under proportional rules would unambiguously be the candidate leading under the current rules only if party unity is high—certainly a rare event. So, as an alternative model of proportionality rules, let us assume nothing about the new winners or losers. Instead, we simply assume that each slate preserves its current party ratios; i.e., each deputy on a slate currently including three PTB and five PFL deputies will now cast the same legislative vote, but it will have one-eighth the original weight. *Paulista* deputies will cast the same votes they currently cast, but each vote will be reweighted by the ratio 114/60. The key element in this "state ratio" method is that we do not know who will be added to the delegations, so we assume current party ratios will hold.

Now let us apply these reallocation rules to some important votes in the Constitutional Assembly of 1987–88. Two of its most important—and most conflictual—issues were the vote over parliamentarism (known as the Humberto Lucena amendment) and the decision to grant the incumbent president a five-year rather than a four-year term. President Sarney lobbied strenuously on both issues. After vigorous debate, presidentialism won, 344–212, and Sarney got his five-year term, 304–223.

How would the two models affect voting on these two issues? Using the state-ratios model, i.e., simply reweighting each vote to reflect the fraction of the delegation added or subtracted, presidentialism still wins, but a five-year term would be defeated by the four-year alternative. Using the party-ratios model, i.e., eliminating those deputies who would not have been elected in states losing members and assuming the new members in states gaining deputies would vote according to their party brethren, the results are the same: presidentialism wins, and the four-year term vanquishes the five-year term. If we take a broader sample of crucial votes in the constitutional assembly, the results are similarly mixed: about one in five changes.[9]

Why are the effects of correct proportionality not more dramatic? Remember that party discipline in the Brazilian Congress in this period was quite low. Only the PT votes as a bloc, and it has never been more than the fourth or fifth largest party in the Chamber, even lower in the Senate. When São Paulo increases its seat share dramatically, center and center-left parties can expect a substantial share of the additions, but these parties rarely cast unified votes, so the additional "progressive" vote will be smaller.

As a final model of the effects of allocation changes, let us imagine what would happen if parties voted as blocs. Suppose we take the position of the majority in each party and then assume that all the party's delegation voted with the majority. We eliminate the delegates from states losing seats and add delegates according to their rank in the substitute list for those states gaining seats. In this case parliamentarism defeats presidentialism, but Sarney gets a five-year term. These results occur because the majority of the PMDB voted parliamentarist but supported PMDBista Sarney on his quest for a longer term. On our broad range of crucial issues in the constitutional assembly, many other outcomes change from what actually occurred.

These results show the importance of considering the context of structural changes in political rules. Reallocating seats according to population sometimes makes an important difference. But since parties are rarely unified, the effects are reduced.

Corruption and Patterns of Vote Distribution

In 1993, an enormous scandal shook the Congress. The racket's basis was simple: deputies submitted, and the Budget Committee approved, amendments to the general budget law, amendments mandating the construction of public works. Only particular companies could build these public works, either because those companies had already initiated the project or because the bidding would be rigged. The companies could afford handsome kickbacks to the deputies, often 20 percent or more of the value of the project, because collusion generated big profits on the project itself. The deputies laundered their kickbacks through the national lottery: they would go to the lottery office, buy a winning ticket for a small premium, and receive "clean" money from the lottery.

The ringleaders of the scheme, a group of Budget Committee deputies known, because of their small stature, as the "seven dwarfs," were investigated by a special committee of inquiry. Most either resigned or were kicked out of the Chamber. One resignee was the former chair of

the Budget Committee, João Alves, a senior deputy from Bahia. Alves
had come to the Congress in 1966 with no money; by the early 1990s he
had millions of dollars in real estate and a $6 million airplane.

Examine figure 4, which displays the 1990 vote distribution of
Deputy Alves. Note that his votes came from widely scattered municipalities, but where he got votes, he got lots of votes. In many of his pock-
ets of support he collected over 70 percent of the municipality's total
vote, but in the municipality next door he might get nothing. How could
this be? If he had the kind of support enjoyed by a local mayor or council
member, a leader with a strong local reputation, Alves would have a single dominant cluster of votes with a gradual tapering off as his local fame
grew faint. It is possible, of course, for a locally based politician to have
more than one cluster of votes. For example, a deputy with family in one
region might build a political career in another. Alves, however, has too
many separate clusters to fit that pattern. Some candidates appeal to a
special bloc of voters and receive small amounts of scattered support, but
Alves *dominates* his bailiwicks.

The pork-barrel *cum* kickbacks scandal depended first on the existence of a highly concentrated civil construction industry, one dominated
by fewer than a dozen huge companies. Without government contracts
they could not survive. Politicians and bureaucrats have traditionally had
great leeway in allocating such contracts. Whether a particular corrupt
project involves local officials or not, the existence of local bosses who
can "deliver" voters en masse is critical to the survival of this kind of
corruption. Deputies get rich with the bribes of the construction giants,
but they have to use part of the money to pay off the local bosses. Although no empirical data are available to support this intuition, the
share going back to the district in the form of personal loans and grants,
petty favors and "walking around" money, probably accounts for a substantial part of the bribes deputies receive.[10] Thus a key part of corruption is the existence, on the one hand, of politicians willing to sell blocs
of voters and, on the other, politicians with the money to buy their support. To illuminate the bases of dominant-scattered distributions, I developed a model of the vote of João Alves. Space constraints prevent the full
presentation of the model's results, but the conclusions are interesting.

The regression model sought the determinants of Alves' vote
among political, economic, and demographic variables. It turns out that
the political characteristics of municipalities are much more important
than their economic and demographic characteristics. João Alves was
more successful, in terms of his share of total municipal votes, where the
municipality's mayor represented the Liberal Front Party (PFL) and
where the fragmentation of PFL candidates was low.[11] And finally, he

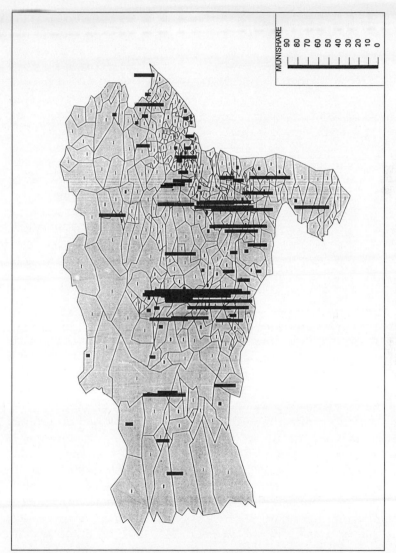

FIGURE 4. *Vote Distributions of the "Budget Mafia"* (Scattered-Dominant)
Municipal Vote Share of Joao Alves, PFL-BA

gained a small increment of votes in municipalities where a higher share of the work force is employed in municipal government.[12] In such municipalities politics is often the only thriving business, and municipal employees understand the importance of remaining in the good graces of the local boss.

Dominance is only possible where people are poor—hence the strong negative relationship between income per capita and municipal vote share. But neither population size nor the percentage of migrants in the municipality matter at all. When the level of absolute poverty is higher, measured by the share of the population earning less than one-fourth the monthly minimum (about $60 at the time), Alves does a bit better, but the relationship is weak.

Overall, the particular kind of dominance enjoyed by deputies accused of corruption results from the combination of poverty with stable, machine-based politics. When deputies dominate a concentrated set of municipalities, they usually represent some family with a long history of political influence. When the dominated municipalities are scattered, we see arrangements with local leaders, bosses seeking the best deals available.

Issue Caucuses and Accountability: Who Represents Whom?

Caucuses of like-minded deputies occur naturally in legislatures. When parties have little control over their members, issue caucuses are likely to cut across party lines. In the U.S. Congress, for example, a legislator may belong simultaneously to the black caucus, the steel caucus, and the women's caucus. Another legislator may belong to the textile and tobacco caucuses. Issue caucuses are an important form of representation in legislatures organized by single-member districts. They help deputies represent the economic, ethnic, and social interests of their constituents.

Remember that seats in the Chamber are filled from multimember districts. Because each state, i.e., district, elects many members, political scientists characterize Brazil as a country with "high district magnitude."[13] Given open-list PR and high district magnitude, communities lose the privileged position they hold in a single-member district system like that in the United States. Any politically mobilized cohort of sufficient size can elect a deputy whose sole function is to represent that cohort.[14]

Observers of the Brazilian Congress have identified at least fifteen caucuses. The largest, with about 100 deputies each, are generally thought to be the agricultural (or rural) caucus, the construction industry caucus, and the health caucus, followed by Petrobrás (the national oil company), Catholics, bankers, evangelical Protestants, and communications, each with 50–80 members. Caucuses of 20–30 members each include education, the welfare system and its employees, state banks, civil servants, multinational firms, auto dealers, and unions (*Veja* 1994).

In the issue caucuses of the U.S. Congress, and in cases like the Brazilian deputy advocating the death penalty, the authenticity of claims to representation is based on the interests of the voters electing that deputy. In the House of Representatives, members of the steel caucus come from steel-producing regions. No one would expect a member of the steel caucus to own a steel mill *personally;* indeed, such a tie would be a conflict of interest. In Brazil, however, such ties are often the exact motivation behind caucus membership. A deputy from Rio Grande do Sul represents the interests of the civil construction industry in the Congress. His vote map in no way reflects a concentration of construction workers or firms; rather, the construction industry supports his campaigns, and he responds by lobbying for their interests. The health caucus includes doctors lobbying for medical facilities as well as hospital-owning doctors lobbying for their personal interests.

The Brazilian Congress, then, shelters multiple bases of representation. Some are direct. The "evangelical" caucus lobbies for subsidies for Protestant churches and schools, but the members of this caucus get their votes from precisely the interest they represent. Direct ties with voters also characterize the union and civil servant caucuses. But self-representation, i.e., representation of groups in which the deputy has personal interest, characterizes many members in such caucuses as health, civil construction, and state banks.

To examine this issue further, consider the rural caucus, usually considered as the strongest organized interest in the Congress. The rural caucus can stop any major agrarian reform. In 1994 its power was so great that the government could not push through its economic stabilization package without bargaining with the caucus on completely unrelated agricultural issues. Caucus members claim, of course, that they represent farm interests, but they really represent their own personal interests. In table 2, we seek the determinants of two votes central to the interests of the rural caucus during the 1991–94 legislature. One issue involved a tax (benefiting the welfare system) calculated in terms of agricultural production; the second concerned a tax increase penalizing nonproductive rural properties. Farm interests opposed both taxes. I combined support for the two rural caucus positions, scoring each deputy as pro- or anti-the rural caucus. The explanatory variables include measures of personal economic interests, region, the economic base of a

TABLE 2

Personal Interest vs. Constituency Interest in the Rural Caucus

| | LOGISTIC ESTIMATION OF SUPPORT FOR RURAL CAUCUS | | |
PARAMETER	ESTIMATE	WALD CHI-SQUARE	PR > CHI-SQUARE
Intercept	−1.783	52.09	.0001
Agricultural interest	1.411	27.95	.0001
Northeast region	−.553	1.74	.1867
South region	.719	1.95	.1630
Rural base	.070	3.75	.0529
PFL	1.155	11.56	.0007
PDS	0.434	.93	.3341
PTB	1.040	3.68	.0552
Evangelical	1.419	4.45	.0348

Likelihood ratio significant at .0001 level, N = 408

deputy's voters, party affiliation, and membership in the evangelical caucus. Biographical directories helped identify deputies who were owners of large estates or significant agricultural enterprises.[15] The indicator "Rural Base" (the inverse of "urbanization") came from the 1980 census. I aggregated the characteristics of the municipalities where each deputy received votes, weighted by the percentage of the deputy's total votes the municipality contributed.

Table 2 contains some striking results. Personal agricultural interests were by far the dominant influence in the votes of deputies on agrarian issues. Owners of rural properties essentially make up the rural caucus, and they defend their personal interests. Region did not matter significantly, although deputies from the supposedly traditional and backward northeast were actually a bit more likely to support agrarian reform than their "modern" southern colleagues.[16] A rural electoral base made deputies more likely to oppose agrarian reform, but the relationship was much weaker than the linkage between support for reform and personal economic holdings. Party mattered. Membership in the PFL or PTB was associated with strong antireform positions. PDS partisans, however, took no clear position, probably because their delegation was split between urban and rural deputies. Finally, evangelicals opposed agrarian reform. Their vote, I suspect, resulted both from their natural conservatism and from their willingness to logroll, i.e., to trade support to the rural caucus for the caucus's support on their bills.

This test of the bases of the rural caucus supports the contention that the rules of the Brazilian electoral system distort representation and accountability. Obviously not all caucuses are self-representing. Such groups as unions, evangelicals, and civil servants trade voting support for real representation. But the caucuses representing the construction industry, telecommunications, and state banks have an entirely different claim to legitimacy.

Open-List Proportional Representation and Party Building

By this point it should be clear that open-list PR personalizes politics and hinders efforts at party building. If, in a given state, 50,000 votes elects a deputy, and if a candidate has 200,000 voters who will follow wherever the candidate goes, then that candidate has enormous power. Whichever party attracts the candidate can be assured of another four seats, i.e., the candidate plus three others elected by the 150,000 "extra" votes. Party leaders, of course, will be very tolerant of ideological deviations between such heavyweight candidates and the party's official program. To explore the problem of party building under these rules, this section examines the incentives for inconsistent cross-party alliances, the consequences of party switching by incumbents, and the weakness of links with social groups.

Multiparty Alliances

Brazil's formula for apportioning legislative seats (the D'Hondt method) hinders the chances of small parties attaining the "electoral quotient" entitling them to a seat. As a result, they often ally with larger parties so that their joint total, which determines whether they reach the quotient, is larger. A candidate with a personal total insufficient to earn a seat—because the total of all the party's candidates is inadequate—may have enough votes as part of a multiparty alliance. These alliances are truly just electoral: they imply no joint legislative action. At the same time, the parties have to agree on a common set of promises—it would be a stretch to call these programs—to offer their electorates during the campaign.

    If electoral alliances are inconsistent across the states, state delegations are less likely to share a common program at the national level. Consider the 1986 election. The PTB allied with the PMDB in Ácre and Pará, but it joined anti-PMDB alliances in Bahia, Goiás, Mato Grosso do Sul, Santa Catarina, and São Paulo. In most states the PFL aligned with the PDS, but in Piauí, Rio de Janeiro, Rio Grande do Sul, and Santa

Catarina the PFL either opposed the PDS or ran a separate slate. The PDC joined the PFL in Bahia, but it allied with the PMDB—against the PFL—in Ceará.

The apparent confusion of state-level alliances results from a conceptual confusion. With the exception of the Workers' Party, parties really exist only at the state level.[17] At the state level, moreover, parties can correspond to traditional factional disputes. Thus politics in Maranhão is either pro- or anti-José Sarney. Bahia's lineup is pro- or anti-Antonio Carlos Magalhães. In the presidential election of 1994, PSDBista Fernando Henrique Cardoso defeated PTista Luís Inácio Lula da Silva in the first round, but in the second round Cardoso supported the PT candidate for governor of Espirito Santo. In most states the PT and PDT are fierce enemies, but in Rio Grande do Sul they cooperate. Leonel Brizola, the PDT's founder, controls the party in Rio Grande do Sul and Rio de Janeiro, but in Paraná he has no influence whatever. An even stranger example is found in São Paulo. Former PMDB governor Orestes Quércia naturally dominates a wing of the *paulista* PMDB, but it happens that he also dominates the *paulista* PFL, which answers to him rather than to the national leaders of the PFL.

Party Loyalty and Party Switching

We have seen how Brazil's version of open-list PR personalizes politics and hinders party development. Party leaders lack the means to discipline deputies seeking the party label; indeed, efforts to rein in individualistic or deviant behavior can be costly to the parties themselves. At the same time, parties do nominate governors, senators, and presidents, and, in spite of their ideological vagueness, many of the major parties (especially the PT, PSDB, PMDB, and PFL) occupy recognized positions on a left-right spectrum. Could partisan affinities develop in spite of the hostile environment of open-list PR? In the absence of survey data adequate to illuminate voters' attachments to parties, let us seek clues about the strength of party loyalties in the electoral fates of deputies who change parties.[18]

Between the elections of 1986 and 1990, 72 deputies left the parties they originally represented and sought reelection under different party labels. Only 16 were reelected in 1990. Since the 1990 success rate of all deputies seeking reelection (both switchers and nonswitchers) exceeded 50 percent, party switching may seem tactically foolish. Do the switchers' failures imply that party loyalties really matter, that party switchers lost because they were unable to carry their voters to their new party? Before we blame party loyalty for the losses of party switchers, we need to assess their chances *if they had remained in their parties of origin*. A place to start is the switchers' individual rankings in their deputy list in 1986. It turns out that high-ranking 1986 deputies had a better chance of winning in 1990, but not by much. Of the 34 party-switching deputies who had finished in the lower half of their states' lists in 1986, 6 won in 1990. Of 36 switchers who had finished in the upper half in 1986, 10 were reelected in 1990. So a higher finish in 1986 helped only a little. Switchers were almost equally likely to have done well or poorly in 1986. Deputies do not change parties because they think their chances with the original party are poor.

Politicians know that some of their voters will support them regardless of their party affiliation, while others will support them only as long as they belong to a given party. Deputies considering a shift ought to examine the spatial configuration of their vote. If their personal vote is highly correlated with the overall party vote (the vote for all members of that party together), then it will be tougher to move their voters to another party.[19] It turns out, however, that in most states party switchers were about as likely as nonswitchers to have received their 1986 votes in party bailiwicks. Switchers were not loners with essentially personal votes. They believed that party loyalties would not cripple their reelection chances.

Finally, did switchers hold on to their 1986 voters in 1990? One answer is found in the correlation between the spatial distributions of deputies' personal vote shares in the two elections. In other words, did deputies get their votes in the same places in the two elections? In Bahia, Rio de Janeiro, and Paraná, party switchers actually held their voters *better* than nonswitchers, and in other states switchers did about as well as nonswitchers in transferring their bailiwicks. But the fact that party-switching deputies maintained the same bailiwicks could indicate merely that deputies contemplating a change in party did not foresee that party loyalty would be a problem. As a result, they failed to extend their campaigns out from their 1986 bailiwicks.

The best way to test party loyalty is to compare the vote gains and losses between 1986 and 1990 of party switchers and nonswitchers from the same party. Deputies leaving the PMDB constitute the biggest group of potential switchers. It turns out that, in almost every state, switchers did much worse in 1990 than nonswitchers. In Bahia, for example, switchers from the PMDB lost an average of 20,550 votes between 1986 and 1990, while nonswitching PMDBistas gained 9,611 votes. In Paraná, switchers lost almost 50,000 votes apiece, while nonswitchers lost only 13,480. In only two states, Rio Grande do Sul and São Paulo, did switchers do better than nonswitchers, and in these states the deputies who did well in 1990 had all been extremely popular vote-getters in 1986.

The poor performance of deputies who changed parties between 1986 and 1990 becomes even more dramatic when we recall that switchers, overall, had previously performed as well in 1986 as nonswitchers. We cannot, in other words, dismiss the failure of party switchers on the grounds that they were merely weak candidates. In addition, few switchers lost their seats in 1990 simply because, even though they personally had about the same totals as in 1990, their new party could not muster enough votes from all its candidates to guarantee their seats. Only about one-third of losing switchers could plausibly argue that their defeat was due to the failure of the party to accumulate enough total votes, rather than to their personal decline.

The surprising strength of party at the mass level is even more dramatic in the context of the PMDB's debacle in 1990. Riding the strength of the Cruzado economic plan in 1986, the party had swept most state assemblies and governorships. It was easily the biggest party in the Chamber of Deputies. But by 1990 the Cruzado was a bitter memory, the PMDB's presidential candidate had finished with only a small percentage of the national vote, and the party was in disarray. Leaving the PMDB should have provided candidates a boost, and many clearly saw switching as a political lifeboat. Apparently they were wrong. Loyalty did pay.

This discovery, that party identification may develop more quickly and may resist poor governmental performance more sturdily than commonly believed, needs some qualification. These results are mainly based on switches of former PMDB members. As the party associated with resistance to the military dictatorship, the PMDB enjoyed the highest levels of partisan identification in Brazilian society. Other parties, except for the PT, are unlikely to do as well. In addition, the decline of the PMDB in recent years suggests that overall levels of partisan identification are dropping in Brazil. Party switching inevitably reinforces that decline.

Society and Party: The Missing Link

We usually classify party systems as "institutionalized" when parties have stable shares of the popular vote, when parties and elections clearly determine who governs, when party organizations have stable rules and structures, and when parties have roots in society.[20] Brazil's parties fail all four tests. The PMDB, the nation's largest party, had 40 percent of the Chamber seats in 1983, 53 percent in 1987, 21 percent in 1991. In

1989, just three years after the PMDB's sweeping legislative and gubernatorial victories of 1986, the party's candidate for president received just 4.4 percent of the national popular vote.[21] Parties and elections do determine who governs in Brazil, at least in the sense that military coups are highly unlikely. But at the national level parties—with the exception of the Workers Party—really do not exist, and the strength of state party organizations varies enormously. Still, these aspects of institutionalization are all fairly obvious. More interesting, and more complex, is the question of roots, that is, the problem of parties and their links to groups in society.

For a political party to have a coherent national program, it must represent essentially the same social groups in each of the major regions of the country, and it must maintain these ties over time. Because Brazil's party system is still evolving, with new parties appearing, old ones fading, and politicians switching parties, we cannot simply chart the correlation between each party's candidates and various socioeconomic indicators.[22]

Let us return to our four-category typology of electoral bases: concentrated-dominant, concentrated-shared, scattered-shared, and scattered-dominant. In an open-list proportional system of Brazil's type, would any single category predominate if the system were evolving in the direction of tighter party-society linkages? Clearly neither of the dominant cells reflects society-party linkages. A scattered-shared pattern usually represents groups like evangelicals or ideological niche fillers. Scattered-shared patterns also reflect candidates relying on narrow social groups like pensioners, but in this case they represent very specific interests. The remaining pattern, concentrated-shared, seems more promising. Given the large size of Brazil's districts, candidates appealing to broad social forces are likely to do so in individual metropolitan areas (encompassing multiple municipalities), and these areas are usually large enough to elect more than one candidate. In such districts, contact between voters and their representatives is actually possible. Thus the PT candidates who share the votes of São Paulo's working class have concentrated-shared bases, but middle-class candidates successfully mine the same metropolitan area for votes. Such distributions, in other words, reflect competition along group or class lines.

How can we determine, over the four elections from 1978 until 1990, the number of candidates with concentrated-shared vote distributions? Suppose we pool all four elections, then divide each dimension by its median. This yields, for the entire universe of deputies serving between 1978 and 1990, a rough balance between the four distributional types. In 1978, 19 percent of the deputies had concentrated-shared distributions. In 1982 this number rose to 27 percent, and by 1990 it reached 33 percent. Some parties deviate from this evolutionary pattern. The PDS (now called the PPB), once the promilitary party and long the largest conservative party, shows no shift at all in the vote distributions of its deputies. In 1986 the PDS lost most of its northeastern adherents to the Liberal Front Party, the PFL. Because those PDSistas who remained in the party tend to have secure, noncompetitive vote bases, the party looks increasingly anachronistic. But the general rise in competitiveness does seem to fit the PMDB. It gained many new members in 1986 and then watched many members defect between 1987 and 1989 to the PSDB, the PTB, and other smaller parties. Since the PMDB lost both dominating and sharing deputies, its overall change is not merely a reflection of the defeat of a particular type; rather, it reflects the overall shift of the universe of deputies. New PMDB politicians were more likely to invade old PMDB bailiwicks, and old PMDB deputies adopted the same campaign style as the newcomers.

In sum, party evolution has reduced the number of traditional, municipally dominant deputies and increased the number of community-based deputies who appeal to broad social strata but face competition. This kind of competition heightens emphasis on delivering pork-barrel benefits to communities. But to the degree that parties shape the behavior of their deputies, it also leaves open the possibility that parties will develop programs responding to their voters' class affiliations.

The Congress

I have argued that the electoral system produces a legislature with a plethora of weak parties and an excess of individualistic deputies. This section demonstrates that the pursuit of pork-barrel politics affects deputies' votes on broader issues as well.

What moves deputies? Political scientists usually assume that reelection is the preeminent objective of all politicians. According to the conventional wisdom, deputies maximize the odds of reelection by staying close to the wishes of their constituencies and by attracting pork. We saw, however, that Brazil's electoral system makes it difficult to decide what the constituency wants. Moreover, it is not obvious that most Brazilian legislators *desire* reelection. Voluntary retirements, i.e., deputies leaving though undefeated, are very common. Members may serve a term, then return to a state assembly. They may leave for bureaucratic or business positions only to return a few years later. They may prefer an executive position.[23] Voluntary retirements combine with electoral defeat to produce a high turnover rate in the Chamber. Unlike U.S. House membership, where turnover is very low, typically about 40 percent of Brazilian deputies are serving their first term.

In the previous section we saw that presidents distribute pork to try to gain deputies' support. Do these efforts succeed? To answer that question, I analyzed the voting patterns of Brazilian deputies when they met in 1987–88 as the National Constituent Assembly (ANC). Constitution-writing is quite different from normal legislative politics. Parties less often define clear-cut positions, and they seldom attempt to discipline their members. Ideological positions are more important in constitutional assemblies than in regular legislatures. As a result, we are likely to come closer to the underlying motivations of deputies in a constitutional assembly.

The analysis of the ANC is built on the pioneering research of Maria D'Alva Gil Kinzo, who fashioned a series of issue scales from key constitutional votes. I selected four scales as indicators of basic dimensions of voting.[24] The four scales include "support for expanded congressional prerogatives," "support for expanded executive authority," "statism-welfarism," and "support for popular democracy." The explanatory variables included measures of the spatial distribution of deputies' electoral support, the wealth and industrialization of their constituencies, career tracks, seniority and electoral strength, strength of state political machine, party, ideological orientation, and orientation to pork barrel. In the interest of brevity, I will focus here only on the results of the measures of pork.[25]

In a single-member system, all deputies should be interested in pork-barrel projects, because all are able to claim credit for the projects built in their districts. In multimember constituencies, the ability to claim credit decreases as the number of vote-getting deputies increases. Brazil's left-leaning deputies often share working-class constituencies, where credit claiming is impossible and where national economic issues take precedence over public works. Thus in the long run pork-oriented deputies tend to be antilabor and proexecutive. In the short run the executive may offer inducements to deputies. President Cardoso, for example, made extensive use of public works projects to recruit deputies on key constitutional reforms, including the amendment allowing his own reelection.

I developed four different measures of the probability that a deputy received a pork-barrel payoff. The variable "Pork Payoff to Municipality" is the probability that a deputy could claim credit for an intergovernmental transfer made in 1988 to municipalities where that deputy received votes.[26] "Pork Payoff to Deputy" refers to a 1988 social assistance program of the Ministry of Planning (SEPLAN). Specific deputies sponsored the program in each municipality. "Radio and TV License" calculates the probability that the Ministry of Communications granted a concession during the ANC to a municipality in which the deputy had an electoral base.[27] Finally, "Ministerial Request" indicates that in 1990 the deputy met with the ministers of infrastructure, agriculture, education, or social action. These meetings, I assume, were not about the weather.[28]

Table 3 presents the model's results for four basic dimensions of voting in the ANC. Focusing only on the results for the "pork" variables, what can we conclude? Overall, deputies receiving pork benefits voted to weaken the legislature and strengthen the executive, and they tended to oppose statism-welfarism and popular democracy. Though a few coefficients are insignificant, the directions are always correct, and the insignificant cases occur on the indicator where it was difficult to identify the deputy benefiting from a public works project. Moreover, without the pork variables the model's R^2 declines by an average of 28 percent. In sum, *pork buys—or at least rents—deputies*.

The Presidency

Given the predominant role of the president as the initiator of most legislation, the ultimate legislative consequences of Brazil's electoral and party systems cannot be understood without an assessment of presidential authority. Suppose we compare the powers of Brazil's presidents with that of other executives. Shugart and Carey (1992) rank presidents according to the powers they wield. *Legislative* powers include the right to veto legislation, issue decrees, control the budget and other policy areas, and propose referenda. *Nonlegislative* powers include the right to name a cabinet without parliamentary interference, avoid parliamentary censure, dismiss cabinet ministers at will, and dissolve the parliament. Currently, Brazilian presidents wield a total or partial veto, issue decrees with the force of law, and play a central role in the budgetary process. Nothing restricts their ability to form cabinets, and the legislature cannot censure them. About the only thing presidents cannot do is dissolve the legislature. Overall, Shugart and Carey place Brazil's presidents among the world's most powerful, and this picture of a strong presidency is not just a recent phenomenon: Brazil's presidents in the 1946–64 period also ranked among the most powerful.[29]

Still, if presidents have so much power, why do they have such a hard time governing? The simple answer is that presidents almost inevi-

TABLE 3

OLS Estimates for Voting in the Constituent Assembly

INDEPENDENT VARIABLES	CONGRESSIONAL POWER	SUPPORT FOR EXECUTIVE	STATISM-WELFARISM	SUPPORT FOR POPULAR DEMOCRACY
Constant	−.176**	.136*	.113	−.076
Municipal dominance	−.110**	.131**	−.037	.002
Clustering in South	.019**	−.024**	.015*	.008
Clustering outside South	.029**	−.009	.025*	.024*
Wealth * high variance	.035	.146	.101	.232
Wealth * medium variance	.061	−.115**	.091	.104*
Wealth * low variance	.104	−.061	.090	−.027
Local career	.033	−.001	.052	−.002
Business career	−.112**	.146**	−.143**	−.158**
Bureaucratic career	−.059	.044	−.046	−.034
Evangelical	−.204	.194**	−.095**	−.126**
Terms in office	−.037	.045**	.007	−.029
Rank in party list	−.005	.113**	.004	.003
Bahia * PFL	−.108**	.087**	−.130**	−.162**
Bahia * PMDB	.103**	−.149**	.116**	.071
Maranhão * PFL	−.028	.076**	−.043	−.032
Maranhão * PMDB	−.011	.036	.027	−.003
ARENA	−.304**	.190**	−.342**	−.266**
Pork to Municipality	−.104**	.059	−.070	−.119**
Ministerial Audience	−.156**	.145**	−.193**	−.182**
Radio–TV License	−.065*	.079**	−.097**	−.141**
Pork to Deputy	−.142**	.215**	−.122**	−.095*
R^2 =	.34	.38	.33	.27
R^2 (without pork variables) =	.17	.28	.24	.18
F =	9.25	10.89	8.87	6.63
N =	403	403	403	403

Entries are standardized regression coefficients.

** $p < .05$, two-tailed test

* $p < .10$, two-tailed test

tably lack a stable base in the legislature. Their search for congressional support is hindered by the electoral system, which, as we have seen, leads to fragmented party support and a proliferation of small parties. Between 1986 and 1990, each of four parties had more than 5 percent of the seats in the Chamber of Deputies. In both the 1991–94 and 1995–98 legislatures, eight parties each had more than 5 percent of the seats, and the largest party held less than 25 percent of the Chamber's seats. So even if all parties were perfectly united behind coherent programs, presidents would have to govern with party coalitions. Since Brazil's parties in fact lack both unity and real programs, and since cabinet selections satisfy regional as well as party demands, presidents are forced to govern with broad, inclusive coalitions.[30]

The president's problem is to calculate the number of legislative votes cabinet ministers can bring from their parties and states. If each cabinet minister could count on the vote of every party member or every state colleague, then a rational executive would invite representatives of the party and state delegations closest to the presidential program until a majority was assured. Given low party cohesion, and given that state political leaders have less than perfect control over their delegations, presidents must construct coalitions much larger than the minimum. In the 1946–64 period, for example, the typical cabinet included parties holding 78 percent of the seats in the Congress.

Because both region and party are important determinants of political outcomes, cabinet appointments must satisfy both criteria. In the 1946–64 period, certain ministries, including justice, labor, foreign relations, and industry and commerce, were regarded as ministries of "political control" (Abranches 1988: 25). Party criteria, mainly favoring the PSD as the largest party, determined the distribution of these ministries. Regional criteria controlled a second group, characterized as "spending" or "clientele" ministries. These ministries, including education and health, transportation and public works, went predominantly to politicians from Bahia or Rio de Janeiro. A third group of ministries—strategic both politically and economically—included treasury, mostly run by São Paulo natives from the PSD, and agriculture, dominated by Pernambucans from the PTB.

Do party and regional criteria still predominate? Compare the cabinets of José Sarney, Fernando Collor de Mello, Itamar Franco, and Fernando Henrique Cardoso. Sarney inherited his first cabinet from Tancredo Neves, who died before taking office. The key economic ministers, from Rio de Janeiro and São Paulo, were appointed to reassure industrialists rather than provide pork. Neves gave the Ministry of Communications, which controls the highly political process of licensing radio and television stations, to Antonio Carlos Magalhães, the most powerful figure in Bahia. Magalhães had built a dominant state machine with the largesse of federal projects. As communications minister, however, his influence was national. Transportation went first to a politician from Paraná, then to Sarney's fellow *maranhense*, José Reinaldo Tavares. Sarney's political career would not end when he left the presidency, so Tavares could facilitate his postpresidential ambitions.[31] Four different ministers ran education, but for almost the whole period the ministry was a fief for the bosses of Sarney's own Liberal Front Party. Health remained mainly in the hands of politicians from Bahia, the same state that dominated the ministry from 1946 to 1964.

Some state and congressional leaders were so powerful they forced President Sarney to swallow painful appointments. His first three ministers of welfare and social assistance, for example, were all political enemies appointed to appease PMDB congressional leader Ulysses Guimarães. Neves had nominated an economist (supported by the ex-governor of Sao Paulo) to head the Planning Secretariat, but when this *paulista* departed, Sarney selected a little-known politician from Minas Gerais. His new minister converted a relatively unimportant economic planning agency into a conduit for social assistance benefits. It turned out that the minister was using these programs to advance his own gubernatorial ambitions. When corruption charges forced out the minister, Sarney replaced him with a technocratically oriented economist. But he allowed Newton Cardoso, the governor of Minas Gerais, to make the actual choice. Since Cardoso was part of the historic opposition to Tancredo Neves, the choice confirmed that President Sarney had broken away from his predecessor's base of support.

The cabinet appointments of Fernando Collor reveal no consistent legislative coalition-building strategy. Indeed, his appointments seem inconsistent with any single motivation except personal loyalty. Two former members of the Congress, both early supporters of Collor's campaign but neither influential in the legislature, received the portfolios of education and health. Labor and social welfare went to a pro-Collor labor leader from São Paulo. An unknown from Alagoas (Collor's home state) ran social action, and a respected nonpartisan technocrat headed infrastructure. A mix of *políticos* and *técnicos,* in other words, headed these ministries. Clearly, the appointments reflected no attempt to maximize legislative support. Rather, Collor—unlike Sarney—appointed people with whom he would be comfortable politically and personally.

Most of Collor's other ministerial appointments had little political clout. The minister of the economy, an early Collor adviser, was an unknown economist. A former university rector became secretary of science and technology. The secretary of the environment was an environmental activist with no party affiliation. Overall, Collor's initial appointments suggest a desire to rule above party. Given his appointments in education, health, social action, and labor, "above party" did not mean "above clientelism"; indeed, charges of corruption and favoritism plagued all four ministers. The appointments do suggest, however, that Collor was betting on his ability to marshall legislative support not by negotiating with party leaders but by dealing directly with individual deputies. In this way Collor's initial cabinet-forming strategy differs sharply from that of his predecessors, reflecting his peculiar mix of populism and arrogance.

The cabinet changes Collor made *during* his term in office demonstrate his belated recognition of the importance of congressional leaders and his response to corruption charges leveled against his first cabinet members. Collor replaced the ministers of labor and social action, for example, with congressional leaders from the PFL. When the justice minister's ineptitude and his romance with the economics minister became too embarrassing, Collor replaced him with a politically savvy senator. But Collor also seems to have enjoyed the tone of respectability lent by well-known technocrats: he replaced the highly political ministers of education and health, both accused of corruption and favoritism, with a university researcher and a famous surgeon.[32]

The cabinet appointments of Itamar Franco obeyed three criteria: personal relationship, party representation, and intraparty faction. Of the seventeen nonmilitary ministers, at least ten were personal friends of the president. The initial cabinet represented seven parties: PFL (4), PMDB (5), PSDB (3), PDT (1), PSB (2), PTB (1), and PT (1). In the case of the larger parties, multiple factions received attention. The two largest elements of the PMDB, for example, the Rio Grande do Sul wing (called the *gaúchos*) and the Quércia-Fleury wing from São Paulo, each received one minister.[33] The PSDB's Ceará wing (Jereissati/Ciro Gomes) garnered the appointment of Jutahy Junior (ministry of social well-being), while the São Paulo wing was represented by Fernando Henrique Cardoso (initially foreign relations, then finance).

Fernando Henrique Cardoso's cabinet is based on the core of his electoral alliance. The right-wing PFL and the centrist PSDB hold most of the key policy-making positions. The ministries of justice and transportation—the latter a prime distributor of pork-barrel projects—went to the PMDB, a party whose support was crucial for Cardoso's constitutional reforms. Cardoso also sought to neutralize Itamar Franco, who remained eligible to run for the presidency in 1998, by making him ambassador to Portugal and by appointing a key Franco adviser to head the postal service, a major repository of political jobs.

What do ministers do with the portfolios they manage? Once again, consider the Collor cabinet. Collor appointed a politician from the state of Rio Grande do Sul to head the education ministry. In the first fifteen months of his tenure, municipalities in this relatively wealthy state were 160 percent more likely to receive a central government grant than if someone from another state had led the ministry. The health ministry went to a former congressman from Paraná, where municipalities soon increased their likelihood of getting a grant by 84 percent. The minister of social action, from Collor's home state of Alagoas, increased grants to Alagoan municipalities by 123 percent.[34] From the politician's perspective, a ministerial appointment provides a good opportunity to advance one's chances for state-level elective office after the ministerial term ends.

This section began by noting that Brazil's presidents enjoy extensive formal powers but struggle to assemble legislative majorities. In the end, are they successful? The question is difficult, because we cannot know the president's true preferences. Sarney had only mixed success in dealing with the Congress, but he managed to defeat parliamentarism and prevent a shortening of his term in office.

Taking another tack, I analyzed the universe of presidential proposals, even those that were never voted on in the Congress.[35] I recorded what the president proposed, when it was proposed, what the legislature did with the proposal, and when that action occurred.[36] Many proposals never get to a vote at all, and *practically nothing gets through the Congress without substantial modification*. It is difficult, in other words, to satisfy both partisan and regional demands in a political system where parties lack both programs and cohesion. Presidents expand the number of ministries and increase the volume of resources devoted to coalition building, but such tactics fail to overcome the inherently centrifigul tendencies of a system of individualistic politicians operating in multiple weak parties.

CONCLUSION

This chapter has emphasized the formal institutions at the heart of Brazilian politics: the electoral system, the legislature, and the presidency. The consolidation of Brazilian democracy depends on these institutions. We should remember, however, that institutions are not created and do not function in a historical and social vacuum. Open-list proportional representation combines with federalism to increase the incentives for local politicians to deliver pork-barrel projects to their supporters and to hinder or delay the adoption of effective policies. Clientelism and state intervention, the "accommodationist state," increase the pool of resources at the disposal of politicians. Programs that impose losses on powerful sectors require compensation, typically in the form of government jobs or the delivery of local pork barrel.

As Brazilians have discovered, it is very difficult to reorient such a state, even when public sentiment overwhelmingly favors such reorientation. The nation's electoral rules motivate candidates for legislative office to campaign individualistically. The high cost of individual campaigning facilitates corruption. In office, deputies deliver jobs and public works to their constituencies and avoid party discipline and party programs. In a sense the electoral system is hyperdemocratic, but it produces a fragmented and weak party system, hinders accountability, and discourages deputies from raising issues of national scope.

Presidents in Brazil can only govern with the support of multiparty coalitions. Because presidents must look to both party and regional criteria in forming their coalitions, and because parties lack discipline, cabinets tend to be very large. As a result, hefty payoffs are required to cement coalitions, and some coalition partners can veto almost any policy the executive proposes.

With most legislators seeking to reward their own narrow constituencies, and with a multiplicity of weak political parties, it is no surprise that the Congress is largely inactive on policy questions. Congress takes an active role in the budgetary process, but critical legislation, even legislation required by the Constitution, remains on hold for years. Mostly, the Congress simply reacts to presidential decrees. But even these reactions are politicized: individual politicians and platformless parties hold up crucial stabilization measures in exchange for bureaucratic jobs or in an effort to hamper the political career of an opponent.

Prospects for Reform

Are there prospects for political reform? In 1993 a referendum offered the Brazilian people a choice between retaining presidentialism or switching to parliamentarism. The parliamentary proposal initially had widespread support from every elite group in the society except the military. Parliamentarism would alleviate the problem of legislative support for the chief executive. It would also reduce the likelihood of military coups. But many Brazilians thought parliamentarism would increase the powers of the legislature, and the Congress (in the wake of the budget scandal) was quite unpopular. A number of state governors supported presidentialism because they had their own presidential ambitions. The PT, though most of its deputies were parliamentarists, supported presidentialism because its rank and file, which cast votes in a straw poll, thought Lula would be the next president. In the end, presidentialism won comfortably.

Electoral reforms have been proposed to reduce the corruption exemplified by the budget scandal. Brazilian politicians and social scientists have extensively debated along the lines of the German "mixed" electoral system. This system, adopted in Venezuela (among other countries), divides the legislature into two parts: half elected in single-member districts, the other half elected by closed-list proportional representation. In theory, the German system would strengthen Brazil's parties through its use of closed-list PR, but it would also maximize local accountability through its use of single-member districts. It would reduce campaign spending, because candidates would campaign as individuals only in the relatively small districts. Whether these gains would really be achieved is uncertain, but it does seem clear that the German system would eliminate the corrupt deputies considered here. Dominant-scattered distributions would be extremely difficult to maintain. Deputies like João Alves could not be elected on the district side, because they could not compete, in any given district, with popular local leaders. On the closed-list side they would have a hard time getting nominated in the first place, and, if nominated, business interests and local bosses would have little incentive to make deals with them. So, regardless of other benefits, the adoption of a mixed German-type system would kill off deputies relying on dispersed deal-making. At the same time, single-member districts would not reduce the interest of deputies in pork. Given the amount of discretionary pork available, the district deputies might come to specialize in local issues, while the PR deputies would focus on national issues.

At this time, the chances of a major electoral reform along the lines of the German system seem remote. Any reform would have to be approved by 60 percent of both houses of the Congress, and incumbents are naturally reluctant to approve anything that increases their political risk.

Less dramatic political reforms remain on the agenda. In 1994 the Congress reduced the president's term from five to four years, so presidential and congressional elections now occur at the same time. With concurrent elections, the president is likely to have more support in the legislature. In addition, the Congress did approve a minimum vote that parties have to reach before they attain congressional representation, though the reform was weakened so that it will have less effect than similar thresholds in Europe.

Institutional Constraints in Perspective

Ironically, the bleak chances for reform at the moment are partly attributable to the optimism surrounding the success of the *Real* economic plan and the incumbent president. President Cardoso was reelected in 1998, but his second term may prove more difficult than the first. The economy is likely to continue to be sluggish. Cardoso's party, the PSDB, is likely to lose some of the governorships it won in 1994, and these losses will weaken its position in the Congress. All the parties will begin jockeying for position for the election of 2002. Thus, Cardoso is likely to quickly become a "lame duck" in his second term. As I have argued in this chapter, the Cardoso administration provides the perfect test of the claim that institutional design plays a large part in Brazil's political problem. Cardoso is an intelligent and creative politician with skilled advisers. At the same time, as conservative forces continue to control the Congress, the alliance with the PFL surely limits the reforms he can propose, and the institutional deficiencies remain. So the question is simple: Can intelligent leadership overcome dysfunctional institutions? The PSDB-PFL alliance guarantees passage of measures opening the economy and privatizing state enterprises, but the partnership has not done well dealing with tax, administrative reform, welfare, and social questions. This does not imply that unless Cardoso's government triumphs against the nation's ills, the country will experience revolution or return to authoritarianism. Brazil will probably remain democratic, and massive social upheaval is unlikely. But in the Brazil of the 1990s, millions of people are condemned to lives of hopelessness and misery. Solutions to the nation's problems, whether they involve antiinflation policy, a new structure of intergovernmental relations, efficient implementation of education and health services, or reduction in governmental waste and corruption, require political choices and carry political implications. Brazil cannot emerge from its crisis merely by "getting the prices right." It also has to get the institutions right for developing a healthy democracy.

NOTES

1. A number of analysts attempting to explain the military coup of 1964, notably Wanderley Guilherme dos Santos (1979), have stressed the legislative im-

mobility of the Congress at the end of the earlier pluralist period, but little serious research on congressional elections or congressional behavior during the 1947–64 democratic period has been undertaken. See, however, Benevides (1976, 1981), Soares (1973), and Souza (1976).

2. For useful discussions of democratic consolidation, see Shugart and Carey (1992), and Mainwaring and Scully (1995).

3. In pre-1973 Chile, by contrast, voting districts cut across provincial lines, so district delegations and local political machines did not match up. Valenzuela (1977) notes that party leaders did choose candidates who were attractive to local voters, but loyalty to the parties' positions on national issues appears to have been a necessary condition for selection.

4. Note that municipal dominance has nothing to do with actually winning seats; whole states, not municipalities, are electoral districts. I have also experimented with conceptualizing dominance solely in terms of votes for candidates of the candidates' own party.

5. For a discussion of Moran's I and other aspects of spatial statistics, see Anselin (1988).

6. The Appendix discusses the construction of the map as well as other data problems.

7. Concentrated-dominant distributions often reflect traditional, clientelistic relationships between voters and politicians, but such distributions can also develop when able local leaders climb through the ranks from such local offices as municipal council to mayor or state deputy.

8. I discuss these "casuismos," or sophisms, in *Political Survival: Politicians and Public Policy in Latin America* (1987).

9. I utilized Kinzo's (1989) indices of crucial votes in the Assembly.

10. A deputy's chief aide once told me during a congressional recess that the deputy had not returned to his district, because he had no money to respond to the hundreds of requests for small financial favors that he would inevitably receive.

11. I subtracted João Alves' own vote from the municipal total before calculating the fragmentation of PFL candidates. In effect, the variable measures the fragmentation of all PFL candidates *except* Alves. Interparty fragmentation was squared, because Alves' connections in Salvador might bring him a slightly bigger share in the capital. Alves also did better in municipalities that simultaneously had PFL mayors and low intraparty fragmentation.

12. Note that there is no "Wagner's Law" effect, i.e., no relationship between population size and employment in municipal administration.

13. Japanese districts, by contrast, send between three and five representatives to the Diet.

14. Deputy Amaral Netto, from Rio de Janeiro state, occupied a unique ideological niche as a defender of the death penalty. His pattern of electoral support was remarkably even: with the exception of a lightly populated area where he campaigned little, Netto received 3–5 percent of the vote in nearly every municipality. Amaral Netto was unsuccessful in promoting the death penalty in Brazil, but no one doubted the authenticity of his ideological base.

15. These sources included *Perfil Parlamentar Brasileiro* (Istoé 1991)and *Repertório Biográfico* (Brasil: Câmara dos Deputados 1987). I also consulted the lists prepared by DIESSE, the union research office in Brasília. Finally, the government agricultural extension agency Embrapa had prepared its own list of deputies who held substantial rural property.

16. In recent years the south has been the site of violent conflicts between huge, modern agricultural operations and the landless poor.

17. I am indebted to Tim Power for help on the nature of state-level factions.

18. Here I ignore the difference between mass loyalties and the loyalties of political bosses. In my "Reverse Coattails" article (Ames 1994), I distinguish empirically, at the municipal level, between mass partisan tendencies and the effects of the political machine.

19. I defined the "overall party vote" as the sum of all party members' shares of each municipality's total vote minus the share of the deputy in question.

20. For an extended discussion of these themes, see Mainwaring and Scully (1995).

21. For an extensive treatment of the 1989 presidential election, see my "The Reverse Coattails Effect: Local Party Organization in the 1989 Brazilian Presidential Election" (1994).

22. Moreover, the votes of city-based candidates would correlate with such characteristics as urbanization and manufacturing whether their votes come from the working class, the upper-middle class, or—as in the case of charismatic candidates—a multiclass coalition. A perfect test of the stability of party-societal ties requires information we simply do not have, i.e., longitudinal survey data in different states.

23. In 1993, for example, about one-fourth of all members of Congress sought election as municipal mayor.

24. Kinzo's (1989) study leaves unclear whether the groups of votes are true scales or merely indices. I applied standard scale tests retaining only those votes meeting scaling criteria. Logit analyses of individual votes were generally consistent with regressions based on the multivote scales, but these scales are preferable because they minimize the effects of absentee voting and other peculiarities specific to particular votes. I call Kinzo's "Economic Conservatism" scale "Statism-welfarism," because the items really measure willingness to support government intervention in the economy and defense of issues championed by unions. I have renamed her "Support for Democratic Values" scale "Support for Popular Democracy," because a number of its items facilitate class-action lawsuits and direct democracy, while others hinder military intervention. The Congressional Power Scale includes nine items; a typical item requires the Congress to approve the federal budget. The Support for Executive scale includes five items; a typical item gave future presidents a five-year mandate. The State Economic Intervention-Welfarism scale included six items; a typical item dealt with indemnities paid to workers fired unfairly by employers. The Support for Popular Democracy Scale included six items; a typical item permitted class-action suits.

25. The complete results are available in Ames (1995b).

26. Municipalities, not deputies, receive intergovernmental transfers. If a deputy wins all the votes in a municipality, then clearly that deputy gets all the credit. Suppose, however, a group of deputies shares a municipality's votes. Do all deputies claim credit equally? Do they divide the credit in proportion to their vote shares? Does the leading vote getter get all the credit? Does the credit go to deputies from the president's party, or is it divided in terms of party vote shares? Most informants believed that either the leading vote-getter of any party or of the president's party would get the pork. I tried various formulations, achieving the best results by assuming that only the leading candidate in a given municipality could claim credit, but that leader could be of any party. If a deputy received credit for pork in a municipality contributing only a minute fraction of the deputy's total state-wide vote, the credit would do little electorally. In aggregating the individual municipal probabilities, I therefore weighted each municipality's probability by the fraction of the deputy's total vote the municipality contributed. In effect, the indicator measures the probability that someone voting for deputy x actually benefited from an intergovernmental transfer. The precise period of pork delivery, May-June 1988, corresponds exactly to President Sarney's campaign for a five-year term and for presidentialism. Longer periods produced weaker but similar results.

27. The calculation was analogous to the "Pork Payoff to Municipality" variable. I adjusted the probability where I knew a particular deputy owned the radio or TV station.

28. The parliamentary liaisons of these ministries maintain lists of deputies meeting with ministers. While requesting that individual names remain confidential, they allowed me to copy the lists.

29. Among Latin American countries, only Paraguay's presidency is classified as more powerful.

30. Abranches (1988), argues that Brazil is the only country in the world combining proportional representation, multipartism, and a strong presidency, i..e., a president whose cabinet can not be controlled by the parliament, with an executive branch based on "grand coalitions." A very sophisticated treatment of the problem of presidential appointment strategies in six Latin American countries is found in Geddes (1994).

31. Ex-president Sarney is now a senator from the lightly populated state of Amapá, but his Maranhão machine still functions. He sought the presidency again in 1994, but his main ambition seemed to be electing his daughter Roseana to the governorship of Maranhão.

32. In Collor's case the corruption was so pervasive that it ultimately led to his impeachment. The extortion scheme masterminded by his confidant, Paulo Cesar Farias, was implemented in part by placing Farias' henchmen in lower-level ministerial positions. These underlings wielded real power; in effect, they made the deals normally arranged by ministers themselves.

33. In 1993, in the middle of the Franco administration, an effort to secure more PMDB support included a cabinet reshuffle. As part of the deal, directorships in state branches of certain federal agencies were put at the disposal of local and state PMDB leaders. This reshuffling led to the replacement of a num-

ber of state directors of the federal environmental agency, IBAMA. There was no doubt, as I discovered during a private consulting project, that the criteria for replacement were purely political.

34. These estimates come from a logistic regression in which the dependent variable was the existence of an education or health transfer agreement with the central government (a *convénio*) between April 1990, and July 1991. Transfers were more likely to go to municipalities that were larger in population, more urban, and poorer. The probabilities above are partial coefficients from the complete model.

35. By the universe of proposals, I mean any proposal important enough to be mentioned in the "Latin America Weekly Report: Brazil," the "Economist Country Report," or the Brazilian financial newspaper *Gazeta Mercantil*.

36. Because the tables I constructed from this data are far too long to be included in this text and are of interest mainly to a more specialized audience, they could not be included here. Readers who are interested in securing this data may contact me at the Department of Political Science of the University of Pittsburgh.

<h2 style="text-align:center">REFERENCES</h2>

Abranches, Sérgio Henrique H. de. 1988. "Presidencialismo de Coalizão: O Dilema Institucional Brasileiro." *Dados*. 31:1, pp. 5–34.

Ames, Barry. 1987. *Political Survival: Politicians and Public Policy in Latin America*. Berkeley: University of California Press.

———. 1994. "The Reverse Coattails Effect: Local Party Organization in the 1989 Brazilian Presidential Election." *American Political Science Review*. (March).

———.1995a. "Electoral Strategy under Open-List Proportional Representation." *American Journal of Political Science* (May).

———.1995b. "Electoral Rules, Constituency Pressures, and Pork Barrel: Bases of Voting in the Brazilian Congress." *Journal of Politics* (May).

Anselin, Luc. 1988. *Spatial Econometrics: Methods and Models*. Dordrecht: Kluwer Academic Publishing.

Benevides, Maria Victória. 1976. *O Governo Kubitschek: Desenvolvimento Econômico e Estabilidade Política*. Rio de Janeiro: Paz e Terra.

Brasil. Câmara dos Deputados. 1987. *Assembléia Nacional Constituinte 1987: Repertório Biográfico*.

Cohen, Youssef. 1994. *Radicals, Reformers, and Reactionaries: The Prisoner's Dilemma and the Collapse of Democracy in Latin America*. Chicago: University of Chicago Press.

DIEESE. 1991. *Pesquisa DIEESE*. August.

DIEESE, 1992. *Pesquisa DIEESE,* April.

Dimenstein, Gilberto, and Josias de Souza. 1994. *A História Real: Trama de uma sucessão*. São Paulo: Editora Ática-Folha de São Paulo.

Dos Santos, Wanderley Guilherme. 1979. "The Calculus of Conflict: Impasse in Brazilian Politics and the Crisis of 1964." Ph.D. dissertation, Stanford University.

Fausto, Boris. 1970. *A Revolução de 1930; historiografia, e história.* São Paulo: Editora Brasiliense.

Geddes, Barbara. 1994. *Politician's Dilemma: Building State Capacity in Latin America.* Berkeley: University of California Press.

Istoé. 1991. *Perfil Parlamentar Brasileiro.* Brasília: Editora Trés.

Kinzo, Maria D'Alva Gil. 1989. "O Quadro Partidário e o Constituinte." *Revista Brasileira de Ciencia Politica.* 1:1.

Linz, Juan. 1973. "The Future of an Authoritarian Situation or the Institutionalization of an Authoritarian Regime: The Case of Brazil." In Stepan, Alfred, ed., *Authoritarian Brazil.* New Haven: Yale University Press.

Mainwaring, Scott, and Timothy R. Scully, ed. 1995. *Building Democratic Institutions: Party Systems in Latin America.* Stanford: Stanford University Press, 1995.

Shugart, Matthew Soberg, and John M. Carey. 1992. *Presidents and Assemblies: Constitutional Design and Electoral Dynamics.* New York: Cambridge University Press.

Skidmore, Thomas. 1967. *Politics in Brazil, 1930–1967.* New York: Oxford University Press.

Soares, Gláucio Ary Dillon. 1973. *Sociedade e política no Brasil: Desenvolvimento, classe e política durante a Segunda República.* São Paulo. Difel.

Souza, Maria do Carmo Campello de. 1976. *Estado e partidos políticos no Brasil.* São Paulo: Alfa-Omega.

Stepan, Alfred. 1973. *Authoritarian Brazil: Origins, Policies, and Future.* New Haven: Yale University Press.

Straubhaar, Joseph, Organ Olsen, and Maria Cavaliari Nunes. 1993. "The Brazilian Case: Influencing the Voter." In Thomas E. Skidmore, ed., *Television, Politics and the Transition to Democracy in Latin America.* Washington: Woodrow Wilson Center Press.

Valenzuela, Arturo. 1977. *Political Brokers in Chile: Local Government in a Centralized Polity.* Durham: Duke University Press.

Veja. 1994. "Bancada de interesse." May 4, pp. 28–30.

6

Caciques and Coups: The Challenges of Democratic Consolidation in the Philippines

Jeffrey M. Riedinger

IN LATE FEBRUARY 1986, unarmed civilians joined military rebels in facing down columns of tanks in the Philippine "People Power Revolution." This event brought to an end the twenty-year rule of Ferdinand Marcos and many of the attendant economic, human rights, and political abuses. A nonviolent popular movement headed by Corazon Cojuangco Aquino, the widow of Marcos's arch political rival, ousted the Marcos regime, restored democratic institutions, and ushered in a regime publicly committed to social and economic reform. Under the Aquino government (1986–92), and the successor governments of Fidel V. Ramos (1992–98) and Joseph Ejercito Estrada (1998 to present), the Philippines has experienced appreciable progress in establishing and consolidating democracy, although significant problems persist. Congressional and local elections were held in 1987, 1992, 1995, and 1998; presidential elections were held in 1992 and 1998. In general, candidates have respected the electoral outcomes, with many offices peacefully changing hands. Increasingly, former communist insurgents, Muslim separatists, and military rebels have renounced armed struggle and are contesting politics in the electoral arena. However, Philippine democracy continues to be marked by electoral fraud, violence, and domination by traditional elites, and characterized by weak parties and factionalism based primarily on personalities and regional and linguistic identities rather than on ideology. Democratic consolidation is stymied further by continuing human rights abuses committed by corrupt police, a politicized military, and the various insurgent movements. Continuing debates over the fundamental constitutional arrangements also call Philippine democratic consolidation into question.

THEORETICAL APPROACHES TO DEMOCRATIC
TRANSITION AND CONSOLIDATION

In the course of this chapter, I separately draw upon scholarly explanations for the processes of democratic transition and consolidation and scholarly criteria for measuring the extent or outcomes of such processes. Scholars analyzing democratic transitions and democratic consolidation have generally favored one of two approaches: structural or contingent. Theorists in the former tradition, most notably Lipset (1959) and Diamond (1992), give primacy to the socioeconomic context in explaining the emergence and persistence of democratic regimes. In particular, these scholars emphasize the positive correlation between economic development and democracy. With the emergence of democratic institutions in many less developed countries as part of what Huntington (1991b) terms the "third wave" of democratization, other theorists have turned to contingent explanations which focus on the "choices of particular political elites and specific historical conjunctures" (Remmer 1991: 483). In response to these competing paradigms, Karl (1990) commends a "structural contingency" approach which recognizes that economic and political structures condition the choice set available to political actors. Following Karl's lead, I review some of the structural features which have shaped the choices available to Philippine political actors in the process of democratic consolidation and then examine the choices key actors have made in practice.

In assessing the extent of democratic consolidation in the Philippines, I follow the lead of Diamond (1996) in distinguishing between *electoral* and *liberal* democracy. Electoral democracy is the selection of political leaders through competitive elections which are free, open, and fair. My focus is on the extent and nature of participation among the adult population and the extent and nature of political contestation (see Dahl 1971). I examine the policies and practices which determine suffrage and the patterns of electoral turnout. I also assess the degree of electoral competition and the presence of credible opposition, including political parties and media outlets.

Diamond (1996: 23–24) identifies a series of characteristics of liberal democracy which distinguish it from minimalist definitions of electoral democracy: (1) real power, in theory and practice, is vested in elected officials and their appointees; (2) executive power is constrained by the constitution and other government institutions; (3) groups which embrace constitutional principles are free to form political parties and contest elections, the outcomes of which are not preordained; (4) the political process is open, in theory and practice, to all groups, regardless of such characteristics as class, culture, ethnicity, or religion; (5) citizens are free to express and represent their interests through a wide variety of political parties, associations, and other groups; (6) citizens have ready access to alternative sources of information, including independent media; (7) individuals enjoy freedom of belief and expression; (8) citizens receive equal protection under the law; and (9) the rule of law and an impartial judiciary effectively protect citizens from unjustified detention, terror, or torture, whether committed by the state or antistate forces. These criteria will be the primary bases for my assessment of the extent of consolidation of liberal democracy in the Philippines. I will supplement them with criteria drawn from Linz and Stepan's (1996) discussion of behavioral, attitudinal, and constitutional features of democratic consolidation.

THE STRUCTURAL CONTEXT FOR PHILIPPINE DEMOCRACY

In their attempts to consolidate Philippine democracy, the Aquino, Ramos, and Estrada governments have confronted a number of contextual problems. To varying degrees, similar features have marked many of the "third wave" democratic transitions. In the Philippine case, the structural constraints have included acute poverty and disparities in wealth, substantial foreign debt, ongoing communist and Muslim insurgencies, and a history of exclusionary politics. The social configuration of the Philippines has posed other problems. Regional and provincial "strongmen" retain considerable power and influence.[1] Among the poor, dependency relations, cultural norms, differentiated interests, repression, and electoral institutions have stood as obstacles to effective mobilization and political participation. Patron-client relations and personal and group identifications along regional and ethno-linguistic lines have continued to shape Philippine politics.[2]

The Philippine transition to democracy occurred in a setting of widespread poverty. The government estimated that over 49 percent of the population nationwide was living below the poverty threshold in 1985. Despite considerable economic growth in the intervening years, over 40 percent of the population still lived in poverty in 1994 (NEDA 1998a). Unemployment similarly has persisted at over 9 percent through much of the period of democratic consolidation, declining modestly to the 7 to 8 percent range in 1996–97 (NEDA 1998b; NSO 1998). High population growth rates continue to outstrip the economy's capacity for employment generation.

The scope for government action also has been limited by substantial foreign debt. As of early 1986, foreign debt exceeded $26 billion; the government faced a large budgetary shortfall, inflation was over 20 percent in 1985; real Gross National Product had fallen 6.8 and 3.8 percent in 1984 and 1985 respectively; and world prices for the principal Philippine agricultural exports (coconut products and sugar) were depressed (NEDA 1986). The Aquino and Ramos governments restored Philippine economic growth, with each government experiencing periods of strong growth interrupted by periods of stagnation or modest growth. For example, Philippine GNP grew 5.7 percent and 6.8 percent in 1995 and 1996 respectively (Hernandez 1996:147; idem 1997: 209), after growth of only 1.2 percent and 2.5 percent in 1992 and 1993 respectively (Riedinger 1994: 143). To date, the currency crises and economic downturns in leading countries in East and Southeast Asia in 1997 have been less pronounced in the Philippines. Nonetheless, the Philippine peso has depreciated substantially relative to the United States dollar, trading at 44 pesos to the dollar in August 1998, down from 26 pesos to the dollar in June 1997. Philippine foreign debt remains substantial-over $45 billion—and debt-servicing obligations are a continuing source of political controversy, particularly with respect to debts incurred by the Marcos government. The new Estrada government thus faces formidable economic constraints.

The Aquino, Ramos, and Estrada governments also have confronted communist and Muslim insurgencies in their quest to consolidate democracy. According to military estimates, the Communist Party of the Philippines (CPP) and its armed wing, the New People's Army (NPA), had "infiltrated" over a tenth of the country's villages and were able to stay for long periods of time with little fear of discovery or attack, at the CPP/NPA's peak in the mid-1980s. In Mindanao and Sulu, Muslim secessionist movements similarly challenged the Philippine state. The Muslim struggle for autonomy dated to Spanish colonialism. Christian encroachment on Muslim lands during the second half of the twentieth century added an economic dimension to religious enmity. A series of rebellions by elements of the Philippine armed forces further complicated the consolidation of democracy.

Exclusionary Political History

For our purposes, one of the most important contextual features for democracy and democratic consolidation in the Philippines was the country's history of exclusionary politics. Even in the nominally democratic pre-martial-law Philippines (1946–72), politics was exclusionary in nature, with traditional regional and local elites exerting substantial political influence while effectively limiting the independent participation of the Philippine poor. This pre-martial-law party system was stable in the sense that two parties dominated Philippine politics. However, the parties lacked coherence and discipline. Reflecting their common origin, there was little of either substance, composition, or constituencies to distinguish the two leading parties, the Nacionalista Party (NP) and the Liberal Party (LP). Each party was built primarily upon vertically linked patron-client networks.[3] Party-switching was frequent as national, provincial, and local leaders (and their coteries) sought advantage in access to government resources. Both Ramon Magsaysay and Ferdinand Marcos switched parties shortly before their respective nominations and elections to the presidency in 1953 and 1965. The parties were noted more for their personalities than for ideological or issue orientation. Elections were typically marred by violence and fraud. Benedict Anderson (1988) aptly described Philippine politics in this era as "cacique democracy."

President Ferdinand Marcos halted the evolution of Philippine democracy with his declaration of martial law in September 1972. After some initial improvements in the law and order situation and several years of impressive economic growth, much of it fueled by foreign borrowing, the promise of martial law, such as it was, gave way to a reality of human rights abuses, corruption, and economic mismanagement. With few restraints on Marcos's power, his family and their cronies gave free rein to their avarice, bankrupting the country in the process. Despite his power, Marcos found it necessary to create the trappings of popular legitimacy, scheduling a series of plebiscites and referenda to approve his 1973 constitution and the continuation of martial law (Hernandez 1985). Many provincial and municipal functionaries of Marcos's political apparatus, the Kilusang Bagong Lipunan (KBL, or New Society Movement), were traditional politicians.[4]

AQUINO'S CONSTRUCTION OF DEMOCRACY

The "People Power Revolution" that formally ousted Marcos was considered an urban, predominantly middle-class phenomenon. In this view, the "revolution" owed relatively little to the left or the rural poor.[5] Although the movement that propelled her to power had populist attributes, Aquino's electoral support primarily reflected public reaction to the abuses of the Marcos years. Aquino's ability to unite the anti-Marcos forces stemmed from her veneration as an almost religious figure.[6]

Judged against the energy devoted to her various tasks, Aquino saw her principal duty in assuming the presidency of the Philippines as the reestablishment of institutions of electoral democracy and, to a lesser extent, institutions of liberal democracy.[7] She used the considerable political capital available to her in the early months of her presidency to effectuate the drafting and adoption of a new constitution and initiation of local, congressional, and ultimately presidential elections. At the outset of her tenure, she also restored the writ of habeas corpus, released political prisoners, and initiated negotiations with communist insurgents and several regional autonomy movements. In all but the negotiations she was successful.

Aquino's First Cabinet

Mrs. Aquino's campaign organization was a diverse coalition which relied in part on traditional Philippine elites, many of whom were tardy critics of the Marcos regime. Contact was also established with the dissident "Reform the Armed Forces Movement" (RAM) within the military.[8] Aquino's first cabinet featured conservative reformists, social democrats, and soldiers (Landé and Hooley 1986: 1091-92; Wurfel 1988: 305-8). The military members were late participants in the anti-Marcos struggle, but their contribution to the ouster of Marcos—initiating the rebellion of February 22-25—was undeniable. These officers were concerned primarily with reserving an area of relative autonomy for the military, notably in the form of military prerogatives and a military approach to the communist and Muslim insurgencies.[9]

Broad opposition coalitions, such as Mrs. Aquino's, risk fragmentation upon assuming power, whether they were previously united in opposition to one political leader or a colonial power. It appears that in her choice of cabinet members Mrs. Aquino insisted on neither allegiance nor ideological unity.[10] Perhaps it was impossible to do so at the outset of her presidency, with so many divergent viewpoints and personalities involved, however belatedly, in the anti-Marcos movement. The abrupt nature of the transition limited Aquino's ability to formulate a coherent, disciplined organization even had she been disposed to do so, which she was not.[11] Aquino did reward social democrats and other noncommunist progressives, the heart of the nonviolent opposition to Marcos, with a number of cabinet and other government appointments.[12]

President Aquino's predisposition to nonparty politics may have been reinforced by the contentiousness surrounding the appointments of new local government officials. In its early months, the new Aquino administration systematically removed Marcos-era provincial and local officials from office, replacing them with appointed officers-in-charge (OICs). The selection process benefited the PDP-LABAN (Philippine Democratic Party—Lakas ng Bayan [Strength of the Nation]), upsetting Salvador Laurel's United Nationalist Democratic Organization Party (UNIDO) and bringing an end to the alliance between the parties. Even apart from this intracoalition conflict, the process of replacing local officials generated considerable controversy.

The Philippine military was among the foremost critics of the OIC appointments (Sacerdoti 1986a). The displaced officials had been elected to their offices—however flawed the Marcos-era elections—and, it was argued, many of them enjoyed sufficient local popularity to make their victory likely in the event new elections were held. Local military commanders and the leadership of the armed forces argued that incumbents better understood local issues, and were thereby able to afford greater aid to the military in combating the insurgency. More cynical interpretations were that incumbent local officials were more easily influenced by the military in the formulation and implementation of counterinsurgency policies, or were sharing the spoils of the local economy with military officers.

In the view of other critics of the appointment process, summary replacement of local officials by the central government was not only antidemocratic, it raised disturbing parallels with Marcos's assumption of the power of local appointment in the early years of martial law.

1987 Constitution

Aquino used her executive powers to appoint all of the members of the Constitutional Commission, attempting to make the commission reasonably representative.[13] No known communists were appointed, but the forty-eight-member Commission included progressives, important figures from the pre-Marcos era, Catholic Church clergy and laity, and five members of Marcos's Kilusang Bagong Lipunan Party (KBL).[14] Despite this diversity, the commission included only one representative of the peasant sector. Once the commission had begun its deliberations, Aquino adopted a hands-off policy. Criticized in some circles for foregoing this opportunity to mandate a specific reform program, Aquino apparently sought to contrast her actions with those of Marcos in 1972–73.[15]

The 1987 Constitution established important constraints on the executive branch. Like many in the anti-Marcos movement, Aquino appeared determined to curtail the powers of the presidency, relative not only to those exercised by Marcos, but to those exercised by earlier Philippine presidents under the 1935 Constitution.[16] The Constitution separated executive, judicial, and legislative functions and restored a bicameral Philippine legislature. The power of judicial review was recognized in an independent judiciary. A congressional Commission on Appointments was vested with confirmation authority over presidential appointments to the cabinet.

The 1987 Constitution reaffirmed the principle of universal adult suffrage. In an effort to promote responsiveness and accountability in government, the Constitution mandated a system of popular initiative and referendum (Art. VI, Sec. 32). The Constitution also provided at least partial representation for smaller political parties and other groups previously excluded from politics, in the form of a "party list" system of proportional representation for 20 percent of the 250 House seats (Article VI, Sec. 5(2)). To further facilitate liberal democracy, the Constitution provided for freedom of speech and of the press, as well as freedom of assembly and association.

In response to these freedoms, there has been a proliferation of newspapers and other media since 1986, particularly in Manila. Philippine media operate with few formal restrictions. However, several journalists investigating drug syndicates have been murdered (U.S. Department of State 1998: 11). The (in)accuracy and (in)adequacy of political coverage also has been an object of complaint, notably from groups outside the political mainstream.

Despite the constitutional guarantee of universal adult suffrage, overseas Filipinos, of whom there are an estimated four million, remain disenfranchised due to congressional failure to pass the absentee voter legislation required by the Constitution.[17] The Philippine Congress similarly has failed to pass implementing legislation for popular initiative and referendum. However, the Congress did enact legislation providing for a unique "party list" system for 51 seats in the Philippine House of Representatives, with the first such elections held in May 1998.

ELITE DOMINATION OF PHILIPPINE POLITICS

By some standards, the Aquino, Ramos, and Estrada regimes have established an *inclusionary* electoral democracy—nearly 40 percent of the population voted in the February 1987 constitutional plebiscite and the May 1987 legislative elections.[18] Voter turn-out for the 1992 and 1995 local, provincial, and national elections was similarly high. However, voter registration for the May 1998 elections, which involved every elected office at the local, provincial, and national levels, declined 12 percent relative to registration for the May 1997 *barangay* (village) elections (Vanzi 1998d). Officially attributed to the purging of duplicate entries and the names of deceased voters on the twelve-year-old voters' list, the decline may also reflect voter disenchantment with the continuing fraud and violence of the electoral process.

Philippine electoral democracy under Aquino, Ramos, and Estrada is most appropriately characterized as *exclusionary,* voter turnout notwithstanding. The accountability and competition in politics ordinarily associated with democratic governance are limited by significant, albeit largely informal, barriers to entry in the Philippines. Rates of electoral participation disguised the continuing importance of "guns, goons, and gold" in Philippine elections, despite improvements in the post-Marcos era (Hutchcroft 1991). Upper-class control is facilitated by the manipulation of rural voting blocs by large landowners and formal or informal restrictions on popular mobilization (cf. Remmer 1985–86: 74–75). The single-member districts for the House of Representatives advantage local socioeconomic elites, who are better financed and better able to mobilize local clientelist networks, and prevent the mobilization of opposition. By putting a premium on the fund-raising capabilities of would-be candidates, the at-large (i.e., nationwide) elections for the Philippine Senate similarly limit entry to members of wealthy families or their agents and to established film and media personalities.

The uncertainty of electoral outcomes—that is, the possibility that an opposition party might win a genuinely competitive election—is one hallmark of electoral democracy. In identifying violations of this norm, analysts typically focus on dominant political parties or other institutional arrangements which effectively preclude opposition victories. In the Philippine context of weak political parties, the uncertainty of electoral outcomes is compromised in a sense not by dominant political parties but by the continuing influence of the traditional elite, regardless of party affiliation. The outcome of the 1987 elections illustrated this dominance: over two-thirds of the members of the 1987 House of Representatives had previously been elected to national office or belonged to "political dynasties"—that is, they were the second or third generation of their family to hold national office (Peterman 1988: 20). The May 1992 House election results confirmed the continuing importance of political dynasties and elites. According to one study, 145 of the 199 members were members of political families and over two-thirds of the members had other relatives in public office (Gutierrez 1994: 4, 12–13). Virtually all members of the Senate had multiple relatives in elective and appointive government positions. The results of the May 1998 local and national elections continued this pattern.

The Philippine legislature has imposed a ban on political advertising in the major media prior to the official campaign period. Intended to limit the campaign expenditures of well-financed candidates, the ban has the effect of limiting the precampaign visibility of nontraditional and less-well-known candidates. Not surprisingly, many of the successful candidates for nationwide office (the presidency and the Senate) in 1998 included figures of established public prominence, whether as incumbent politicians or as media or film personalities. Moreover, powerful candidates can skirt the campaign ban with relative impunity.

Elite domination of sectoral politics has been reinforced by the failure to enforce conflict-of-interest laws for legislators. For example, in 1993, 19 of the 40 members of the Committee on Banks and Financial Intermediaries had past or present interests in the banking industry. Twelve of the 29 members of the Committee on Agrarian Reform had substantial agricultural interests.

1987 Elections

The May 1987 congressional elections presented the best opportunity for President Aquino to democratically institutionalize "People Power." Aquino resisted all calls to do so. Disdainful of traditional politics, she headed no political party, commanded no systematically organized political apparatus. Rejection of the Marcos legacy of single-party rule and "personality cult" politics may partially explain her refusal to consolidate her popularity in a political organization. Yet in choosing to act (or, more accurately, not act) as she did, Mrs. Aquino relinquished a critical opportunity to promote democratic consolidation through the foundation (and eventual institutionalization) of a stable party system with substantive and organizational coherence. Such party systems appear to be a requisite of democratic consolidation (Mainwaring 1998; Diamond et al. 1990: 25–28).

Formation of the 1987 electoral alliance was left largely to the president's brother, Jose "Peping" Cojuangco, Jr. Peping fashioned a rebirth of the pre-martial-law network of provincial bosses, relying on them to restore the economy and address the local law-and-order situation. Among those recruited to Cojuangco's PDP-LABAN banner were many Marcos loyalists (Anderson 1988). One measure of the influence of these former Marcos supporters within the Aquino congressional coalition was provided by the progressive Institute for Popular Democracy. Using political affiliation as of the 1984 national assembly elections as the benchmark, the IPD identified 18 (of 56) heretofore Marcos supporters as having run under an Aquino-affiliated party. Had political affiliation been defined as of 1980, the IPD claimed that the number of "blue wearing yellow" — Marcos supporters turned nominal Aquino backers — would be "overwhelming" (IPD 1987: 4–5).

1992 Elections

The results of the May 1992 elections, in which local, provincial, and national offices were contested, suggested important elements of continuity in Philippine politics while providing evidence that traditional political practices had lost some of their efficacy. Election spending remained high, and congressional, provincial, and local results reflected the continuing importance of political patronage and political dynasties. More encouraging was the success of the ban on the display of guns by politicians and their bodyguards, which appeared to reduce election-related violence and coercion sharply. A generational shift was increasingly evident in the national legislature, as well as in provincial and local offices, although in a number of cases the victorious candidates were simply younger members of political dynasties.

The presidential election of May 1992 afforded some evidence that liberal democracy had been strengthened. A record number (eight) of candidates contested the presidency, indicating both an opening of political competition and a disturbing fractionalization of the party system. A more positive sign was the growing visibility of nongovernmental organizations (NGOs) and cause-oriented groups in the electoral process. Such groups began to emerge in the final years of the Marcos administration, with many of them involved in the anti-Marcos struggle. Benefiting from the liberalization of the rights of association since 1986, thousands of NGOs had been established to promote causes such as agrarian reform, environmental protection, the rights of indigenous peoples, and an end to violence against women. Hundreds of these social organizations aligned themselves with the 1992 Ramos and Salonga presidential campaigns. Citizens had a wider array of organizational channels for representing their interests in the political arena, albeit at the cost of severe party fragmentation.

The poor showing of presidential candidate Ramon Mitra, former Speaker of the House, was widely viewed as a rebuff for traditional politicians (*trapos*). Miriam Defensor-Santiago's second place finish, despite limited resources and a near-absence of party organization, pointed to the popularity of her anticorruption campaign theme and the reduced importance of the traditional political parties.

Fidel V. Ramos's narrow plurality victory carried a mixed message. Ramos benefited enormously from the endorsement of Corazon Aquino. Moreover, Ramos switched party identification in the preelection period. Ramos's actions were eloquent testimony to the weakness of political party discipline, and his victory was testimony to the continuing importance of personalities in Philippine politics. The continuing regional strength of Marcos loyalists was evident in the third-place finish of presidential aspirant Eduardo "Danding" Cojuangco (Landé 1996: 20–26). More generally, the 1992 elections demonstrated the continuing importance of linguistic and regional identities in explaining national electoral outcomes (Landé 1996).

1995 Elections

The results of the May 1995 mid-term elections suggested little cause for optimism about the direction of Philippine electoral democracy. At stake were all seats in the House of Representatives and one-half of the Senate seats, as well as all local government positions apart from *barangay* (village) officials. There was considerable electoral choice, with 60,311 candidates contesting the roughly 17,342 positions. However, a disquieting number of congressional and local government positions were uncontested, the result of preelection deals among heretofore competing political parties (Hernandez 1996: 142–43). After the relative peace of the 1992 elections, there was an appreciable upswing in political violence in 1995: at least 55 people were killed in election-related violence. This violence was most evident in local and provincial contests (Landé 1996: 108; see also Sidel n.d. 104–7). The continuing role of political dynasties also was evident: Senators Gloria Macapagal-Arroyo, Ramon Magsaysay, Jr., and Sergio Osmeña III traced their political lineage to past Philippine presidents. Although Ferdinand Marcos, Jr., failed in his Senate bid, his mother, Imelda, captured a House seat. Moreover, the elections, particularly those for the Senate, were marked by significant fraud. Recounting ballots in nearly one-fifth of the country's precincts, a Senate Electoral Tribunal discovered that one candidate had been awarded victory on the basis of nearly 250,000 nonexistent votes, in a process known as "Dagdag-Bawas" (addition-subtraction). Notwithstanding the fraud, the candidate remained in office, fueling public cynicism about the electoral process (U.S. State Department 1998: 12).

Preparations for 1998 Elections

The Election Modernization Act (Republic Act 8437) provided for a number of measures to improve electoral democracy, including computerization of voter registration lists and elections. Comelec had hoped to fully computerize voter registration lists by 1998. The change was intended to assure that voter lists were current; outdated lists had disenfranchised qualified voters and facilitated voting fraud in earlier elections. However, in February 1998, Comelec abandoned efforts to computerize the May elections in all regions except the Autonomous Region of Muslim Mindanao, citing delays in congressional approval of funding. Comelec's own footdragging and its decision to retain manual counting of ballots were condemned as "preparing the ground for cheating" (*Philippine Daily Inquirer* 1998).

The Party-List System Act (Republic Act 7941) finally instituted the party list provision of the 1987 Constitution. The law sets aside 51 seats in the House of Representatives for sectoral groups or minor parties. In theory, this system will enhance the electoral voice of historically marginalized and underrepresented groups such as peasants, fisherfolk, workers, and women. Traditional political parties are barred from contesting these seats and participating parties are limited to a maximum of three seats.

Comelec approved the applications of some 60 sectoral parties to contest the party list elections. However, following the election, Comelec adopted a conservative interpretation of the law, applying the threshhold requirement of 2 percent of the vote to each party-list seat. Only 12 parties met this minimum and only 13 seats were awarded (one party received more than 4 percent of the party-list vote). Comelec's narrow interpretation is likely to be challenged in court. Party-list groups view the law as setting a 2 percent minimum for the first party-list seat with additional seats (up to three) awarded proportional to the number of votes received. Even in the event the more liberal interpretation is accepted, this intentional extreme fragmentation of the party system would seem ill-suited to the promotion of a stable and coherent party system upon which to consolidate democracy (see Diamond et al. 1990: 27). Some proponents of the party-list system also have expressed concern that the representative intention of this electoral system will be vitiated by the participation of nominal sectoral parties which they allege to be progeny of the traditional parties. Such parties, it is argued, will merely reinforce the dominance of traditional political elites.[19]

Electoral and liberal democracy in the Philippines is also threatened by continuing election-related violence. In the runup to the May 1998 elections, the armed forces of the Philippines identified 285 "problem areas" out of the country's 1,605 municipalities and cities. The military and the police were particularly attentive to potential for election-related violence in these areas (Vanzi 1998b). To further forestall violence, candidates and local government officials were prohibited from carrying guns, as they were during the 1992 and 1995 election campaigns. Comelec also has prohibited candidates from employing security personnel or bodyguards, as such employees have been the source of much of the violence in prior elections (Vanzi 1998a).

Weak Party System

Huntington attributes the legislative dominance of traditional elites in competitive polities to the absence of effective political organizations (1968: 402). To similar effect, Mainwaring (1998: 74–76) argues that democratic consolidation is impeded by the personalism, lack of accountability, and electoral volatility which characterize polities where party organizations are weak (see also Diamond et al. 1990). In the Philippine case, the leading parties are personality-based coalitions of politicians with independent power bases. As the parties provide few campaign resources, candidates have limited incentives to "toe the party line." Nominal party control over campaign endorsements apparently has done little to strengthen party discipline.

During the Aquino era, the largest political party, Lakas ng Demokratikong Pilipino (LDP), was identified with the president, but she held no office in the party.[20] Furthermore, the party lacked any defining ideology or agenda. The LDP was generally left to its own devices, and at several key junctures it failed to honor Aquino's wishes.

Frequent party-switching further undermines party discipline. Between the 1992 general elections and June 1993, 71 members of the House switched parties to join President Ramos's Lakas-National Union of Christian Democrats-United Muslim Democrats of the Philippines (Lakas-NUCD-UMDP). On paper, the 159-member coalition afforded President Ramos a solid legislative majority. In practice, weak party discipline made executive-legislative cooperation extremely problematic. The situation was worse in the Senate, where initially Laban ng Demokratikong Pilipino (Laban) accounted for 17 of the 24 members and Lakas-NUCD held only two seats. Despite subsequent party switching, executive-legislative relations have frequently been marked by gridlock. In the early years of his presidency, President Ramos was regularly frustrated by congressional delays on crucial elements of his legislative agenda, including economic and tax reform.

Lakas-NUCD candidates fared very well in the May 1995 elections, capturing 9 of the 12 Senate seats and nearly 90 percent of the 204 House seats up for election (Hernandez 1996: 143). In the final years of his presidency, Ramos's party claimed the allegiance of 20 of the 24 Senators. However, executive-legislative cooperation, such as it was, apparently had been purchased through a variety of discretionary mechanisms for allocating sizable amounts of the national budget to individual legislators. These allocations were identified with rampant graft and corruption. The 1996 disclosure of these allocations occasioned extensive media and popular condemnation. (See, e.g., Doronila 1996; Nocum 1996.) Such congressional allocations continued in 1997 and 1998.[21]

MILITARIZATION OF PHILIPPINE POLITICS

Objective civilian control of the military is another essential element of liberal democracy. Huntington (1995: 9–10) identifies the central features of such control as including: high levels of military professionalism; civilian preeminence in basic foreign and military policymaking; and the minimization of military involvement in politics and of civilian political interference in the area of professional military competence. In the Philippines, as in many "third wave" democracies, civilian rule is threatened by the military. Establishing civilian control is problematic: democratic leaders risk military backlash in the event they move to rein in the military and punish military leaders for past human rights abuses, yet failure to take such measures leaves civilian rule incomplete.

Martial Law

The political role of the Philippine military increased markedly during the martial law era. Everything from promotions to troop deployments reflected Marcos's political interests. Loyalty replaced merit as the basis for promotion. Equally important, the roles of the Presidential Security Command and of the National Intelligence and Security Agency were dramatically increased. These forces became a privileged elite within the Philippine military.[22] Both trends—loyalty-based promotions and enhancement of the intelligence/Manila security apparatus—came at the expense of sound military strategy and adequate field support. Junior officers, dissatisfied with this state of affairs, created the Reform the Armed Forces Movement (RAM) in 1981–82. It was RAM which catalyzed Marcos's downfall with a preemptive military rebellion in February 1986. This evolution has important parallels to a phenomenon

Stepan (1988) has described in the Latin American context: military re-actions to the growing influence of intelligence services leading to the formation of military-civilian alliances and ultimately precipitating tran-sitions to democratic rule.

Private Armies and Civilian Militias

During the Marcos era, the private armies of local landowners and the Civilian Home Defense Forces (CHDF) were widely regarded as the worst violators of human rights. Shortly after Aquino came to power, the number of private armies was estimated at 260 (Mydans 1987). Some of the armies were controlled by Marcos loyalists, others by local, ostensi-bly pro-Aquino, landed elites. CHDF units, created during martial law, were often indistinguishable from the private armies. Marcos cronies such as Eduardo Cojuangco (Corazon Cojuangco Aquino's cousin) and Armando Gustillo maintained huge private armies (1,600 and 1,200 men, respectively; Simons 1987: 169).

During her presidential campaign, Aquino pledged to abolish the CHDF units and disband private armies. Both represented instruments of local domination, the removal of which would increase the political space for political activism and competition. These private armies are prohibited by the 1987 Constitution (Article 18, Section 24), but Aquino made little effort to disband them.[23] Indeed, after the breakdown in ne-gotiations with the NPA, she adopted a policy of "total war" and offered conditional praise of vigilante groups.[24] This policy shift reflected the growing autonomy of the military in waging the counterinsurgency cam-paign. Aquino's praise was taken by some as carte blanche approval of abusive vigilante groups and private armies, as well it might be in the absence of effective enforcement of government guidelines on the opera-tion of anticommunist civilian groups. The Aquino government did little to prosecute members of vigilante groups or the armed forces (see LCHR 1988).

Aquino did order the disbanding of the CHDF in March 1987. However, the directive was immediately changed in response to strong reaction within the military. The revised directive called for recommen-dations from the military as to the future of the CHDF. In the end, the CHDF was essentially converted into the new Civilian Armed Forces Geographical Units (CAFGUs).[25]

The problem of private armies was largely ignored until July 1993, when President Ramos launched an effort to abolish all private armies within sixty days. The deadline was subsequently extended. As of mid-

September 1993, the government claimed to have disbanded 283 of an estimated 558 armed groups and accepted the surrender of over 3,600 weapons (out of an estimated total of 11,200). Most of the surrendered weapons were of World War II vintage and the majority of the disbanded groups were small. Critics claimed the government was ignoring the large armies of prominent Filipinos. The initiative has received little government attention since late 1993.

Military and Police Involvement in Criminal Activities

In addition to their role in other human rights abuses (detailed below), elements of the Philippine armed forces and the national police are widely believed to be involved in criminal activities, including kidnaping for ransom. This perception has received confirmation from the Ramos government's kidnaping task force (U.S. Department of State 1998: 5). Kidnaping syndicates (and insurgent forces) have targeted members of the Chinese-Filipino business community, who play a prominent role in the Philippine economy. To partially address the problem, Ramos initiated a purge of miscreant elements of the Philippine National Police (PNP) in 1993. The PNP is the successor organization to the Philippine Constabulary, which Ramos directed during martial law. The forced retirement of senior PNP officers and rank-and-file PNP personnel have had little apparent impact on police misconduct. Since 1993, and despite public protests by Chinese businessmen and human rights organizations in 1997, the government has done little to curb military and police involvement in criminal activities, issuing few indictments against implicated personnel.

Coup d'État Attempts

In the aftermath of martial law, Aquino confronted a very politicized military. The specter of prisoner releases that included the founder of the CPP/NPA, campaign promises of negotiations with the insurgents and punishment for human rights abusers within the military, and the exclusion of the military from the early cease-fire negotiations with the NPA all antagonized a military whose loyalty was suspect from the start.[26] The military was well positioned to protect its interests, having played a critical role in Aquino's ascension to power. Moreover, Aquino lacked an institutionalized popular base with which to contest the actions and demands of the military.

What followed were seven coup attempts, several of which seriously threatened the survival of the Aquino regime and democratic institutions. On July 6, 1986, Arturo Tolentino, Marcos's vice presidential candidate, was joined by several hundred troops in seizing the Manila Hotel for three days. Although the rebellion bordered on the comical, it signaled Aquino's (and General Ramos's) inability to command loyalty among all segments of the armed forces. Aquino's inability or unwillingness to crack down on military disloyalty was evident in the punishment meted out to the rebels: they were forced to do push-ups.

A more serious threat was uncovered on November 23, 1986. The discovery led to the discharge of Juan Ponce Enrile, a leading figure in the military rebellion against Marcos in February 1986, from the cabinet. As one of the prices of military loyalty during this period, two of the most progressive cabinet members, labor minister Augusto S. Sanchez and local government minister Aquilino Q. Pimentel, were also dismissed. Human rights investigations also were downgraded and a variety of military prerogatives restored and demands met (Thompson 1990: 5).

Coup attempts on January 27 and April 18, 1987, amounted to little, although the former involved seizure of Manila's largest television station for sixty hours. Charges were eventually filed against 6 officers and 136 soldiers; all were allowed to retain their weapons.

On August 28, 1987, Colonel Gregorio Honasan launched the most serious threat to that point, with the support of several hundred soldiers. The rebels attacked the presidential palace and a variety of other targets. As a result of the fighting, fifty-three soldiers and civilians died, hundreds more were wounded. A thousand rebel soldiers were eventually captured or surrendered. Honasan initially eluded capture, was then jailed and, with the collusion of his navy guards, finally escaped. Military loyalty to Aquino during an August 1987 coup attempt again carried a price: Executive Secretary Joker P. Arroyo, President Aquino's closest adviser, and her special legal counsel, Teodoro L. Locsin, Jr., were both dismissed from their positions, tarred as leftists by military and business leaders. Aquino appointed Fidel V. Ramos as secretary of national defense. Responding to rebel complaints, Aquino awarded pay hikes of 60 percent to the armed forces (Steinberg 1994: 162).

Following two years of relative quiescence among the military, Honasan initiated another coup attempt on December 1, 1989, this time involving over 3,000 rebel troops, many from elite units. Nearly 100 soldiers and civilians were killed, almost 600 wounded. At the height of the fighting, the rebels controlled access to two television stations, had closed the Manila airport, and were launching air attacks on the presidential palace. At Aquino's request, the United States Air Force intervened from

Clark Air Base in Central Luzon, grounding the rebel aircraft. The rebels held out for eight days, seizing commercial buildings and international hotels in the Makati business district. A settlement was finally negotiated by Philippine Military Academy superintendent, General Arturo Enrile (a cousin of Juan Ponce Enrile and Ramos's successor as chief of staff of the armed forces).

Finally, on October 6, 1990, Colonel Alexander Noble, a veteran of the December 1989 rebellion, staged a fifty-four-hour revolt in Mindanao. Regardless of the severity of this or earlier coup attempts, each undermined the principles of democratic governance and civilian control and fostered an image of a regime barely able to govern. With each uprising, the Aquino government moved further to the right politically, eventually acceding to many of the rebel demands.

A Silent Coup

Judging from the absence of coup attempts against his government, President Ramos enjoyed greater success in establishing civilian control over the armed forces than did Aquino. However, in what amounted to a "silent coup," Ramos appointed a large number of former military officers to key government and public sector positions, particularly in government-owned or controlled corporations. Real power may still have been vested in elected officials and their appointees, per Diamond's criterion for liberal democracy (1996: 23). At issue, however, was the nature of those appointments. Fewer *serving* officers were in political positions, but many *recently retired* officers were appointed to such positions (see Huntington 1995: 12). The most prominent appointee was presidential security adviser and National Security Council director general Jose T. Almonte, widely viewed as Ramos's foremost adviser. Other key appointees included: Bureau of Customs commissioner Colonel Guillermo Parayno; Commission on Human Rights commissioner General Samuel Soriano; Export Zone Processing Authority administrator Tagumbay Jardiniano; Government Service Insurance Corporation chairman General Jose Magno; National Steel Corporation chairman General Luis Mirasol; Philippine Airlines board of directors member Major General Loven Abadia; Philippine Ports Authority general manager Captain Rogelio Dayan; Philippine National Railroad general manager Colonel Jose Dado; and Social Security Service administrator Colonel Renato Valencia.[27] By some accounts, public reaction to these appointments was muted because they remained modest relative to Marcos's appointments during martial law (Reyes 1993: 6). Nonetheless, the list of such appointees was extensive.

Former military officers have been similarly active in their pursuit of electoral office. Numerous retired officers ran for national and local offices in the 1992 elections. Five former officers ran as part of Miriam Defensor Santiago's senatorial slate, eight ran on Imelda Marcos's ticket. Salvador Laurel's slate included former military rebel, Brigadier General Edgardo Abenina, prominent for his involvement in the August 1987 and December 1989 coup attempts. Other former military rebels ran for local office as independents or under Santiago's party label. Ramos was the only presidential candidate who did not have retired military officers on his senatorial slate.[28] However, a number of retired military officers ran for governorships under his banner. In the 1995 midterm elections, Gregorio Honasan successfully ran for a seat in the Philippine Senate. Other former military rebels ran for local office.

Ramos attributed much of the Philippines' economic success and social unification to the leadership and stabilizing influence of the military, the coup attempts notwithstanding. He traced military involvement in developing country politics to its role in responding to the imperialist pressure from the West. In his words, a country's "officer corps came to understand the West better than did its bureaucrats. The military became the nation's intelligentsia and political conscience."[29] Stepan (1988) has termed this the "new professionalism," a focus on internal security which entailed an "expansion of military-mission definition, organizational reach, and comparative power" (Stepan 1988: xii). In Ramos's view, the Philippine military came to recognize that social reform and economic growth, rather than a purely military response, were the keys to addressing insurgency and other internal threats (1995: 35).

At the same time, the Philippine military has had to bear increasing responsibility for external defense following the termination of the Philippine-U.S. Military Bases Agreement and the withdrawal of American military forces in 1992. The dispute with China and several Southeast Asian nations regarding claims to the Spratly Islands has heightened consciousness of this external role. In turn, Ramos initiated a major modernization of the Philippine armed forces. Huntington identifies such modernization and reorientation in the military's mission as two (of ten) crucial actions for promoting military professionalism and curbing military power (1991a: 251–52).

During the 1998 presidential campaign, Estrada gave little public attention to the military, promising only to demilitarize the government bureaucracy. Estrada's ability to control the politicized Philippine military in the face of economic and social challenges to the nation will be a crucial test of his presidency and the consolidation of Philippine democracy.

To promote civilian control of the military in the post-transition era, Stepan (1988: 129–30) recommends the formation of a civilian institution specializing in military affairs as a means of providing support personnel so the legislative body might properly perform the requisite military and intelligence oversight of political society. To date, efforts in this regard in the Philippines have been quite modest.

BRINGING INSURGENTS INTO THE DEMOCRATIC FOLD

One hallmark of democratic consolidation is that "all politically significant groups in a new democracy acknowledge its political institutions as the only legitimate arena for political contestation" (Gunther et al. 1996: 153). In this regard, the Aquino, Ramos, and Estrada governments have faced formidable challenges as communist insurgents, Muslim secessionists, and rightist rebels within the military threatened the Philippine state. The Ramos and Estrada governments have benefited from a combination of declining popular support for the insurgents and varying progress in negotiating settlements to the conflicts. In 1993, the National Unification Commission (NUC) began negotiations with all three rebellious elements. Negotiations with the National Democratic Front (NDF), the united front for the Communist Party of the Philippines (CPP), have been complicated by a major factional split within the rebel movement. The Manila Rizal Regional Committee and regional committees in the Visayas and Mindanao have broken from the Maoist line of CPP-founder Jose Maria Sison, who remains in exile. Sison loyalists remain committed to a rural-based protracted people's war; the break-away groups give greater emphasis to an urban struggle. Still other elements have renounced armed struggle in favor of democracy.

Recent negotiations with the NDF have periodically broken down over safety and immunity measures for the rebel negotiators. Government negotiators also have balked at other NDF demands, including a total review of government policies on agrarian reform, repayment of international debt, participation in the World Trade Organization (WTO), and the expanded value-added tax.

Similar factionalism has partially frustrated government efforts to peacefully resolve the conflicts with Muslim rebels. Building upon a 1993 cease-fire agreement, the Ramos government signed a peace accord with the Moro National Liberation Front (MNLF) led by Nur Misuari in 1996. As part of the agreement, the Southern Philippine Council for Peace and Development (SPCPD) was established for fourteen provinces in Mindanao. These provinces (originally thirteen, now fourteen) had been slated for Muslim autonomy under the terms of the 1976 Tripoli Agreement negotiated by the Marcos government. With support from President Ramos's Lakas party, Misauri and the MNLF won elections in the Autonomous Region for Muslim Mindanao. Misauri became chairman of the SPCPD, which includes representatives from the Muslim, Christian, and Lumad (indigenous non-Muslim) communities. Over the next three years, the SPCPD is to facilitate economic growth in the region and the development of a provisional autonomous government. A referendum will then determine the nature of autonomy in the region. As Muslims now constitute a majority of the population in only five of the fourteen provinces, there is little expectation that the autonomous region will resemble that envisioned in the 1976 accord.

Despite this progress toward peaceful resolution of the Muslim-Christian conflict, a large breakaway faction, the Muslim Islamic Liberation Front (MILF), was involved in a series of armed encounters with government troops in 1996–97. A 1997 cease-fire accord between the government and the MILF has not stopped military action in several Mindanao provinces. The MILF ordered its supporters to boycott the 1998 elections as part of a broader rejection of the Philippine Constitution (Vanzi 1998c). Thousands of families have been displaced by the conflict, many of them suffering from periodic acute food shortages. Both sides to the conflict have been guilty of human rights abuses.

The NUC also began negotiations with former military rebels, the Rebolusyonaryong Alyansang Makabansa-Soldiers of the Filipino People-Young Officers Union (RAM-SFP-YOU), in 1993. Under his amnesty program, Ramos released several hundred military (and communist) rebels. After several years of exchanging recriminations with government officials over delays in their negotiations, the former military rebels signed a peace agreement in early August 1995. The former rebels have focused their energies on electoral reform and broadening political participation, supporting calls for prohibitions against political dynasties, establishment of a party-list system, year-round voter registration, and computerization of voter lists.

A Compromised Judicial System

Legal institutions which provide neutral, predictable, and timely adjudication of disputes are essential to effective governance and liberal democracy. In recent decades, the Philippine legal system has been ill-equipped to serve as a neutral and timely arbiter of disputes. Judges, as the sole arbiters of litigation (there are no jury trials in the Philippines), are the targets of political influence and bribery.

Justice also is often effectively denied in the Philippines because it is so frequently delayed. Reflecting both a shortage in the number of judges and prosecutors and the delaying tactics of some litigants, there is a massive backlog of cases (U.S. Department of State 1998: 8). This backlog typically disadvantages the poor claimant or defendant. The costs of protracted litigation, in legal fees, time away from work, and travel costs, are considerable. Moreover, with the appellate courts situated in Metro Manila, poor Filipinos resident elsewhere in the archipelago are effectively barred from access to the higher courts. Judicial proceedings are often a war of attrition, with wealthy litigants much better equipped to go the distance. This backlog similarly hampers efforts to curb graft and corruption, as suspected officials retain their offices pending the outcome of the proceedings.

Following the lead of the United States, judicial review is an accepted practice in the Philippines. Under martial law the once independent and respected judiciary was made subservient to Marcos. With the transition to the Aquino regime, legal and judicial reforms were introduced in an effort to restore public confidence in the law and its application. Mrs. Aquino's second presidential proclamation restored the writ of habeas corpus. She also released political prisoners and abolished Marcos-era decrees that had permitted indefinite detentions. In reorganizing the judiciary, Mrs. Aquino appointed 11 of the 15 Supreme Court justices, 42 of the 51 Court of Appeals judges, and 9 new judges to the Sandiganbayan—the ombudsman court (Timberman 1991: 222). The 1987 Constitution included a number of provisions designed to restore the independence of the judiciary: giving the judiciary fiscal autonomy (Art. VIII, Sec. 3); giving the Supreme Court administrative supervision over all courts and court personnel (Art. VIII, Sec. 6); and creating a Judicial and Bar Council to recommend lists of potential judicial appointees (Art. VIII, Sec. 8). Still, public confidence in the judicial system remains low, reflecting the lengthy delays in bringing matters to trial, unwieldy and expensive procedures, corruption, and the government's unwillingness or inability to curb human rights abuses.

CRACKDOWN ON CRIMINAL ACTIVITIES OF GOVERNMENT OFFICIALS

To consolidate Philippine democracy, President Ramos sought to curb corruption, cronyism, and criminal activities among public officials.

These efforts met with mixed success. The most notable milestone was the September 24, 1993, conviction of Imelda Marcos for violations of the Anti-Graft and Corrupt Practices Act. At least ninety criminal and civil cases are still pending against Mrs. Marcos. The indictments against Mrs. Marcos and others have done little to reduce the pervasive cronyism and corruption. Moreover, the charges have had only modest impact on Mrs. Marcos's political career. She won election to the House of Representatives in 1995. Reprising her 1992 bid, Mrs. Marcos campaigned briefly for the presidency in 1998.

In 1994, by Executive Order 151, Ramos established a Presidential Commission Against Graft and Corruption, with authority to handle complaints involving presidential appointees. The Supreme Court also upheld the power of the Aquino-era Presidential Commission on Good Government (PCGG) to investigate all cases of graft or corruption. However, government auditors attributed losses of over P239.5 million to ineptness and abuses in the PCGG.

There is continuing evidence that the Philippine legal system does not provide equal justice when public officials are involved. As of early 1998, the Sandiganbayan had not tried the police implicated in the 1995 "rub out" (assassination) of the Kuratong Baleleng robbery suspects. Key witnesses, a judge, and a senator urging prosecution were subjected to death threats, while senior police officials were reinstated in their jobs rather than being charged for their alleged involvement in the crime (U.S. Department of State 1998: 3).

There are some signs of progress, however, in the application of Philippine justice. Widely publicized allegations of criminal misconduct have prompted the suspension, dismissal, or prosecution of a number of public officials. For example, in 1993, Mayor Antonio Sanchez (Calauan, Laguna) and five henchmen were tried on rape and murder charges in connection with the brutal slayings of two university students. At the same time, the entire Calauan police force was suspended for serving as Sanchez' private security force. In an unrelated case, Ramos suspended Ilocos Norte Governor Rodolfo Farinas following accusations of misconduct and abuse of authority. In 1997, in response to widespread media attention, a member of congress was jailed and was being tried for the alleged rape of an eleven-year-old girl.

OBSTACLES TO PEASANT POLITICAL INFLUENCE

The transition to the Aquino government meant a reopening of political space for peasant activism. Nongovernmental organizations, many representing previously marginalized segments of Philippine society, have proliferated under the Aquino, Ramos, and Estrada governments. Many NGOs concentrate on delivery of basic social services, often with support from the government and foreign donors. Other NGOs have become active in policy advocacy at the local, provincial, or national levels. Although historically slow to respond to grassroots initiatives in tailoring its policies, the Philippine government now acknowledges the positive contributions NGOs can make to an equitable and sustainable development process. However, NGOs still find it difficult to make their voices heard on public policy issues.

The obstacles confronting attempts to convert majority interests into political organizations and, in turn, political power and redistributive policies, are considerable.[30] There are both objective and subjective constraints on the emergence of a perception of shared interests among the lower classes. Yet, models of democratic class struggle (as well as Marxist analysis) presuppose that class is the most politically salient identity (Jackman 1986). Where it is not, strong, class-based political parties are unlikely to emerge to pursue fundamental political and social reform. Even where class is the operative identity, there are differing interests among Philippine peasants.[31]

Where peasants perceive themselves to have common interests, they may nonetheless abstain from costly (in terms of finances, time, and the risks of reprisals) union or party membership in the belief that individual contributions will have no perceptible impact on the political process. Collective action places a premium on effective leadership and the provision of incentives sufficient to bring individual and collective interests into alignment (Popkin 1981). The pool of potential union or party organizers is limited by the minimal economic rewards, scarce organizational resources, and threats of physical harm that leaders confront. Landowners' private armies have long been an instrument of oppression in rural Philippine society. The proliferation of vigilante organizations in the late 1980s increased the risks of repression even further.

Dependency relations and fear of reprisals also influence the behavior of potential members. In settings of multiple dependency-relations peasants must generally avoid alienating powerful people (Herring 1981). If not voting at the specific behest of a local patron, many of the rural electorate continue to vote in terms of actual or perceived patronage.[32] In an archipelago such as the Philippines, these voters are often physically isolated, making it difficult to be informed about rural policy, let alone reach or influence state leaders. They generally lack the contacts and wherewithal to independently publicize their position (Esman and Uphoff 1984).

The conversion of an organizational base into effective political power is also hampered by the limited resources of the peasant membership. Moreover, as latecomers to Philippine politics, peasant organizations and NGOs must challenge established patterns of political behavior and state action. In so doing, these and other self-described "peoples' organizations" have found themselves regularly branded "leftist," "subversive," or "communist" by antireform rural and national elites. By manipulating the terms of public discourse, opponents of political and social reform have worked to portray reform proponents as extremists who threatened the well-being of the nation.

Repression of Peasant Organizations

Institutionalization of the organizational work of NGOs and peasant organizations is ultimately dependent on community volunteers. These nonremunerated volunteers face many of the same suspicions, and are subject to greater threats of punishment—enjoying neither the guarantee of external employment nor the physical security attendant to the institutional affiliation of the NGO personnel—than those who organize them. NGO personnel can always flee hostile locales. Peasant activists, by contrast, must generally live—or, in the case of numerous organizers and Basic Christian Community leaders, die—with the consequences of their activities.

After a brief hiatus in the early months of the Aquino government, human rights abuses resumed under the Aquino and Ramos governments, belying images of liberal democracy. These abuses continue to the present, albeit at a declining level. The targeted "subversives" include members of the church community and union activists. Members of militant organizations such as Kilusang Magbubukid ng Pilipinas (KMP, Peasant Movement of the Philippines) and the National Federation of Sugar Workers (NFSW) have been subjected to harassment, torture, and, in some cases, execution (Amnesty International 1991).

Extrajudicial killings continue, most of them committed by the police, prison personnel or the military, or by insurgent forces (U.S. Department of State 1998: 2–4). Other Philippine citizens continue to be victimized by "disappearances" or torture. Philippine prisons are characterized by the abuse of prisoners and corruption among prison officials, as well as by overcrowding, inadequate food, and poor sanitation (idem 1998: 5–7).

Labor relations in provinces such as Negros Occidental remain tense. In the case of NFSW, a successful Negros-wide strike in 1990 was countered by increasing repression from the *hacenderos* and Philippine

military. Utilizing a "divide and rule" strategy, the military deployed special operations teams to individual sugar haciendas. In exchange for
"surrendering"—that is, renouncing communism and the NFSW—farm
workers were granted safe conduct passes for use in areas of military activity.[33] In some cases, torture was used to extract the "surrender" agreement (farm worker interviews, Hacienda Mandayo, February 11, 1991).

In Mindanao, the Christian-Muslim conflict similarly has been
marked by human rights abuses by the Philippine military, the Muslim
insurgents (notably the MILF), and CAFGUs. These abuses continue, albeit on a diminished scale, despite the 1996 peace accord between the
Ramos government and the MNLF and 1997 ceasefire between the government and the MILF. Among the victims in 1997 were a bishop and
a volunteer worker for the Catholic Church (U.S. Department of State
1998: 3–4).

CHALLENGES TO THE PHILIPPINE CONSTITUTION

The continuing debate over constitutional arrangements with respect to
the basic structure of Philippine government is another visible indication
that significant steps remain in the consolidation of Philippine democracy. Faced with legislative gridlock and the weak party system, prominent Philippine politicians have urged a switch from a presidential to a
parliamentary system, fusing the executive and legislative branches.[34]
The debate over presidential versus parliamentary forms of governance
has a long history in the Philippines, dating back to the independence
movement of the late 1800s (Santos et al. 1997). The current campaign
for constitutional reform received its impetus from members of the
House of Representatives who formed the Parliamentarians Bloc in 1991
and a December 1991 National Conference on Parliamentary Government sponsored by the (German) Konrad Adenauer Foundation and the
(Philippine) Local Government Development Foundation. In his June
1992 inaugural address, President Ramos promised to ask Congress to
convene as a Constitutent Assembly for the purpose of amending the
Philippine Constitution, to adopt some variant of parliamentary government.

Under the terms of the 1987 Constitution, changes can be made to
the Constitution if: three-quarters of the members of Congress vote to
convene as a Constituent Assembly; or two-thirds of the members of
Congress vote to call a Constitutional Convention; or a majority of the
members vote to submit the question of calling a Constitutional Convention to the public. The first two requirements are complicated by confu-

sion over whether the relevant percentage of votes for Congress is considered as a whole or for each chamber of Congress. There is little expectation that the Senate would approve either measure. The slow and expensive nature of constitutional conventions makes the latter two options unappealing to proponents of rapid constitutional reform, particularly those who had urged amendments in the mid-1990s to extend the term of President Ramos beyond 1998. The response was a public signature campaign (detailed below) to hold a public initiative on proposed constitutional changes.

In late September 1995, a thirty-five-page draft constitution was revealed to the media by Father Joaquin Bernas, a longtime confidant of Mrs. Aquino. The draft was widely attributed to the National Security Council, despite repeated denials by NSC head Jose T. Almonte. A series of authoritarian features of the draft were promptly and widely criticized. In marked contrast to most parliamentary systems predicated on responsible government, the draft made no provision for a vote of no-confidence, question hour, or dissolution of parliament. There appeared to be no provision for holding the executive accountable to the parliament. Equally disquieting were several provisions related to civil rights: the draft permitted the suspension of habeas corpus "when public safety requires" and contained no limit on the duration of martial law.

The debate over constitutional reform quickly became identified with, and in important ways subsumed by, a concurrent campaign to eliminate the constitutional provisions limiting terms of office for members of the executive and legislative branches. Under the 1987 Constitution, the president is limited to a single six-year term, members of the House are limited to three consecutive terms (of three years each), and members of the Senate are limited to two consecutive terms (of six years each). Of the 217 members of the 1995–98 House, 87 were barred from reelection, as were 8 of 24 Senators. Ramos regularly disavowed any interest in remaining in power beyond his six-year term. However, prominent members of his entourage were at the forefront of the efforts to amend the Constitution and abolish term limits. They cited President Ramos's "indispensability" to the course of Philippine economic and political progress in explaining their support for the proposed changes. They argued that continuity was best served by retaining Ramos as executive. Their actions seemed to belie Ramos's stated disinterest in continuing in office.

The effort to abolish term limits was led by the People's Initiative for Reform, Modernization and Action (PIRMA ["signature" or "sign"]), formed in early December 1996. PIRMA enjoyed the support of a variety of social organizations, including several Protestant and evangelical groups. As of mid-March 1997, PIRMA had collected nearly six million signatures in support of a national initiative on the term-limit question. That month, in a split decision (9–5), the Philippine Supreme Court rejected PIRMA's petition for a people's initiative. The court ruled that no initiative could be put to the people in the absence of legislation implementing the 1987 constitutional provision for such initiative. The court enjoined Comelec from accepting such initiatives. In July 1997, Comelec unanimously (7–0) dismissed PIRMA's petition.

Even some proponents of parliamentary government cautioned against making the change at the time. They were concerned that the change would fuel the ruling party's aspirations to remain in power and would distract public and congressional attention from more urgent policy matters, notably further economic reform. By these accounts, the constitutional reform must also be preceded by a strengthening of the political party system and the bureaucracy (Abad 1997).

Those opposing changes to the 1987 Constitution or an end to term limits included former president Aquino, archbishop of Manila Cardinal Jamie Sin, 1986 Constitutional Commission chair and former Supreme Court chief justice Celia Muñoz Palma, University of the Philippines president Jose Abueva, former director of the National Economic Development Authority (NEDA) Solita Monsod, and retired chief of the armed forces Rodolfo Biazon. On October 15, 1995, the eighth anniversary of the signing of the 1987 Constitution, Mrs. Aquino and others founded Demokrasya, Ipagtanggol ang Konstitusyon (DIK), the principal organization of opposition to constitutional reform. Another organization challenging PIRMA's efforts was Bury the Useless Reform Agenda (BURA ["erase"]). In March 1997, the Catholic Bishops' Conference of the Philippines voiced its opposition to constitutional reform. A variety of opposition parties similarly denounced the proposed constitutional changes, among them the Liberal Party, Nacionalista Party, PDP-Laban, Laban ng Demokratikong Pilipino, and People's Reform Party. Several progressive groups also condemned the proposed constitutional reforms, including BAYAN (Bagong Alyansang Makabayan, New Nationalist Alliance). Then vice president Joseph Estrada and members of the Senate voiced opposition to a related proposal to shift to a unicameral legislature, the latter motivated in part by concern for their positions.

Opponents of the changes challenged the premise that President Ramos was crucial to Philippine economic and political development. In their view, Ramos had been inappropriately credited for many reforms initiated under the Aquino and Marcos governments. They expressed doubts about Ramos's commitment to further economic or political reform. Moreover, they argued that extending Ramos's term would fuel unrest rather than promote democratic continuity. They cited the parallels between the proposed changes and Marcos's efforts to extend his term in the early 1970s. Public opposition to the proposed changes was substantial: 69 percent opposed the changes in a December 1996 poll (Hofeliña 1997).

The constitutional reform effort suffered several significant setbacks in 1997. PIRMA failed to collect sufficient signatures and obtain Comelec certification for their initiative by their self-imposed deadline of March 1997. PIRMA had hoped to stage the initiative vote concurrent with the 1997 elections, thereby minimizing the costs of holding the initiative vote and the attendant difficulties of obtaining the requisite congressional funding. Proponents of constitutional reform were dealt a further setback by a massive public rally in opposition to such reforms. In an act of great symbolism, rally organizers, led by Mrs. Aquino, staged the event on September 21, 1997, the twenty-fifth anniversary of Marcos's declaration of martial law.

In the aftermath of these setbacks, supporters of President Ramos increasingly turned their efforts toward identifying and electing a candidate who could carry on the Ramos legacy. For much of 1997, Renato de Villa, former secretary of national defense under Presidents Aquino and Ramos and former armed forces chief of staff, was touted as Ramos's heir apparent. However, de Villa, who enjoyed little public support, lost the Lakas-NUCD party nomination to House Speaker Jose de Venecia. De Venecia obtained the endorsement of President Ramos, as well as that of prominent former military rebels, including Senator Honasan. De Venecia's poor electoral showing in the May 1998 election was testament to the weakness of Ramos's political organization.

Joseph "Erap" Estrada's movie-screen image as an anticrime figure and his pledge to help the poor and revitalize Philippine agriculture endeared him to the Philippine masses. His presidential campaign built upon this charismatic and populist image. Estrada was the clear victor in the May 11, 1998, elections, notwithstanding allegations of electoral fraud. Estrada ran under the LaMMP (Laban ng Makabayang Masang Pilipino [Fight of Nationalist Filipino Masses]) banner, capturing 46.4 percent of the vote in a ten-candidate contest. His nearest challenger was Jose de Venecia, who garnered only 17.1 percent of the vote. De Venecia's running mate, Senator Gloria Macapagal Arroyo, daughter of a former president of the Philippines, won the vice presidency with 50.2 percent of the vote. Estrada's running mate, Senator Edgardo J. Angara, finished a distant second, with 24.5 percent of the vote. The split presidential/vice-presidential ballot is further evidence of the continuing weakness of Philippine political parties.

CONCLUSION

The processes of democratic transition and consolidation which began in 1986 in the Philippines differ from those in "third wave" democracies which had not previously experienced democratic rule. In the main, Filipinos acted in 1986 to end the authoritarian rule of Ferdinand Marcos and restore previous Philippine democratic institutions. With few exceptions (noted above), the shortcomings of those earlier institutions received little overt attention from the political actors shaping the transition process. Not until nearly a decade after the transition would these issues command public attention.

The scholarship on democratization distinguishes between negotiated transitions—those involving "pacts" between various political actors regarding the terms of transition—and insurrectionary transitions—those involving dramatic collapses of the prior regime in the face of massive popular opposition (O'Donnell and Schmitter 1986: 37–47). The former types of transition are thought to bring less transformation of social and economic inequalities. Less examined is the question of whether the institutional arrangements of democracy receive more specific and more critical attention in negotiated transitions. The Philippine case would suggest that insurrectionary type transitions involve less explicit attention to the institutional details of the successor regime, at least during the transition.

The events of February 1986 ushered in a series of reforms which restored central elements of electoral democracy in the Philippines. Competitive elections for all levels of government have been held on several occasions since 1986. The electoral process has been open to a range of candidates and virtually all adults in the country. Voter turnout has been uniformly high. With some notable exceptions, the electoral results have been honored as fair. However, this return to democratic governance is characterized by the continuing prominence of traditional political elites, weak political parties, notable incidents of electoral fraud, election-related violence, and factionalism based primarily on personalities and ethno-linguistic affiliations rather than ideology.

Over time, Philippine electoral democracy under President Aquino became increasingly problematic in the face of rightist threats from within the military, leading to substantial concessions to the military and the avoidance of controversial political and social reforms. Encouragingly, the Aquino government survived a series of coup attempts and successfully handed power to an elected successor. Former military rebels largely have turned to the electoral arena to contest government policies. President Ramos placated the armed forces at least temporarily with a program of modernization (materiel and training). Ramos also appointed a significant number of retired officers to key government positions. At this writing, the Estrada government is still in its infancy. Its likely legacy with respect to establishing civilian control over the military is unclear.

If we revisit Diamond's (1996: 23–24) characteristics of liberal democracy, we find that the governments of Corazon Aquino, Fidel Ramos, and Joseph Estrada have taken significant strides in consolidating Philippine democracy. In theory, and to a considerable degree in practice, executive power is constrained by the constitution and other government institutions. Groups which now embrace constitutional principles are free to form political parties and contest elections, with little regard to their prior political actions—including armed challenges to the Philippine state. In theory, and to a lesser degree in practice, the political process is open to all groups, regardless of such characteristics as class, culture, ethnicity, or religion. With the transition from authoritarian rule in 1986, Philippine citizens enjoy greater liberty to express and represent their interests. The range of choice of political parties has increased. The number and range of nongovernmental organizations have dramatically increased. Many alternative sources of information exist and the Philippine media are largely free of government interference. In theory and to a lesser extent in practice, Philippine citizens enjoy freedom of belief and expression.

However, the country still falls short of liberal democracy in a number of important regards. Given the continuing importance of the political role of the Philippine military, real power is incompletely vested in elected officials and their civilian appointees. Regional and provincial elites continue to hold considerable sway over the course of electoral politics. Among the poor, dependency relations, cultural norms, differentiated interests, repression, and existing electoral institutions stand as obstacles to effective mobilization and political participation. Many rural communities remain largely beyond the reach of the various independent media. The media's coverage of nontraditional political movements and organizations also bears improving. Individuals and organizations challenging the prevailing order still find themselves subject to detention, torture, disappearance, or extrajudicial killings at the hands of the police, military, paramilitary organizations, and insurgent groups. Many of the conditions around which the communist and Muslim insurgencies so successfully organized in the past persist. Particularly notable are the continuing human rights abuses and the extreme inequalities in wealth, both between socioeconomic classes and between Christians and Muslims. Philippine citizens do not receive equal protection under the law.

The legal system is marked by lengthy delays in judicial proceedings, corruption, and a bias in favor of individuals and corporations of influence and wealth. Notwithstanding the considerable progress in the Philippines, the imagery of democratic transition and consolidation thus masks important continuities with the authoritarian rule of Ferdinand Marcos and the exclusionary legacy of earlier "democratic" rule in the Philippines.

In the Philippines, as elsewhere, structural features constrained the democratic transition. The persistence of some of these features and the shortcomings of democratic consolidation in the Philippines reflect in part the contingent choices of leading political actors. The strong role of the Philippine military before and during the transition to democratic governance, the weakness of Philippine political parties, and the lack of democratic lower-class mobilization shaped and limited the processes of democratic transition and consolidation. At crucial junctures, key Philippine political actors have chosen not to address these constraints. As a result, Philippine democracy remains incomplete. To further the process of democratic consolidation, Philippine politicians must work to strengthen the capacity for civilian oversight of the military. They also must build upon the proliferation of nongovernmental and cause-oriented organizations to mobilize the electorate through disciplined and coherent parties. Failing this, the Estrada government and its successors will be ill-equipped to address the nation's myriad economic and social problems.

NOTES

1. This pattern of local and regional caciquism reflects the fragmented nature of precolonial Philippine society and the mode of Spanish and American colonial rule—indirect rule through collaborating elites. American introduction of elections in the early 1900s reinforced this local "bossism" (Sidel n.d.).

2. Landé 1996. With the exception of the Christian-Muslim conflict in Mindanao, ethnic diversity in the Philippines is dispersed, rather than centrally focused (Horowitz 1985). In turn, ethnic conflict tends to be localized rather than systemic, posing less threat to the Philippine state. Nonetheless, the ethnolinguistic diversity and attendant subnational loyalties hinder national and democratic consolidation.

3. On the similarities in the class composition and ideologies of the two parties, see Wurfel (1962); and Milne (1969). On patron-client dyads, see Landé (1977).

4. Discussions of martial-law-era politics can be found in Noble 1986; and de Guzman et al. 1977.

5. This interpretation is widely, though not universally, accepted. By contrast, Jose María Sison, founder of the CPP, emphasized the role of BAYAN and cause-oriented organizations of the left, the "hard core," in sustaining the revolutionary demonstrations at EDSA and in pressuring Malacañang. Remarks of Jose María Sison in Mercado 1986: 243.

6. Doeppers 1987: 280. One longtime observer of Philippine politics characterized the Aquino following as a "genuine populist movement," but attributed her popularity to the "affection and love that people have for her as a kind of Joan of Arc figure" (Shaplen 1986: 69; idem 1987: 57). Cardinal Jaime Sin used the same Joan of Arc imagery in his conversation with Mrs. Aquino when she first announced to him her intention to run for the presidency (Crisostomo 1987: 157).

7. The events of 1986 in the Philippines thus centered around a restoration of prior democratic institutions, distinguishing it from "third wave" transitions in countries which had never experienced democratic or semidemocratic rule. Mrs. Aquino identified her primary objective as "restoring democracy" (*Philippine Daily Inquirer,* March 1, 1986). This commitment can also be seen in the agenda Mrs. Aquino outlined for her first 100 days in office during a February 3, 1986, campaign speech. She promised a constitutional convention, an end to presidential decree-making authority, and the restoration of the writ of habeas corpus. She further pledged to end the media's progovernment bias and repeal legal prohibitions on the right to strike (*New York Times* 1986). Mrs. Aquino's second presidential proclamation restored the writ of habeas corpus (*Proclamation No. 2,* March 2, 1986).

8. Thompson 1989: 5. RAM members expressed concerns about corruption within the military and the Marcos government and the ineffectiveness of the military as a fighting force. RAM members attributed this ineffectiveness primarily to military leadership which rewarded loyalty over merit. Not coincidentally, the "overstaying" generals—those kept on by Marcos beyond retirement age—were blocking career advancement for the younger officers associated with RAM.

9. The military was thus particularly suspicious of two of Aquino's closest advisers, executive secretary Joker Arroyo and presidential spokesman Rene Saguisag. Both were leading human-rights lawyers in the Marcos years. Within the Aquino government both supported amnesty for erstwhile insurgents and punishment of military officers for human rights abuses.

10. The closest Mrs. Aquino came to promoting unity through her appointments was the prominence she accorded the so-called "Jesuit Mafia," Jesuit-trained advisers. Yet even among this group there existed significant ideological differences. Most notable of the Jesuit advisers were Jaime V. Ongpin, minister of finance, and Joaquin G. Bernas, president of Ateneo de Manila University. In addition to Ongpin, government appointees with strong Catholic ties included: Teodoro L. Locsin, Jr., minister of public information; Solita Collás-Monsod, minister of economic planning; and Aquilino Q. Pimentel, minister of local government. See Henares 1986; Youngblood 1987: 1248–49.

11. As the nonpolitical "housewife" of a martyred opposition figure, Mrs.

Aquino may have been acceptable to other prominent members of the opposition precisely because of her disinterest in politics. Her lack of political ambition left open the possiblity that these other figures could ascend to leadership in the post-transition regime.

12. Among the social democrats appointed were Jose Diokno (human affairs commissioner), Joker P. Arroyo (presidential executive secretary), Augusto S. Sanchez (minister of labor), Rene Saguisag (presidential spokesman), and Aquilino Pimentel (minister of local government). Thompson 1990: 4.

13. Despite the broad range of viewpoints represented in Aquino's selections, the appointment process drew criticism from Marcos loyalists and others. The critics urged election of the constitutional commissioners. In May 1986, the Catholic Bishops' Conference of the Philippines issued a pastoral exhortation in support of the selection process. Church officials and organizations, Catholic and Protestant, were also instrumental in facilitating public hearings on the new Constitution. Youngblood 1987: 1249–50.

14. Sacerdoti 1986b. Progressives included Jaime Tadeo, head of Kilusang Magbubukid ng Pilipinas (KMP, Peasant Movement of the Philippines) and Sister Christine Tan, a leading figure working with Manila's poor. Leading figures from the pre-Marcos era included Jose Laurel, former minority leader of the lower house, Celia Muñoz Palma, a retired Supreme Court Justice, and Napolean Rama, former vice-president of the 1971 Constitutional Convention (until his arrest under martial law). The Catholic Church was represented to varying degrees by Bishop Teodoro C. Bacani, Jr., Joaquin G. Bernas, S.J., president of (the Jesuit) Ateneo de Manila University, and Bernardo Villegas, a free-market economist. The KBL party members were: Blas Ople, former labor minister, and former members of Congress, Alejandro Almendres, Teodulo Natividad, Regalado Maambong, and Restituto de los Reyes.

15. In the event, Aquino nonetheless was criticized for her use of executive power in selecting the 1986 Constitutional Commission. Marcos's involvement in the constitutional deliberations of 1972–73 was of a quite different nature. A Constitutional Commission (ConCom) was elected in 1970, but was still meeting in late 1972. The drafting process was extremely slow, reflecting weak leadership and the enormous number of resolutions under consideration. The deliberations suggested widespread hostility to any changes (including shifting to a parliamentary system) that might facilitate continuation of Marcos's rule; this despite Marcos's sizable cash contributions to ConCom delegates regarded as pliable. With martial law came the arrest of more than a dozen ConCom delegates. Thereafter, a new constitutional draft was prepared in close consultation with the president and was quickly approved. Marcos thereupon decreed the existence of new "Citizens' Assemblies," convened the assemblies and obtained ratification of the new constitution. Though the Supreme Court held that this procedure did not comply with applicable constitutional provisions, it dismissed legal challenges to the constitution in acknowledgment of Marcos's dominance through force (Wurfel 1988: 106–17).

16. To this extent, the early period of democratic consolidation involved an explicit consideration of alternative institutional arrangements for Philip-

pine democracy (see Brillantes 1988: 127–28). Under the influence of Manuel Quezon, the 1935 Constitution provided Philippine presidents with an array of powers—among them explicit emergency powers, wide discretion in the issuance of executive orders, and general control of local government—not found in the United States.

17. U.S. Department of State 1998:12. Newly elected President Estrada (1998—2004) has proposed legislation which would enfranchise overseas Filipinos.

18. In Remmer's schema the degree of political inclusiveness is determined by formal rates of electoral participation—inclusive democracies are those in which 30 percent or more of the total population participates in elections (1985–86).

19. Conversations with Akbayan party officials, February 16, 1998. This concern does not appear to have been borne out by the 1998 election results, but it may be in future elections.

20. Identified with the LDP were 186 of the 204 members of the Philippine House of Representatives and 7 of the 24 Senators.

21. During the 1998 campaign, presidential-aspirant Estrada pledged to abolish these discretionary accounts.

22. General Fabian Ver, the Marcos-loyalist par excellence, concurrently commanded the Presidential Security Unit, the National Intelligence and Security Authority, and the National Intelligence Board. Ver's chief rival within the military was General Fidel V. Ramos, head of the Philippine Constabulary (and a cousin of Marcos).

23. For discussions of the status and abuses of vigilante groups, private armies, civilian armed forces, and the military, see LCHR 1988; idem 1990; and van der Kroef 1988.

24. The most notable occasion being a speech made in praise of Alsa Masa (variously translated Risen Masses, Masses Uprising, or Masses Arise) on October 23, 1987, in Davao City, Mindanao (*Manila Chronicle* 1987). In October 1987, government guidelines on anticommunist citizens' groups were released, which provided among other things that membership be voluntary, that members be "thoroughly screened," and that such groups operate "exclusively for self-defense." See LCHR 1988: xvi.

25. Executive Order No. 264, July 25, 1987 ("Providing for Citizen Armed Force"). For a discussion of the overlap between CHDF and CAFGU personnel, see Asia Watch 1990: 41–44.

26. General Fidel V. Ramos was constantly cautioning Mrs. Aquino about a possible backlash within the military in the event she initiated prosecutions for human rights. Interviews with Congressman Florencio B. Abad, June 21, 1989, and Congressman Bonifacio H. Gillego, June 17, 1989. The late Gaston Ortigas ascribed the concern with the fragility of the Aquino coalition to her advisers rather than to Aquino personally (interview, June 22, 1989). Ultimately Aquino was responsible for the policy decisions of her government; she chose the path of concessions to the military.

27. I am indebted to Sheila Coronel and her colleagues at the Philippine

Center for Investigative Journalism for compiling this list and making it available to me. See also Reyes 1993.

28. Jovito Salonga's slate included only one retired officer.

29. Ramos 1995: 34. As Bienen notes in another context, one of the central lines of argument intended to legitimize military involvement in political and economic development is that the "military is often, but not always, the most modern institution in terms of its advanced technology, educated elite, absorption of rational norms, division of labor, and exposure to western influence" (1968: xv, citing Pye 1962). See also Huntington 1968: 201.

30. This discussion owes much to Kohli 1987: 43.

31. For example, the agrarian reform-related interests of landless agricultural laborers and tenant farmers are not synonymous, as reform outcomes in other settings have demonstrated. The redistribution of the coastal sugar haciendas in Peru directly benefited the permanent agricultural laborers, while temporary and migratory laborers were largely denied land rights (McClintock 1981: 63, 73). The redistribution of tenanted holdings in Kerala State, India, benefited tenants, frequently at the expense of the landless laborers who actually cultivated the affected parcels (Herring 1983: 180–216).

32. This has been a repeated theme in interviews with landless and near-landless peasant cultivators since 1986. See generally, Doronila 1985; Landé 1977. Sidel (n.d.) and Landé (1996) argue that these relationships have become increasingly instrumental, with immediate material gains figuring more prominently in the calculations of the poor and disadvantaged "clients."

33. McCoy 1991. The teams conducted a three-day, live-in seminar, gathering the entire labor force together to view pictures of NPA atrocities and screen films such as "The Killing Fields," which depicted communist atrocities in Pol Pot's Cambodia. The military typically described the NFSW as a communist-front organization. At the seminar's end the workers were pressured to "surrender" and pledge allegiance to the Aquino government in a mass "graduation" ceremony. See Rutten 1992.

34. Similar debates have marked many "third wave" democratic transitions: African countries frequently have chosen parliamentary systems, Latin American countries generally have chosen presidential systems. The scholarly arguments in support of parliamentarism are summarized in Abad 1997; Linz 1990a; idem 1990b; Stepan and Skach 1993. The merits of presidentialism, particularly when coupled with electoral rules that favor the emergence of effective legislative majorities, are discussed in Jones 1994a; idem 1994b; Mainwaring and Shugart 1997; Shugart and Carey 1992.

REFERENCES

Abad, Florencio. 1997. "Should the Philippines Turn Parliamentary: The Challenge of Democratic Consolidation and Institutional Reform." In Soliman M. Santos, Jr., Florencio Abad, Joel Rocamora, and Chay Florentino-

Hofileña, eds. *Shift,* pp. 48–89. Manila: Ateneo Center for Social Policy and Public Affairs.

Amnesty International, 1991. *Philippines: Human Rights Violations and the Labour Movement.* New York: Amnesty International. June.

Anderson, Benedict. 1988. "Cacique Democracy in the Philippines: Origins and Dreams." *New Left Review* 169 (May/June), pp. 3–31.

Asia Watch, 1990. *The Philippines: Violations of the Laws of War by Both Sides.* New York: August.

Bienen, Henry, ed., 1968. *The Military Intervenes: Case Studies in Political Development.* New York: Russell Sage.

Brillantes, Alex B., Jr. 1988. "The Executive." In Raul P. de Guzman and Mila A. Reforma, eds., *Government and Politics of the Philippines,* pp. 113–31. Singapore: Oxford University Press.

Crisostomo, Isabelo T. 1987. *Cory: Profile of a President.* Boston: Branden Publishing.

Dahl, Robert A. 1971. *Polyarchy: Participation and Opposition.* New Haven: Yale University Press.

de Guzman, Raul P., Arturo G. Pacho, Ma. Aurora A. Carbonell, and Vicente D. Mariano. 1977. "Citizen Participation and Decision-Making Under Martial Law Administration: A Search for a Viable Political System." *Philippine Journal of Public Administration* 21, no. 1 (January): 1–19.

Diamond, Larry. 1992. "Economic Development and Democracy Reconsidered." *American Behavioral Scientist* 35 (May-June).

——. 1996. "Is the Third Wave Over?" *Journal of Democracy* 7, no. 3 (July): 20–37.

Diamond, Larry, Juan J. Linz, and Seymour Martin Lipset. 1990. "Introduction." In Larry Diamond, Juan J. Linz, and Seymour Martin Lipset, eds. *Politics in Developing Countries: Comparing Experiences with Democracy.* Boulder: Lynne Rienner, pp. 1–37.

Doronila, Armando. 1985. "The Transformation of Patron-Client Relations and Its Political Consequences in the Philippines." *Journal of Southeast Asian Studies* 16, no. 1 (March): 99–116.

——. 1996. "Pork Corrupts Budget." *Philippine Daily Inquirer.* August 4, p. 1.

Esman, Milton J., and Norman Uphoff. 1984. *Local Organizations: Intermediaries in Rural Development.* Ithaca: Cornell University Press.

Gunther, Richard, P. Nikiforos Diamandouros and Hans-Jürgen Puhle. 1996. "O'Donnell's 'Illusions': A Rejoinder." *Journal of Democracy* 7, no. 4 (October): 151–59.

Gutierrez, Eric. 1994. *The Ties That Bind: A Guide to Family, Business and Other Interests in the Ninth House of Representatives.* Pasig, Metro Manila: Philippine Center for Investigative Journalism.

Henares, Hilarion M., Jr. 1986. "Snow White's Seven Dwarfs: The Jesuit Mafia." *Philippine Daily Inquirer.* March 22.

Hernandez, Carolina G. 1985. "Constitutional Authoritarianism and the Prospects of Democracy in the Philippines." *Journal of International Affairs* 38, no. 2 (Winter): 243–58.

———. 1996. "The Philippines in 1995: Growth Amid Challenges." *Asian Survey* 26, no. 2 (February): 142–51.

———. 1997. "The Philippines in 1996: A House Finally in Order?" *Asian Survey* 27, no. 2 (February): 204–11.

Herring, Ronald J. 1981. "Embedded Production Relations and the Rationality of Peasant Quiescence in Tenure Reform." *Journal of Peasant Studies* 8, no. 2 (January): 131–72.

———. 1983. *Land to the Tiller: The Political Economy of Agrarian Reform in South Asia.* New Haven: Yale University Press.

Florentino-Hofileña, Chay. 1997. "Tracking the Charter Amendment Debate: 1995–Mid-March 1997." In Soliman M. Santos, Jr., Florencio Abad, Joel Rocamora, and Chay Florentino-Hofileña, eds., *Shift*, pp. 134–69. Manila: Ateneo Center for Social Policy and Public Affairs.

Horowitz, Donald. 1985. *Ethnic Groups in Conflict.* Berkeley: University of California Press.

Huntington, Samuel P. 1968. *Political Order in Changing Societies.* New Haven: Yale University Press.

———. 1991a. *The Third Wave: Democratization in the Late Twentieth Century.* Norman: University of Oklahoma Press.

———. 1991b. "Democracy's Third Wave." *Journal of Democracy* 2, no. 2 (Spring): 12–34.

———. 1995. "Reforming Civil-Military Relations." *Journal of Democracy* 6, no. 4 (October): 9–17.

Hutchcroft, Paul. 1991. "Oligarchs and Cronies in the Philippine State: The Politics of Patrimonial Plunder." *World Politics* 43, no. 3 (April): 414–50.

Institute for Popular Democracy (IPD). 1987. *Encore: Between Honesty and Hope.* Manila: IPD, May 30.

Jackman, Robert. 1986. "Elections and the Democratic Class Struggle." *World Politics* 39, no. 1 (October): 123–46.

Jones, Mark P. 1994a. "Electoral Laws and the Survival of Presidential Democracies," Ph.D. diss., University of Michigan.

———. 1994b. "Presidential Elections and Multipartism in Latin America." *Political Research Quarterly* 47, no. 1 (March): 41–57.

Karl, Terry Lynn. 1990. "Dilemmas of Democratization in Latin America." *Comparative Politics* 23 (October): 1–21.

Kohli, Atul. 1987. *The State and Poverty in India: The Politics of Reform.* Cambridge: Cambridge University Press.

Landé, Carl H. 1977. "Networks and Groups in Southeast Asia: Some Observations on the Group Theory of Politics." In Steffen W. Schmidt, James C. Scott, Carl Landé, and Laura Guasti, eds., *Friends, Followers, and Factions: A Reader in Political Clientelism*, pp. 75–99. Berkeley: University of California Press.

———. 1996. *Post-Marcos Politics: A Geographical and Statistical Analysis of the 1992 Presidential Election.* Singapore: Institute of Southeast Asian Studies and New York: St. Martin's Press.

Landé, Carl H., and Richard Hooley. 1986. "Aquino Takes Charge." *Foreign Affairs* 64, no. 5 (Summer): 1087–107.

LCHR (Lawyers Committee for Human Rights). 1988. *Vigilantes in the Philippines: A Threat to Democratic Rule.* New York: LCHR.

———. 1990. *Out of Control: Militia Abuses in the Philippines.* New York: LCHR. September.

Linz, Juan J. 1990a. "The Perils of Presidentialism." *Journal of Democracy* 1, no. 1 (Winter): 51–69.

———. 1990b. "The Virtues of Parliamentarianism." *Journal of Democracy* 1, no. 4 (Fall): 84–91.

Linz, Juan, and Alfred Stepan. 1996. "Toward Consolidated Democracies." *Journal of Democracy* 7, no. 2 (April): 14–33.

Lipset, Seymour M. 1959. "Some Social Requisites of Democracy: Economic Development and Political Legitimacy." *American Political Science Review* 53, no. 1 (March): 69–105.

Mainwaring, Scott. 1998. "Party Systems in the Third Wave." *Journal of Democracy* 9, no. 3 (July): 67–81.

Mainwaring, Scott, and Matthew S. Shugart. 1997. "Juan Linz, Presidentialism, and Democracy: A Critical Appraisal." *Comparative Politics* 29, no. 4 (July): 449–71.

Manila Chronicle. 1987. "Cory Backs Alsa Masa." October 24.

McClintock, Cynthia. 1981. *Peasant Cooperatives and Political Change in Peru.* Princeton: Princeton University Press.

McCoy, Alfred. 1991. "The Restoration of Planter Power in La Carlota City." In Benedict J. Kerkvliet and Resil B. Mojares, eds., *From Marcos to Aquino: Local Perspectives on Political Transition in the Philippines,* pp. 105–42. Quezon City: Ateneo de Manila University Press.

Mercado, Monina A. 1986. *People Power: An Eyewitness History of the Philippine Revolution of 1986.* Manila: James B. Reuter, S.J., Foundation.

Milne, R. S. 1969. "The Filipino Party System." In José V. Abueva and Raul P. de Guzman, eds., *Foundations and Dynamics of Filipino Government and Politics,* pp. 181–87. Manila: Bookmark.

Mydans, Seth. 1987. "Right-Wing Vigilantes Spread in Philippines." *New York Times* April 4.

NEDA (National Economic and Development Authority). 1986. *Medium Term Development Plan 1987–1992.* Manila: NEDA, November.

———. 1998a. "Poverty and Equity Indicators." http://localweb.neda.gov.ph/~ioneda/cgi-b . . . national/income/poverty__equity__indicators__a.sc.

———. 1998b. "Employment Indicator." http://localweb.neda.gov.ph/~ioneda/cgi-b . . . national/labor/employment__indicators__a.sc.

NSO (National Statistics Office). 1998. "Quikstat-March 1998." http://www.census.gov.ph/data/quikstat/qs9803tb.html.

New York Times. 1986. "Aquino Gives New Policy Details and Labels Marcos a 'Pharaoh.'" February 4.

Noble, Lela Garner. 1986. "Politics in the Marcos Era." In John Bresnan, ed.,

Crisis in the Philippines: The Marcos Era and Beyond, pp. 70–113. Princeton: Princeton University Press.

Nocum, Armand. 1996. "P7-B Pork Went to Public Works." *Philippine Daily Inquirer.* July 27, p. 1.

O'Donnell, Guillermo, and Philippe C. Schmitter. 1986. *Transitions from Authoritarian Rule: Tentative Conclusions about Uncertain Democracies.* Baltimore: Johns Hopkins University Press.

Peterman, John. 1988. "Democracy and the Dynasties." *Far Eastern Economic Review* January 14, pp. 19–21.

Philippine Daily Inquirer. 1998. "Comelec Fails Test." Editorial. February 8.

Popkin, Samuel L. 1981. "Public Choice and Rural Development: Free Riders, Lemons, and Institutional Design." In Clifford S. Russell and Norman Nicholson, eds., *Public Choice and Rural Development*, pp. 43–80. Washington, D.C.: Resources for the Future.

Pye, Lucian W. 1962. "Armies in the Process of Political Modernization," in John J. Johnson, ed., *The Role of the Military in Underdeveloped Countries.* Princeton: Princeton University Press.

Ramos, Fidel V. 1995. "Catalyst for Change," *Asiaweek* January 20, pp. 34–35.

Remmer, Karen L. 1985/1986. "Exclusionary Democracy." *Studies in Comparative International Development* 20, no. 4 (Winter): 64–85.

———. 1991. "New Wine or Old Bottlenecks? The Study of Latin American Democracy." *Comparative Politics* 24, no. 1 (July): 479–95.

Reyes, Wilfredo G. 1993. "Is There an Issue at All?" *Business World* March 15, p. 1.

Riedinger, Jeffrey M. 1994. "The Philippines in 1993: Halting Steps Toward Liberalization," *Asian Survey* 34, no. 2 (February): 139–46.

Rutten, Rosanne. 1992. "'Mass Surrenders' in Negros Occidental: Ideology, Force and Accommodation in a Counterinsurgency Program." Paper presented at the Fourth International Philippine Studies Conference. Canberra, July 1–3.

Sacerdoti, Guy. 1986a. "Shadow of the Past." *Far Eastern Economic Review* May 29, pp. 42–43.

———. 1986b. "Cory's basic-law makers." *Far Eastern Economic Review* June 5.

Santos, Soliman M., Jr., Florencio Abad, Joel Rocamora, and Chay Florentino-Hofileña, eds. 1997. *Shift.* Manila: Ateneo Center for Social Policy and Public Affairs.

Shaplen, Robert. 1986. "Reporter at Large: From Marcos to Aquino." *The New Yorker.* August 25 and September 1.

———. 1987. "Reporter at Large: The Thin Edge." *The New Yorker.* September 21 and 28.

Shugart, Matthew S., and John M. Carey. 1992. *Presidents and Assemblies: Constitutional Design and Electoral Dynamics.* Cambridge: Cambridge University Press.

Sidel, John T. n.d. *Coercion, Capital and Crime: Bossism in the Philippines.* Forthcoming. Palo Alto: Stanford University Press.

Simons, Lewis M. 1987. *Worth Dying For.* New York: Morrow.

Steinberg, David Joel. 1994. *The Philippines: A Singular and a Plural Place.* Boulder: Westview Press.

Stepan, Alfred. 1988. *Rethinking Military Politics: Brazil and the Southern Cone.* Princeton: Princeton University Press.

Stepan, Alfred, and Cindy Skach. 1993. "Constitutional Frameworks and Democratic Consolidation: Parliamentarianism versus Presidentialism." *World Politics* 46 (October)ı 1–22.

Suh, Sangwon, and Antonio Lopez. 1998. "At the Starting Blocks." *Asiaweek* (February 20): 16–18.

Thompson, Mark R. 1989. "Cory and 'the Guy': Reformist Politics in the Philippines." Field Staff Reports Asia No. 16. Universities Field Staff International. March.

——. 1990. "The 'Little Left' in the Politics of the Philippines." Field Staff Report No. 17. Universities Field Staff International. April.

Timberman, David G. 1991. *A Changeless Land: Continuity and Change in Philippine Politics.* New York: M. E. Sharpe.

United States Department of State. 1998. "The Philippines Country Report on Human Rights Practices for 1997." (January 30). (http://www.state.gov/www/global/human_rights/1997_hrp_report/philippi.html).

Van der Kroef, Justus M. 1988. "The Philippines: Day of the Vigilantes." *Asian Survey* 28, no. 6 (June): 630–49.

Vanzi, Sol Jose. 1998a. "No Guns, No Bodyguards for Candidates." *Philippine Headline News Online* (http://www.interlog.com/~leeq/fccs/199801/pe/pe000136.htm). January 3.

——. 1998b. "285 Towns are Election 'Hot Spots.'" *Philippine Headline News Online* (http://www.interlog.com/~leeq/fccs/199801/pe/pe000174.htm). January 28.

——. 1998c. "MILF Orders Election Boycott." *Philippine Headline News Online* (http://www.interlog.com/~leeq/fccs/199802/pe/pe000187.htm). February 6.

——. 1998d. "More Candidates, Fewer Voters in '98." *Philippine Headline News Online* (http://www.interlog.com/~leeq/fccs/199803/pe/pe000265.htm). March 18.

Wurfel, David. 1962. "The Philippine Elections: Support for Democracy." *Asian Survey* 2, no. 3 (May): 25–37.

——. 1988. *Filipino Politics: Development and Decay.* Ithaca: Cornell University Press and Ateneo de Manila University Press. (Page citations are to Ateneo University Press edition.)

Youngblood, Robert L. 1987. "The Corazon Aquino 'Miracle' and the Philippine Churches." *Asian Survey* 27, no. 12 (December): 1240–55.

7

"Waiting for Democracy" in Mexico: Cultural Change and Institutional Reform

Howard Handelman

El problema de la democracia mexicana hoy se puede resumir así: la élite no quiere y la sociedad no puede.
(The problem of Mexican democracy today can be summed up as follows: the elite doesn't want it and society can't achieve it)
    Lorenzo Meyer (1992: 175)

FOR MORE THAN TWO decades Mexico has been moving slowly and unevenly from a one-party-dominant, authoritarian system to a semidemocratic one.[1] Institutional reforms since the mid-1970s have facilitated the registration of opposition parties, mandated ever-greater opposition representation in Congress, restructured the Supreme Court, established independent oversight of the electoral process, and, for the first time, permitted serious electoral challenges to the official party (the PRI) at the state and national levels (Alonso, Aziz and Tamayo 1992; Dresser 1996).

As a result, the 1994 presidential election (or at least the vote count), won by PRI candidate Ernesto Zedillo, was the cleanest in modern Mexican history. More significantly, in the 1997 congressional elections, the PRI lost control of the Chamber of Deputies (the more powerful, lower house of Congress) for the first time since the country's ruling party was founded in 1929. Opposition parties also won the high-profile governorship in Mexico City (a position previously named by the president) and two of six gubernatorial elections. Thus, while the official party still controls the all-powerful presidency, nearly seventy years of hegemonic rule by the PRI-state may finally be drawing to an end.[2] For now, however, the country still suffers from a measure of political repres-

218

sion, government-influenced media coverage, local and state electoral fraud, and other manifestations of a semiauthoritarian regime (Pérez Barbosa 1994).

Not long ago, one of Mexico's leading intellectuals, Lorenzo Meyer, compared his country's anticipation of democracy to Samuel Becket's *Waiting for Godot*. Two characters alternate between hope and despair, expecting the arrival of the mysterious Godot. As the play ends, Godot has not arrived but the protagonists still have not abandoned hope (Meyer 1986; 1991: 2). Despite Meyer's pessimism (more recently expressed in the opening quotation, above) it may be that, for Mexico, Godot is finally arriving.

During the late 1970s and early 1980s, when bureaucratic-authoritarian (BA) regimes still prevailed in Brazil and South America's southern cone (Argentina, Chile, and Uruguay) and repressive military dictatorships dominated much of Central America, Mexico's hegemonic party-state, for all its flaws, was considered one of the region's less authoritarian regimes. Today, after a wave of democratization has swept the hemisphere, Mexico's political system ranks as one of the region's least democratic. To be sure, Mexico is no more authoritarian than it was a decade ago. To the contrary! But as most Latin American countries have moved toward reasonably competitive national elections, Mexico seemed to have been passed by, at least until 1997. Though never as repressive as Argentina, El Salvador, or Guatemala in their dark, recent pasts, Mexican politics is still marred by intimidation and substantial human rights violations, particularly outside the country's urban centers (as evidenced by the December 1997 massacre of nearly fifty peasants, mostly women and children, in the state of Chiapas).

In response to a series of challenges—from the massive student protest (and the massacre of several hundred protestors) in 1968, through a sharp decline in presidential legitimacy in the 1970s, the debt crisis of the 1980s, a particularly tainted presidential election in 1988, the 1994 Zapatista guerrilla uprising in Chiapas, renewed economic collapse in 1994–95, massive corruption, narco-politics, and a series of high-profile but yet unsolved political assassinations at the close of the Salinas administration (1988–94)—the ruling political establishment has been forced to liberalize the political system and open the field to opposition candidates. Increasingly, election results have been fairly tallied, but electoral races remain unfairly contested. As just noted, in recent years opposition candidates have won the governorship of Mexico City and a majority in the Chamber of Deputies. And the major opposition party on the right, the PAN (National Action Party), now holds six gubernatorial posts. But the PRI's string of presidential victories, in a system dominated by the executive, remains unbroken. And, it is still not clear whether an opposition presidential victory is possible in the near future.

THE NATURE OF MEXICO'S AUTHORITARIAN SYSTEM

Before examining the prospects for Mexican democracy, I first need to outline the major characteristics of the country's embattled authoritarian regime. The party-state regime has differed from Latin America's authoritarian norm in that it is civilian dominated (with fairly well established control over the armed forces). And, unlike communist or fascist regimes, it has allowed, even encouraged, opposition parties. Consequently, many important works on Latin America's democratic transition pay relatively scant attention to Mexico (O'Donnell and Schmitter 1986; Malloy and Seligson 1987; Huntington 1991; Przeworski 1991; Diamond and Plattner 1993).[3] Indeed, because of the appearances of electoral contestation, Mexico's party-state hegemony prior to the 1990s was sometimes mistakenly labeled as quasi-democratic.

The centerpiece of the nation's modern political system has been the official party, founded in 1929 to restore order after the carnage of the revolutionary war (1910–20) and its aftermath. Its initial purpose was "the control of *caudillos* and *caciques* [regional and local strongmen]" and rationalizing the party system (González Casanova 1970: 34). In time, the party developed a corporatist structure that afforded representation to the major social groups in the revolutionary coalition: peasants, unionized blue-collar workers and white-collar employees (especially those in the state sector), and a wide range of middle-class groups. For nearly sixty years its primary objective has been winning elections, regulating the circulation of political elites, mobilizing popular support for the president and his policies, and legitimizing the regime. Into the 1980s, the PRI succeeded admirably in all of those goals. But, while it created new channels for mass mobilization, the party's corporatist structure also enabled Mexico's political elite to weaken and exclude contending labor unions, peasant groups, and middle-class organizations that might challenge the official party's dominance.

Unlike Leninist systems, Mexico's party-state, even in its most authoritarian formulation, did not impose a single-party system. To the contrary, its leaders long encouraged controlled opposition in order to maintain the facade of competitive elections and thereby increase regime legitimacy (Molinar Horcasitas 1996). As Alan Riding (1984: 135) has observed: "Without formal opposition, elections would be meaningless. And without elections the system would lose its mask of democratic legitimacy." Opinion polls from the 1960s (Almond and Verba 1963) into the 1980s indicate the effectiveness of this strategy. While Mexicans have doubted the integrity of their electoral process—in one 1988 poll only 8.3 percent of all respondents expressed confidence in it (Morris 1995: 130)—at least until recently most continued to support the PRI and to tell pollsters that they believed that the electoral process was important.

It is one thing, however, for the PRI-state to foster opposition. It is quite another to allow the opposition to win. Unlike hegemonic party systems such as Japan's or Sweden's, until recently Mexico's opposition parties had no realistic chance of winning major offices. Using patronage, state subsidies, vote-rigging, and, when necessary, intimidation, the PRI never faced a serious presidential challenge nor did it loose a single senatorial or gubernatorial election until 1988.

Before the 1978 electoral reform law, the only authentic opposition party permitted was the PAN (National Action Party) whose presidential vote slowly grew from 7.8 percent (1952) to 15.7 percent (1982). A few left-of-center, parastatal or "satellite" parties provided an extremely loyal "opposition," generally endorsing the PRI presidential candidate. But when both parastatal parties backed the PRI in the 1976 presidential race and the PAN chose not to run, PRI nominee José López Portillo was put in the embarrassing position of winning over 92 percent of the valid vote (table 1). Two years later, desiring to resuscitate a legitimizing opposition, Congress passed legislation facilitating the registration of additional political parties, effectively legalizing authentic (nonparastatal) opposition parties on the left (Molinar Horcasitas, 1996).

THE FOUNDATIONS OF HEGEMONIC SURVIVAL

Following the collapse of communist rule in the Soviet Union, the PRI became the world's most enduring ruling party. PRI-state hegemony has now lasted for seventy years. As the country has developed economically and socially, its failure to democratize correspondingly has seemingly defied many critical assumptions of modernization theory. As of 1990 Mexico had a real GDP (PPP) per capita of nearly $6,000, an adult literacy rate of 88 percent, and a Human Development Index (HDI) of .805 (UNDP 1993: 135). On these and other standard measures of development Mexico falls within the upper ranks of Latin American and other third-world countries. Its literacy rate and GNP per capita have long passed the thresholds beyond which democracy becomes probable (Seligson 1987).

Similarly, Mexico apparently failed to fulfill expectations that a

TABLE 1

Mexican Presidential Election Results: 1929–1994

YEAR	PRI	PAN	FDN OR PRD	OTHER*
1929	93.55	—	—	6.45
1934	98.19	—	—	1.81
1940	93.89	—	—	6.11
1946	77.90	—	—	22.10
1952	74.31	7.82	—	17.87
1958	90.43	9.42	—	0.15
1964	88.82	11.05	—	1.03
1970	84.13	13.85	—	2.03
1976	92.27	—	—	7.63
1982	71.00	15.68	—	15.89
1988	50.74	16.80	32.50	—
1994	53.40	28.60	18.00	—

* Includes votes for parastatals and invalid votes.

Sources: Pablo González Casanova, *El estado y los partidos políticos en México,* 3d edit. (México, D.F.: Ediciones Era, 1986), pp. 132–34; Dale Story, *The Mexican Ruling Party* (New York: Praeger, 1986), p. 52; María Amparo Casar, *The 1994 Mexican Presidential Elections* (London: Institute of Latin American Studies, 1995), pp. 14 and 18; Comisión Federal Electoral and Instituto Federal Electoral; Ann Craig and Wayne Cornelius, "House Divided: Parties and Political Reform in Mexico," in *Building Democratic Institutions: Party Systems in Latin America,* ed. Scott Mainwaring and Timothy Scully (Stanford: Stanford University Press, 1995), p. 258.

growing working class would become a powerful force for democratization (Rueschemeyer, Huber Stephens, and Stephens 1992). The country's industrial takeoff—from the early 1940s into the 1970s—produced one of Latin America's largest working classes, with a significant portion of urban workers organized into labor unions. Today labor unions represent about 20 percent of the urban EAP (down somewhat from the 1970s), a level somewhat higher than that of the United States (Bizberg 1993: 303). Yet, excepting a small independent sector, Mexico's boss-controlled labor movement has been a pillar of the PRI machine and one of the most vigorous opponents of democratic reform.

In short, at least until recently, Mexico's long-standing authoritarianism has seemed to defy the country's relatively advanced socioeconomic and institutional development. Why has Mexico been so resistant to democracy? How has the PRI-state regime managed to maintain its hegemony for so long? And, what are the prospects for a successful democratic transition in the near future? The following section focuses on several explanatory factors: corporatist institutions that foster an unusual form of inclusionary authoritarianism, the PRI-state's mixture of co-optive and coercive techniques, and a conservative political culture.

Inclusionary Authoritarianism

Most authoritarian governments in Latin America, particularly the bureaucratic-authoritarian regimes that governed from the 1960s through the 1980s, have been exclusionary, prohibiting mass demonstrations and other independent political gatherings, banning unions and political party activity, and terminating electoral politics. In fact, a fundamental objective of the BA regimes in Argentina, Brazil, Chile, and Uruguay was the demobilization of labor unions and leftist political parties (Collier 1979). Mexico's modern political system, on the other hand, has been purposefully inclusionary from its inception. The government nurtured the growth of urban labor unions and developed peasant federations while incorporating both groups into the PRI (along with the growing urban middle class and, for the party's first decade, the military). As a leading Mexican analyst, Denise Dresser, notes (1996: 178), "the groups incorporated into the [party] were highly representative of society at the time, and this lent exceptional legitimacy to the PRI." In time, organized groups as diverse as small businessmen, mariachi bands, taxi drivers, and shoe-shine men were incorporated.

Furthermore, unlike most authoritarian regimes, Mexico's party-state has usually favored co-optation over coercion, when feasible, as a mode of political control. Consequently, militant peasants, labor, and student groups often dance a delicate minuet with government officials in which the former must demonstrate their capacity to mobilize support and to pressure the government while at the same time being careful not to push authorities too far. The state, in turn, lays out limits as to what type of political protest it will tolerate, while offering payoffs to groups (or their leaders) amenable to abiding by the rules of the game. In her discussion of Mexican rural politics, Judith Hellman (1979: 109–19) describes "the politics of tamales," that very balance between independent peasant mobilization and the willingness to work within the system at the appropriate time. Hellman focuses on the communist-led Central Union of peasants in the cotton-growing Laguna region. Over the years, the union moderated its demands and its tactics, eventually reaching a beneficial accommodation with the regime, "opposing the government less, but winning more in the way of economic benefits for its constituency." More recently, Marxist-led peasant organizations such as UNORCA (National Union of Autonomous Regional Peasant Organizations) have reached similar accommodations with the system (Harvey 1991). And, after an initial period of repression, the national government has responded to the 1994 Chiapas uprising and the continuing standoff with the Zapatista rebels (the EZLN) with traditionally co-optive tactics (though state and local party-state officials have been far more repressive).

In dealing with student protest, the government has demonstrated a similar blend of repression and co-optation. When the student demonstrations of 1968 exceeded the regime's tolerance limits, army troops murdered over 200 protestors in the traumatic Tlatelolco massacre. Where possible, however, the regime prefers co-optation. Indeed, whereas university student leaders were until quite recently the primary targets of rightist death squads in neighboring Guatemala, Mexico's student activists have often been brought into the PRI-state apparatus. For example, Manuel Camacho, the first government negotiator with the Zapatista rebels and initially a leading contender for the PRI 1994 presidential nomination, was a student activist in the 1968 protest demonstrations.[4]

Corporatism and Patronage

Until the 1990s opportunities for individual membership in the PRI were limited. Instead, the party's corporatist structure captured unions, peasant federations, and professional associations into each sector's hierarchy. As the Mexican economy expanded rapidly from the 1940s into the 1970s, the state benevolently dispensed patronage and other financial benefits to organized groups that demonstrated their loyalty to the PRI. In rural villages and urban slums throughout the country, the PRI faithful have been rewarded with agricultural credits, roads, irrigation, schools, potable water, paved streets, and public housing. The party-state not only dispenses government jobs, but controls licenses for taxi drivers, shoe-shine men, newspaper vendors, and many others who dutifully work for the PRI during every election. Other public goods such as subsidized food and gasoline prices have also been used to augment public support for the regime.

In the wake of Mexico's deep economic depression in the 1980s, President Carlos Salinas introduced the National Solidarity Program (PRONASOL), a massive public-works and grass-roots mobilization program in low-income urban neighborhoods and peasant communities. Designed to restore some of the sharp cuts in social spending that had transpired earlier in the decade, the program allocated up to $2.5 billion

(2 percent of GDP) annually to school construction, public health and nutrition programs, electrification, paving of streets and roads, and extending potable water (Cornelius, Craig and Fox 1994: 8 and 89). PRONASOL's political objectives were to restore popular support for the government (following Carlos Salinas's weak performance in the 1988 presidential election) and to provide the president with a power base somewhat independent of the PRI, both of which it accomplished quite successfully.[5] Funds were targeted particularly toward states where the PRD, the major left-of-center opposition party, had fared well in earlier elections. Following a renewed economic collapse at the end of 1994, the Zedillo administration (1994 to present) initiated more modest, targeted efforts aimed at ameliorating the costs of economic stabilization.

Caciquismo and Political Repression

Although Mexico's national political leaders have increasingly turned to co-optive tactics to bind the lower classes to the PRI, many local and state political bosses still control their populations through intimidation, particularly in the countryside. Local *caciquismo* (bossism) long predates the revolution but has been practiced by the official party as well. As with machine-dominated systems worldwide, it is ironically the most vulnerable members of society, those who benefit least from the social-political order, who generally most loyally support the ruling party at the polls. Thus, the PRI vote is strongest in rural areas and in states with the most impoverished and most heavily indigenous (Indian) populations. In the 1988 presidential election, many rural districts in the states of Chiapas, Nuevo León, Guerrero, Oaxaca, Veracruz, Sinaloa, Puebla, and Yucatán allegedly cast *all* of their votes for the PRI, sometimes casting more votes than the number of registered voters (Aziz Nassif and Molinar Horcasitas 1990: 170). In that election Salinas received his most overwhelming victory margin in Chiapas, the nation's poorest state, where, according to the official tally, more than 90 percent of the voters supported the PRI candidate a scant six years before the same state spawned the Zapatista rebellion.

While the peasants' need for government-supplied or state-subsidized goods and services underlies the party's heavy rural support, fear and intimidation play important roles as well. In many communities local bosses and their extended families wield virtually absolute economic and political power. A National Autonomous University (UNAM) sociologist involved in rural development projects recently told me of his experience working in a coastal community in Oaxaca, one of Mexico's poorest and most indigenous states. When village fisherman and farmers organized to challenge the town *cacique*'s monopoly over local transport, their leader was killed in broad daylight by several of the *cacique*'s relatives. They murdered the protest leader with a machete in front of a number of witnesses and then quartered his body. Elsewhere, local-level violence and intimidation have escalated when *caciques* involve themselves with the drug trade and establish links to powerful cartels.

Violence is most prevalent in the country's poorest states where peasants, particularly Indians, are often evicted from their lands, harassed, or physically attacked. Periodically, political activists who have tried to organize against such abuses have been tortured or killed (Bonfil 1988; Nagengast et al. 1992). As political repression has receded in much of Latin America, international human rights groups such as Amnesty International and Americas Watch increasingly have focused their attention on Mexico, charging it with "problems of executions, routine use of torture, violence related to land disputes, and violations of press freedom" (Sikkink 1996: 71). A recent Amnesty study of human rights violations in Oaxaca and Chiapas concluded that "a number of peasants . . . have apparently been the victims of deliberate political killings." While AI did not blame the national government for these deaths, it concluded that "local authorities have been involved in murders and . . . criminals regularly act with impunity. . . . Informants say that the killings are the work of assassins hired by landowners and *caciques* who have close ties to the local power elites" (Nagengast et al. 1992: 9).

In recent years there have also been more extensive massacres of dissident peasants in Guerrero, Chiapas, and other impoverished states. In several cases, the governor appears to have been directly involved. To be sure, political repression has never reached the massive proportions recently experienced in Guatemala and El Salvador, nor has it been as systematic and centralized as it was in Chile or in Argentina. But precisely because its origins are decentralized it has been difficult to expose and eradicate. Furthermore, since political violence is primarily directed toward peasants rather than urban intellectuals or labor leaders (major targets in the southern cone), state torture and murder are less likely to attract national or international outrage (Centro de derechos humanos 1992).

Within urban areas, however, the most frequent victims of assassination have been urban political activists and journalists. Human rights monitors have also been harassed or attacked (Americas Watch 1991). The emergence of the first serious left-of-center challenge to PRI hegemony provoked a wave of violence against activists in the Party of the

Democratic Revolution (PRD). More than two hundred PRD militants were murdered from the 1988 through the 1994 presidential elections (Rodríguez and Ward 1994: 121). In 1994, a truck mysteriously crashed into the car carrying the PRD's gubernatorial candidate in Chiapas. The crash took place at the very spot where a PRD worker had been hit by a truck not long before.

Fifty-one Mexican journalists were murdered between 1970 and 1988, and many more were attacked or threatened. That pace has continued unabated ever since. Often the victims had been investigating politically sensitive topics: election fraud or violence; police corruption and misconduct; or narcotics trafficking. Most recently there have been numerous police attacks against journalists and other independent investigators examining ties between narcotics traffickers and government authorities. Police units trying to apprehend drug lords have sometimes been attacked by other police defending the dealers. Between 1990 and 1992 alone, a total of 270 federal justice department officials and federal judicial police agents were charged with corruption or abuse of power (U.S. Department of State 1992: 4). Unfortunately, corruption has permeated the highest levels of law enforcement and the number of officials actually charged undoubtedly represents a small percentage of those who are tainted.

The NAFTA debate, the Zapatista uprising, and narcotics-related police violence have intensified foreign scrutiny of Mexico's human rights record, especially in the American media, and made the national government more sensitive to that issue's adverse effect on Mexico's image abroad. Thus, for example, shortly before meeting with George Bush to launch the NAFTA initiative, President Salinas created a National Commission for Human Rights (the CNDH) to demonstrate his administration's concern in this area. While human rights groups such as Amnesty International and Americas Watch have been impressed by the CNDH's integrity, its powers have been fairly limited.

Salinas also made apparent efforts to clean up the notoriously abusive antinarcotics division of the federal police and the attorney general's office. But progress was limited and perhaps undermined by the president's brother's links to drug lords. Despite President Zedillo's commitment to reform, it does not appear that he has been notably more successful. Zedillo did take a bold step when he appointed a respected PAN lawyer, Antonio Lozano, as the first opposition-party figure ever to hold the politically sensitive post of attorney general (he has since stepped down). But while the national government has tried to reduce new human rights violations, it has hesitated to prosecute past abusers, effectively allowing them to operate with relative legal impunity. Zedillo has removed the governors of Guerrero and Chiapas after they either initiated or covered up official involvement in peasant massacres. Ironically, however, his commitment to decentralizing political power and limiting presidential reach (obvious prerequisites for greater democracy) has opened up new opportunities for corrupt and repressive state and local officials.

A Conservative Political Culture

Characterizing a national political culture is always difficult and risky, particularly so in the case of Mexico. A range of local, regional, and national attitudinal surveys often have produced controversial or conflicting results.[6] But most analysis, be it data-based or drawn from anthropological case studies, suggests that postrevolutionary Mexican political culture has generally been conservative and cynical. Those feelings have been expressed in widespread apprehension about fundamental political change along with the belief that no matter how corrupt and unresponsive PRI rule has been, opposition-party government would be no better.

Fear of change and a propensity to support a deeply flawed status quo are largely reactions to the cataclysm of violence that swept the country during the early decades of the twentieth century. The Revolution (1910–20) took a shocking toll in lost lives and suffering. Out of a national population of sixteen to seventeen million people, between one and two million died in the insurrection (Cumberland 1968: 241 and 245). Millions more were wounded or uprooted from their homes. Hundreds of villages disappeared from the face of the earth. Bloody civil war continued through the late 1920s (the *Cristero* rebellion) and violence extended into the following decade. In addition, from 1912 to 1928 a series of Mexican revolutionary leaders and presidents were assassinated, most notably Emiliano Zapata, Pancho Villa, and presidents Francisco Madero, Venustiano Carranza, and Alvaro Obregón. Not surprisingly, when the surviving revolutionary leadership created a ruling party in 1929, the primary purpose was restoring political stability and order.

Well into the 1970s many Mexicans, or their parents or grandparents, had stories of revolutionary and postrevolutionary violence emblazoned in their memories. For example, in a survey of northern factory workers, almost 60 percent of all respondents reported that they had frequently been told stories of the Revolution in their youth, with over 50 percent noting that such stories were still told. "Slightly over one-quarter . . . had a recollection of death, physical injury, or property loss [within their own family] during the Revolution, three generations after the event" (cited in Stevenson and Seligson 1996: 68). Consequently, the legacy of that era has been a "culture of fear." Some 45 percent of those polled indicated that stories of the Revolution had made them fearful of violence in Mexico. More significantly, there was a powerful correlation between that fear and the belief that an "anti-PRI vote leads to the eruption of violence."

These concerns have not only bolstered PRI electoral strength (as the party of the status quo) but, more insidiously, have led many Mexicans to identify democracy with chaos. Indeed, the country's two most democratically elected administrations until 1994—Juárez's and Madero's—were identified with civil war or revolution. Thus, Levy and Bruhn (1995: 209) note that "anarchy is particularly frightening to many Mexicans, perhaps because of the nation's history, and many have felt they could little afford democracy." This is a fear that the PRI has skillfully manipulated. For example, years ago, during a national congressional campaign, I noted political posters hung throughout Mexico City and Guadalajara warning that a PRI defeat would mean "foreign domination, hunger and disorder." While recent elections clearly suggest that Mexicans are becoming less fearful of fundamental political change and more receptive to opposition-party victories, a substantial number of PRI supporters in the two most recent presidential elections told pollsters that their vote was still greatly influenced by fear that an opposition victory would produce political and economic disorder.[7]

Thus, in a perverse way, the 1994 Zapatista uprising and the (unrelated) assassination of the PRI's presidential candidate, Luis Donaldo Colosio, several months later ultimately strengthened the ruling party's electoral hand by renewing the specter of violence and insecurity. "In a political climate tainted by suspicion, uncertainty, increased public insecurity, and fear of the future, the PRI handily marketed itself as a guarantor of stability and continuity" (Dresser 1996: 161). Indeed, many analysts considered el voto de miedo ("the fear vote") an important factor propelling PRI candidate Ernesto Zedillo to victory in the 1994 presidential race (Fox 1994).

Others have noted additional authoritarian characteristics within Mexico's political culture. For example, Rafael Segovia's (1982) extensive national survey of Mexican school children illuminated nondemocratic aspects of the political socialization process. At least until recently, the school system has failed to instill democratic values in many of its charges. School children in poor neighborhoods and villages generally have been inculcated with deferential political outlooks. And some Mexican anthropologists insist that Mexican youth are raised to accept unquestionably their father's authority. When they grow up, it is argued, they transfer that obedience to the nation's president and other authority figures (Turner 1995: 209).[8]

THE ROOTS OF POLITICAL PLURALISM

The first important challenge to PRI hegemony, according to most analysts, was the massive student-led protests of 1968. Originally intended to protest police brutality against student activists, the movement gradually broadened its objectives to include a generalized indictment of political repression and social injustices. Drawing on considerable working- and middle-class support, the student movement mobilized as many as 300,000 participants in its protest marches. Faced with the prospect of substantial losses in urban support and embarrassing demonstrations during the impending summer Olympics, the Díaz Ordaz government ordered troops to open fire at protesting throngs in Mexico City's Plaza of the Three Cultures (Tlatelolco). Some 200 people died and 2,000 were arrested. The massacre and associated repression shocked the Mexican middle class and undermined the regime's legitimacy, particularly within the country's intellectual community (Smith 1991: 359–62).

Others, however, would identify the first modern confrontations between civil society and the party-state as the labor protests of the late 1950s and early 1960s. Railroad workers, miners, teachers, and medical interns all carried out major strikes (Handelman 1976). But both the labor and student movements could, in turn, be traced back to the broad transformation of Mexican society begun in the early 1940s. During its postwar economic boom (the so-called "economic miracle"), featuring average annual GDP growth of 6–7 percent from 1940 to 1970, Mexico had become far more urban, more industrialized, and more literate (Ramírez 1989: 14). From 1940 to 1990 the proportion of Mexicans living in cities more than tripled and the literacy rate nearly doubled (table 2). The number of students attending secondary schools and universities also mushroomed. And, social-economic modernization, in turn, swelled the ranks of the middle class, which emerged as the country's most powerful political force. At the same time, the PRI's most dependable and compliant constituency, the rural poor, diminished in size.

From the 1960s onward, the PRI-state regime fell victim to both the successes and the failures of its own development model. Impressive economic growth and modernization produced a larger and more politically articulate urban middle class and a larger, unionized working class. In time, many in these sectors of society were repelled by the nation's

TABLE 2

Mexico's Socioeconomic Development: 1940–1990

	1940	1990
Percentage Urban	22	72
Percentage in Agriculture	65	24
Percentage Literate	52	96
Kilometers of Roads	10,000	235,000

Source: Miguel Basáñez, *El pulso de los sexenios* (Mexico City: Siglo XXI, 1990), pp. 345–59.

sharp income inequality, extensive poverty, rampant corruption, and periodic political repression. The debt crisis of the 1980s and the country's 1995 financial collapse intensified popular disenchantment and generated support for both the left and right opposition.

From the ranks of the middle class emerged the student activists of the 1960s and 1970s. More recently, many middle-class voters, particularly in Mexico City, have supported the PRD. At the same time, the business community and members of the independent middle class — most notably in Mexico's northern cities — became the backbone of the conservative National Action Party (PAN).

Because the country's labor movement has been so tightly controlled by the PRI and so dominated by corrupt and politically conservative union bosses, the working class has played a less pivotal role in the democratization process than Rueschemeyer, Huber Stephens, and Stephens (1992) found elsewhere in Latin America, in Western Europe, and in the Caribbean. However, in recent decades dissident movements or unions representing, among others, electrical-power workers, steelworkers, nuclear-power workers, bank employees, university employees, and auto workers have mounted serious challenges to labor bosses and to the PRI's corporatist structure.

CONTINUING CRISES AND THE POLITICS OF ACCOMMODATION

The quarter century from 1968 to 1994 was marked by a seemingly unending series of crises for the Mexican political establishment.[9] Following the Tlatelolco massacre of 1968, President Luis Echeverría's fiscal mismanagement (1970–76) and clashes with the business community provoked a financial crisis and rumors of a military coup. The 1982 external debt crisis and subsequent depression ended the postwar economic boom and seriously eroded the regime's legitimacy. The government's inept response to Mexico City's massive earthquake in 1985 further exposed the state's inefficiency and corruption. The 1988 presidential election brought the first significant challenge to PRI's electoral hegemony, a race many Mexicans still believe was really won by PRD candidate Cuauhtémoc Cárdenas. In 1994, the Chiapas rebellion and the subsequent assassinations of PRI presidential candidate Luis Donaldo Colosio and party secretary general, José Francisco Ruiz Massieu, called the political system's stability into question. And, most recently, the 1995 financial crisis brought the economy's mild recovery to an end and, once again, plunged much of the population into economic despair. At the same time, revelations that President Salinas's brother had somehow acquired over $100 million and Raul Salinas's imprisonment on charges of having masterminded the Ruiz Massieu assassination increased public cynicism.

Throughout, however, Mexico's political elite have been remarkably adept at co-opting opposition, making strategic concessions, and liberalizing the authoritarian regime without actually democratizing it. Each of the aforementioned crises was followed by electoral reform, government efforts to regain the support of alienated constituencies, or new social programs. Important posts, such as the governor of Mexico City, previously appointed by the president, were opened to electoral contestation. As far back as 1964, the government had set aside a relatively small number of "party seats" in the Chamber of Deputies for opposition parties.

When pressure for democratic reform intensified in the 1970s, following the Tlatelolco massacre and a sharp economic downturn, party registration rules were eased to allow leftist parties to compete, and opportunities for opposition congressional victories were enlarged. In recent years, opposition parties were offered greater (though still limited) access to the media and to campaign funds. More importantly, a growing portion of the Chamber of Deputies has been elected through proportional representation, with those seats largely allocated to opposition parties (whereas almost all deputies were formerly elected from single-member districts, then still totally dominated by the PRI).[10] Since 1986, 40 percent of the Chamber's members have been elected to those plurinominal seats (Middlebrook 1986; Molinar Horcasitas 1996).

In 1993, electoral reforms enlarged the Senate, introduced plurinominal senate elections in each state, and awarded one-fourth of the upper chamber's seats (one from each state) to the parties whose candidate slates finished second in that state. Consequently, opposition parties are guaranteed 25 percent of that body. As Juan Molinar Horcasitas (1996: 141–42) has noted, prior to 1997 these reforms meant that "the regime was able to incorporate increasing numbers of opposition members into the Chamber of Deputies [and, more recently, into the Senate] without inflicting defeat on the official party."

In recent years, reforms have focused on electoral procedures, most notably reducing electoral fraud. Modest efforts also have been made to reduce the enormous advantage that the PRI enjoys in media access. A PRI-dominated national election commission has been replaced by a respected independent body, the Federal Electoral Institute (IFE). Sophisticated voter identification cards and an extensive system of randomly selected poll watchers have been introduced to guard against the multiple voting, ballot stuffing, and electoral miscounts that characterized many past elections such as the disputed 1988 presidential race.

In addition, thousands of unofficial observers from the independent watchdog, Civic Alliance, now blanket the nation's polling stations. In the 1994 and 1997 elections, they were joined by several hundred foreign observers whom the government had reluctantly accepted in a bow to considerable international pressure. All of these reforms have produced the most honest ballot counts in Mexican history, though some irregularities still remain, particularly in the countryside (Handelman 1997: 82–83; Dresser 1996). The confluence of greater citizen awareness, increased popular discontent over government performance, and more open electoral procedures has produced a steady erosion in PRI congressional dominance. Whereas the official party received 85.2 percent of the national vote for the Chamber of Deputies in 1976 (and 82 percent of the seats), that portion dropped to 50.4 percent in 1988 (52 percent of the seats) and 38 percent of the vote (48 percent of the seats) in the historic 1997 election that established an opposition majority in the lower house of Congress.

A CHANGING POLITICAL CULTURE

Elsewhere in this volume, Scott Mainwaring notes that while socioeconomic modernization is generally conducive to democracy, the correlation between those two variables is weaker in Latin America than in other regions of the world. Like Mainwaring, I am suggesting here that progress toward democracy in Mexico must be understood in both structural and cultural terms. Growing educational levels and the greater emergence of the Mexican middle class have coincided with a series of challenges to regime legitimacy dating at least to the student and labor unrest of the 1960s. An authoritarian or semiauthoritarian order that was once accepted as both inevitable and necessary for stability (a "culture of fear") is now being challenged.

In their review of contemporary survey data on Mexican public opinion, Domínguez and McCann (1996: 28) found compelling evidence of progress toward a democratic political culture. "Our review . . . suggests that support for authoritarianism may have weakened between the 1960s and the 1980s, perhaps to the point where majority support would exist for democratic values." Since most Mexican surveys find that the respondents' democratic values correlated positively with their educational levels, there is reason to believe that rising educational levels and other aspects of modernization in recent decades have contributed to a more democratic political culture.

At the same time, citizens' interest in politics and their willingness to engage in political discussion seem to have grown as well. Gallup surveys conducted in 1959 and 1991 indicate an increased number of Mexicans who "talk freely about politics with anyone" and a growing number who were attentive to political campaigns. Indeed, by the 1980s "the level of political interest expressed by Mexicans was similar to that expressed by citizens of several advanced industrial democracies," equal to that of Germany and Greece, and higher than political interest levels in Britain, Canada, and France. And Mexico's political culture had become more homogeneous as differences in the level of political interest across regions, educational strata, class, and gender had narrowed considerably (Domínguez and McCann 1996: 30–31, 34). As levels of commitment to democratic values grew, and society's political interest and willingness to discuss politics intensified, the PRI's grip on the electorate weakened.

Deteriorating economic conditions also contributed to the official party's decline. An unknown, but significant, proportion of the PRI's support and the regime's legitimacy is now performance-based. Thus in the 1988 presidential election, following over five years of national economic crisis, over 80 percent of those Mexicans who believed that a PRI win would bode better for the economy than would an opposition victory voted for Salinas. Conversely over two-thirds of the voters who felt that the economy would fare better under an opposition government voted for the PRD or PAN candidates. In the absence of an immediate stimulus to the "fear vote" (such as the Zapatista uprising and the Colosio assassination in the run-up to the 1994 election), this economic calculus was a stronger predictor of voting preference in the 1988 election than was the respondent's degree of anxiety about social unrest in the event of an opposition-party victory (Domínguez and McCann 1996: 101). By the time of the 1997 congressional election and Mexico City's concurrent gubernatorial contest, the hopes raised by Salinas's economic recovery had been dashed and the country once again was mired in a deep depression. This time, performance-based evaluations seem to have superseded lingering anxieties over possible social unrest, producing a stunning opposition victory.

CONCLUSIONS

I have suggested that Mexico suffered a cultural lag in which authoritarian or semiauthoritarian values persisted in the political culture despite several decades of impressive socioeconomic modernization (1940s– 1970s). As we have seen, some of that lag may be attributed to pervasive popular apprehension concerning political contestation and social disorder, a fear stemming from the devastation brought on by the Mexican Revolution. That "culture of fear" has been skillfully manipulated by the PRI and its predecessors and cast its shadow as recently as the 1994 national elections when Ernesto Zedillo benefited from voter concerns over the Chiapas rebellion and the Colosio assassination.

In addition, the party-state's corporate structure long penetrated deeply into society (most notably through the trade-union movement and the rural government bureaucracy), creating a vast network of patron-client relationships and citizen dependency on the regime. As long as Mexico enjoyed a dynamic, expanding economy the state could dispense public goods to a wide spectrum of social groups. Even peasants, the victims of a highly inegalitarian development model, received benefits through the *ejido* structure.

During the 1980s and early 1990s, two factors greatly reduced the resources which the regime could draw upon for co-optive purposes. First, the debt crisis and related structural adjustment and stabilization programs substantially reduced state expenditures. Second, privatization and other neoliberal reforms during the de la Madrid and Salinas administrations diminished the size of the state. The result was the weakening of patronage politics and the deterioration of the corporatist state (Dresser 1996: 168). As a consequence, by the time of the 1988 presidential election the PRI's labor and peasant sectors could no longer control and mobilize their members' votes as they had before. Salinas and now Zedillo began to dismantle the party's corporatist structure built around its labor, peasant, and "popular" sectors.[11]

With the decline of the PRI's performance-based legitimacy, voters were less inclined to overlook the regime's authoritarianism and pervasive corruption. By the 1994 presidential campaign these issues had become paramount in the voters' minds. These are also the major issues that facilitate congressional cooperation between the otherwise divergent opposition parties, the neoliberal PAN and the left-nationalist PRD. Finally, as the PAN and the PRD won local elections in a substantial number of municipalities and as a number of PAN and, more recently PRD governors took office, a substantial minority of the Mexican population lived under opposition-party government for the first time. Fears that PRI defeats would bring political disorder dissipated.[12]

The results of the 1997 congressional elections notwithstanding, Mexico has yet to achieve full procedural democracy. At the state and local levels, particularly in the nation's poorer states such as Oaxaca, Chiapas, and Quintana Roo, election fraud, rampant corruption, and *cacique* intimidation and gangsterism continue. As I have noted, the governors of Chiapas and Guerrero have recently been implicated in the massacres of dissident peasants.

While national election counts are now fairly clean, the campaigns that precede them are not yet conducted on a level playing field. For one thing, the PRI enjoys a massive advantage in campaign funds and routinely ignores legal spending limits (though measures have been taken to reduce party use of government revenues). For example, "in Tabasco's 1994 gubernatorial race, the PRI spent $70 million to court a mere 500,000 voters, out-spending the opposition by a margin of 60 to 1. . . . In the 1994 national elections the PRI spent more than three times as much as all of its opponents combined" (Handelman 1997: 86). The official party also benefits from more extensive and more favorable media coverage. This is particularly true of television where most Mexicans get their news. The nation's dominant network, *Televisa,* which attracts 85 percent of the country's television audience, is blatantly biased in the PRI's favor (Arrendondo Ramírez 1992: 39–66).

Finally, alternation of the all-powerful presidency between parties remains problematic as long as the opposition vote is divided between PAN and the PRD. While the two parties have collaborated on political reform and while talks are underway regarding a possible joint slate in the 2000 national elections, the wide policy and strategic gaps that divide them make a joint candidacy highly unlikely.

Still, the longer-term prospects for further democratization remain strong as the "culture of fear" is being replaced by a political culture more hospitable to contested electoral politics. And even though the economy has once again begun to recover, the pared-down, neoliberal state lacks the resources to reconstitute effective corporatist controls.

NOTES

1. Portions of this chapter previously appeared in Howard Handelman (1997).

2. The phrase "PRI-state" (or "party-state") refers to the intertwined corporatist ruling party (whose major function is legitimization and mobilization) and the state's bureaucratic apparatus, both of which work in tandem. The ruling party had several earlier names and structures before becoming the PRI (Institutional Revolutionary Party) in 1946. For simplicity sake, I will refer to the party ever since its inception as the PRI.

3. The portion of *Transitions from Authoritarian Rule* that contains Latin American case studies includes a chapter on Mexico by Kevin Middlebrook. However the theoretical volume by O'Donnell and Schmitter makes only a single passing reference to that country.

4. Camacho, who has held several key cabinet posts, eventually left the PRI, but did so only after outgoing President Carlos Salinas failed to select him as his successor and the party's hegemony appeared threatened.

5. To be sure, Salinas's high approval ratings plummeted after he left office as support for him and the PRI suffered from the renewed economic crisis after 1995. Salinas was further tarnished by evidence of rampant corruption and perhaps murder by his own brother. But before Salinas stepped down, PRONASOL's popular success contributed to the PRI's 1994 electoral victory.

6. See Craig and Cornelius (1980) for a sharp criticism of the characterization of Mexico in *The Civic Culture*. Craig and Cornelius also offer a valuable review of the survey research on Mexican political culture available at that time.

7. *Voz y Voto* and *Este País* are two excellent Mexican journals that regularly report the results of their public-opinion polls.

8. It should be noted that scholars are sharply divided regarding the extent to which Latin American cultural traditions present independent roadblocks to democratization and regarding the degree of authoritarianism in the region's contemporary political culture (Diamond and Linz 1989: 9–14). Examining data from the early 1980s, Booth and Seligson (1984) disputed the widely held contention that Mexico still labored under an authoritarian political culture at that time.

9. For examples of the scholarly literature depicting Mexico as being in an ongoing crisis or "on the brink," see Basáñez 1990; Castañeda 1986; Hellman 1979).

10. In the first three elections held under the mixed single-member and plurinominal system (1979, 1982, 1985), *all* of the latter seats were allocated to the opposition.

11. The "popular sector" was a catchall branch of the party representing a wide variety of middle-class and urban, lower-class groups, especially unionized white-collar state employees. Under the PRI's traditional structure, all members of affiliated labor unions and of villages represented in the National Confederation of Peasants (CNC) have automatically been considered party members.

12. Initially at least, many opposition-controlled state and local governments, especially those led by the PRD, faced formidable resistance from the national government and even from PRI-affiliated unions of local government employees (for example, disruptive strikes by sanitation workers). Even so, opposition victories did not produce the dire consequences that some had predicted and many PAN or PRD governments have maintained considerable voter support.

REFERENCES

Almond, Gabriel A., and Sidney Verba. 1963. *The Civic Culture*. Princeton: Princeton University Press.

Alonso, Jorge, Alberto Aziz, and Jaime Tamayo, eds. 1992. *El Nuevo Estado Mexicano—II. Estado y Política*. Mexico City: Nueva Imagen.

Americas Watch. 1991. *Unceasing Abuses: Human Rights in Mexico One Year After the Introduction of Reforms*. New York: Americas Watch.

Arrendondo Ramírez, Pablo. 1992. "El Estado y la comunicación." In Jorge Alonso, Alberto Aziz, and Jaime Tamayo, eds., *El Nuevo Estado Mexicano—IV: Estado y Sociedad,* pp. 39–66. Mexico City: Nueva Imagen,

Aziz Nassif, Alberto. 1992. "La reforma electoral: adecuaciones a una democracia tutelada." In Jorge Alonso, Alberto Aziz, and Jaime Tamayo, eds., *El Nuevo Estado Mexicano—II: Estado y Política*.

Aziz Nassif, Alberto, and Juan Molinar Horcasitas. 1990. "Los resultados electorales." In Pablo González Casanova, ed., *Segundo informe sobre la democracia: México el 6 de Julio de 1988*. Mexico City: Siglo XXI.

Basáñez, Miguel. 1990. *El pulso de los sexenios: 20 años de crisis en México*. Mexico City: Siglo XXI.

Bizberg, Ilán. 1993. "Modernization and Corporatism in Government-Labor Relations." In Neil Harvey, ed., *Mexico: Dilemmas of Transition*. London: Institute of Latin American Studies, University of London.

Bonfil, Guillermo. 1988. *México Profundo*. Mexico City: Secretaría de Educación Pública.

Booth, John A., and Mitchell A. Seligson. 1984. "The Political Culture of Authoritarianism in Mexico: A Reexamination." *Latin American Research Review* 19 (no. 1), pp. 106–24.

Castañeda, Jorge G. 1986. "Mexico at the Brink." *Foreign Affairs* 64 (Winter 1985–86), pp. 278–96.

Centro de Derechos Humanos Miguel Agustín Pro. 1992. "Los Derechos humanos: Nuevo campo de la lucha social en México." In Jorge Alonso, Alberto Aziz, and Jaime Tamayo, eds., *El Nuevo Estado Mexicano—II. Estado y Política*, pp. 225–72.

Collier, David. 1979. *The New Authoritarianism in Latin America*. Princeton: Princeton University Press.

Cornelius, Wayne A., Ann L. Craig, and Jonathan Fox, eds. 1994. *Transforming State-Society Relations in Mexico*. La Jolla: Center for U.S.-Mexican Studies, the University of California, San Diego.

Craig, Ann L., and Wayne A. Cornelius. 1980. "Political Culture in Mexico: Continuities and Revisionist Interpretations." In Gabriel A. Almond and Sidney Verba, eds., *The Civic Culture Revisited*, pp. 325–93. Boston: Little, Brown.

Cumberland, Charles. 1968. *Mexico: The Struggle for Modernity*. New York: Oxford University Press.

Diamond, Larry, and Juan J. Linz. 1989. "Introduction: Politics, Society, and Democracy in Latin America." In Larry Diamond, Juan J. Linz, and Seymour Martin Lipset, eds., *Democracy in Developing Countries: Latin America*, pp. 1–59. Boulder: Lynne Rienner.

Diamond, Larry, and Marc F. Plattner, eds. 1993. *The Global Resurgence of Democracy*. Baltimore: Johns Hopkins University Press.

Domínguez, Jorge I., and James A. McCann. 1996. *Democratizing Mexico: Public Opinion and Electoral Choices*. Baltimore: Johns Hopkins University Press.

Dresser, Denise. 1996. "Mexico: The Decline of Dominant-Party Rule." In Jorge I. Domínguez and Abraham F. Lowenthal, eds., *Constructing Democratic Governance: Mexico, Central America, and the Caribbean in the 1990s*, pp. 159–84. Baltimore: Johns Hopkins University Press.

Fox, Jonathan. 1994. "The Mexican Elections: What Does the 'Fear Vote' Mean?" Paper presented at the Meeting of the New England Council on Latin American Studies, Cambridge, Mass.

González Casanova, Pablo. 1970. *Democracy in Mexico*. New York: Oxford University Press.

Handelman, Howard. 1976. "The Politics of Labor Protest in Mexico: Two Case Studies." *Journal of Interamerican Studies and World Affairs* 18 (August): 167–94.

———. 1997. *Mexican Politics: The Dynamics of Change*. New York: St. Martin's Press.

Harvey, Neil. 1991. *The New Agrarian Movement in Mexico, 1979–1999*. London: Institute of Latin American Studies.

Hellman, Judith Adler. 1979. *Mexico in Crisis*. New York: Holmes and Meier.

Huntington, Samuel P. 1991. *The Third Wave*. Norman: University of Oklahoma Press.

Levy, Daniel C., and Kathleen Bruhn. 1995. "Mexico: Sustained Civilian Rule without Democracy." In Larry Diamond, Juan J. Linz, and Seymour Martin Lipset, eds., *Politics in Developing Countries: Comparing Experiences*, pp. 171–217. Boulder: Lynne Rienner.

Malloy, James M., and Mitchell A. Seligson, eds. 1987. *Authoritarians and Democrats.* Pittsburgh: University of Pittsburgh Press.

Meyer, Lorenzo. 1986. "La democracia politica: esperando a Godot." *Nexos,* no. 100 (April).

———. 1991. "México o los límites de la democratizacíon neoliberal." Paper delivered at the University of California, San Diego Center for U.S.-Mexican Studies, May 15, 1991.

———. 1992. *La segunda muerte de la Revolución Mexicana.* Mexico City: Cal y Arena.

Middlebrook, Kevin J. 1986. "Political Liberalization in an Authoritarian Regime: The Case of Mexico." In Guillermo O'Donnell, Philippe C. Schmitter, and Laurence Whitehead, eds., *Transitions from Authoritarian Rule,* pp. 123–47. Baltimore: Johns Hopkins University Press.

Molinar Horcasitas, Juan. 1996. "Changing the Balance of Power in a Hegemonic Party System: The Case of Mexico." In Arend Lijphart and Carlos H. Waisman, eds., *Institutional Design in New Democracies: Eastern Europe and Latin America.* pp. 137–60. Boulder: Westview Press.

Morris, Stephen D. 1995. *Political Reformism in Mexico.* Boulder: Lynne Rienner.

Nagengast, Carole, Rudolfo Stavenhagen, and Michael Kearney. 1992. *Human Rights and Indigenous Workers.* La Jolla: Current Issues Brief, Center for U.S.-Mexican Studies, University of California, San Diego.

O'Donnell, Guillermo, and Philippe C. Schmitter. 1986. *Transitions from Authoritarian Rule: Tentative Conclusions about Uncertain Democracies.* Baltimore: Johns Hopkins University Press.

Pérez Barbosa, Raúl. 1994. *Volverá a caerse el sistema.* Mexico City: Grupo Editorial Planeta.

Przeworski, Adam. 1991. *Democracy and the Market.* New York: Cambridge University Press.

Ramírez, Miguel. 1989. *Mexico's Economic Crisis: Its Origins and Consequences.* New York: Praeger.

Riding, Alan. 1984. *Distant Neighbors.* New York: Vintage.

Rodríguez, Victoria E., and Peter M. Ward. 1994. *Political Change in Baja California: Democracy in the Making?* Lajolla: Center for U.S.–Mexican Studies, University of California, San Diego.

Rueschemeyer, Dietrich, Evelyne Huber Stephens, and John Stephens. 1992. *Capitalist Development and Democracy.* Chicago: University of Chicago Press.

Segovia, Rafael. 1982. *La politicización del niño mexicano,* 2d ed. Mexico City: El Colegio de México.

Seligson, Mitchell A. 1987. "Democratization in Latin America: The Current Cycle." In James M. Malloy and Mitchell A. Seligson, eds., *Authoritarians and Democrats,* pp. 3–12. Pittsburgh: University of Pittsburgh Press.

Sikkink, Kathryn. 1996. "The Emergence, Evolution, and Effectiveness of the Latin American Human Rights Network." In Elizabeth Jelin and Eric Hershberg, eds., *Constructing Democracy: Human Rights, Citizenship, and Society in Latin America,* pp. 59–84. Boulder: Westview Press.

Smith, Peter H. 1991. "Mexico Since 1946: Dynamics of an Authoritarian Regime." In Leslie Bethell, ed., *Mexico Since Independence*, pp. 321–96. New York: Cambridge University Press,

Stevenson, Linda S., and Mitchell A. Seligson. 1996. "Fading Memories of the Revolution: Is Stability Eroding in Mexico?" In Roderic Ai Camp, ed., *Polling for Democracy,* pp. 59–79. Wilmington: Scholarly Resources.

Turner, Frederick C. 1995. "Reassessing Political Culture." In Peter H. Smith, ed., *Latin America in Comparative Perspective.* pp. 195–224. Boulder: Westview Press.

UNDP (United Nations Development Program). 1993. *Human Development Report 1993.* New York: Oxford University Press.

U.S. Department of State. 1992. *International Narcotics Control Strategy Report 1992: Mexico.* Washington, D.C.: 1992.

8

Arab Women and Political Liberalization: Challenges and Opportunities

Laurie A. Brand

ALTHOUGH THE "third wave" of democratization, as it has been called, actually began in Southern Europe, by the late 1980s it had reached into Eastern Europe and the former Soviet Union. The dramatic nature of the events in Eastern Europe overshadowed further extensions of this wave, involving political liberalizations or redemocratizations in other parts of the world where the transitions were less thoroughgoing but still significant. Perhaps least noted were a number of developments in the Middle East/North Africa (MENA) region where, beginning in the late 1980s, leaderships in several countries were forced by the power of economic crisis and long years of political malaise to open up their domestic political systems. Morocco, Tunisia, Algeria, Jordan, Yemen, Syria, and Kuwait in varying forms and to differing degrees all experienced such processes.

Rather than examine the MENA transitions in general, the discussion that follows will focus on the relations between women and the state during these transitions.[1] Several elements account for the selection of this particular set of relationships as a focus. First and foremost, unlike economic liberalization or market transformations, which have been criticized for their impact on the poor and other sectors of society, politi-

The author is grateful to CAORC, SSRC, and AIMS as well as the School of International Relations at the University of Southern California for research grants and support for the fieldwork that made this project possible. This article is part of the author's larger work (*Women, the State and Political Liberalization*, Columbia University Press, 1998), which looks at the experiences of women in Jordan, Morocco, and Tunisia under liberalization, testing these experiences against those of women in Latin America and Eastern Europe.

242

cal liberalization or democratization is, generally, implicitly assumed by the literature and by commentators to produce only winners (with the possible exception of the repressors from the previous regime, who may be punished). Yet, a brief examination of women's experiences with the liberalizing or democratizing regimes in Eastern Europe, for example, reveals a retreat in women's rights to work and to control their reproductive fates as well as a decline in their presence in formal representative structures. Thus, an examination of women's status provides a corrective to what are clearly erroneous generalizations, at least in other regions.

Attention to the relationship between women and the state will also address deficiencies in pertinent bodies of theoretical literature. For example, while women's fates in the Eastern European and Latin American transformations have been examined by a growing feminist literature (Moghadam 1993; Funk and Mueller 1993; and Rai, Pilkington, and Phizacklea 1992), mainstream "transitology" has shown no inclination to treat gender as a significant category, and the limited literature on these transitions in the MENA region has all but ignored women.[2] Further, some of the civil society literature argues that women's organizations may in fact be among the most important moving forces pushing for greater democratization, and this proposition needs more systematic testing (Norton 1995). Hence, there are important gaps in the literature from both a theoretical and an empirical point of view. An examination of how women have fared under the more limited and/or brief liberalizations in the Middle East and North Africa should contribute to our ability to determine what is generalizable about transition outcomes across regions.

More broadly, the prevailing wisdom regarding the MENA region is that its regimes are for some reason(s)—implicitly or explicitly argued to be cultural—impervious or immune to democratic change. The durability of authoritarian regimes in the Middle East is worthy of close consideration, and a discussion of notable, if ultimately stalled or reversed, openings can serve as a potential window on the broader question of the staying power of these regimes. Examining MENA cases with these larger questions in mind lifts the region's states out of what is often an externally imposed ghetto and forces their consideration in the realm of more broadly comparative politics.

The discussion that follows will examine, by necessity briefly, the experiences of women with the state in two MENA countries during periods of political liberalization: Jordan, which experienced a notable opening beginning in April 1989, only to suffer substantial retreat since the summer of 1994; and Tunisia, which despite the heralding of a new era of pluralism after the unseating of Bourguiba, soon descended into a contest between state and Islamists which has gradually consumed any opposition, loyal or otherwise. Both are small in size and population, both have had leaderships with generally forward-looking and pro-Western stances on political and development issues, and both experienced transitions that were triggered (in the immediate sense) by a single shock, rather than by gradual pressures from below. In this final respect they certainly share a key characteristic with a number of the Eastern European cases. Each country section will provide a recounting of the opening, including introductions to the cast of characters. The discussion will also examine several events or developments which are intended to serve as examples of the broader nature of the relationship between women and the state during these critical periods.

JORDAN

It was economic riots protesting the lifting of petroleum-related subsidies in April 1989 that led to the decision to begin to liberalize the kingdom's political system. By late July the king had ordered that preparations begin for new parliamentary elections, the first in twenty-two years, to be held in November. By mid-September, unprecedented public debate had begun about the upcoming voting and the candidates (*Middle East International* [*MEI*], September 22, 1989).

Among the field of candidates were twelve women, a development which a number of Islamists criticized in the press (Eury 1991: 43). Not unexpectedly, none of the women candidates won, although in the wake of the voting the king did appoint one woman, Layla Sharaf, the former minister of information (1984–85), to the Senate. However, the most controversial story of the election period surrounded one of the failed candidacies, that of Toujan Faisal. Faisal, who had run for the ethnic minority Circassian seat in the fifth district (north, outside Amman), had worked as a television broadcaster for eighteen years, during which time she presented a series on women's affairs. She was also known as a writer and columnist who had raised the ire of conservatives on a number of occasions for programs challenging established Islamic or traditional practice (Gallagher 1993: 7–8).

The story which is of interest here concerns an op-ed piece she authored prior to officially declaring her candidacy. On September 21 she published an article in the Arabic daily *al-Ra'i* entitled "They curse us and we elect them" as part of an ongoing debate on women's role in society and their competence in handling national issues. In it, Faisal, who is well-versed in Islamic law, criticized "those" who hold women to be intellectually deficient and in need of being treated like minors. Faisal's larger political point was that those who believed in discrimination on any basis could not be entrusted with a family, an extended household, or a nation. And women were in a position to use their influence not to seat those who in effect denied them their humanity. It was a powerful and straightforward indictment of both Islamists and other traditionalists, but it was not intended to be an indictment of religion: her references were always to Islamists and not to Islam itself.

Two weeks after the appearance of her article, Faisal was visited by two bearded men who demanded that she apologize for the article and withdraw from the election or they would take her to court. She refused (Gallagher 1993: 10–15). She subsequently received a subpoena to appear in a south Amman *shariʿa* (Islamic law) court, charged with apostasy by an assistant mufti and a private in the armed forces. The suit sought to declare Faisal legally incompetent, dissolve her marriage, reject any repentance should she offer it, deny her all rights, ban her writings, and give immunity to anyone who shed her blood. Many activists described the suit as an attempt to "stifle the women's movement in Jordan at a time when women were running in elections for the first time in the kingdom's history." A group of women and other political activists, lawyers, university professors, and journalists submitted a petition to the king denouncing the charges against Faisal as "intellectual and psychological intimidation which will reflect badly on Jordan's image and on the democratic atmosphere for the elections" (*Jordan Times [JT]*, November 4, 1989). In a very short time more than 700 signatures were collected (Gallagher 1993: 17).

The day following the hearing, at which the plaintiffs presented their case and as a result of which the judge set a second session for November 9 (the day following the elections), the Jordanian press reported the story and triggered international interest. Journalists scrambled for interviews with Faisal and the case became a cause celebre. It could not have been lost on the king that the first case of apostasy ever raised in the kingdom was coming at a time when Jordan was trying to hold its first democratic elections since the 1950s and maintain or rebuild an image of a forward-looking, modernizing country.

Both plaintiffs in fact withdrew the case after the Amman *shariʿa* court ruled five days before the elections that the case was beyond its jurisdiction. Observers viewed the swift ruling as stemming from popular indignation and high-level pressure to put an end to the controversy as soon as possible. Nonetheless, ʿAbdallah Shamaylah, the lawyer for the two plaintiffs, subsequently filed an appeal himself, on the grounds that the original lawsuit had been filed on behalf of the "public right"

(*JT,* February 22–23, 1990). Shamaylah claimed that certain groups in the armed forces had forced the two original plaintiffs to withdraw the case. The story continued until February 1990, when a *shari'a* appeals court found Faisal not guilty of apostasy, although the plaintiff said he planned to file a new lawsuit.

There seems little question that the case was an embarrassment to the king, as it detracted from the showpiece free campaign period and free elections. Another key consideration during this period was that the regime was involved in drawing boundaries regarding what kind of activity would be permitted in a new, more open, era. The fact that the Muslim Brotherhood (also known as the Ikhwan), the largest Islamist group in the kingdom, stayed out of the fray—whatever their real feelings about Faisal—made the problem much easier to solve. One should not, therefore, interpret the treatment of the case as indicative of a special concern on the part of the palace to protect women or women's rights. In the wake of the Faisal case, the crown prince did select a group to study possible changes to the Personal Status Law, the law that governs many of the issues most basic to considerations of women's rights, such as marriage, divorce, inheritance, and child custody. But the appointment of such study and recommendation committees has generally been a strategy of "adopt and defuse," or demobilize, rather than "adopt and act." That seriously addressing women's concerns was not a primary consideration was clear from the composition of the committee, which initially had no women members.

To return to the election outcome and its import for the future of politics in the kingdom, the most striking element was the unexpected scale of the success of the Islamists, who, of various stripes took some thirty of the parliament's eighty seats.[3] Although their victories apparently came as a surprise to the authorities, the reasons for the Islamists success were no mystery. Over the years, the Jordanian regime had allowed them a great degree of freedom of action, if not active encouragement. The Muslim Brotherhood had been recognized as a social organization, and hence was not subject to the same restrictions as political parties, which had been declared illegal in 1957. As a result, it was able to expand its network of mosques as well as social, medical, and educational services, and in the process develop a positive reputation as well as a tangible presence among large numbers of average Jordanians. In addition, in contrast to many who had run for parliament, the Islamists generally had no prior governmental experience, no direct association with the corruption perceived to have plagued the previous regime. The "Party of God," as one analyst called them,[4] was a new commodity as a parliamentary representative, and for many average Jordanians there was little reason not to embrace the Islamists' slogan "Islam is the answer."

Following the elections, on December 4, Mudar Badran, former head of the Intelligence Services and former prime minister known for his good relations with the Ikhwan, was selected by the king to assume the prime ministership. Badran proceeded to hold discussions with members of the Brotherhood as part of his consultations aimed at forming a government. However, the Ikhwan's insistence upon being given the education portfolio was not acceptable to the new prime minister and, therefore, while he ultimately did include six independent Islamists (justice, labor, health, social affairs, *awqaf,* and a minister of state for government affairs) in his cabinet, none was a member of the Brotherhood.

Badran won the parliamentary confidence vote easily and then began to make good on the liberalization-related and other promises he had made in his opening policy speech. The process of releasing confiscated passports began (many who had required official permission to travel were allowed to travel without being subjected to such measures), and more political prisoners were released. Ministries were also directed to begin rehiring those who had been dismissed for political reasons. Badran's government also began moving to end martial law, the defense laws, the military courts, and the anticommunism law.

In February, work began on a national charter, called for by the king and intended to be a supplement to the Constitution. The new document was to serve as the basis for a new ordering of state-civil society relations. A royal commission to draft the charter was then assembled, comprising sixty members from across the political spectrum. (While work proceeded on the document, it was delayed by the Gulf crisis and its ratification did not come until June 9, 1991, following the war. In its final form, it guaranteed a pluralistic political system, but also required the acceptance of the Hashemite monarchy.)

In the meantime, with a plurality in parliament, the Islamists began to push for parts of their announced program. Without warning, in early May 1990 the press reported that the Ministry of the Interior would begin to enforce a ban on male hairdressers. Initially the ministry denied that such an order existed, but later admitted that it was in keeping with the "general feeling in the country." While never taking credit officially for advocating the ban, the Ikhwan did state that they welcomed it because "it increased women's employment chances" (*JT,* May 15, 1990). However, the reaction in the press and among the intelligentsia was strong and negative. Some charged the government with following a policy of appeasement regarding the Ikhwan, while a group of women met to plan a strategy to pressure the authorities not to enforce or pass the decision, arguing that this was just the first step in a longer-term strategy against the mixing of the sexes (*JT,* May 8, 1990). Despite an announced scaling back of the application of the ban, by May 18 the ministry was forced to rescind it altogether.

The new parliamentary session began in November 1990, convened in the shadow of the growing Gulf crisis and the popular mobilization that attended it. Rumor had it that the Ikhwan had presented a list of twelve demands, including application of *shariʾa* and obtaining certain ministerial portfolios. Then again, quietly, much like what had happened with the hairdresser incident, the Legal Committee of the House approved a law changing the formula according to which Miri (state) land could be inherited. Prior to the passage of this law, women and men had been eligible to inherit equal shares of such land. The new law made these lands subject to *shariʾa,* thereby reducing a woman's share to one-half that of her brother(s). The law was proposed and passed by the House so quickly that there was no public reaction until after the fact, when it went to the Senate, where it also passed, virtually unchallenged. Indeed, the Islamists were joined by a cohort of non-Islamists who saw nothing detrimental to their interests in a proposal which compromised women's rights.

In January 1991, an awaited cabinet shake-up was finally announced, and this time it was not independent Islamists but five members of the Muslim Brotherhood who were included in Badran's cabinet. The inclusion of the Ikhwan in the cabinet was described by observers as reflecting both the group's power and the government's desire to coopt it (*JT,* May 23–24, 1990). The Islamist ministers, especially ʿAbdallah ʿAkaylah (education) and Yusuf al-ʿAthm (social development) proceeded to implement a number of policies, including sex segregation of their employees, which alienated many in upper-middle-class and upper-class Amman society. The scope and importance of the uproar their attempts at change triggered should not be underestimated, for it is credited in part with bringing down the Badran government.

Shortly after ʿAkaylah was appointed minister of education, he began to institute a series of new measures. In his first meeting with ministry employees he told women that he did not want to have them working in sensitive and important places. Sources also reported that he ordered the "cleansing" of the ministry by segregating the sexes. He then began firing some of the higher-ranking employees and replacing them with Islamists. ʿAkaylah also introduced a series of measures to Islamicize education. He limited the freedom of schools to close on Christian holidays, set midterm exams during Christian holidays, and attempted to ban books deemed incompatible with the kingdom's "moral and religious ethics" (*JT*, May 23–24, 1990).

He then moved to bar male sports instructors from working with female students, while his colleagues in parliament submitted a proposal to ban the mixing of the sexes in all educational facilities. None of this appeared to have a broad impact, nor was there any noticeable public reaction. The controversy was triggered on April 30, when ʿAkaylah issued a decision forbidding fathers to attend their daughters' sporting events. The minister argued that the young girls were often scantily clad for such events and that they therefore would not have total freedom to display their skills without embarrassment if males were present. It was this move that triggered a public outcry and which may well have heralded the beginning of the end for Ikhwan participation in cabinets. Parents reacted swiftly and angrily, forming an ad-hoc PTA of sorts. One legislator who was approached by a concerned parent assisted in drafting a petition, for which more than 5,000 signatures were collected protesting the proposed measure.[5] In mid-June, a delegation of parents angry over the ministers' decisions met with Badran, insisting upon their right to choose on the issue of mixing of the sexes and rejecting the imposition of the minister's will (*JT*, June 13–14, June 1991). Badran resigned only a few days later.

Similar stories were reported about the minister of social affairs, Yusuf al-ʿAthm. He took advantage of the beginning of the Gulf war, as people were upset and distracted, to begin to segregate offices by sex. He instituted separate meetings with male and female staff, and when he met with female staff, he reportedly did not discuss work-related matters. Instead, he admonished them about their style of dress, telling them they should wear less makeup, that he preferred but would not require Islamic dress, and urging them not to wear heels that would click as they went up and down the stairs.[6]

It is difficult to say how important these policies, particularly in the case of the uproar created by those of ʿAkaylah, were in the decision by the king to change prime ministers and exclude the Ikhwan from the next cabinet. Badran was succeeded by Tahir al-Masri. The appointment of al-Masri, known as a liberal, was certainly reassuring to a politically and economically significant sector of Amman society which had been alienated by Badran's ministers' controversial policies. King Husayn certainly prided himself on Jordan's image as a moderate and forward-looking country—and the edicts of the two Ikhwan ministers certainly clashed with that image. Yet, it seems more likely that foreign policy or security considerations played the primary role in the ouster of the Ikhwan from the cabinet.

In the period just before Badran's dismissal, it became increasingly clear that U.S. pressures to convene a comprehensive Middle East peace conference would succeed and that Jordan would participate. Masri was the first prime minister in many years to identify himself and be identified by others as a Jordanian of Palestinian origin and hence to be viewed as a natural choice to lead the government: only a Palestinian would have the necessary legitimacy to undertake such a step, and no Transjordanian would have wanted to be in the position, lest he be charged by Palestinians with being a traitor.

Thus, from the point of view of both domestic and foreign policy, the stage was set for at least the reduction of Ikhwan influence if not their exclusion from the cabinet. For their part, in response to the disquiet their domestic policy initiatives had elicited from some quarters, the Islamists complained that the Jordanian political system (a non-Islamic government) had prevented them from achieving many of their goals (*JT,* June 22, 1991). In any case, with the retreat in the role of the Ikhwan in the government, concern about possible new socially conservative parliamentary initiatives receded. Indeed, women's issues, along with many other domestic economic and political issues, were—for better or worse—slated to take a back seat as the kingdom moved seriously into the Arab-Israeli peace process.

TUNISIA

During his last years in power, Habib Bourguiba, president since 1956, had grown increasingly erratic and arbitrary in his behavior, and political malaise had set in as Tunisians wondered how and when the aging leader would pass from the scene. At the same time, relations between the government and the country's Islamists had deteriorated severely. Islamist journals were closed, and the MTI (Mouvaement de la Tendance Islamique) leaders were arrested and interrogated (*Annuaire de l'Afrique du Nord* [*AAN*], 1987: 650). The move by Zine al-ᶜAbdine Ben ᶜAli against Bourguiba on November 7, 1987, the constitutional coup, as it is called (*changement,* in French; *al-tahawwul,* in Arabic), is generally attributed to his belief in the immediate possibility of an Islamist move against the state.

Prior to taking power, Ben ᶜAli had served as director of military security, minister of the interior, and prime minister, assuming the last post only a month before deposing Bourguiba. Hence, it was not clear whether in his new role as president he would have the will or the power to change the system, as his initial promises indicated he would (Dwyer

1991: 149). What was clear was that he needed to consolidate his own position. This required dealing with three main forces: the ruling Parti Socialiste Destourien (PSD), which Ben ʿAli had joined only in 1984 and to many senior members of which, as a military man who had ousted Bourguiba, he must have appeared threatening; the Islamists; and the leftist and secular opposition. His strategy, at least in hindsight, appears to have been first to defuse the Islamist challenge and offer hope to the secular opposition as he set to work on a process of revival and renewal in the PSD. For that he needed a period of relative social quiet.

Ben ʿAli took a number of steps immediately following the November 7 removal of Bourguiba that seemed to promise a new beginning for politics in Tunisia and which bought him time with both the Islamists and the secular opposition (Tessler 1990: 169–84). The lifetime presidency was abolished and the president's tenure limited to three five-year terms. Some exiled politicians began to return home, and several opposition newspapers were allowed to resume publication. Contacts were also initiated by the government with the opposition parties regarding a new political parties law.

However, the new president also initiated an Islamization of official discourse. He condemned the extent of his predecessor's secularism and argued that, as a result, the free expression of religious faith had been compromised. At the same time, he began to stress the government's role as defender of Islam and morality. The national radio and television began broadcasting the five daily prayers, the autonomy of the Islamic Zitouna University was restored, and Ben ʿAli and his entourage began to take advantage of every occasion to demonstrate their attachment to Islam by appearing at mosques on Fridays and days of celebration. Perhaps Ben ʿAli believed he could truly co-opt all religious elements by such gestures and put an end to the divisions that had increasingly plagued Bourguiba's rule. More likely, he may have thought that he could co-opt at least enough of the pious elements to, in effect, undermine the Islamists.

Having made initial conciliatory gestures to both Islamists and secularists, Ben ʿAli moved to push through changes in the PSD, where support for his program of reconciliation and renewal was by no means universal. The central committee of the party met in late February 1988, chose a new name, the Rassemblement Constitutionnel Démocratique (RCD), and embarked on a path of change. The president took charge of the RCD (a move denounced by the opposition parties), proceeded to choose 122 of 200 members of the RCD Central Committee and reduced the number of political bureau members from fifteen to six. In so doing, he purged some of the old guard who were staunch defenders of the *ancien régime* (*AAN*, 1988: 745). This merging of party and government was a warning of things to come.

In early 1988, the change in regime practices and discourse triggered a heated exchange between Islamists and secularists. The Islamists called for an amendment to the Constitution that would make Islam the state religion. The secularists responded by circulating a petition expressing their concerns about any further concessions to the Islamists, who then responded by denouncing the separation of mosque and state (Ahnaf 1989: 98–105). In the midst of the exchange, in March 1988, the president made his first clear statement on the Personal Status Code (CSP),[7] the symbol of laicism and a centerpiece of Bourguiba's modernization program. The CSP had given Tunisian women a legal status that made them the envy of many Arab or Muslim women, since, among other provisions, the code outlawed polygamy and gave women more equal access to divorce. As a result, the CSP was an issue on which secularists and Islamists were in clearly opposing camps. Ben ʿAli reassured the secularists that there would be no retreat from the code; however, his position was "the code, but nothing but the code," meaning that women could also expect no further reforms.

Shortly thereafter, a new Political Party Law was announced, permitting the establishment of additional opposition parties as long as they were not founded on the basis of language, race, ethnicity, or religion. This, of course, continued to exclude the MTI. However, in a move similar to those that have taken place in other regimes undergoing political transitions (Jordan being a case in point), Ben ʿAli opened a dialogue in the fall of 1988 with opposition politicians, as well as leaders of the main national organizations (labor, employers, farmers, women's unions), with the goal of producing a national pact. The final text guaranteed basic freedoms and the right to form political parties, but also emphasized the consensual nature of Tunisian politics and the country's Arab/Islamic identity. This last aspect, Ben ʿAli's apparent reaching out to Islamists, certainly altered the MTI members' perception of the government (*Economic Intelligence Unit Quarterly Report* [*EIU*], *Tunisia*, no. 4, 1988: 7).

The MTI was, at least officially, making all the right statements to render itself eligible for legalization, including changing its name to al-Nahdah ("renaissance") in early 1989 to address the Party Law's condition that parties not be based on religion. And, although the official press multiplied its attacks against the Islamists, the government made a number of overtures to them (*AAN*, 1989: 682–83). Yet, each time the MTI's leaders sought to take part in negotiations with the government leading to further recognition, new barriers were raised.

The state's temporizing with the Islamists should perhaps have been read as an omen for the transformation of the political system more broadly. The form of the new liberalization was only briefly matched by content, as most observers seem to agree that by the time of the parliamentary elections of April 1989, and certainly by the beginning of 1990, significant political indicators pointed in the direction of a renewed authoritarian swing. Freedom of expression and association were gradually constricted, and members of legal political parties—loyal opposition by most anyone's definition—were increasingly harassed. Accusations of maltreatment and torture, not to mention death while in custody, were widely reported.[8] Just as serious for the long term was the fact that, contrary to the Bourguibist tradition of keeping the military out of politics, Ben ʿAli gradually insinuated the army into positions of civilian power (Leveau 1989: 6).

The 1989 elections, which were legislative and presidential, were a great shock and revelation. In the first place, Ben ʿAli, the only candidate for president, presented himself as the guarantor of both religion and modernity. The powerful electoral machine of the PSD turned RCD, combined with the state's monopoly of information and the meager resources of the opposition parties, led the RCD to win all the seats. At the same time, the opposition bitterly complained of electoral abuses. Only the Islamists, who had to run as independents, made a respectable showing, gaining as much as 30 percent of the vote in some large industrial and urban areas, especially Tunis, thereby confirming that they were the only credible opposition force (*AAN* 1989: 685–86).

A complete rehearsal of all of the twists and turns, carrots and sticks of this period in the relationship between al-Nahdah and the state is beyond the scope of this presentation. What seems clear is that following the elections of April 1989 the state's policy toward the Islamists began to change. The message of Ben ʿAli's subsequent *changement* anniversary speech was one of closure, not opening. The president insisted that it was the state that would determine the framework and the climate needed for political competition and dialogue. It was then up to civil society to accept the state's determination and, beyond that, to oppose any actions which ran counter to the (regime-defined) *national* consensus (*AAN,* 1990: 793). His only "concession" was the establishment of a government Higher Commission on Human and Basic Rights.

Only a few weeks later, at the end of November, it was announced that a cell of Islamic terrorists who had intended to overthrow the state had been rounded up. Al-Nahdah claimed noninvolvement, but arrests of its members followed (*AAN* 1990: 793). As the crackdown on al-Nahdah continued, unease in the opposition ranks grew. On January 12, 1991, the legal opposition parties issued a joint statement declaring their deep concern over "the diminution of political liberties and the trend toward violence." The statement called on the government to lift restrictions on opposition groups, both licensed and unlicensed (*EIU*, no. 1, 1991: 11). In the meantime, al-Nahdah continued to press for its own legalization.

The point of no return came a few months later, on March 22, 1991, when Islamists attacked and set fire to an RCD office in the Bab Souika district in Tunis, just outside the medina. People were outraged by the violence, in which one person was killed and another badly burned. Some 800 people were picked up, including most of al-Nahdah's leadership not already in jail or in exile, although the group initially denied any responsibility. At the end of the roundups, only three members of its executive committee were left at liberty in Tunis, and they subsequently announced that they were freezing their membership because of the violence. New state claims about the discovery of arms and explosives, as well as antiregime tracts, made it clear that a full-scale battle was underway.

The story of the place of women in the maneuvering and bargaining that took place under Ben ʿAli began immediately after the *changement*. Just as women and the CSP were a central part of the legitimacy formula of the Bourguiba regime, so they became under the new president. As in the case of Jordan, several developments will be examined here to explore the relationship between women and the state during the period of liberalization and its aftermath.

Early moves by Ben ʿAli to relax the laicism of his predecessor's regime put women on the defensive and led some to conclude that a competition had developed between the PSD and the MTI over who was more Islamist (Ghanmi 1993: 120). Indeed, the state's initial silence in the face of the MTI's post-*changement* questioning of women's status was interpreted as meaning that a rollback of certain CSP provisions might be on the horizon. The swift move to Islamize state discourse seemed equally threatening (Dargouth-Medimegh 1992: 144).

Growing concern with the power of the Islamists and the Islamization of state discourse led to the coalescing of a group of democratic, liberal, reformist, and leftist women and men. On March 8 (International Women's Day), 1988, many who were concerned with the apparently new direction in regime policy organized a series of activities to celebrate the CSP, women's other gains, citizenship, and laicism more broadly. Perhaps this is the reason that Ben ʿAli's March 20, 1988 address closed the book on any discussion of revising the CSP and presented the state as the guarantor of the code. However, the president's position was also intended to show concern for traditionalist sensitivities. His phrase,

"Tout le CSP, mais rien que le Code," captured the new approach to women's rights: what had been granted would be preserved, but no amendments were envisioned.

The discussions surrounding the National Pact further revealed the ongoing secularist-Islamist battle. The government and others clearly wanted the Islamists to renounce both violence and their desire to turn the clock back on the CSP and related issues. The MTI's primary goal, on the other hand, was simply to secure legal political party status, and it was willing to compromise to achieve it. The "bargain" that was finally struck to include the Islamists as signatories to the pact involved their acceptance of the designation of the CSP as an "irreversible civilizational gain" in exchange for including in the text a phrase insisting upon Tunisia's Arabo-Islamic identity, the meaning of which was never specified. More problematic for non-Islamist women, the president declared that women were responsible for safeguarding this identity. As had long been the case during the Bourguiba years, women's rights had been (re)defined by the state to serve its interests (Ghanmi 1993: 122–23).

But it was not only the discourse and program of the Islamists that non-Islamist women found threatening; it was also the behavior of some MTI members. Despite their adherence to the National Pact, some of the more radical members of al-Nahdah did not hesitate to attack Tunisia's secularism in general, as well as the CSP in particular on the issues of divorce and polygamy. The fact that their meetings attracted large and youthful crowds around the country worried secularist men and women alike (*EIU*, no. 3, 1989: 8).

At the same time, the women did not have the support of all the secularists, as even some members of the government took stands during this period which indicated, if not a sympathy for the Islamists, a clear antagonism toward women. The most notable example occurred during the December 1989 parliamentary discussions of the 1990 budget. During the discussion of the budget for the Ministry of Justice, Deputy Hamza Saʿid called into question Tunisia's laws on polygamy, making clear his antagonism toward women. During the discussion of the Ministry of Higher Education's budget, some deputies contended that the increasing feminization of the educational structure was significantly hurting standards. It was suggested that women's work in education should be regulated by law and that women should be forbidden to give birth during the academic year. Another deputy stated in a newspaper interview that girls should play sports only with other females, thus making clear his preference for segregation according to sex (*Al-Sabah* [Tunis], December 28, 1989).

In addition, however, shortly after the *changement*, members of the

Parti Communiste Tunisien (PCT) launched a campaign in the press attacking, not just the fundamentalists, but also the "deviationist" projects of the women they called westernized feminists. At first, the Association Tunisienne des Femmes Démocrates (ATFD), an independent but largely leftist group of secular women, refused to respond, but subsequently appealed to the Ligue Tunisienne des Droits de l'Homme (LTDH), the nongovernmental human rights organization, on the grounds that the leftists were attacking women's freedom of expression and organization through a form of intellectual terrorism. Not surprisingly, the communists argued that the women's efforts should be part of the struggle of the masses against capitalism and fascism. Women's concerns with the rising power of the Islamists had instead led them to throw their lot in with the *state*, a position which the PCT strongly opposed. They argued that a women's movement independent of the official women's union, the Union Nationale des Femmes Tunisiennes (UNFT), *and* the ATFD should evolve to emphasize and fight *two* forms of fascism: destourian (the state) and fundamentalist (Ghanmi 1993: 124–25).

As noted above, despite the MTI's formal acceptance of the CSP through its adherence to the National Pact, Islamist candidates during the campaign for the April 1989 elections regularly attacked the code, often attracting large, supportive crowds. The Islamists placed women center-stage in their program, campaigning on the theme of "women and morals," lambasting "the modern woman" and glorifying "the veiled woman" (Dargouth-Medimegh 1992: 145). In response, on March 31, 500 women participated in a demonstration led by the still unlicensed ATFD, although the president of the government union, the UNFT, was also present. Slogans called for no retreat on women's rights and for equality (*Al-Sabah,* April 1, 1989).

In the end, the RCD received 77.7 percent of the female vote (39.8 percent of eligible women), and 70.5 percent of the male vote (47.3 percent of the eligible men) in the April elections. Six RCD women were elected; the previous parliament had had seven. The success of the Islamists, who ran as independents, was estimated officially at 13 percent of the vote; however, as noted above, the percentage was actually much higher, especially in the urban areas (Dargouth-Medimegh 1992: 154, 158, 181). Ben ʿAli was apparently alarmed by their strong showing, and, as was argued above, these elections marked the beginning of the end of regime willingness to treat with the Islamists.

One of the most interesting characteristics of the early Ben ʿAli period is the degree to which regime policy toward the Islamists became increasingly inseparable from its policy toward women. The important place that women and the CSP had had in Bourguiba's modernizing and laicist project meant that, almost by definition, they would be a primary target of Islamists seeking to restore Islam and women to their "proper place" in society. Beginning with an apparently ambivalent attitude toward women's concerns as he Islamized state discourse, Ben ʿAli gradually came to view women as a natural first defense line against the Islamists. With no where else to go, the women had little choice but to seek the protection of the state. Once the state decided to crack down on the Islamists—for its own reasons—it was able to use its demonstrated concern for women as a justification for its policy and as proof, especially to the outside world, of its continuing commitment to modernity and human rights despite the strong criticisms that came from abroad regarding the brutality of the anti-Islamist drive.

Conclusions

In the two case studies considered above, the initial period of liberalization offered both new opportunities as well as challenges or threats to women and women's rights. The greater freedom of expression allowed by the political openings meant the empowerment and/or legalization of a range of actors, some new, some preexisting but unlicensed. In both these cases, the opening allowed growing Islamist movements the opportunity to participate in national politics in an unprecedented way. And, during the initial period of the liberalization, as the regimes sought out new allies in their drive to consolidate power, the Islamists, or at least traditional elements, clearly imposed themselves as forces with which to be reckoned.

In the case of Jordan, the fact that the regime had long had a relationship of coordination with the Muslim Brotherhood meant that the process of co-optation or inclusion was relatively smooth. And it was in this period that the demands of the new Islamist deputies and the position of the government on these demands made some women feel increasingly uneasy. In the end, it appears that a combination of overplaying their hand and a new foreign policy direction (with the latter probably far more important in the end than the former) led to the Islamists' exit from parliament and to the apparent end of the new, direct threat they posed to women's status.

In Tunisia the situation was quite different, in large part because of the antagonistic relationship that had long existed between the Bourguiba regime and religious elements, whether the MTI or others. As a result, when Ben ʿAli took power and saw the need to establish a separate, new legacy for himself, the temptation to roll back at least some aspects of the secularism of the previous regime was too great to resist. It was at this point, again, in the very early period of the new regime, that women's rights (as represented by the CSP) appear to have been in greatest danger, precisely because they were one of the hallmarks of the Bourguiba era. Only with the electoral successes of the Islamists in April 1989, elections in which women had taken a strong pro-RCD stance, and against the backdrop of an ascendant Islamist movement next door in Algeria, did Ben ʿAli finally move to end the policy of co-optation on the margins in favor of suppression of the center. In the process the CSP was upheld and even later (1993) improved. Lost in the equation, however, was the broader, earlier commitment to pluralism and tolerance.

The Tunisian case shows most clearly that a swift break with the previous leadership, combined with equivocal (or negative) attitudes of the new leadership toward the old, may well open the legacy of the previous regime to criticism and expose its achievements to possible reversals as a calculated part of the consolidation process. The parallel with many of the Eastern European transitions is striking here: in Eastern Europe, the socialist policies of women's rights to work and reproductive choice were among the first elements to be denigrated, challenged, and overturned under the transitional or consolidating regimes.

The question of break versus gradual transition is also important. Gradual transitions operate in less of a crisis mode. The need to reconsolidate is less urgent or perhaps not present at all. The more serious the reconsolidation issue, the more likely the new regime will be to seek new allies. Although the actual transitions were managed from above, both Tunisia and Jordan can be placed in the category of shock transition; that is, an unexpected event rather than a slow evolution brought about the change.

Beyond this, however, the two cases diverge, based on each regime's prior relationship with the new opposition. While Islamists emerged as the primary opposition force in both Tunisia and Jordan, in Jordan this "opposition" had long had a close relationship with the regime and consequently had less to gain from a political opening. Moreover, social policy in Jordan has been conservative, the Westernized veneer of the country and its leadership notwithstanding. As a result, the Islamists were less concerned with overhauling social policy (although they certainly had plans for it) than with making sure that political freedoms were reinforced, and this in turn meant that Jordanian women, relatively, had less to lose from an increase in Islamist influence. In Tunisia, by contrast, the relationship between the regime and the Islamists had long been tense and contentious. Moreover, a cornerstone of the regime's image, the CSP, was seen by Islamists as objectionable at best and heretical at worst. For these reasons, women and their rights were at greater risk in Tunisia: women had more to lose and the Islamists' previous exclusion from the political game gave them less to lose.

This said, the challenges or threats that women faced during these periods were clear and substantial. The ultimate outcomes represent in most cases at best a reinforcement of the status quo; that is, no retreat in the realm of women's rights. In Jordan, the initial challenges were resisted by the regime, perhaps largely for reasons of external image and preventing internal dissent. In the end, the combination of the Islamists' close relationship with the regime and their disaffection owing to Jordan's major foreign policy initiative of the period, the peace treaty with Israel, greatly reduced the possibilities for confrontation or for a substantial impact of their voice. In the case of Tunisia, the CSP was preserved, but the state's battle against the Islamists made victims of many other civil and political rights.

The major unifying theme of these observations is that improvements in women's status and rights continue to depend on initiatives from above. A related theme is that political liberalization may increase the opportunities available to Islamists and other conservative political forces opposed to such improvements. In such a situation, one in which women have not been able or allowed to establish organizations with mobilizational power that must be taken into account by the state, rights will continue to be bestowed rather than "earned," i.e., wrested from below. While the importance of state protection and sponsoring of women's rights should not be underestimated, the lack of an independent source of power and the continuing contentiousness of questions related to women's rights means that women will continue to find themselves beholden to the state and hence on the frontlines of the political battles that accompany political transitions—be these revolutions or managed political liberalizations. It is a position that offers both tremendous possibilities and dangerous challenges.

NOTES

1. This article does not pretend to analyze the experiences of all Tunisian and Jordanian women. It focuses on negotiations among political actors at the national level and the impact they had upon women. The rationale behind this choice was that at this level state intent (as opposed to unintended outcomes) is clearest; and understanding the relationship between women and the state was the primary goal of this research. Women were and continue to be differentially affected by such negotiations and their outcomes. The impact examined here was

certainly felt more directly by urban and, in particular, better-educated and often middle- to upper-class women.

2. The only such treatment of which I am aware is Hatem 1995.

3. Actually, the number of Islamists varies, depending upon the source, that is. The problem lies in who is defining "indepedent Islamist." I found as many as 34 cited, and as few as 28. Most oftern 28 or 30 is cited as the figure. What seems most important is that even if one takes the lower figure, Islamists controlled more than one-third of the eighty-seat lower house.

4. This was a term I first heard used in the Jordanian context in English by Dr. Mustafa Hamarneh, director of the Center for Strategic Studies, Jordan University. It does not refer to the Lebanese "Hizballah," which means Party of God.

5. From an off-the-record interview with a Jordanian legislator. I was assured that this petition campaign had had an impact on discussions in policy circles.

6. From an off-the-record interview with a Ministry of Social Development employee.

7. The CSP and its counterparts in other Arab countries regulate those issues associated with the family, marriage, inheritance, children, divorce, and so forth. It is also the law that generally draws most heavily from Islamic law.

8. See Amnesty International reports for the period.

REFERENCES

Ahnaf, M. 1989. "Tunisie: un débat sur les rapports Etat/religion." *Maghreb-Machrek* 126 (October-December): 98–105.

Dargouth-Medimegh, Aziza. 1992. *Droits et Vécu de la Femme en Tunisie.* Paris: L'Hermès Edilis.

Dwyer, Kevin. 1991. *Arab Voices: The Human Rights Debate in the Middle East.* Berkeley: University of California Press.

Eury, Pascaline. 1991. *Jordanie: les élections législatives du 8 novembre 1989.* Beirut: Centre d'Etudes et Recherche sur le Moyen Orient Contemporain.

Funk, Nanette, and Magda Mueller, eds. 1993. *Gender Politics and Post-Communism.* New York: Routledge.

Gallagher, Nancy. 1993. "Gender, Islamism and Democratization in Jordan: The Case of Tujan al-Faysal." Unpublished paper.

Ghanmi, Azza. 1993. *Le mouvement féministe tunisien: terminologie sur l'autonomie et la pluralité des femmes, 1979–1989.* Tunis: Editions Chama.

Hatem, Mervet. 1995. "Political Liberalization, Gender, and the State." In Rex Brynen, Bahgat Korany, and Paul Noble, eds. *Political Liberalization and Democratization in the Arab World,* vol. 1. Boulder: Lynne Reinner.

Leveau, Remy. 1989. "La Tunisie du Président Ben Ali: équilibre interne et environnement arabe." *Maghreb-Machrek* 124 (April-June): 6.

Moghadam, Valentine M., ed. 1993. *Democratic Reform and the Position of Women in Transitional Economies.* Oxford: Clarendon Press.

Norton, R. Augustus. 1995. "Introduction." In R. Augustus Norton, ed., *Civil Society in the Middle East,* vol. 1. Leiden: Brill.

Rai, Shirin, Hilary Pilkington, and Annie Phizacklea, eds. 1992. *Women in the Face of Change: The Soviet Union, Eastern Europe and China.* New York: Routledge.

Tessler, Mark. 1990. "Tunisia's New Beginning." *Current History* (April 1990): 169–84.

9
Democratic Concern and Islamic Resurgence: Converging Dimensions of the Arab World's Political Agenda

Mark Tessler

DEMOCRACY AND ISLAM are two critical dimensions of political life in the present-day Arab world. A concern for democracy has become prominent during the past decade, both as a focus for political reforms introduced by a number of Arab regimes and as a central theme in Arab political discourse. Islam, while not a new factor, has in recent years assumed a much more influential position in Arab societies through the growth of new Muslim cultural associations, social institutions, and political organizations. While these two trends are pivotal to understanding political developments in the Arab Middle East, the relationship between them has been strongly debated.

In particular, there is considerable disagreement concerning the compatibility of the Islamic resurgence and the push for more accountable government. Some observers assert that democracy and Islam are two competing ideological perspectives. While democracy requires openness, competition, pluralism, and tolerance of diversity, Islam is said to encourage intellectual conformity and an uncritical acceptance of established authority. But many others point out that Islam is characterized by a wide and disparate range of prescriptions, and that Muslims have historically attached legitimacy to diverse interpretations on issues of

Preliminary research for this chapter was done while the author was a visiting scholar at Rand in August 1994. He wishes to express his thanks to the Rand Greater Middle East Studies Center, and to its former associate director, Mary Morris. He also wishes to record his thanks to Laurie Brand, Emile Sahliyeh, and Jodi Nachtwey for valuable comments on earlier versions of this chapter.

law and morality. As a result, openness, tolerance, and progressive innovation are well represented among the traditions associated with the religion.

Turning from Islam to Islamism, here defined as the pursuit of political power in order to govern in accordance with a strict interpretation of Muslim law, there is even greater disagreement about the implications for democracy of the growth in popular support for Muslim political movements. On one hand, many observers allege that these movements do not respect democratic processes. They fear that Islamist organizations will use any influence or power they acquire to advance an ideology that is monolithic and intolerant of dissent, thereby subverting the democratic process from within the political system. Others challenge this assessment, however, both questioning the motives of those who reject any possibility of sharing power with Islamist movements and suggesting that meaningful democratization is impossible if organizations with broad public support are excluded from the political process. These analysts conclude that the real danger to democracy lies in the banning of Muslim political groups, not in allowing them to participate in an open and competitive political process.

Against the background of these issues and debates, the present chapter examines the relationship between democracy and Islam by explicating the factors fueling democratization and the region's Islamic resurgence. It is impossible to offer definitive evidence, which is the reason, or course, that disagreements exist. Nor is it necessarily the case that uniform conclusions apply to the whole of the Arab world. Nevertheless, with these cautions in mind, the discussion to follow addresses the subject of democracy and Islam in an effort to foster critical thinking about some of the most important dimensions of present-day Arab politics.

DEMOCRATIC TRANSITIONS AND THEIR LIMITS

The Arab world's growing interest in democracy can be seen in the political experiments undertaken in a number of states in the mid- and late-1980s. These include Egypt, Morocco, Tunisia, Jordan, Algeria, and Yemen, whose combined population totals more than 130 million men and women.

In Tunisia, for example, Zine el-Abidine Ben ʿAli, at the time prime minister, assumed the presidency through a constitutional coup in November 1987, after a panel of doctors had certified that the existing president, Habib Bourguiba, was no longer able to perform his duties. Ben ʿAli promised political reform in his inaugural address, and the national assembly soon adopted measures consistent with this pledge. These included abolition of the State Security Court, which Bourguiba had used to suppress critics, passage of a more liberal press law, and plans for new presidential and legislative elections. In anticipation of the balloting, scheduled for April 1989, the government granted legal status to two new opposition parties.

In Jordan, another important case, the announcement in April 1989 of the lifting of subsidies on petroleum and petroleum products led to the outbreak of rioting in the southern city of Ma'an, after which disturbances spread throughout the kingdom. The prime minister resigned, and after a brief interlude it was announced that the first parliamentary elections since 1967 would be held in November 1989. This was followed by the enactment and implementation of a number of important measures, including provisions for greater freedom of expression.

Democratic concern was also evident in Arab political discourse. According to one knowledgeable scholar, writing early in 1992, "the demand for human rights, participation and democracy comes from across the political spectrum. . . . The call for democracy is the subject of meetings, conferences and academic studies" (Kramer 1992: 23). One such meeting was a pan-Arab conference, held in Amman, Jordan, in 1991 and attended by prominent intellectuals. Participants called for a "new Arab order" and declared in their final communique that "democracy should take priority in the pan-Arab national project. It should not be sacrificed for any other value or cause—including Arab unity itself" (Halasa 1991).

This is not to say that democracy has taken root in the Arab world. In both Tunisia and Jordan, as well as Egypt and other countries, transitions to democracy slowed significantly during the mid- and late-1990s. In Tunisia, the retreat from the democratic path has been particularly striking, with the Ben ʿAli government becoming increasingly intolerant of dissent. Recent developments in Jordan suggest movement in the same direction.

Some democratic experiments have been abandoned altogether. The Algerian political system, for example, closed abruptly in early 1992. The Islamic Salvation Front (FIS), an Islamist party, had scored a decisive victory in the local and provincial elections of June 1990, and it was leading after the first round of balloting in the parliamentary elections held eighteen months later, in December 1991. The government canceled the second round of balloting, however, rather than risk losing control of the National Assembly. Further, under pressure from the military, the president then resigned and handed over power to a hastily formed High Security Council. The military arrested many FIS leaders in the weeks that followed, not only bringing Algeria's democratic experiment to a definitive end, but also initiating a civil war that has steadily grown more brutal.

Accordingly, the mood in the Arab world today is radically different than it was at the beginning of the decade. Surveying the remnants of democratic openings, one prominent scholar describes the situation as "exceptionally bleak . . . from the spectacular crash and burn of Algeria's liberalization to Tunisia's more subtle but no less profound transformation into a police state, from Egypt's backsliding into electoral manipulation [and repression of Islamic political movements] to the obvious reluctance of Palestinian authorities to embrace human rights" (Anderson 1999: 6).

It remains to be seen whether, and in what way, democratic experiments will resume in the Arab world. While the situation at present is not encouraging, popular demands for more responsive and accountable government remain strong and can be expected to exert pressure for renewed movement in this direction (Quandt 1994; Zartman 1995; Norton and Wright 1995). So, too, do global currents, including, especially, pressures for economic liberalization. In most Arab countries, including those where there is little overt movement toward democratization, economic liberalization is introducing new patterns of political and economic influence and creating the conditions for greater pluralism and independence in interest articulation (Solingen 1996: 151; Henry 1996). Finally, the presence of a growing number of civil society organizations is also relevant in this connection (Norton 1996). Many of these civic associations have been established for the explicit purpose of influencing public policy and extracting resources from the state. Thus, despite the stalemate as the millennium approaches, it is likely that issues of governance in general and democratization in particular will retain a place of prominence on the Arab world's political agenda.

ORIGINS OF DEMOCRATIC CONCERN

Western observers frequently assume that democracy has been placed on the Arab political agenda by external influences. On the one hand, they argue that there has been a diffusion of democratic currents from other parts of the world, including Latin America and some parts of Asia and sub-Saharan Africa. According to one scholar, "there is a 'contagion' of democratic development: events in some countries clearly impact on neighboring ones" (Zacek 1993). Observers also frequently emphasize the end of the cold war and the collapse of the Soviet Union in this connection. They point out, correctly, that these events have discredited centralized and authoritarian models of development, while at the same time reducing external support for some of the Arab world's most dictatorial regimes.

But these developments are of secondary importance so far as domestic politics in the Arab world is concerned. Pressures for political liberalization both preceded the fall of communist regimes in Eastern Europe and have evolved independently of circumstances in other regions of the Third World. Political reforms undertaken in the mid- and late-1980s were first and foremost a response to the demands for more responsive government articulated by ordinary men and women. Many Arab countries, and most notably those that subsequently implemented political reforms, experienced riots, violent confrontations, and other forms of popular unrest during this period. These outbursts, revealing public discontent with established power relationships and existing patterns of governance, created pressure for change that could not be ignored (Tessler 1991).

Events in Tunisia, Algeria, and Jordan, as well as elsewhere, provide support for the assertion that domestic pressures, rather than external influences, have been the most important stimuli for political reform. Tunisia, for example, was shaken by a week of rioting in 1984 when students, workers, and unemployed young men attacked symbols of authority and wealth in several major cities. Algeria also experienced unrest during this period, culminating with intense and widespread rioting in 1988. In Algiers, Oran, Constantine, and several other cities, thousands of young people came into the streets to vent their anger over worsening economic and social conditions. In Jordan, riots broke out in April 1989, beginning in the southern city of Ma'an and spreading quickly throughout the kingdom. The unrest shocked the country, forcing the king to rush home from an overseas visit to address the crisis.

Immediate grievances were the same in all of these countries, and similar to those in many other Arab countries as well. Masses of people live in impoverished conditions, and for much of the population, especially the young, the prospects for social mobility and a higher standard of living have been declining rather than growing brighter. Unemployment is a particularly severe aspect of this problem, and accordingly, with no other way to occupy themselves, legions of young men while away their days on street corners or in coffeehouses, becoming ever more disillusioned and embittered (Moffett 1989; Tessler 1993). In Algeria, for example, they are sometimes called "homeboys" (*houmistes*), boys from the neighborhood, or "wall boys," (*hittistes*), unemployed youth who have nothing to do and so "hang out," leaning against the walls that line many city streets (Brown 1993).

Further, there is a large and growing gap between rich and poor, meaning that the burdens of underdevelopment are not shared equitably and that, despite economic difficulties, there are islands of affluence and privilege. A related complaint is that elite membership is determined in most instances not by ability, dedication, or service to society but, rather, by personal and political connections. Resentment of those who benefit from this situation was reflected during the riots of the 1980s in attacks on shops selling luxury goods and incursions into fashionable elite neighborhoods. Anger was directed at the consumption-oriented middle and upper classes, population categories which were perceived to be prospering at a time when the circumstances of the masses were steadily deteriorating. These favored elements, it was also charged, supported their indulgent lifestyles with resources needed for national development, while giving the country little or nothing that might justify their privileged positions.

Anger was directed in equal or even greater measure at political leaders, whose lethargy and corruption were held to be largely responsible for economic and social problems. Politically conscious citizens not only complained about governmental systems in which patronage and clientelism predominate, but also about the inability of the populace to remove politicians whose performance is unsatisfactory, or even to exert meaningful influence in political decision-making. According to a journalistic investigation in Jordan, for example, "many people were unwilling to tighten their belts to pay for an economic crisis which they felt was the result of widespread corruption," and that among the elite "a system of cronyism is persuasive," with opportunities for enrichment channeled by insiders to their friends and with top positions always going "to the same old faces, families and clans" (Amawi 1992: 27).

Against this background, it is clear that there has been popular pressure for meaningful political change. Ordinary men and women may not have well-developed and coherent notions of democracy. Indeed, as explained by a prominent Moroccan sociologist, *dimuqratiyya,* as the term is usually rendered in Arabic, often appears foreign, confusing, and perhaps even slightly threatening to many of the very citizens who are demanding political change (Mernissi 1992: 42–45, 53). Nevertheless, there can be little doubt that people want greater accountability and responsiveness from their leaders. They want the ability to express their complaints through effective and legitimate channels, in ways that empower and give them political influence. They also want political alternatives so that leaders who do not deal sincerely and wisely with the requirements of ordinary citizens can be replaced. As expressed by a Jordanian journalist, there are indications throughout the Arab world of "a profound desire for change—for democracy and human rights, for social equity, for accountability on the part of public officials, for morality in public life" (Khouri 1990).

Public opinion polls have also documented this desire for political change and accountable government. For example, surveys carried out in the West Bank and Gaza during 1995 found that respondents overwhelmingly favored a free press, a multiparty system, fair elections, and a right to criticize the government (Shikaki 1996). A 1988 survey in Egypt found that 68 percent of the urban population believes the government usually ignores the needs of the people, and that 71 percent thinks public officials usually pursue their personal interests before those of the people (Tessler and Sanad 1994). Surveys carried out in Morocco in the early 1980s report that "while the state is feared, it is also often resented, if not hated . . . [and is] widely recognized as not representative of the people" (Suleiman 1987).

A final point about the origins of democratic concern is the view of many Arabs that while the West claims to be encouraging political reform, its actions are in fact designed to preserve the status quo. The Gulf Crisis of 1990–91 confirmed this proposition for many in the Arab world. As expressed by one Arab scholar, "the U.S. has supported the transition to democracy in Eastern Europe and Latin America, but it fought a war to restore the traditional monarchy in Kuwait and has not subsequently exerted pressure on the Gulf states for democratization and political change" (Al-Suwaidi 1995: 102–3).

The U.S.-led action to oust Iraq from Kuwait also provoked large demonstrations of opposition in many Arab countries, most notably, moreover, in states that had experienced a measure of democratization (Labib 1991: 195). The charge of protesters, as well as many Arab intellectuals, was that the anti-Iraq coalition was acting in defense of corrupt and undemocratic regimes to preserve the existing political and economic order. It was an imperialist coalition fighting not for change, as it pretended, but rather for business as usual (Zghal 1991: 161–62; Bennani-Chraibi 1993: 392–436; Pollock 1992: 31, 35).

In conclusion, even if these criticisms of Western governments are exaggerated, as they sometimes are, it remains clear that the actions of ordinary Arab citizens, not external powers or worldwide trends, have been primarily responsible for putting democracy on the Arab world's political agenda.

THE ISLAMIC RESURGENCE

The current Islamic revival in the Arab world began during the 1970s. This religious resurgence has been characterized by the formation of cultural associations and study groups, by the growth of Muslim social institutions, including welfare societies and financial establishments, and by an increase in such public manifestations of religious observance as mosque attendance and veiling. The religious resurgence has also been marked by growing support for Islamist political movements, organizations which not only seek to foster greater piety and conformity to Islamic prescriptions among individual Muslims, but which also work for the establishment of governments that will rule in accordance with Islamic law. These movements have been particularly successful in recruiting followers among the young, including highly educated as well as socially disadvantaged, and women as well as men. By the late 1970s, Muslim groups were not only active but had in most cases displaced leftist organizations as the primary vehicles for political activity on high school and university campuses.

Muslim political movements became an important vehicle in the 1980s for the expression of discontent at the failure of Arab governments to deal satisfactorily with domestic economic and political problems. As noted, the anger of ordinary men and women was visible in explosions of unrest during this decade, and in some cases during the mid- and late-1970s. This anger soon found expression as well in the support of these citizens for Islamist political movements. These movements called for the replacement of current rulers and regimes and campaigned under the banner "Islam is the solution."

In Jordan, for example, the riots of 1989 were followed by the resuscitation of parliamentary life, which included elections in which the Muslim Brotherhood emerged as the largest block in the parliament. In Algeria, as discussed, the Islamic Salvation Front prevailed in both the local and provincial elections of 1990 and in the truncated parliamentary elections of 1991. The Tunisian case provides another illustration. Although the government refused to grant legal status to the Renaissance Party, or al-Nahda, the country's principal Muslim political movement, party candidates ran as independents and performed impressively in the 1989 parliamentary elections. According to government figures, individuals affiliated with the party received about 14 percent of the total vote and one-third or more of the votes in Tunis and other urban centers. al-Nahda sources put the figures even higher, insisting they had actually won a majority in several locations.

The origins of this resurgence are diverse, rooted to a significant degree in the enduring religious attachments of ordinary Muslims, but shaped to an equal or even greater extent by events that have been transforming the political landscape of the Arab world. The Arab-Israeli War of 1967, for example, brought to the Arabs a crushing defeat and thus cast doubt on the socialist development ideologies of those states, particularly Egypt and Syria, that had led the struggle against Israel. Another important factor was growing disenchantment with foreign development models, including capitalism as well as socialism. Complaints against Western ideologies included not only a failure to reduce poverty or increase political freedom, but also the charge that they had produced in the Arab world such undesirable characteristics of Western society as crime, alcoholism, sexual permissiveness, and the alienation of youth. Together, these failures led many to conclude that an indigenous normative system, Islam, should be given greater weight in the search for a strategy of social and economic change.

It is important to recognize the commonalities that underlie the Islamic resurgence and the concern for democracy in the present-day Arab world. Each trend has for the most part been driven forward by the same underlying stimulus, namely a deep dissatisfaction among ordinary citizens with established patterns of governance and prevailing political and economic relationships. The impact of the Arab defeat in June 1967 should be understood in this context; it provoked a crisis of confidence in leaders and ideologies based not on religious lapses or cultural deviation but on a perceived inability to deal effectively with temporal problems.

Opposition to the political and economic status quo is similarly at the root of popular support for Islamist movements. As recently expressed by two American scholars of Algerian origin, "economic deprivation, social exclusion, and political under-representation [have] encouraged the development of Islamist movements not only in Algeria but also in many other Muslim countries" (Layachi and Haireche 1992: 76). Often, therefore, the electoral gains of Islamist parties reflect votes *against* the government and the status quo, as much as, or even more than, votes *for* the platform of Muslim political parties. For example, according to several analyses of the 1990 and 1991 Algerian elections, many men and women cast "rejection votes," or, as one journalist put the matter, many voted for the FIS "out of revenge" (Y. Ibrahim 1990). Thus, although it may appear as a contradiction to those unfamiliar with the Arab world, a desire for economic and above all political change is producing both support for democratization and support for political Islam.

It is also necessary to ask why large numbers of ordinary Arabs are concluding that they can best work for political change by giving their support to Islamist movements. Islam is appealing because of its familiarity, of course, and because it offers a constitution for societal organization, but also prominent among the reasons for the success of Islamist movements are the organizational and political advantages that these groups enjoy. For one thing, in the undemocratic environment that has prevailed in most Arab countries, mosques and other religious establishments offer opportunities to recruit and organize followers that are unavailable to more secular movements. In addition, quiet but sometimes considerable support from Arab governments also enabled a number of Muslim groups to expand their influence. This was the case in Egypt, Jordan, and Morocco, for example. In these as well as several other countries, governments took a relatively tolerant attitude toward Islamist organizations in order to build up a counterweight to leftist opposition movements, from which in the past had come the most serious challenges to many Arab regimes. Israel pursued a similar policy in the West Bank and Gaza, giving latitude to Islamist movements in the hope that they would draw support away from the PLO.

In some countries, Islamic groups have also built support through the provision of social services and through community assistance projects. Clinics, schools, day-care centers, and welfare distribution programs are among the most common of these activities. Also, in addition to these efforts aimed primarily at the urban poor, some Islamic groups have established publishing societies, investment companies, and even banks. Such efforts require a measure of organization that political authorities have little choice but to tolerate because they are carried out in the name of religion, even though the resulting institutions may foster a belief that Islamic groups are more dedicated to helping ordinary men and women than are government officials. As reported by an American scholar of Egyptian origin, groups associated with political Islam use socioeconomic institutions and programs to "participate in the political process within the official parameters of permissible action, while working to extract concessions from the state to allow the [Islamist] movement greater access to the masses and through them access to power" (Karawan 1992: 172).

An additional factor working to the advantage of Islamist movements, and in some ways the most important, is the absence of alternative opposition parties with a credible platform. In particular, with a few partial exceptions, most Arabs no longer regard parties of the political left as suitable vehicles for the mobilization and expression of opposition to existing regimes. This was evident in the Tunisian elections of April

1989, for example, where the leading socialist party received less than 4 percent of the vote. Leftist parties also fared poorly in the Algerian election of June 1990, about which one study concludes that gains made by the FIS reflect not only social and economic grievances but also, in combination, an "inability of the traditional secular opposition to channel popular demands" (Layachi and Haireche 1992: 76). The situation in Egypt was summed up by a socialist leader who complained in an interview with the author that while "Islam may not be able to solve the country's problems, Muslim groups at least have a credible slogan. They may be without a real solution, but we [Socialists] are without even a pretend solution."

The conclusion to be drawn from this analysis is that the major reasons for the Islamists' success are to be found in the domain of politics and organization, and only secondarily in that of spirituality. As summarized in a recent study of Egypt, Islamist groups have distinct advantages: "they have access to mosques, operate charitable societies, and promote Islamic banks and investment companies. They run medical clinics and literacy programs, provide low cost clothes and books for students, and contribute food and even cash for the indigent. Given the deterioration in the quality of government services since the 1970s, the Islamic charities fulfill important needs. [At the same time,] government restrictions on the formation of civic and political groups have disproportionately hampered liberal and left movements, thus leaving loopholes for the religious groups" (Kramer 1992).

DEMOCRACY IN ISLAMIC THEORY AND PRACTICE

The origins of both the growing concern for democracy and the resurgence of Islam are to be found in the political crisis that has been buffeting the Arab world. Whether there is tension between these two trends, despite their common origins, is a question that preoccupies many analysts with an interest in the Arab world. Some observers, particularly Western ones, express doubt that greater responsiveness to the will of ordinary citizens is likely to lead to democracy in countries where the population has a strong attachment to Islam. Indeed, some predict that Arab democratic experiments are destined to fail precisely because they will empower men and women with neither a knowledge of, nor an interest in, the secular values that are a prerequisite for democracy. Those who take this position usually contend that two interrelated aspects of Islam are incompatible with democracy. The first concerns civic values and the second concerns the institutions of government.

With respect to the civic values, democracy requires a political culture that accepts or even welcomes political and ideological pluralism, and which is thus hospitable to independent judgment, dissent, and political bargaining. But these values are held to be absent in Islam. According to this analysis, the Muslim religion insists on social and intellectual conformity and on the uncritical acceptance of established authority, whereas democracy demands a political culture "that is less monistic and more tolerant of diversity and compromise" (Huntington 1984: 214; also Huntington 1993).

With respect to the institutions of government, Islam is said to be antidemocratic because it prohibits the establishment of representative and parliamentary political systems, viewing these as man-made constructions that have no place in a polity where the revealed word of God is the only authoritative source of law and political authority. In the view of some, this means that Islam "has to be ultimately embodied in a totalitarian state" (Choueiri 1996: 21–22; also Lewis 1994: 54–56). A related consideration is the contention that Islam requires rulers to be obedient to God alone. As one scholar explains, democracy ceases to exist in a situation where the ruler is accountable only to God, and where it is the ruler's responsibility to guarantee the continued harmonious integration of each individual and group into the community (Anderson 1987: 221).

These propositions about the antagonism between democracy and Islam are not accepted by all observers, however. So far as civic values are concerned, Islam is monolithic in the sense that its sole foundation is the word of God as revealed to the Prophet Mohammed and set down in the Koran, and thereafter, for orthodox Muslims, the words and deeds of the Prophet as recorded in the *Sunna*. But this does not take one very far. As a guide to action and the living of life, not as a text to be recited and revered but as a legal code to be put into practice, the word of God requires neither more nor less than what the community of believers and its religious leaders interpret it to require. And since Muslims have over the course of nearly fourteen centuries advanced varying interpretations of Islamic doctrine, it is a futile exercise to search for the *true* Islam, or to inquire about the religion's *true* attitude toward complex and changing social issues, such as those pertaining to governance and democracy.

Many scholars, therefore, view unidimensional characterizations of Islam with suspicion (Halliday 1995: 116; Esposito and Piscatori 1991). They emphasize that there is considerable variation in the interpretations of religious law advanced by Muslim scholars and theologians, and that among these there are even expressions of support for democracy (Abed 1995: 127–28). They insist that openness, tolerance, and progressive innovation are well represented among traditions associated with the religion, and that these values and orientations thus are entirely compatible with Islam (Hamdi 1996; Mernissi 1992; al-Dajjani 1987).

A forceful exposition of this thesis is offered by Fatima Mernissi, who points out that there are two great historical traditions in Islam and that neither is more authentic than the other. As Mernissi states in *Islam and Democracy,* the religion has been marked throughout its history by an intellectual trend that encouraged rational inquiry and speculated on the philosophical foundations of the world and humanity, as well as by an obscurantist trend that condemned philosophy, reduced ordinary citizens to intellectual apathy, and left political challengers no resort but force. The central preoccupation of the former tradition is discussion, or *kalam,* defined as the exercise of reason and stimulated not only by the logical exposition of arguments but also by "new ideas [that] poured into the souks and became a preoccupation of the masses" (p. 36).

Another Arab scholar makes the same point, placing particular emphasis on the issue of cultural borrowing and adaptation. He notes, in an essay also entitled "Islam and Democracy," that from its earliest stages Islam was marked by "heated debates between those who defended openness and accommodation to non-Muslim political, social and even metaphysical world views, and those who looked upon these same views with suspicion and disapproval." Further, like their premodern counterparts, contemporary Arab and Muslim intellectuals are divided between those who reject foreign political concepts, including democracy, and those who do not ask "*whether,* but rather *how,* it is possible to remain a Muslim while acquiring new, non-Muslim values" (Abed 1995: 119).

Equally important, progressive Muslim thinkers not only contend that Islam is open to new ideas, many argue that in most cases these concepts actually are not foreign at all. According to Rifat al-Tahtawi, for example, a leading nineteenth century Egyptian modernist, "what is called freedom in Europe is exactly what is defined in our religion as justice [*adl*], right [*haqq*], consultation [*shura*], and equality [*musawat*]. . . . This is because the rule of freedom and democracy consists of imparting justice and right to the people, and of the people's participation in determining their destiny" (Abed 1995: 119). More recently, in a book entitled *al-dimuqratiyyah fi'l-islam* (Democracy in Islam), the celebrated Egyptian intellectual Abbas Mahmoud al-Aqqad stressed the similarity between the liberal stream in Islamic thought and the elements of democracy that are found in Western political theory.

Turning to political institutions, it is the view of Muslim traditionalists that the laws governing human affairs come only from God. For men and women to enact such laws is to be guilty of *shirk,* or association, the substitution of human judgment for that of the Deity. If interpreted literally, this means that representative democracy is indeed impossible in a Muslim polity, and that national assemblies can never be more than vehicles for advice and consultation.

Again, however, this is not the only or even the most common interpretation advanced by knowledgeable and devout Muslims. Nor is it consistent with the experience of a large number of Arab states that have adopted constitutions establishing Islam as the religion of state. In some cases, such as the kingdoms of Morocco and Jordan, the constitution also fuses religious and political authority in the person of the monarch. Yet this situation has not prevented these Arab governments from establishing democratic institutions and practices. Nor has it brought significant criticism either from countries that have chosen a different path in the name of Islam or from mainstream local Islamists. Indeed, so far as the latter are concerned, governments are as likely to be criticized for the timidity or superficiality of their movement toward democratization as for any alleged deviation from the true Islamic path.

There is also diversity within Islam with respect to the theory and practice of political leadership. One particularly important aspect of the more liberal and philosophical tradition within Islam is the requirement that leaders be held accountable and judged according to their performance in temporal matters. In the philosophy of Alfarabi, for example, those who rule "do so by the will of the ruled, and the rulers follow the wishes of the ruled . . . in truth, there is no distinction between ruler and ruled" (Najjar 1972: 99–102; Abed 1992: 7). Put differently, God is infallible and his power absolute, but Islam prohibits the attribution of such qualities to mortals, including both political and religious leaders. These leaders are owed obedience only if they are just, and only if they follow the *shari'a,* which is the path not only to spiritual fulfillment but to "happiness, harmony, and prosperity" in the present life (Mernissi 1992: 33).

To be sure, some Arab leaders have claimed religious authority for the exercise of unrestrained power. Moreover, these men have frequently received support from religious officials. As one Arab scholar observes, "there are numerous examples of *ulama* manipulating Islamic teachings to the advantage of political leaders . . . they have [often] offered doctrinal interpretations that are deliberately designed to justify the behavior of political leaders" (Al-Suwaidi 1995: 87). But such pronouncements are motivated by political calculations rather than a search for religious truth. They are also the product of human intelligence, and thus are no closer to the true intent of God's word than are the interpretations of those Muslim scholars and intellectuals who insist that absolutism has no place in Islam.

In the arenas of both values and institutions, then, with respect to theory as well as practice, there are differing Islamic traditions with persuasive and historically validated claims to legitimacy. The more progressive of these traditions prevailed during the early Islamic centuries, when the "Gate of *Ijtihad*," or Interpretation, was considered to be open. More recently, the progressive tradition within Islam has been championed by modernists and reformers who, beginning in the nineteenth century, have sought to rescue the religion from the more narrow and obscurantist orientation that gained prominence during the religion's middle centuries (Hourani 1962).

The alternative tradition, with its more restricted and fundamentalist perspective, is no less authentic. It prevails today among many associated with "establishment Islam," including many of the jurists and administrators who exercise influence through the religion's public institutions. It is also promoted by many Islamist movements and theologians. But this more conservative tradition, while no less Islamic, is also neither *more* Islamic, and that is the critical point. In the final analysis, that which is advanced and implemented in the name of Islam will depend on the judgments and interpretations of the Muslim community and its leaders, on judgments and interpretations that are not predetermined and hence invariable, but rather have themselves varied, and will continue to vary, as a function of the experiences and circumstances of Muslims.

Thus, to conclude, civic values and institutional arrangements antithetical to democracy are no more, although also no less, an integral part of Islam than are norms and structures that are fully consistent with democratic governance.

ISLAMISM IN THE PUBLIC MIND

Islam is not of necessity antidemocratic by virtue either of its theology or of the political institutions that have emerged in Arab states with large Muslim majorities. But the fact that large numbers of Arab men and women support Islamist political movements might suggest that this is of no more than theoretical relevance; while Islam possesses traditions hospitable to democracy, as well as antidemocratic traditions, the behavior of Muslim Arabs in recent decades might suggest that the latter set of traditions is clearly dominant at the present historical moment.

This would not be an accurate inference, however. Support for Islamist movements is to a large extent instrumental in character. The leaders of these movements may have more existential concerns, seeking governance in accordance with God's law as an end in and of itself, essential because it is what the Creator commanded and thus requiring no secular or temporal justification. But this is not the way that Islamist organizations make their case among ordinary citizens, or the primary reason they are supported by many of the latter. Rather, Islamist parties offer themselves as vehicles for political change. They campaign under the banner "Islam is the Solution," and the problems they claim to be able to solve are first and foremost those of political economy and governance.

Public opinion data from Egypt provide evidence in support of this conclusion. A large survey carried out in 1988 revealed only a weak correlation between personal piety and support for Islamist political movements. Many pious respondents did not express support for these groups, while more than one-third of those with a favorable attitude toward political Islam reported that they themselves are not very devout. In addition, support for political Islam was correlated strongly with support for expanded political participation and greater democracy. These findings indicate that for many Egyptians support of political Islam derives not from a desire for spiritual fulfillment but from a desire for political change. Moreover, the study was replicated in Kuwait with similar results, suggesting that the pattern is not unique to Egypt or to countries with similar political and economic problems (Tessler and Grobschmidt 1995; Tessler 1997).

Other findings from the surveys in Egypt and Kuwait lend additional support to this thesis. For example, again in both countries, those who express support for Islamist political movements but are not personally devout are disproportionately likely to disagree with the statement that "Western values have led to moral erosion in our society." This, too, suggests that it is the search for an alternative to the political and economic status quo, rather than an attraction to the spiritual content of Islamist slogans, that has produced much of the support which Muslim political groups currently enjoy.

This assessment is also illustrated by the voting patterns displayed in several recent elections. Perhaps the clearest case is Algeria, whose elections in 1990 and 1991 were among the most free in the Arab world. While the principal Islamist party, the Islamic Salvation Front, was victorious in both elections, the strong showing of the FIS did not necessarily mean that most Algerians favored governance based on a strict interpretation of Islamic law. Rather, as noted earlier, many and perhaps most who voted for the FIS were motivated by more temporal considerations.

According to a journalistic investigation carried out in 1992, the FIS gained ground by winning converts "among victims of the corruption and inequality evidenced by the [gap between the] comfortable life of the old political leadership and the appalling housing and other conditions in which most citizens live" (Abramson 1992: 20). According to another study, "the majority of the [FIS] voters (between 55 and 82 percent depending on the parameters used) were not identifiable with the hard core of Islamist themes," meaning that the election results were much more a defeat for the government than a victory for the Islamists (Burgat and Dowell 1993: 281).

Similar conclusions are advanced about the origins of support for political Islam in other Arab countries. As one knowledgeable analyst writes of Tunisia, for example, the growth of the Islamist movement is "only a symptom of a deeper malaise within Tunisian society" (Vandewalle 1988: 617). According to another, writing about Morocco, radical groups with an Islamist ideology will be able to attract support only so long as "the problems of social disadvantage and deprivation and of political marginalization" remain unaddressed and become increasingly severe (Seddon 1989: 263). And yet again, according to a political scientist from the United Arab Emirates, "As long as Arab governments resist political participation and refuse to tolerate different political opinions, the strength of Islam as an alternative political ideology will continue to grow" (Al-Suwaidi 1995: 92).

A particularly interesting illustration is provided by the March 1992 election for the Chamber of Commerce in Ramallah, in the Israeli-occupied West Bank. Candidates associated with the Islamist Hamas movement handily defeated those identified with secular nationalism and the PLO. According to press reports, Palestinians complained of PLO officials who live lavishly and whose bank accounts contain funds that should be spent in the occupied territories, and it is for this reason, at least in part, that Hamas was victorious in "a city with a large number of Christian Palestinians who normally would never vote for an Islamic fundamentalist" (Y. Ibrahim, 1992b).

The Gulf Crisis of 1990–91 offers another opportunity to examine the factors shaping popular attitudes; and a rejection of the status quo, rather than a specific desire for governance based on Islam, again emerges as a central motivating factor. Saddam Hussein received considerable support from the rank and file in many Arab countries, and this is primarily because he succeeded in presenting himself as an agent of political change.

Despite the Iraqi leader's history of opposition to radical Islam, many of those who had expressed support for Islamist organizations on other occasions came into the streets to demonstrate in favor of Saddam and against the coalition ranged against him. In Algeria hundreds of thousands marched in Algiers and other cities following the attack on Iraqi forces in January 1991. Pro-Saddam sentiments were no less present in Morocco, even though the country's leader, King Hassan II, had sent troops to Saudi Arabia as part of the U.S.-led force put in place under U.N. auspices. A crowd that some observers estimated at 300,000 took to the streets of Rabat in February 1991 to demand the withdrawal from Saudi Arabia of all allied forces, including those from Morocco.

It is doubtful that many Algerians, Moroccans, and other Arabs actually approved of the Iraqi invasion of Kuwait. Rather, the Gulf Crisis served as a proxy for a very different set of grievances and gave ordinary citizens an occasion to express once again their intense desire for change, the very same sentiments producing support for political Islam. According to one study of the attitudes of young Moroccans, and also of the popular slogans and jokes that circulated in Morocco during the crisis in the Gulf, Saddam was represented as a man of action among those who saw themselves as powerless and marginalized, whereas there was little sympathy for Kuwait, which was judged to be arrogant and selfish (Bennani-Chraibi 1993: 392–436). A Moroccan scholar offers a similar assessment. She writes that while many Western commentators interpreted the protest as "a demonstration by xenophobic fundamentalists" and an expression of "obscurantist fanaticism," many different groups participated, including "all the branches of the Moroccan Left and thousands of independents of all persuasions" (Mernissi 1992: 17). Thus, she concludes, the massive demonstrations were above all a call for democracy.

These themes were also repeatedly stressed at a colloquium on the Gulf Crisis held in Tunis in March 1991. Academics and other intellectuals from a number of Arab countries came together for two days of discussion, and articulated frequently was the view that the war divided the Arab world's rich and poor and at its core was a confrontation between supporters and opponents of political change (*La Geurre du Golfe* 1991).

A final set of observations bearing on the meaning of popular support for political Islam is the ideological distance between the practices and conceptions of ordinary Muslims on the one hand and the doctrine espoused by Islamist leaders on the other. According to a number of contemporary accounts, many ordinary citizens, including many who are devout, have only a vague notion of the system of government called for by Islamists. One American scholar argues that "a politicized conception of Islam differs radically from how Islam is normally understood by ordi-

nary Muslims" (Munson 1992: 19). The same point is made by a scholar
from the United Arab Emirates, who concludes that "ideologically, the
reasoning of religious groups and their socio-political programs are
too political to appeal to traditional mainstream Muslims" (Al-Suwaidi
1995: 93).

In offering such judgments, these and other analysts seek to provide
additional evidence that a specific and conscious desire for Islamist solutions is at best only a secondary factor shaping the political attitudes of
the Arab rank and file. It is true, of course, that assertions which proclaim Islam to be the solution strike a responsive chord for other reasons
as well. Islam is an indigenous belief system, familiar to almost all Arabs,
even those who are Christian. It has shaped the Arabs' history, it helps
to define their collective national identity, and it gives spiritual meaning
to the lives of millions, including many who are not personally devout.
Equally significant, by its very nature, as a legal system and as the cultural foundation of a major world civilization, as well as a religion, Islam
presents Muslims with a coherent blueprint for the construction of a just
political community. All of this makes the Islamist platform appealing
for existential reasons.

Nevertheless, popular support for activist Muslim movements cannot be explained exclusively, or even primarily, by Islam's familiarity and
considerable normative attraction. In the final analysis, the Islamist appeal is instrumental; political Islam draws support from men and women
who believe, or hope, that it offers them an effective vehicle for the expression of their anger at existing governmental regimes and a way to
exert pressure for political and economic change. This is evident in the
weak correlation between personal piety and support for political Islam,
in the enthusiasm of ordinary citizens for non-Islamic instruments of
protest and change, when these are available, and in the normative distance between the politicized conceptions of Islamist groups and the
faith and practices which characterize Islam at the level of everyday life.

ISLAMISM IN THE POLITICAL PROCESS

Even if many of the men and women who support Islamist groups do not
seek governance based on a politicized conception of Islam, and do not
themselves understand or practice their religion in this manner, it is very
likely that political liberalization would, in the short run at least, increase
the political influence of parties and movements that campaign under the
slogan "Islam is the solution." These movements would probably be well
represented in the national assembly, for example, which would not only

give them a prominent platform for the expression of their views but would also enable them to make gains through participation in legislative bargaining. There is also a strong possibility that Muslim political groups would become members of the ruling coalition in some Arab countries. Thus, quite apart from assessing the nature and consequences of popular religious sentiments, it is necessary to ask about the implications of any increase in the political power of Islamist movements that would result from democratization.

More particularly, the question is whether Islamist political groups would seek to subvert from within the very democratic process that enabled them to gain influence or power. Some observers, including some Arab governments, insist that Islamist movements reject political and ideological pluralism, and that they will use any influence they acquire to work for the establishment of "a quasi-totalitarian and theological state" (Al-Suwaidi 1995: 93). The presumed danger, as expressed in an article in the *Economist*, is that "the first people delivered to power by democracy will in fact be intent on dismantling it" (January 1992). "One man, one vote, one time" is the way this danger is sometimes cynically characterized.

Following this line of argumentation, some Arab governments offer the protection of democracy and pluralism as a justification for the suppression of Islamist movements. The cases of Algeria and Tunisia illustrate this tendency. In Algeria, the government initially accorded legal status to the FIS and sanctioned its participation in the political process, only to suspend movement toward democracy when the party scored successes in both local and national elections. In Tunisia, the government refused to sanction participation in the electoral process by al-Nahda, the country's major Islamist movement, and thereafter arrested al-Nahda's leaders and activists.

The principal justification provided by both the Algerian and Tunisian regimes was that Islamists could not be trusted to respect the democratic process. In Algeria, the government and its supporters asserted that FIS politicians had used coercion and intimidation to secure votes in the balloting of 1990 and 1991, and that many of the municipalities which came under FIS control in 1990 interfered in the parliamentary elections of December 1991. More recently, the government has also insisted that the FIS is a terrorist organization, pointing out that extremist elements within its ranks are responsible for the assassination of hundreds of prominent Algerians with whom they disagree, as well as dozens of foreigners.

In at least some cases, these assertions are put forward by those whose own commitment to democracy is questionable, including government and party leaders who themselves are prepared to restrict democracy rather than relinquish their privileges and political primacy. This alone does not make their arguments inaccurate, however. As indicated in the *Economist* article cited above, there are also disinterested opinions and independent scholarly analyses that see a genuine danger in permitting Islamist movements to participate in the political process. As expressed by one of the Arab scholars quoted earlier, "the authoritarianism of current Arab regimes will become the quasi-totalitarianism of a theological state if religious opposition groups seize power" (Al-Suwaidi 1995: 93).

Such an outcome is by no means certain, however. Many Arab and other analysts argue that it is inappropriate to generalize about how Islamist groups would behave were they to acquire a measure of power through participation in the democratic process. For one thing, it is essential to differentiate between Islamist movements that are radical, extremist, or militant, on the one hand, and those that are moderate, pragmatic, or accommodationist, on the other. According to one Arab scholar, Muslim groups which are "legalist" or "political" differ from those that are "radical" or "militant" in that they renounce violence, emphasize incrementalism, and "focus on propagating *al-da'wa* [the call] and on 'purifying' individual minds and social beliefs from traces of secularism." Moreover, he continues, it is groups of the latter type, rather than those that are more extreme, which have been most effective in attracting followers and gaining influence. This is the case in Egypt, Syria, Jordan, Tunisia, Morocco, and Algeria (Karawan 1992: 172).

This difference is also reflected in the writings and speeches of Islamist theoreticians and political leaders. As noted in connection with Muslim political theory more generally, some insist that Western-style democracy has no place in Islam because it puts man on God's throne. Others, however, adopt a much less negative attitude toward democracy. Rashid al-Ghannoushi, leader of the outlawed al-Nahda movement in Tunisia, is one influential Islamist theoretician who speaks in positive terms about democracy: "We accept [the fact that we must] work within the legal framework with the hope of improving it by making it more democratic and pluralistic." And again, "We believe in giving everyone the chance to run for the government and we believe in giving the people the right to choose through voting in an environment of democracy and human rights." There is no guarantee that such statements are sincere, of course. But the gap between rhetoric and performance is hardly unique to Islamist politicians. Moreover, so far as rhetoric and ideology are concerned, the prodemocracy statements of Ghannoushi and other prominent Islamists have the important consequence of legitimizing democracy among their supporters and thereby, to at least some extent, undermining the antidemocratic arguments of more radical Islamist theoreticians.

It is thus essential to understand that there are important differences among Muslim political movements and that Islamist politicians do not speak with a single voice on the question of democracy or other issues of governance. It is also important to avoid unidimensional and simplistic conclusions about the consequences of permitting Islamist groups to take part in democratic elections, of running the risk, in other words, that they might acquire a significant measure of political influence, or even political power. While it is possible that this might in some instances reduce the prospects for continued democratization, leading to a situation where only Muslim parties would be permitted to run candidates in future elections, there are reasons to conclude that such a scenario is unlikely.

In Algeria, for example, the FIS controlled a significant number of local governments between 1990 and 1991, and by all accounts they made a serious effort to govern effectively, using technical rather than religious criteria when making appointments. Another example, also at the local level, concerns the performance of Muslim political groups in the West Bank and Gaza and in Arab villages in Israel. In each of these cases, as in Algeria, Islamist factions have displayed some or all of the following: a concern to build support through service delivery rather ideological appeals, a willingness to bargain and form coalitions with nonreligious parties, and a willingness to accept defeats as well as victories in the electoral process.

The most clear-cut case is that of Jordan, where the Muslim Brotherhood emerged as the largest block in parliament following the 1989 elections, and thereafter displayed neither an ability nor a desire to undermine the democratic process. Although the Brotherhood opposed Jordan's participation in peace talks with Israel, it accepted King Hussein's June 1991 decision to name a new cabinet to lead the country into these negotiations. Of equal or even greater significance, the party accepted the loss of half of its parliamentary seats in the election of November 1993, suggesting that Islamists who gain power through the ballot box are not necessarily unwilling to surrender that power.

These and other illustrations suggest that Islamist participation in the political process is not necessarily a prescription for the end of democratic experiments. Some suggest that participation in the democratic process may even to some degree alter the views and leadership structure of Muslim political movements, further moderating and "normalizing" those Islamist groups that acquire a share of legitimate political power. According to a recent analysis of Jordan, for example, the Islamist movement has been at the forefront of political liberalization "not because the movement is made up of Jeffersonian democrats, but rather because greater democratization has served its organizational and political interests" (Robinson 1997: 374). Members of the movement recognize that by encouraging greater political openness, they have a greater opportunity to pursue their own policy goals.

This conclusion is also advanced by other analysts, both Western and Arab. An American scholar asserts, for example, that many Islamists are not "unbending dogmatists" but, on the contrary, are "at ease with the complex political calculus of means and ends, constraints and values which we in the West assume to be the normal stuff of politics" (Piscatori 1991: 23). Thus, in the judgment of a seasoned Lebanese political observer, "Islamist movements are capable of being absorbed into the political mainstream" (quoted in Wright 1991: 140). And according to a prominent Egyptian scholar, the Muslim Brotherhood in Egypt "is becoming a fairly respectable movement, like Christian Democrats or Euro-Communists. They're learning how to win and lose gracefully" (quoted in Miller 1992: 42).

There is a final important point about the alleged Islamist threat to democracy. Specifically, it is necessary to recognize that the relative strength of these movements is highly variable and that the popular support they enjoy at present may decline significantly in the future. For one thing, the influence and popularity of Muslim political groups have historically been variable, waning in the 1950s and 1960s and surging more recently at least partly in response to the crisis of secular leadership, including the failure of Arab nationalist regimes to hold themselves accountable and provide for meaningful political participation. But while Islamist groups have been greatly strengthened by the absence of democracy, they might lose much of their appeal should political systems become more open and governments more accountable. Indeed, although the situation is more complex, this to some extent accounts for the relatively poor performance of the Muslim Brotherhood in the most recent Jordanian elections.

A related point is that democracy and political liberalization may erode support for Muslim political groups by exposing the deep political and ideological cleavages that exist among those who proclaim Islam to be the solution to the Arab world's problems. This is one of the conclusions of a recent study of Islamic "fundamentalisms" in four Arab states, the Israeli-occupied West Bank and Gaza Strip, Iran, and Pakistan (Brumberg 1991: 187, 195).

Perhaps most important is the different way that Islamist movements are likely to be viewed once they are permitted to enter the arena of legitimate politics and, if successful, to share responsibility for dealing with unresolved political and economic problems. Under these circumstances, Muslim groups will become much less attractive as vehicles for the expression of political discontent and a rejection of the status quo. Even more critical, their claim that Islam is the solution will lose much of its appeal if, as seems inevitable, the problems confronting ordinary men and women persist.

Support for these conclusions is provided by accounts of Jordan and Algeria, where there has been public dissatisfaction with the performance of Islamist politicians who acquired national or local leadership after their parties scored successes in the elections of 1989 and 1990, respectively. In the latter case, for example, several recent studies report that leaders of the Islamic Salvation Front were criticized for serious shortcomings in the operation of local government and for failing to deliver on a number of the promises they made in the electoral campaign. And this is all the more significant in view of the efforts of the FIS to deal with local problems. In the former case, the Muslim Brotherhood was hurt by disenchantment with the performance of some of its cabinet ministers, including the minister of education, who attempted to implement unpopular policies based on a very conservative interpretation of Islam.

Yet another example is that of Sudan; Islamists have come to power, and university students, once their passionate supporters, have largely turned against the ruling National Islamic Front. Thus, overall, as expressed by a senior Egyptian scholar, "the early results [of democratization] show that when Islamic activists gain power and in fact exercise it, they will not necessarily fare much better than the liberals before them, or the socialists before them or the nationalists before them. They will make their mistakes" (quoted in Wright 1991: 144).

These observations do not invalidate the arguments of those who see serious challenges and even dangers in the opening that democratization may give to Islamist political movements. They do suggest that such concerns may be significantly exaggerated, however, or at least that they offer only a partial view of the possible results of genuine political openings.

More generally, challenges and dangers notwithstanding, the conclusion to be drawn from the present analysis is that democracy and Islam are not of necessity incompatible, or in contradiction by definition. Indeed, thus far at least, it is not from Islam, or even Islamist political movements, that have come the greatest obstacles to serious democratization. On the contrary, the most important impediment is the continuing resistance of established political regimes, whose leaders frequently espouse the language of democracy but rarely permit political liberalization beyond that which they can orchestrate and control. This gap between rhetoric and performance equals or exceeds that which may be attributed to Islamist politicians, and is at present the most serious obstacle to meaningful democratization in the Arab world.

REFERENCES

Abed, Shukri. 1992. "Democracy in the Arab World." Unpublished paper.

Abed, Shukri. 1995. "Islam and Democracy." In David Garnham and Mark Tessler, eds. *Democracy, War and Peace in the Middle East*. Bloomington: Indiana University Press.

Abramson, Gary. 1992. "Rise of the Crescent." *Africa Report* (March-April).

Amawi, Abla. 1992. "Democracy Dilemmas in Jordan." *Middle East Report* 174 (January/February): 26–29.

Anderson, Lisa. 1999. "Politics in the Middle East: Limits and Opportunities in the Quest for Theory." In Mark Tessler, with Jodi Nachtwey and Anne Banda, eds., *Area Studies and Social Science: Strategies for Understanding Middle East Politics*. Bloomington: Indiana University Press.

——. 1987. "Lawless Government and Illegal Opposition: Reflections on the Middle East." *Journal of International Affairs*, 40 (Winter/Spring): 219–33.

Bennani-Chraibi, Mounia. 1993. *Les Représentations du Monde des Jeunes Marocains*. Paris: Thèse de doctorat de l'Institut d'Etudes Politiques.

Brown, Kenneth. 1993. "Lost in Algiers." *Mediterraneans* 4 (Summer): 8–18.

Brumberg, Daniel. 1991. "Islamic Fundamentalism, Democracy, and the Gulf War." In James Piscatori, ed., *Islamic Fundamentalisms and the Gulf Crisis*. Boston: The American Academy of Arts and Sciences.

Burgat, François, and William Dowell. 1993. *The Islamic Movement in North Africa*. Austin: The University of Texas Press.

Choueiri, Y. 1996. "The Political Discourse of Contemporary Islamist Movements." In Abdel Salem Sidahmed and Anoushiravam Ehteshami, eds., *Islamic Fundamentalism*. Boulder: Westview Press.

al-Dajjani, Ahmad Sidqi. 1987. "Tatawwur mafahim al-dimuqratiyya fi'l-fikr al-arabi al-hadith" (The Evolution of the Concept of Democracy in Modern Arab Thought). In *Azmat al-dimuqratiyya fi'l-alam al-arabi* (The Crisis of Democracy in the Arab World). Beirut: Markiz Dirasat al-Wihdah al-Arabiyya.

"The Democracy Agenda in the Arab World." *Middle East Report* 174 (January/February 1992).

Halasa, Serene. 1991. "Arab Scholars Call for New Order Based on Democracy, Urge End to Iraq Sanctions." *Jordan Times* (May 30–31).

Halliday, Fred. 1995. *Islam and the Myth of Confrontation: Religion and Politics in the Middle East*. London: I. B. Tauris.

Hamdi, Mohamed Elhachmi. 1996. "Islam and Democracy: The Limits of the Western Model." *Journal of Democracy* 7 (April): 81–85.

Henry, Clement. 1996. *The Mediterranean Debt Crescent: Money and Power in Algeria, Egypt, Morocco, Tunisia, and Turkey.* Gainesville: University Press of Florida.

Hourani, Albert. 1962. *Arabic Thought in the Liberal Age.* Oxford: Oxford University Press.

Huntington, Samuel. 1993. "The Clash of Civilizations." *Foreign Affairs* (Summer).

———. 1984. "Will More Countries Become Democratic?" *Political Science Quarterly* 99 (Summer): 193–218.

Ibrahim, Saad Eddin. 1987. "Masadir al-shariyyah fi anzimat al-hukm al-arabi" [The Origins of Legitimacy for the Arab Regimes]. In *Azmat al-dimuqratiyya fi'l-alam al-arabi* [The Crisis of Democracy in the Arab World]. Beirut: Markiz Dirasat al-Wihdah al-Arabiyya.

———. 1990. "Militant Muslims Grow Stronger As Algeria's Economy Grows Weaker." *The New York Times* (June 25).

———. 1992a. "Jordan Feels Change Within As Muslims Pursue Agenda." *The New York Times* (December 26).

———. 1992b. "PLO Is Facing Growing Discontent." *The New York Times* (April 5).

———. 1994. "Palestinian Religious Militants: Why Their Ranks Are Growing." *The New York Times* (November 8).

Karawan, Ibrahim. 1992. "'ReIslamization Movements' According to Kepel: On Striking Back and Striking Out." *Contention* 2 (Fall): 161–79.

Khouri, Rami G. 1990. "The Arab Dream Won't Be Denied." *The New York Times* (December 15).

Kramer, Gundrun. 1992. "Liberalization and Democracy in the Arab World." *Middle East Report* 174 (January/February): 22–25.

Labib, Taher. 1991. "L'intellectuel des sept mois." In *La Guerre du Golfe et l'Avenir des Arabes: débats et réflexions.* Tunis: Cérès Productions.

Lalor, Paul, and Floresca Karanasou. 1993. "Case Study: Egypt's Islamic Resurgence." *Middle East Peace Notes* (American Friends Service Committee) 15 (November): 3–6.

La Guerre du Golfe et l'Avenir des Arabes: débats et réflexions. 1991. Tunis: Cérès Productions.

Layachi, Azzedine, and Abdel-kader Haireche. 1992. "National Development and Political Protest: Islamists in the Maghreb Countries." *Arab Studies Quarterly* 14 (Spring/Summer): 69–92.

Lewis, Bernard. 1994. *The Shaping of the Modern Middle East.* New York: Oxford University Press.

Mernissi, Fatima. 1992. *Democracy and Islam.* Reading: Addison-Wesley.

Miller, Judith. 1992. "The Islamic Wave." *The New York Times Magazine* (May 31).

Moffett, George D. 1989. "North Africa's Disillusioned Youth." *The Christian Science Monitor* (May 17).

Munson, Henry. 1992. "Islamist Political Movements in North Africa." Paper presented at a workshop on "Politico-Religious Movements and Development in the Near East." Washington, D.C.: U.S. Agency for International Development.

Muslih, Muhammad, and Augustus Richard Norton. 1991. "The Need For Arab Democracy." *Foreign Policy* 83 (Summer): 3–19.

Najjar, Fawzi. 1972. "The Political Regime of Alfarabi." In Ralph Lerner and Muhsin Mahdi, eds., *Medieval Political Philosophy: A Sourcebook*. Ithaca: Cornell University Press.

al-Nasir, Khalid. 1983. "Azmat al-dimuqratiyya fi al-watan al-arabi (The Crisis of Democracy in the Arab Homeland). *Al-Mustaqbal al-Arabi* 55 (September).

Norton, Augustus Richard. 1995. *Civil Society in the Middle East*. Leiden: Brill.

Norton, Augustus Richard, and Robin Wright. 1995. "The Post-Peace Crisis in the Middle East." *Survival* 36 (Winter): 7–20.

Piscatori, James. "Religion and Realpolitik: Islamic Responses to the Gulf War." 1991. In James Piscatori, ed., *Islamic Fundamentalisms and the Gulf Crisis*. Boston: The American Academy of Arts and Sciences.

Pollock, David. 1992. *The "Arab Street"? Public Opinion in the Arab World*. Washington, D.C.: The Washington Institute for Near East Policy.

Quandt, William. 1994. "The Urge for Democracy." *Foreign Affairs* 73 (July–August): 2–7.

Robinson, Glenn. 1997. "Can Islamists Be Democrats? The Case of Jordan." *Middle East Journal* 51 (Summer): 373–87.

Seddon, David. 1989. "The Politics of 'Adjustment' in Morocco." In Bonnie K. Campbell and John Loxley, eds., *Structural Adjustment in Africa*. New York: St. Martin's Press.

Shikaki, Khalil. 1996. "The Peace Process, National Reconstruction, and the Transition to Democracy in Palestine." *Journal of Palestine Studies* 25 (Winter): 5–20.

Solingen, Etel. 1996. "Democratization in the Middle East: Quandaries of the Peace Process." *Journal of Democracy* 7 (July): 139–53.

Suleiman, Michael W. 1987. "Attitudes, Values and the Political Process in Morocco." In I. William Zartman, ed., *The Political Economy of Morocco*. New York: Praeger.

Al-Suwaidi, Jamal S. 1995. "Arab and Western Conceptions of Democracy: Evidence from a UAE Opinion Survey." In David Garnham and Mark Tessler, eds., *Democracy, War and Peace in the Middle East*. Bloomington: Indiana University Press.

Tessler, Mark. 1980. "Political Change and the Islamic Revival in Tunisia." *The Maghreb Review* 5: 8–19.

——. 1991. "Anger and Governance in the Arab World: Lessons from the Maghrib and Implications for the West." *The Jerusalem Journal of International Relations* 13: 7–33.

——. 1993. "The Alienation of Urban Youth." In I. Wm. Zartman and Mark

Habeeb, eds., *State and Society in Contemporary North Africa*. Boulder: Westview Press.

——. 1997. "The Origins of Popular Support for Islamist Movements: A Political Economy Analysis." In John Entelis, ed., *Islam, Democracy, and the State in North Africa*. Bloomington: Indiana University Press.

Tessler, Mark, and Marilyn Grobschmidt. 1995. "The Relationship Between Democracy in the Arab World and the Arab-Israeli Conflict." In David Garnham and Mark Tessler, eds., *Democracy, War and Peace in the Middle East*. Bloomington: Indiana University Press.

Tessler, Mark, and Jamal Sanad. 1994. "Will the Arab Public Accept Peace with Israel: Evidence from Surveys in Three Arab Societies." In Gregory Mahler and Efriam Karsh, eds., *Israel at the Crossroads*. London: I. B. Tauris.

Vandewalle, Dirk. 1988. "From the New State to the New Era: Toward a Second Republic in Tunisia." *Middle East Journal* 42: 602–20.

Watt, Montgomery. 1968. *Islamic Political Thought*. Edinburgh: Edinburgh University Press.

Wright, Robin. 1991. "Islam's New Political Face." *Current History* (January).

Zacek, Jane S. 1993. "Prospects for Democratic Rule." *In Depth: A Journal for Values and Public Policy*, vol. 3, no. 1 (Winter): 257–77.

Zartman, I. William. 1995. "A Search for Security and Governance Regimes." In David Garnham and Mark Tessler, eds., *Democracy, War, and Peace in the Middle East*. Bloomington: Indiana University Press.

Zghal, Abdelkader. 1991. "La guerre du Golfe et la recherche de la bonne distance." In *La Guerre du Golfe et l'Avenir des Arabes: débats et réflexions*. Tunis: Cérès Productions.

10
Democracy and Its Discontents: Constraints on Political Citizenship in Latin America

Eric Hershberg

I. INTRODUCTION

DISCUSSION OF CONTEMPORARY Latin American politics invariably highlights the proliferation of democratic regimes throughout the region over the past decade and a half. Whereas at the beginning of the 1980s only a handful of countries boasted formally democratic governments, today Cuba is the only unabashedly authoritarian regime remaining in power, and even there an eventual *apertura* is likely. Democracy remains far from perfect in most countries, but this should not obscure the fact that competitive politics are emerging in societies that until recently appeared condemned to suffer endless cycles of dictatorship and repression. Tentative but meaningful steps toward political democratization have been achieved even in such unlikely settings as Guatemala and El Salvador, Haiti and Paraguay. Nor has change been limited to the realm of formal political institutions. Actors on both the left and right of the ideological spectrum increasingly espouse democratic norms as an end in themselves (Barros 1986), while new patterns of associational life are emerging along territorial and functional lines (Chalmers, Martin, and Piester 1997). And, the discourse of human rights is no longer articulated solely by opposition movements: From the southern cone to the

Earlier versions of this paper were presented at a May 1997 conference on Democracy and its Limits, held at the University of Wisconsin-Milwaukee, and a November 1997 seminar in the Latin American Studies Program at Princeton University. The author is grateful for the numerous suggestions offered by commentators at both workshops.

Caribbean, repressed activists of the 1970s and 1980s are found not in prison cells or enforced exile but in positions of leadership. Some even reside in presidential palaces.

Notwithstanding these remarkable signs of progress, popular dissatisfaction is pervasive throughout all but a few corners of the region. A degree of *desencanto* is perhaps inevitable following the outburst of civic enthusiasm that typically accompanies democratic transition (O'Donnell and Schmitter 1986), but both the breadth and depth of disillusionment in Latin America surpass levels that might be anticipated given the impressive extent of political reform. It is hardly a surprise, then, that recent academic writings about Latin American politics emphasize the persistent obstacles to democratic change (e.g., Diamond 1996). For the most part, the focus is no longer on the vulnerability of fledgling democracies faced with continuing threats of coups by dissatisfied military officers and their allies among civilian elites. Rather, the emphasis nowadays is on the incompleteness of political democracy, on the multiple "enclaves" of authoritarianism which inhibit change (Garreton 1996; Hagopian 1993), or on the inability of important segments of the population to gain access to democratic political institutions (O'Donnell 1993). The continuing influence of authoritarian institutions inherited from the past and the emergence of potent new ones, as well as the fragility of democratic institutions, coincide with stubborn traditions of clientelism and patrimonialism. Together, these phenomena complicate efforts to extend political citizenship to all sectors of the population, and dampen prospects for extending the dynamic of democratic regime change into the spheres of economy and society.

The economic dimension is especially troublesome. The distribution of income and the extremes of poverty in many Latin American countries remain such as to undermine the practical significance of formal political equality. More than 200 million Latin Americans lived below the poverty line in 1995, and 100 million were classified as indigent in a recent analysis by the Economic Commission for Latin America (O'Donnell 1996). Implementation of a variety of market-oriented economic reforms has failed to counteract the worsening maldistribution of wealth. To the contrary, insertion into the global economy has tended to reinforce historic patterns of inequality in all but a handful of countries. Even where modest gains may have been achieved in recent years, as in Chile, 1998 opened amidst growing fears that instability in global financial markets may compel governments to enact fiscal and monetary policies that exacerbate inequality.

At first glance these issues appear irrelevant to a narrow consideration of the fortunes of political democracy. Political democracy involves a set of procedures for making collective decisions, but rather than imply any particular set of outcomes, democracy entails the institutionalization of political uncertainty (Schmitter and Karl 1991; Przeworski 1986). Yet the connections between economic precariousness and democracy become apparent when we recall that the existence of a democratic polity presupposes citizenship. For democracy to flourish, individuals must be capable of articulating political preferences, organizing collectively in civil society, and participating, both individually and through civic associations, in the political process. To the extent that extreme economic vulnerability or social exclusion inhibit people from political deliberation and organization, the possibility for democratic citizenship is called into question. In such an environment, economic and social dimensions of collective life take on renewed importance for the study of political democracy.

This chapter is concerned both with the degree to which Latin American countries have instituted democratic regimes, and with the principal issues that must be confronted if political citizenship is to become more than illusory for the majority of Latin Americans. We take as our point of departure the notion that the weakness of Latin American democracy is best understood not in terms of the prospects for regime survival—which though far from guaranteed appears less problematic than at any time in the recent past—but in terms of the failure of political systems to operate on the basis of citizen preferences and to translate those preferences and needs into policy. Weak representative institutions curtail opportunities for political participation, mechanisms for enforcing accountability are woefully inadequate, and many states lack minimal degrees of sovereignty vis-à-vis domestic and international actors. Each of these factors diminishes the capacity of citizens to share in the benefits of democratic political life. Equally problematic is the elusiveness of economic development strategies that enable national and regional economies to engage the increasingly globalized world trading system in a manner that promotes growth without exacerbating inequality. Only such a development model affords any prospects for Latin America to overcome the obscene levels of inequality that marginalize vast segments of the population and effectively deny them opportunities for self-determination.

The next section of the chapter presents a framework for conceptualizing political democracy and introduces some complexities that are particularly vexing for contemporary Latin America. This framework is used to compare political systems in the region and to classify them according to their proximity to polyarchy. The third section analyzes four variables highlighted by this classificatory scheme: accountability, representation, sovereignty, and mode of insertion into the world economy. The conclusion addresses prospects for overcoming the principal obstacles to deepening democracy and extending political citizenship to broader segments of the population.

II. DEMOCRACY IN LATIN AMERICA:
DEFINITIONS AND DIFFERENTIATIONS

Political scientists typically define democracy in terms of what Robert Dahl (1971) has labeled polyarchy, that is, competition for power among different groups of elites accompanied by institutionalized means through which citizens can participate freely and autonomously, both in the selection of those elites and in the articulation of political viewpoints. Critics of this formulation have questioned whether the degree of popular rule brought about through satisfaction of these two criteria is sufficient to qualify a regime as democratic (Pateman 1970). These doubts are especially relevant to the extent that in some settings specific underlying conditions constrain possibilities for elite competition to take place freely or for popular participation to shape the course of political events. Similarly, the term polyarchy refers to characteristics of political regimes, rather than to the civil societies with which regimes interact, and it is possible that formally competitive political institutions will be distorted in a context of authoritarian social relations, or they will be polarized. Notwithstanding these reservations, few observers have offered compelling measures of democracy that enable us both to go beyond polyarchy and to avoid relegating the concept of democracy to a purely ideal typical category, attractive in theory but unattainable in practice.

Reflecting on the vast literature devoted to democratic regimes in recent years, Collier and Levitsky (1997) advance a number of useful analytical tools for differentiating various forms of democracy. These tools help us to avoid falling into the trap of "conceptual stretching," whereby vastly different cases are fit into a particular category (e.g., democracy), stripping the conceptual category of its specificity and thus its utility. This chapter employs two such strategies: First, I propose two *diminished subtypes* of democracy in Latin America, "pseudo-democracies," and "tutelary democracies," to classify regimes in which elements of democracy are present but in which the minimal criteria for categorization as polyarchies are not satisfied (See Table 1). This exercise involves consideration of whether regimes meet procedural definitions of democracy, conceptualized in terms of contestation and participation, the two principal elements of polyarchy. Second, I employ the strategy

TABLE 1

Diminished Subtypes

Pseudo-Democracies	Tutelary Democracies
Mexico	Colombia
Peru	Ecuador
	Guatemala
	Honduras
	Paraguay

that Collier and Levitsky (1997: 442–45) refer to as *precising,* and which I prefer to label *tailoring,* whereby generally accepted definitions of a concept—e.g., polyarchy—are refined to reflect conditions that are particularly salient in a given setting and that hence determine whether its minimal conditions are likely to be met in practice. This interpretive exercise leads me to advance an additional category of democratic regime in Latin America, "incomplete democracies," located along a continuum bounded by pseudo-democracies and full-fledged polyarchies (Table 2).[1] Tailoring our conceptualization of polyarchy to the specific conditions of Latin America compels us to devote attention not only to contestation and participation, but also to a series of factors that determine whether these objectives are likely to be achieved in practice. Specifically, it brings into the analysis issues of accountability, representation, sovereignty, and economic equity.

Pseudo-Democracies

As suggested in the introductory section of the chapter, only one Latin American regime, Cuba, stands out as unequivocally nondemocratic (i.e., nonpolyarchic) in the mid-1990s. Since soon after the 1959 revolution that brought Fidel Castro to power, Cuba has been governed by a single-party regime in which the existence of competition between elites is deemed illegitimate and in which participation is present in many settings but strictly limited with regard to the political system. This is not to deny the remarkable achievements of the revolutionary regime, many of which have been profoundly democratizing from a societal perspective. Indeed, if we were to gauge democratic development in terms of access to health and education, or equity across categories of race, gender, and class, criteria that are highly relevant to *societal* democracy as op-

TABLE 2

Incomplete Democracies	Functioning Polyarchy
Argentina	Chile
Bolivia	Costa Rica
Brazil	Uruguay
Venezuela	

Perhaps another category should be added here: basket-case democracy, including Nicaragua, and perhaps Venezuela and Honduras, in which economic and social breakdown render strictly political dynamics misleading.

posed to *political* democracy, Cuba until recently would surpass most—if not all—Latin American countries by notable margins. Yet this volume is concerned principally with democracy at the level of political regime, and in this sense only a quite unconventional, though by no means implausible (Macpherson 1966), definition of democracy would encompass the political system in Cuba.[2]

Two contemporary regimes in Latin America, Mexico and Peru, exhibit varying degrees of contestation and participation but fail in important respects to meet both of the central conditions of polyarchy. These systems can be described as "pseudo-democracies," a diminished subtype of regimes which in fundamental respects remain nonpolyarchic. The authoritarian system established in Mexico over the past seven decades has made significant steps toward liberalization in recent years. Elections are more competitive than ever; beginning in the mid-1980s, the ruling Partido Revolucionario Institucional (PRI) increasingly—but not always—recognized victories of opposition parties at the state and local levels, and gradually diminished its hegemony in the Congress. In the historic elections of 1997, the opposition gained a majority in Congress and took control of crucial mayoralties across the country, most notably in the capital. Nonetheless, the corruption of electoral processes remains widespread and the harassment of political opposition has if anything intensified in recent years. These indices of contestation and participation testify to the persistence of institutionalized impediments to polyarchy in Mexico. The case of Peru is more ambiguous. The elections of 1990 featured significant degrees of both elite contestation and popular participation, and on paper this was the case in 1995 as well. Yet the circumstances under which the latter contest took place diminish its democratic credibility. President Fujimori's 1992 "auto-golpe" entailed the unilateral suspension and then rewriting of the Constitution by the executive, who in the process dismissed both the Congress and the

Supreme Court. On this as on other occasions, the authoritarian actions of Peru's neopopulist president, as well as popular support that such behavior elicited, underscored the truncated character of democratic institutions in the country (Panfichi 1997).[3]

The role of public opinion in sustaining or undermining pseudo-democratic politics has been contradictory. On the one hand, popular dissatisfaction with limitations on political competition and widespread revulsion toward human rights violations in which the PRI has been implicated constitute one of the principal pressures compelling the ruling party in Mexico to inch reluctantly toward broader democratic change. In contrast, in Peru the auto-golpe met with broad public support, and the electorate has repeatedly endorsed measures that undermine prospects for furthering democratization. Numerous factors help to account for these differences, but one in particular merits note at this juncture, for it will resurface below in the discussion of "incomplete" democracies. Throughout the region, public perception of intolerable crises, typically economic in nature but encompassing broader concerns about personal and collective security, generates demands for decisive action by political leaders. Fujimori's autocratic style of rule resonated with a society desperate for relief from extreme levels of economic hardship and physical insecurity. Impatient with political institutions that demonstrated no capacity whatsoever to confront that situation, citizens cried out for someone to act decisively to eradicate a multiplicity of ills, ranging from terrorism to inflation to congressional and judicial corruption. Similarly, in Mexico, demands for political opening stem in part from disillusion with a regime that once managed to provide a sense of security to the bulk of the population, but that has clearly lost the capacity to do so. Whether the threat is perceived to come from macroeconomic instability or street crime or guerrilla insurrection, the experience of insecurity has sparked demands for political change. More often than not, these demands result in support for powerful leaders who promise to purge polity and society of intolerable threats; neither the methods needed to restore stability nor their implications for the formalities of political democracy tend to be matters of grave public concern (Caldeira 1996).

Tutelary Democracies

Tutelary democracies are those in which satisfaction of one or both criteria for polyarchy is profoundly in doubt due to the influence of the armed forces over the political system and the dubious autonomy of civilian politicians with regard to the conduct of domestic and foreign policy. In Colombia, Guatemala, Ecuador, Honduras, Paraguay, and perhaps El Salvador, the disproportionate role played by the military is sufficient to question whether polyarchy has been achieved. It is especially unclear whether contestation for power is present when the military remain as de facto arbiters, and sometimes central participants, in the contest for power between competing elites.[4]

The Central American cases present a particularly complex situation, one in which increasing hopefulness (witness the results of the March 1997 legislative and municipal elections in El Salvador) coincides with trepidation stemming from decades of military domination of political life. The size and budget of the military has fallen sharply throughout the region, and in striking peace accords with leftist opponents conservative civilian presidents in both El Salvador and Guatemala have demonstrated surprising autonomy from the armed forces. Civilian supremacy over the armed forces is no longer implausible, and for the first time in decades it is unclear whether and in what domains the military retains veto power over decisions of (now freely elected) governments (Hershberg and Menjivar 1998). Yet it is too early to tell whether these positive trends will continue, particularly in light of the military elite's powerful role in the private sector and lingering uncertainties associated with the reincorporation into civilian life of excombatants in both Guatemala and El Salvador (Morales 1998).

Elsewhere in Latin America, military interference in domestic politics takes on various forms. Paraguayan democracy is unusual to the extent that it traces its origins to a military coup aimed at unseating an entrenched authoritarian regime. This circumstance facilitated the transition to democracy, but it has also served to boost the popularity of the armed forces and to cloud distinctions between civilian and military authority. This ambiguity nearly caused the system to break down in 1996, when a faction of the military sought to dictate appointments to the cabinet of the elected civilian president and again in 1999. Absent intervention from neighboring countries, popular mobilization in support of democratic institutions might not have sufficed to avoid interruption in that country's fragile democratic experiment.

Similarly, in Ecuador, the military has long been understood to enjoy exceptional autonomy and broad influence over domestic policies, owing partly to its reformist past but also to the sorry record of civilian political elites. The prominence of the military was evident during the institutional crisis that culminated in the peaceful removal of President Bucaram in early 1997, only months after his receipt of a majority of the votes cast in a free and fair election. Popular support for the bizarre populism of Bucaram, a political maverick known by friend and foe alike

as "El loco," is comprehensible only when we take into account the
depth of dissatisfaction with established political actors in Ecuador (Rial,
personal communication, 1993).[5] Yet this support evaporated quickly
once the new president unveiled a harsh program of economic restructuring and revealed himself to be unusually (and blatantly) corrupt. The
ensuing street demonstrations and strikes would not have been sufficient
to oust the government had relations between the new president and the
military been cordial. They were not, however, and this motivated the
political class to take advantage of popular repudiation of Bucaram. The
Congress declared him mentally unfit for office and proclaimed his
ouster, but constitutional provisions for succession were dangerously
vague, and for several days the country found itself with three different
people—Bucaram, his vice president, and the head of the Congress—
claiming legitimate rights to the presidency (New York Times, Feb. 6,
1997). That the conflict was resolved quickly and without bloodshed apparently owes as much to the military's clear preference for congressional
leader Alarcon as to any constitutional or legislative provisions. The outcome was felicitous, at least in the short term, but from start to finish the
crisis was handled in a manner that was hardly consistent with conventional understandings of properly functioning polyarchy.

Finally, in Colombia, state of emergency measures have granted the
military vast powers across most of the national territory, prerogatives
that are rationalized in some instances by the need to confront persistent guerrilla activity and in others by the security threats posed by drug
trafficking syndicates. Not only has this resulted in impunity for members of the military engaged in human rights abuses, it has also facilitated
the consolidation of alliances between the armed forces and paramilitary
groups that compete with the state for sovereignty over contested areas
of the country (Reyes Posada 1991). It is not unknown for these groups
to take over key functions of the central government, including collection of taxes, imposition of additional fees on residents, and even the
provision of public services. By early 1998, many observers estimated
that the state actually exercised control over less than half of the national
territory.

Tailoring definitions

Reliance on the concept of polyarchy is not such a grand concession, even
for the most demanding democrat, if one insists on a rigorous, practical
application of both of Dahl's criteria. Indeed, close attention to the dynamics of everyday political life in Latin America and the Caribbean in-

dicates that few countries in the region satisfy both dimensions of poly-archy. The principal shortcomings involve the accountability of elites, which relates to the dimension of contestation, and the *de facto* incapacity for many citizens to access representative institutions or to influence significant policy outcomes through political participation. However modified to reflect conditions in the real world, any theory of political democracy must accommodate the need for accountability of governors vis-à-vis the citizenry, and for free participation of citizens in the selection of decision-makers. In most of Latin America and the Caribbean the mere acknowledgment that these goals are legitimate constitutes a significant achievement in and of itself, and suggests that the prospects for polyarchy are in fact greater than at many moments in the past. In practice, however, accountability and participation remain limited by institutional and societal impediments. Decades of effort and experimentation, as well as a significant dose of good fortune, will be needed in order for polyarchy to become generalized in the region.

But we must also confront two additional, and perhaps more intractable, prerequisites for democratic politics in Latin America. The first concerns state sovereignty, the absence of which strips regime-type of much of its underlying significance. It means little for citizens to be able to choose among competing elites, to participate in the selection of those elites, or even to articulate policy preferences, if the state toward which their efforts are directed lacks the capacity to enforce its will. Yet Latin American states face a growing crisis of sovereignty. The problem is reflected in the incapacity of states to assert prerogatives vis-à-vis both domestic and external pressures. At the domestic level, the quest for democratic rule is complicated immensely by the proliferation of powerful actors which challenge the state's monopoly on the instruments of coercion. As noted above, virtually everywhere in Central America, and in several Andean countries, military forces retain implicit or explicit veto power over civilian authorities. Moreover, a growing number of governments are unable or unwilling to confront criminal and/or paramilitary organizations which exercise de facto authority over broad expanses of territory and population, and which increasingly penetrate the state itself. The growing influence of transnational drug trafficking networks is a particularly dramatic illustration of the impotence of formally democratic political systems throughout Latin America, and creates a further impediment to their becoming more responsive to popular sentiment. Not only in Latin America, but in several other "developing" regions, political democracy is rendered highly problematic by what Thomas Callaghy (1997) has referred to as "failing" and "flailing" states.

The challenges to state sovereignty are not exclusively internal, however. Throughout the world, the globalization of economic transactions has called into question the capacity of governments to influence market-driven allocations of resources (Sassen 1996; Tilly 1996). To be sure, market-oriented democracies have never resolved fully the structural contradiction articulated by Charles Lindblom (1971) a quarter-century ago: The private sector is constitutionally subordinate to democratic political institutions, yet its economic influence grants the modern corporation a de facto exemption from democratic control. These difficulties are well known in Latin America, where even moderately progressive governments have been undermined repeatedly by overwhelming volumes of capital flight, but they are accentuated in the contemporary context of the region. Astronomical debt levels inherited largely from the period of military rule combine with chronic balance of payments difficulties and low domestic savings rates to compel governments to seek capital through loans and investment from abroad. As a result, Latin American governments are particularly vulnerable to external "shocks" stemming from the decisions of First World investors, multilateral lending agencies, and foreign governments (Goodman and Pauly 1993). The reverberations of the Mexican peso crisis of late 1994, and the continuing uncertainties stemming from the Asian crisis that emerged during the fall of 1997, underscore the degree to which Latin American governments face severe economic policy constraints owing to external vulnerability (Castañeda 1994). This situation has profound consequences for the capacity of states to exercise minimal control over domestic allocation of resources. In turn, this calls into question the continued sovereignty of Latin American governments over their own internal affairs.

A second, and even more elusive prerequisite for fulfilling the promise of polyarchy in Latin America concerns implementation of models of economic development that take advantage of the opportunities opened up by global markets without exacerbating the deeply rooted inequities that render participation virtually impossible for much of the region's population. As noted above, the record to date is not encouraging. From 1980 to 1995 inequality worsened in every country in the region except for Costa Rica and Uruguay (Filgueira 1995), and only Chile and Colombia have made significant progress toward reversing this trend during the 1990s.

It is beyond the scope of this essay to develop a comprehensive argument concerning the potential for Latin American countries to combine growth with equity in the context of globalization. Nonetheless, several points are relevant to our consideration of the potential strengthening of democracy in the region. First, a principled stance premised on resistance to economic globalization or a return to the import substitution industrialization (ISI) strategies of the postwar period is not a viable response to the challenges facing Latin America. Autarchy does not hold the potential of providing for the economic welfare of the population, and ISI itself was in most instances detrimental both to long-term growth and distributive equity (Bulmer-Thomas 1995). Second, a determination to engage the world market does not require withdrawal of the state from economic intervention or from regulation of private economic transactions. Rather, what is needed is a streamlined state capable of selective and efficient intervention to overcome market failures and to redistribute assets in a manner that is both equitable and "market-friendly."[6] Finally, a desirable economic model must elicit, and be sustained by, broad support from a cross section of social actors channeled through political institutions. This is a critical stipulation, for as we discuss further in the third section of this chapter, economic policy has increasingly become the restricted domain of technocratic elites insulated from democratic political institutions and representative institutions in society. The implications of this separation go beyond doubts about the sustainability of policies from which key stakeholders remain alienated, though these are not to be underestimated. Equally important, from the perspective of this chapter, are the climate of political alienation and the exclusionary forms of governance that result from the widespread conviction that societal engagement with policy processes is impossible or undesirable.

To summarize, the second section of this chapter has suggested that Latin American political systems typically exhibit a series of deeply-rooted features which militate against simplistic assertions that political democracy—polyarchy—has become generalized across the region. Where the most basic underpinnings of polyarchy are absent despite the presence of some of the institutional trappings of democracy, the concepts of "pseudo-democracies" and "tutelary democracies" may be useful to specify the conditions that separate political systems from the norms of polyarchy. Elsewhere, in what we label "incomplete democracies," the minimal conditions for polyarchy are present, at least in principle, but a variety of factors, including institutional forms and practices which limit accountability, ossified representative structures and structural economic inequalities which obstruct free political participation, and limited degrees of state sovereignty, generate a political reality which bears little resemblance to ideal-typical notions of polyarchy. The next section examines these issues in greater detail, for they are critical to understanding the constraints on democracy in all but the handful of countries in the region which have achieved something resembling polyarchy. Indeed, as depicted in tables 2 through 4, an admittedly loose application

TABLE 3

Incomplete Democracies

	ACCOUNTABILITY	PARTICIPATION	STATE SOVEREIGNTY	GROWTH/EQUITY STRATEGY
Argentina	Medium	Medium	High	Low
Bolivia	Medium	Medium	Low	Low
Brazil	Medium	Medium	High	Low
Venezuela	Medium	Medium	Medium	Low

of our criteria for classification suggests that only three countries, Chile, Costa Rica, and Uruguay, boast political systems that function in practice as polyarchies. "Incomplete Democracies," such as Argentina, Brazil, Bolivia, and Venezuela, fall short of this exacting standard because of relative deficits in accountability, representation, and/or economic equity. Recognition of the importance of such variables is essential not only to understand the widespread malaise that characterizes political life in the southern zones of the hemisphere, but also to address the prospects for reforming Latin American political systems in order to augment the number of regimes that merit consideration as polyarchies.

Tables 3 and 4 compare Latin America's incomplete democracies and its polyarchies in terms of: accountability of the state to its citizenry, level of citizen participation, degree of state sovereignty, and the extent to which the state's economic development model tries to combine growth with equity. Rankings for each category are based on my own subjective observations and those found in the leading literature.

III. IMPEDIMENTS TO EXTENDING DEMOCRACY IN LATIN AMERICA: ISSUES IN INCOMPLETE POLYARCHIES

Lack of accountability

It is ironic that there exists no precise Spanish or Portuguese translation for the English term "accountability," for few problems are more widely lamented in Latin America than the weakness of mechanisms to ensure it. New democracies inevitably suffer some deficits in this regard: even under the best of circumstances, it takes time for institutions to be established and to begin to function effectively. Yet in Latin America this problem is compounded by the fact that in many countries there is no historic precedent for the principle that political and economic elites

TABLE 4

Polyarchies

	ACCOUNTABILITY	PARTICIPATION	STATE SOVEREIGNTY	GROWTH/EQUITY STRATEGY
Chile	Medium	Medium	High	High
Costa Rica	Medium	High	Medium	High
Uruguay	Medium	High	High	High

must be held accountable for the effects of their actions on society as a whole. Nowhere are the enduring effects of this deficit more evident than in the sphere of law. At a very basic level, democracy entails the integrity of individual citizens and the existence of the rule of law to which they can resort in the event that their basic civil and political rights are violated. In much of Latin America, however, citizens lack recourse to judicial institutions, which are either entirely nonexistent or practically inaccessible to those with limited social or economic resources. Nor does the judiciary function effectively or in a neutral fashion in all those places where it is present institutionally. Partly as a result, powerful actors continue to violate the rights of weaker individuals and groups with relative impunity.[7] This is most strikingly evident in the violence inflicted by official and quasi-official security forces on marginalized youth and slum dwellers, in urban areas, and on land-hungry peasants in the countryside, phenomena that have been especially well documented in Brazil but that occur frequently in all but a handful of Latin American countries (Pinheiro 1996; Caldeira 1996).

There are also a variety of less vivid ways in which the absence of accountability hinders political democracy in Latin America. At least three areas are worthy of mention. First, the problem of corruption, which like that of continuing human rights abuses is connected both to the weakness of judicial institutions and to the widespread persistence of an illiberal culture of power, in the sense that those who have power often wield it without regard for the existence of limits on its practice. Though the phenomenon is hardly unique to the region, corruption in some parts of Latin America is so vast that it undermines public confidence in the possibility that political institutions can be used in the common interest. To be sure, leaders can no longer count on absolute freedom to raid the public coffers: incredible excesses have led to the downfall of elected presidents in Brazil, Ecuador, Peru, and Venezuela. But corruption has remained widespread in these countries as in most others in Latin America, and the public tends to believe, often justifiably, that elected and nonelected officials alike treat public resources as their private domain. The adverse consequences for political legitimacy are enormous.

The second and third aspects of the accountability gap—the weakness of legislatures vis-à-vis executives and the insulation of policymaking technocrats—are more specifically institutional in nature. There is a long tradition of highly centralized presidential rule in Latin America, often coinciding with authoritarian styles of leadership by charismatic populists, but also evident in settings in which personalism plays a lesser role. Presidentialism is likely to endure: despite the urgent calls for reform by numerous political scientists, and the incipient moves toward political decentralization, there is little evidence to suggest that the region is heading toward the establishment of parliamentary or hybrid systems of government. While there is no incompatibility between presidentialism and democracy, political contestation is best preserved in a political order in which no actor or institution, including the president or the executive branch of government, enjoys absolute power vis-à-vis competitors. Yet limits on both the legitimate and illegitimate exercise of presidential power have been woefully inadequate in one country after another over the past decade.

As noted in the earlier discussion of "pseudo-democracies," the absence of checks on executive power in Latin America must in part be understood as a product of systemic crisis. The case of Argentina during the Menem administration is instructive. Routinely bypassing congressional and judicial prerogatives, the president responded to the hyperinflationary crisis inherited from the Alfonsin government by presiding over a massive overhaul of the Argentine economy and welfare state. The neo-Peronist president's openly disdainful treatment of other branches of government and of organized opposition in civil society, as well as his tendency to dismiss the concerns of civil libertarians, human rights activists, and anticorruption voices in the media, elicited widespread support from an electorate exhausted by the atmosphere of uncertainty and chaos which had characterized much of the post-transition experience in Argentina. Similar phenomena were evident in Brazil under President Collor, and continue in Venezuela under Chávez. To be sure, responsibility for presidential excess and for the widespread public support it receives lies in part with legislatures and judiciaries themselves, which are often riddled with corruption and which fail to exercise constitutionally mandated controls. Nonetheless, in ruling by decree, in a personalist and charismatic manner, elected leaders reproduce some of the worst aspects of the populist and demagogic politics that many observers hoped could be overcome as a result of democratic transitions. Delegative democracies, to use O'Donnell's (1994) apt categorization of this kind of incomplete democracy, are a substantial improvement over the dictatorships they replaced, but they are not full-fledged polyarchies, and it is entirely possible that they will not be transformed into such democracies.

The issue of accountability arises in a more limited sense when we consider the ways in which institutions involved in policy making are subjected to popular control. Two factors have combined over the past decade or so in Latin America to produce an unprecedented (under democratic circumstances) expansion in the capacity of unelected technocrats to shape the fundamental direction of public policy from positions that are largely insulated from popular control. First, a corollary of the disproportionate authority vested in executive branches of government is that presidential appointees, cabinet secretaries, and other officials dependent on the executive branch experience a similar expansion in autonomy. Second, this logical outcome of the concentration of power in the executive branch is accentuated during moments of severe economic crisis and subsequent structural adjustment. Indeed, observers of the political economy of stabilization and adjustment in the aftermath of the 1980s debt crisis have shown that the imperative of carrying out rapid and painful adjustment creates incentives for power to be concentrated in technocrats in the executive branch, particularly in ministries of finance which take on the role of superministries, effectively superseding the authority of other cabinet secretaries and leaders of a myriad of agencies dependent on the ministry of finance for resources. According to some accounts, the painful measures associated with stabilization are most likely to be implemented by governments in which power is concentrated in the executive, yet the long-term success of economic reform requires a gradual dispersion of power to a broader array of actors and institutions (Haggard and Kaufman 1994; Montesinos 1993). Balancing these conflicting imperatives is hardly simple, however, and in the regimes we have labeled incomplete democracies, it has yet to come about.

A final issue, relevant everywhere in Latin America, concerns the absence of accountability in nongovernmental organizations (NGOs) which, in the aftermath of neoliberal adjustment, are increasingly called upon to supply a variety of public goods traditionally considered the responsibility of the state. When governments provide social, educational, and health services, develop local infrastructures, or provide for community development, elections can serve as a mechanism for ensuring at least some degree of accountability on behalf of consumers of those services. This is no longer the case when private organizations, rather than the state, take on these quintessentially public roles. Analyzing the conditions for effective citizenship in contemporary societies, Arbós and Giner (1996) have noted the importance of accountability not only for political institutions but also for the intermediate associations which provide channels through which societal interests are articulated. Their principal referents are political parties and interest groups of all kinds, and it is well known that in Latin America clientelism and hierarchical relations of power permeate these institutions just as they do the state itself. More novel are the challenges posed by the growing responsibilities of NGOs, which underscore the urgent need to establish mechanisms of public control over nonstate institutions. [8]

Constraints on participation and representation

Legal constraints on participation have largely been overcome in Latin America as a result of the recent wave of transitions to more open political systems, which consistently recognize the right to political association and expression and the importance of regular elections based on universal suffrage. Proscriptions on opposition political parties that accept the legitimacy of the overarching regime have virtually disappeared—Cuba remains the noteworthy exception—and in some instances opportunities for participation and representation have expanded even further. Thus, several countries have strengthened elected goverments at the local and regional levels; popular referendums have decided crucial policy issues in Uruguay; and constitutions in a number of countries, including Bolivia, Colombia, and Guatemala, have devised innovative mechanisms, above and beyond those based on territorial or populational criteria, for democratic incorporation of minority groups. Despite these achievements, an array of factors continue to limit levels of participation throughout Latin America, and in much of the region this diminishes the scope and breadth of popular involvement in democratic political life to such a degree as to call into question whether polyarchies have been achieved.

Once again, much of the problem lies with institutional weakness, not only at the state level but also in civil society, and these insufficiencies are exacerbated by the persistence of powerful economic constraints on the effective participation of the poorest of the poor. Almost by definition, concentration of power in the hands of unelected technocrats removes significant policy domains from the influence of both the electorate and organized interest groups (Connaghan 1992). Excessive centralization is an additional source of separation between state and society, as is the fact that even where recent efforts to decentralize government structures have been most impressive, lower levels of government seldom have access to the resources needed to respond meaningfully to local demands.

Equally problematic, political parties and interest associations remain poorly institutionalized and ill-suited to the task of representing constituent interests in the broader political arena. To be sure, parties are weakening throughout the world, but as Kircheimer (1966) noted three decades ago the trend is troublesome for democratic politics, for the social cleavages which parties ideally represent have not disappeared. The is particularly relevant in regions undergoing changes of the magnitude of those which have swept Latin America in recent decades. Nonetheless, as epitomized by the cases of Brazil (with the exception of the embattled Workers Party), and Argentina (with the possible exception of the recently established Alliance, which defeated the Peronists in parliamentary elections during 1997 and may well unseat them in the 1999 national elections), programmatic political parties have had little success in incomplete democracies, and indeed in much of the region.[9]

The declining fortunes of unions is also a worldwide phenomenon which has especially adverse implications for representation in Latin America. Historically, unionization rates compared favorably to those in regions of similar levels of economic development, and unions constituted important channels for popular sector participation in the public sphere, for constructing collective political identities, and for extending social and economic citizenship (Collier and Collier 1992). For precisely this reason organized labor was typically one of the principal targets of repression under the authoritarian regimes of the past quarter-century (Drake 1996), but despite regime change the union movement has generally failed to reemerge as a powerful force for coalescence, and no substitute has arisen to replace it (Hagopian 1993). Indeed, neoliberal reforms carried out over the past decade, including privatizations, trade liberalization, and restructuring of employment-based pension systems have undermined further the traditional bases of trade-union power.[10] Nor has the variety of social movements that played a pivotal role in galvanizing societal opposition to dictatorships and in demanding democracy served as a substitute for traditional mechanisms for agglomerating interests and expressing collective demands vis-à-vis the democratic regime. Human rights organizations, progressive church groups, community associations, and the like continue to play important roles in isolated instances in which the particular issues that sparked their initial formation reemerge, but they are not well suited to the task of building and sustaining broad coalitions to address the variety of policy domains that concern the public outside the exceptional circumstances of dictatorship.

Growth without development

The introductory section of this chapter referred to the exceptionally unequal distribution of wealth in Latin America and argued that this has potentially profound implications for the plausibility of political contestation and participation. As pointed out in that section, even where economic growth has occurred following implementation of market-oriented reforms, the 1990s generally have not witnessed a reversal of the regional trend toward polarization of income. In a few countries, targeted social policies have helped to alleviate the plight of the poorest of the poor, but economic insecurity, often involving situations of desperation, remains the lot of vast segments of the population. Without significant progress toward combining growth with equity, there is little that can be done to make political systems less exclusionary.

In the countries we have classified as incomplete democracies, long unequal patterns of income distribution (excepting Argentina) have grown more unequal since the military left power or, in the case of Venezuela, since the debt crisis of the early 1980s. In Argentina, which had boasted one of the most advanced welfare states in the hemisphere, much of the state apparatus which shaped allocations of resources has been dismantled, despite widespread popular protest. While annual rates of economic growth have subsequently soared as high as 8 percent, unemployment also has skyrocketed, and the country is suffering poverty rates that have not been seen since the early days of Peronism. A similar trajectory is evident in Venezuela, where a reliance on ever-increasing oil export revenues to service excessive borrowing brought the economy to a standstill a decade ago. Popular mobilization has sometimes deterred Venezuelan governments from enacting neoliberal policies, most notably in the so-called *Caracazo* of 1989, but policy paralysis has produced precisely the outcomes feared by the rioters. Brazil has followed a different path: in contrast to Venezuela, its economy is highly diversified, and democratic governments have been able to avoid or postpone carrying out many of the reforms called for by the "Washington consensus." The result has been a comparatively modest deterioration in living conditions for the poor, most notably since the triumph over hyperinflation following the Real plan of 1995, but the country began this period as one of the most dualistic societies in the world, and it has made little progress toward overcoming that distinction.

No magic formula is available for Latin American polities seeking to redress historically unequal patterns of income distribution. Indeed, while the three countries we have classified as polyarchies have performed relatively well in this regard, they have done so following quite different sets of policies. Chile, which remains one of the most liberalized economies in the region, has relied on a combination of rapid market-driven growth and narrowly targeted compensatory social policies to achieve a substantial reduction in poverty rates (Hershberg 1997). By contrast, Costa Rica and Uruguay have liberalized much more deliberately, in large part in response to popular pressure expressed not only at the polls but also through organized efforts by an array of political parties, unions, and civic associations. Both countries have assigned priority to maintaining their historically ambitious welfare states, albeit with significant cutbacks, and to preserve coverage for as broad a segment of the population as possible. Though their growth rates during the 1990s may have lagged relative to those of some of the more dynamic Latin American economies, Costa Rica and Uruguay have been more successful than any of the other countries in preserving distributive equity and limiting poverty (Filgueira 1995; Cordero and Mora 1998).

IV. Extending Democracy

There is little debate in Latin America today about the desirability of democratic rule, but discussions about the poor quality of democracy are ubiquitous both in the region and in scholarly analyses of Latin American politics. Many of the complaints are typical of those voiced about virtually any political democracy, for as noted earlier, the utopian vision of rule by the people is more elusive in practice than in theory. Given the burdens imposed by its traditions of authoritarianism, social exclusion, and poverty, it is only natural that the road to democratic governance in Latin America has been rife with obstacles. Some of what ails democratic politics in the region can be addressed over time, and indeed is being addressed, by policy innovations and popular initiative, but some of the travails of Latin American democracy are but symptoms of much deeper structural problems which even the most optimistic observer must acknowledge will take generations to overcome.

The fundamental objective must be to enhance political citizenship and to extend it as broadly as possible to all social groups. Citizens must be assured of the right to freely choose among competing elites and to engage the state, and one another, in noncoercive relationships in the public sphere. Citizens must have sufficient autonomy to enable them to freely form opinions and reach decisions about public matters, and they must have the resources, social and economic, as well as political, without which that autonomy cannot be exercised. In what O'Donnell (1993) refers to as the low-intensity citizenship that characterizes much of present-day Latin America, the promise of democracy to coincide with human dignity and autonomy is frustrated. This chapter concludes with a brief exploration of some potentially promising strategies for raising the intensity of citizenship and, in so doing, for deepening Latin American democracy and extending its benefits to broader segments of the polis.

Accountability

At a very basic level, solutions to the accountability gap in Latin America require profound changes in what we might think of as the culture of governing, and of the culture of power more generally. Leaders and public officials are more likely to be accountable to the public if they believe that they should be accountable, and if accountability is routinely demanded of them. This point goes to the core of the concept of citizenship, for citizens not only enjoy rights as individuals, they also incur obligations to their fellow citizens. Those who are committed to expanding accountability in the region are wise to insist on the matter, and in doing so in recent years a number of political leaders in Latin American democracies may well make their greatest contribution to the long-term prospects for democracy.

Accountability may be advanced by a favorable culture of power, but it is made possible by institutions, and there is an urgent need to strengthen such institutions throughout the region. In addition to reform of the judiciary, which must become more accessible as well as more equitable and transparent in its operation, new mechanisms are needed to provide oversight of elected and nonelected officials, at national and subnational levels alike. As Przeworski notes (1997), promising experiments are underway in several countries, encompassing the activities of human-rights ombudsmen, the strengthening of legislative commissions, and the establishment of independent agencies responsible for monitoring the performance of public and quasi-public institutions, including nongovernmental organizations carrying out public functions. The potential importance of political decentralization for accountability is especially noteworthy: motivated by pressure from international financial institutions, virtually all countries of Latin America have begun to decentralize delivery of a variety of public goods, including such basic services as education. If local and regional governments are endowed with the authority and resources to make significant decisions, and if control over those governments is devolved to local residents, the existence of institutional controls over the actions of public officials in relevant agencies could be of enormous benefit to the citizenry.

Participation

Just as decentralization could conceivably open new opportunities to engineer accountability, it offers novel avenues for political participation. In principle, citizen involvement is facilitated by proximity to government, and such involvement makes possible closer monitoring of government activities. At the same time, decentralization poses serious risks, as evidenced by the clientelist practices associated with many of the targeted social policy initiatives that have emerged throughout the region in recent years.[11]

Enhancing opportunities for participation also requires a reinvigoration of existing political parties and interest groups and the creation of new ones. Concern about governability during the fragile moments of democratic transition led many observers to discourage the proliferation of political parties, but in many countries today the greater risk is not the disunity of prodemocratic parties but rather their lack of responsiveness to citizen demands. Some of the most encouraging signs of democratic creativity in the region are associated with newly established parties, in strong democracies (e.g., Uruguay) and weak democracies (e.g., Mexico, Colombia) alike. Just as important, there is a need to democratize the internal functioning of parties and interest associations. Indeed, one widely cited explanation for the weakness of many traditional interest associations is the absence of accountability and participation within those organizations themselves. Expanded use of primary elections to select party candidate slates constitutes a welcome response to this concern.

Sovereignty

Few contemporary issues are as vexing for social scientists, as well as for citizens, as that of sovereignty. Sovereignty is called into question everywhere in the world, as the nation-state is eroded from above by processes of globalization and by the growing influence of international conventions, and from below by the proliferation of local and regional identities that do not take the state as a central point of reference. The impact of the former on Latin America is addressed elsewhere in this chapter, but the presence of the latter phenomenon must be acknowledged as well: transnational migration, as well as the resurgence of collective identities articulated along racial and ethnic lines, call into question the hegemony of the state in collective life. Despite incontrovertible evidence that sovereignty is in flux, there is no clear consensus about how to reconceptualize its relationship to democracy and to politics at the state level more generally.

Two possible dimensions of the changing nature of sovereignty are worthy of mention, however. First, while we tend to associate the decline in sovereignty with diminished opportunities for democratization in developing countries, in some respects the contrary argument may be equally compelling. As Sikkink (1996) argues, international pressures are increasingly imposing powerful constraints on governments engaged in human rights abuses of various kinds. Such pressures were a key element behind Peruvian president Fujimori's agreeing to elections after his "auto-golpe," and some observers have concluded that concern about international reaction persuaded the Salinas administration not to respond with unreserved force when the Zapatista movement burst upon the scene on New Year's Day of 1994. It is entirely possible that, over time, the emergence of a transnational civil society, at least as much as the actions of foreign governments, may help to ensure respect for the rights of vulnerable groups ranging from street children to battered women to landless peasants.

Increasing interest in regional integration schemes represents a second trend related to the changing nature of sovereignty. It is premature to speculate as to whether arrangements such as Mercosur might replicate the trajectory that culminated in establishment of the European Union, but clearly there exists a precedent for programs of economic integration evolving into broader efforts encompassing political goals as well. If this were to occur, there could be important consequences for the fabric of democratic institutions in participating countries. As evidenced by the debates concerning the relationship of Mercosur countries to NAFTA and to U.S. proposals for a hemispheric free-trade zone, integration may also prove significant for the manner in which Latin American countries confront an increasingly globalized economic system. Indeed, one factor motivating the present drive toward greater integration is the vulnerability of individual national economies in the face of the global economy, and particularly in relation to hegemonic powers.

Combining economic growth and equity

The sudden collapse of a succession of East Asian economies during the second half of 1997 suggests that economics is not the sphere for miracles, but this does not stop us from drawing lessons from the accumulated experience of developing countries during the postwar era. Three issues emerge as critical to the prospects for sustaining high levels of economic growth in Latin America and for promoting just distribution of the ensuing benefits. Adequate treatment of these issues would require a separate essay, but they can be summarized as follows: First, just as the excessive reliance on import substitution industrialization (ISI) hamstrung Latin American economies during the half-century following the Great Depression, and particularly beginning in the 1970s, a single-minded focus on export-led-growth invites numerous problems. All too often, the push for international competitiveness culminates in a race to the bottom in terms of cost, rather than continual upgrading of processes and products. The consequence is a pattern of growth based on cheap and overexploited labor, hardly a recipe for equitable development. Regrettably, despite localized exceptions, this is the pattern that is emerging in Latin America. Appropriate government responses need not involve "picking winners" or repeating the mistakes of the failed industrial policies of the past, but there is room for market-friendly public policies designed to help firms to become competitive. Such measures are few and far between at the moment, but there is increasing awareness of their importance. Whether effective competitiveness policies are developed in response to these needs will provide tangible evidence of how far the region has advanced beyond the free-market platitudes of the neoliberal era.

Second, in the absence of sufficient human capital, that is, of an educated population, a globally integrated economy inevitably is relegated to low value-added segments of production, or to capital intensive industries. In either case, the benefits accruing to labor, and the opportunities for employment, are relatively low. Once again, these are glaring problems in Latin America today: the few sectors in the region that are internationally competitive, and hence dynamic, are based almost exclusively on capital-intensive large firms, in which high productivity is predicated on replacing workers with state of the art machinery. There are no short-term solutions to this crisis, but in the long run progress can result from concerted efforts to improve educational systems and to broaden access to training. That there is consensus on this issue, both in the region and among officials of the multilateral lending institutions that must play a role in financing educational reform, is one of the most hopeful signs of progress toward combining growth and equity in the future.

Finally, fiscal reform is another crucial area. Latin American states fail to tax sufficiently and they rely disproportionately on indirect taxes, such as value-added taxes, rather than taxes on income and wealth. There is a need not only to restructure the tax systems along more progressive lines, but also to increase the tax burden substantially; in some instances the goal should be to double the portion of GNP available to enable democratic governments to carry out their functions. One reason that citizens should participate in the political process is to shape the multiple interventions that governments ought to pursue in an effort to improve the life-chances of their people. Governments can only peform these functions if they dispose of the necessary resources; quite understandably, citizens grow disillusioned with democracies that are fiscally unable to meet their most basic demands.

CONCLUSION

The past fifteen years or so have witnessed an unprecedented opening of political systems in many Latin American countries that long suffered under repressive regimes that systematically denied political access to most of the population. Democratization has meant much more than the institutionalization of an improved package of rules—competitive elections—for selecting government leaders: by acknowledging an array of political rights that traditionally were suppressed, democratization has meant tangible changes in people's lives. In most of Latin America today, people can express diverse political views, organize political associations, criticize rulers, and hold public demonstrations without concern for their physical safety. In a significant number of countries, moreover, institutional channels through which individuals and social groups can exercise influence over policy processes continue to be strengthened, and a variety of innovations are emerging to increase the scope of citizen participation in public affairs, particularly at the local level. To be sure, in some settings, politics remains a life-and-death matter, particularly in areas of the countryside where political cleavages are defined largely in terms of struggles over land. Nonetheless, it is far from trivial that in most of the region state-sanctioned violence no longer constitutes the principal response to social conflict, and basic political activities that were once held to be subversive have come to be viewed as normal and legitimate features of public life. A comparison between the present situation and that of the late 1970s, when dictatorships predominated in all but a couple of countries and appeared likely to remain in power indefinitely, testifies to the remarkable progress that has been made despite difficult odds.

At the same time, democratization remains partial and uneven, and, at least so far, it has enjoyed only minimal success in addressing some of the most pressing issues facing Latin American societies. The institutions through which democracies operate in the region, and the democratic regimes themselves, remain weak and subject to a variety of distortions. More problematic still is the fact that democracy has done little to alter the outrageous levels of social and economic exclusion that persist in virtually every country in the hemisphere. Inequalities undermine the capacity of much of the population to take advantage of potential opportunities to intervene in the political arena, and constitute the most serious obstacle to constructing societies in which democratic citizenship is shared by all. The seeming intractability of poverty and socioeconomic polarization despite advances toward political democracy offers powerful support for those who conclude that the glass is merely half full, that democracy has failed to deliver on its promise to improve the quality of collective life in Latin America. Indeed, the scarcity of credible proposals for simultaneously advancing economic growth and improving distribution augurs poorly for the prospects of extending the logic of democracy beyond the narrow sphere of the polity to encompass the related arenas of the society and economy. Yet twenty years ago the notion that democratic regimes would become nearly universal in the region by the end of the twentieth century would have appeared utopian. No one could have predicted the political changes that have taken place since then. Those changes will be all the more meaningful if the next twenty years of Latin American development witness similar progress toward resolving the notorious social question.

NOTES

1. By suggesting that we think in terms of a continuum I do not mean to imply that there is any necessary trajectory of change in one direction or another. Political systems may become more democratic over time, or less so, and the fact that a transition has been achieved or sustained does not mean that a country cannot become "less" democratic over time. This is one reason, though not the

only one, that this essay avoids the concept of "democratic consolidation." For a useful critique of this widely used term, see O'Donnell (1997).

2. As such, the Cuban case does not constitute a diminished subtype of democracy: it belongs to an entirely different category.

3. We also harbor great doubts as to whether Peru passes a minimal threshold for polyarchy in terms of civilian control over the military and/or guarantees for civil liberties. Similarly, Mexico remains some distance away from having achieved polyarchy: Even if elections were to pass the threshold, the weakness of the rule of law, the absence of accountability, and the inadequacy of protections of civil liberties remain highly problematic.

4. We concur with Rabkin (1992–93) that the Chilean case does not qualify as a tutelary democracy. Though it is true that the armed forces enjoy special prerogatives bestowed upon them by the 1980 Constitution, these privileges arguably do not endow the military with veto power over decisions of elected officials.

5. Public opinion data reviewed by Juan Rial in the early 1990s (personal correspondence) indicated that the church and the military were the only institutions that enjoyed widespread popular support in Ecuador, and indeed, the trend was widespread throughout the Andes.

6. The literature on these points is massive and growing. Important contributions include Williamson (1993), who insists on the compatibility of interventionist policies with the "Washington consensus" often attributed to him; Bresser et al. (1993), argues for a streamlined yet powerful state to guide economic policy; Díaz (1996), and Portes (1997) echo this view, noting that neoliberalism aspired to dismantle an outdated statist development model but lacked any conception of how to restructure Latin American economies over the long run. Castañeda (1993) calls upon Latin American progressives to combine the best of Japanese managerial capability with a European social democratic sensibility to negotiated bargaining over distribution and technological innovation.

7. The concept of impunity has of course been used in reference to another of the major sources of discontent in recently established Latin American democracies, namely, the inability of legitimate authorities to prosecute perpetrators of human rights violations under military regimes. A substantial literature has engaged the highly charged question of how impunity for past crimes limits the potential for justice in new democracies (see the essays in Part 1 of Jelin and Hershberg 1996).

8. Our interpretation of the significance of NGOs perhaps differs slightly from the relatively optimistic view put forth, albeit cautiously, by Chalmers et al. (1997). Much work remains to be done before we understand fully how important associative networks are becoming across different domains and how horizontal, as opposed to vertical, are the relations of power that characterize those networks.

9. One system we have classified as a polyarchy, Chile, arguably has the most highly developed party system in the region. Though their clientelist tendencies should not be underemphasized, parties in Uruguay and Costa Rica are

also highly institutionalized. The emergence of a third party as a serious competitor for power in Uruguay, the Broad Front, testifies to the continuing capacity of that polyarchy to evolve in response to public sentiment. A similar dynamic may be unfolding today in Argentina, with the rise of the Alliance.

10. In the medium term, emerging constellations of interests may develop new organizational channels for articulating political demands, and some observers detect promising signs of such innovations in several countries that we have labeled incomplete democracies (Chalmers et al. 1997).

11. It is commonly argued that the dismantling of central state agencies responsible for various aspects of social policy strips government officials of crucial instruments for patronage. This may well be the case, but the experience of initiatives such as PRONASOL, in Mexico, testifies to the very real possibility that clientelist practices will be reproduced by the new institutional frameworks. As one author has noted, decentralization can "consolidate the power of local traditional elites . . . weaken popular social organizations and . . . diminish participation in social affairs" (cited in Rivera 1998).

References

Arbós, Xavier, and Salvador Giner. 1996. *La Gobernabilidad: Ciudadanía y democracia en la encrucijada mundial.* Madrid: Siglo XXI.

Barros, Robert. 1986. "The Left and Democracy: Recent Debates in Latin America." *Telos,* vol. 68, no. 2 (Summer).

Bresser, Perreira, Luiz Carlos, J. M. Maravall, and A. Przeworski. 1993. *Economic Reforms in New Democracies.* New York: Cambridge University Press.

Bulmer-Thomas, Victor. 1995. *An Economic History of Latin America.* New York: Cambridge University Press.

Caldeira, Teresa. 1996. "Crime and Individual Rights: Reframing the Question of Violence in Latin America." In Elizabeth Jelin and Eric Hershberg, eds., *Constructing Democracy: Human Rights, Citizenship, and Society in Latin America.* Boulder: Westview Press, 197–211.

Callaghy, Thomas. 1997. "Failing States and Flailing States." Memorandum prepared for the Program on International Peace and Security of the Social Science Research Council.

Castañeda, Jorge. 1993. *Utopia Unarmed.* New York: Alfred P. Knopf.

———. 1994. *The Mexican Shock.* New York: The New Press.

Cerdas, Rodolfo. 1993. *El desencanto democrático: Crisis de partidos y transición democrática en Centroamérica y Panamá.* San José, Costa Rica: Red Editorial Centroamericana.

Chalmers, Douglass, Scott Martin, and Kerianne Piester. 1997. "Associative Networks: New Structures of Representation for Popular Sectors?" In Chalmers et al., eds., *The New Politics of Inequality in Latin America.* New York: Oxford University Press. 543–582.

Collier, David, and Ruth Berins Collier. 1992. *Shaping the Political Arena.* Princeton: Princeton University Press.

Collier, David, and Steven Levitsky. 1997. "Democracy with Adjectives: Conceptual Innovation in Comparative Research." *World Politics,* 49(3): 430–51.

Connaghan, Catherine. 1992. "Capitalists, Technocrats and Politicians: Economic Policy Making in the Central Andes." In Scott Mainwaring, Guillermo O'Donnell, and J. S. Valenzuela, eds., *Issues in Democratic Consolidation.* Notre Dame: University of Notre Dame Press, 199–242.

Cordero, Allen and Mora Minor. 1998. "Costa Rica: El mercado de trabajo en el contexto del ajuste." In Juan Pablo Pérez Sáinz and Edward Funkhouser, eds., *Mercado Laboral y pobreza en Centroamérica.* San José, Costa Rica: FLACSO.

Dahl, Robert. 1971. *Polyarchy.* New Haven: Yale University Press.

Diamond, Larry. 1996. "Democracy in Latin America: Degrees, Illusions and Directions for Consolidation." In Tom Farer, ed., *Beyond Sovereignty: Collectively Defending Democracy in the Americas.* Baltimore: Johns Hopkins University Press.

Díaz, Alvaro. 1996. "Hacia el post-neoliberalismo? El caso Chileno." Paper presented at the Mellon Foundation Fellows Conference, University of Texas at Austin.

Drake, Paul. 1996. *Labor and Dictatorships in the Southern Cone.* Baltimore: Johns Hopkins University Press.

Epstein, Edward. 1993. "Labor and Political Stability in the New Chilean Democracy: Three Illusions." *Revista de Economía y Trabajo,* 1(20): 47–64.

Filgueira, Fernando. 1995. "Política, desempleo económico y desarrollo social en América Latina, 1980s–1990s." Paper presented in Montevideo, Uruguay, at an August 1995 workshop sponsored by the Institute for Development and Research of Canada (IDRC).

Garreton, Manuel Antonio. 1996. "Human Rights in Processes of Democratization." In Elizabeth Jelin and Eric Hershberg, eds., 1996. *Constructing Democracy: Human Rights, Citizenship and Society in Latin America.* Boulder: Westview Press, 39–56.

Goodman, John, and L. W. Pauly. 1993. "The Obsolescence of Capital Controls? Economic Management in an Age of Global Markets." *World Politics,* 46(1): 50–82.

Haggard, Stephan, and Robert Kaufman. 1995. *The Political Economy of Democratic Transitions.* Princeton: Princeton University Press.

Hagopian, Frances. 1993. "After Regime Change: Authoritarian Legacies, Political Representation and the Democratic Future of South America." *World Politics,* 45(3): 464–500.

Hershberg, Eric. 1997. "Market-Oriented Development Strategies and State-Society Relations in New Democracies: Lessons from Contemporary Spain and Chile." In Douglass Chalmers, Scott Martin and Kerianne Piester, eds., *The New Politics of Inequality in Latin America.* New York: Oxford University Press. 337–59.

Hershberg, Eric, and R. Menjivar. 1998. "Prólogo" to Juan Pablo Pérez Sáinz,

Victor Bulmer Thomas, and Bryan Roberts, eds., *Centroamérica en Reestructuración*, 3 vols. San José, Costa Rica: FLACSO, 7–14.

Huntington, Samuel. 1991. *The Third Wave*. Norman: University of Oklahoma Press.

Jelin, Elizabeth, and Eric Hershberg, eds. 1996. *Constructing Democracy: Human Rights, Citizenship, and Society in Latin America*. Boulder: Westview Press.

Kircheimer, Otto. 1966. "The Transformation of the West European Party Systems." In Joseph Lapalombara and M. Weiner, eds., *Political Parties and Political Development*. Princeton: Princeton University Press, 177–200.

Lindblom, Charles. 1977. *Politics and Markets*. New York: Basic Books.

Macpherson, C. B. 1966. *The Real World of Democracy*. Oxford: The Clarendon Press.

Montesinos, Veronica. 1993. "Economic Policy Elites and Democratization." *Studies in Comparative International Development*, 28(1): 25–53.

Morales, Abelardo. 1998. "Ciudadanía social y reinserción de la población ex-combatiente en Nicaragua y El Salvador." In Bryan Roberts, ed., *Ciudadanía social y politica social*. San José, Costa Rica: FLACSO.

O'Donnell, Guillermo. 1993. "On the State, Democratization and Some Conceptual Problems." *World Development*, 21(8): 1255–69.

———. 1994. "Delegative Democracy." *Journal of Democracy*, 5(1): 56–69.

———. 1996. "Poverty and Inequality in Latin America: Some Political Reflections." *Kellogg Institute Working Paper*, 225 (July).

———. 1997. "Illusions about Consolidation." In Larry Diamond et al., eds., *Consolidating the Third Wave Democracies*. Baltimore: Johns Hopkins University Press, 40–57.

O'Donnell, Guillermo, and Philippe Schmitter. 1986. *Tentative Conclusions about Uncertain Democracies*. Baltimore: Johns Hopkins University Press.

Panfichi, Aldo. 1997. "The Authoritarian Alternative: 'Anti-politics' in the Popular Sectors of Lima." In Douglass Chalmers, et al., eds., *The New Politics of Inequality in Latin America*. New York: Oxford University Press, 217–36.

Pateman, Carole. 1970. *Participation and Democratic Theory*. New York: Cambridge University Press.

Pinheiro, Paulo Sergio. 1996. "O passado nao esta morto: nem passado e ainda." Introduction to Gilberto Dimenstein, *Democraçia em pedaços: direitos humanos no Brasil*. Sao Paulo: Companhia das Letras.

Portes, Alejandro. 1997. "Neoliberalism and the Sociology of Development: Emerging Trends and Unanticipated Facts." *Population and Development Review*, 23(2): 229–59.

Przeworski, Adam. 1986. "Some Problems in the Study of Transition to Democracy." In Guillermo O'Donnell, P. Schmitter, and L. Whitehead, eds., *Transitions from Authoritarian Rule*. Baltimore: Johns Hopkins University Press, 47–63.

———. 1997. "Democratization Revisited." *Items*, 51(1): 6–11.

Rabkin, Rhoda. 1992–93. "The Aylwin Government and 'Tutelary' Democracy:

A Concept in Search for a Case?" *Journal of Interamerican Studies and World Affairs,* 119–94.

Reyes Posada, Alejandro. 1991. "Paramilitares en Colombia: Contexto, aliados y consecuencias." In Gonzalo Sánchez and Ricardo Peñaranda, eds., *Pasado y presente de la violencia en Colombia,* 425–35.

Rivera, Roy. 1998. "La descentralización y la realización de la ciudadanía social en América Central." In Bryan Roberts, ed., *Ciudadanía social y politica social.* San José, Costa Rica: FLACSO, 197–234.

Sassen, Saskia. 1996. *Losing Control: Sovereignty in an Age of Globalization.* Columbia University Press.

Schmitter, Philippe, and Terry Karl. 1991. "What Democracy Is, and Is Not." *Journal of Democracy,* 2: 75–88.

Sikkink, Katherine. 1996. "The Emergence, Evolution and Effectiveness of the Latin American Human Rights Network." In Elizabeth Jelin and Eric Hershberg, eds., *Constructing Democracy: Human Rights, Citizenship, and Society in Latin America.* Boulder: Westview Press, 59–84.

Stavenhagen, Rodolfo. 1996. "Indigenous Rights: Some Conceptual Problems." In Elizabeth Jelin and Eric Hershberg, eds., *Constructing Democracy: Human Rights, Citizenship, and Society in Latin America.* Boulder: Westview Press, 141–60.

Tilly, Charles. 1996. "Globalization Threatens Labor's Rights." *International Labor and Working Class History,* 47: 1–23.

Touraine, Alain. 1997. "Exitos y limites de la democratizacion en America Latina." *LASA Forum,* vol. 28, 2: 17–24.

Whitehead, Laurence. 1992. "Alternatives to Liberal Democracy: Perspectives from Latin America." *Political Studies.* Special Issue on Democracy, edited by D. Held, 146–59.

Williamson, John. 1993. "Democracy and the 'Washington Consensus'." *World Development,* 21(8): 1329–36.

11

The Painful Gradualness of Democratization: Proceduralism as a Necessarily Discontinuous Revolution

Edward Friedman

IN RECENT DECADES, political changes in parts of Asia and Latin America have focused our attention on democratic transitions and the ongoing struggle to achieve and maintain democracy. Too often, however, such analysis has offered misleading generalizations about a different aptitude for democracy of Asian versus Western societies. This chapter explores the question, "Why is democratization so difficult?" The answer suggests that the conventional wisdom limiting the difficulties of democratization uniquely to the non-Western world is not credible. "The inhabitants of countries such as Russia and Ukraine . . . often used [the word 'democracy'] as a synonym for . . . 'Western civilization,' but it is meaningless" (Touraine 1994: 175). Democracy is slow and difficult in "the West" too. Only a mythology of the West which presents its culture as uniquely democratic and obscures the actual histories of Germany, France, Italy, Spain, Greece, et al. hides this general truth. Democratization is so revolutionary as to be a contingent process full of vicissitudes and setbacks anywhere and everywhere, including the West.

To begin with, the question, "Why is democratization so difficult?" cannot be addressed without clarifying the content of democracy. In the conventional Schumpeterian wisdom explicated in the influential work of Samuel Huntington (1991), democracy means competitive elections. At times this notion of competitive elections is supposedly made more precise by adding notions such as the inclusion of most people (or males) as the eligible voters. That is, elections are not deemed democratic if they are not found fair and inclusive.

But which groups have to be included before elections are fair enough to be deemed democratic? That is not agreed upon. After all, if one insists on women voting as part of a definition of democracy, since women often constitute a majority of the adult population, then even France was not democratic until after World War Two. Yet the mainstream literature treats France's Third Republic as democratic. In fact, even if just the inclusion of virtually all adult males is essential to democracy, then, given the brutal and systematic exclusion of African-Americans from voting in the U.S. South, the United States could not be considered democratic until after the implementation of the 1965 voting rights act, that is, at the earliest 1968. But virtually no study of democracy insists that America only became democratic in 1968.

Consequently, the standard Schumpeterian understanding of democracy does not stand up to minimal scrutiny. It does not mesh with the conventional understanding of what is democratic. Or, to put the same point another way, for polities in the "West," quite undemocratic governments still have been counted as democratic. Is it possible that "non-Western" governments labeled nondemocratic are measured by a double standard which raises the bar far higher than in France's Third Republic and in the United States before its civil rights revolution?

Further complicating the notion of conceptualizing democracy, a standard political science approach often defines an institutionalized democracy as the result of a competitive election process producing two peaceful transfers of power among opposing political parties. From that perspective, in 1997 neither Japan nor Taiwan was yet democratic. That misunderstanding of what makes for a democratic polity is as absurd an idea as that France was never democratic before 1945 or the United States not before the 1968 elections. Thus, apparently even minimalist notions of democracy, that is, abstract definitions of competitive elections understood in the Schumpeterian sense are fatally flawed.

There is no escape from addressing matters of values (Berkowitz 1996) and historical subjectivity in comprehending liberal democracy. That is, in reality, notions of fairness change. What seems inclusive and fair at one time, may at another time appear exclusionary and unfair. In England, in the seventeenth century, it seemed reasonable to exclude from the ballot and from officeholding people who did not own land or who did not pay taxes or who were from dissident Protestant churches or who were Catholic or Jewish or Muslim. A long political struggle, as part of a public dialogue, would eventually persuade ruling elites to embrace new standards of fairness and inclusion (Friedman 1998). Democratization consequently involves an ongoing political discussion on fairness and inclusion, an open-ended process, a struggle of groups, ideas, and interests, which can, however, also be won by exclusionists, people who reverse democratic achievements. England's transition to democracy was so patently revolutionary that it was long-drawn-out and nearly lost (Rueschemeyer, Huber Stephens and Stephens 1992). Nonetheless, anti-democrats certainly considered Britain's parliamentary polity to be democratic even before the 1832 reforms. No democracy is without flaws, even huge ones. All democracies require further democratization.

In the United States census of 1790, the only category besides white and free was "other." And the "others" were excluded. These were not few in number. By 1920 white southern elites in America could get the census to drop categories of African by percentage (octoroon, etc.) because "coloreds" to be excluded were disappearing. In an atmosphere of racialistic social Darwinism, the census began to count so-called "races"—Negroes, Hindus, Filipinos, etc.—to facilitate northwest European "white" dominance that blocked and even reversed the painful process of democratization. It would be decades before the unfairness of this system would be exploded. These vicissitudes reveal "how fragile and contingent the conditions of a liberal polity are" (Thomas 1997: 40). Indeed, "No one can say that democracy ['even our democracy'] is permanent" (Singer 1997: 32). The standard dichotomy of the West as the home for consolidated democracies and "the rest" as lesser, merely fledgling democracies makes no sense. A comparative understanding of democratization requires abjuring romantic and idealized notions of the West.

If the system could long evolve in an undemocratic direction, that is, if many of the gains of the American Civil War were rolled back, as they were, does it seem logical to describe the American polity as a consolidated democracy? Ignoring erosions of democracy in countries such as France and the United States, " 'consolidology' is no more than a label for the study of new democracies" (Schedler 1998: 102) The late-twentieth-century scholarly focus on "consolidology" (Carothers 1997: 117) which has proved so misleading for the non-Western world is just as misleading for "the West." Not long ago, Conor Cruise O'Brien maintained, regarding the Enlightment:

> How secure is that heritage? I think not all that secure. . . . John Paul II's aim is the repeal of the Enlightenment. . . . democracy has its specific weakness . . . the short term . . . quest for popularity. . . . the survival of democracy seems to have depended on the emergence, at moments of supreme crisis, of leaders capable of risk-

ing their popularity. . . . To an uncomfortable degree, therefore, the survival of democracy would appear to be a matter of luck. (O'Brien 1994: 18, 24, 48, 54)

Given how much a democratic government can never control overwhelming forces such as war and depression, it is impossible that democracy can be so secure as to never be capable of erosion or breakdown. Democratization can achieve monumental gains, but there are no final consolidations of democratic breakthroughs. Indeed, the very term "consolidation" itself may be incoherent. That is, the opposition of consolidated Western democracies and fledgling democracies elsewhere is pure ideology, a binary that misleads. The West is just like the rest. The dynamics of power explored by political science do not work differently in Japan or Britain any more than do other lawful generalizations. Treating the West incorrectly as an easy and natural instance of democratization elides the important European debate of the nineteenth century over whether massively flawed liberal democracies were meaningfully democratic.

Because democracies exclude so many for so long from participating in the project of political empowerment, many observers over the years have found liberal democracies in the West to be no democracies at all. Imagining full inclusiveness as impossible under the extant rules seen as entrenching a particular power structure, such critics often embraced some other value (e.g., equality, group solidarity, socialism) as of true worth, in contrast to "mere" liberal democracy seen as but an ideological mask for rule by some entrenched elite (e.g., capitalists, whites, east-coast Anglo-Saxon Protestants, males). That misunderstanding, however, has been a threat to what a struggle for democratization in a really existing democracy, warts and all, achieves. As the French sociologist Alaine Touraine (1994: 173) put it in his book, *What Is Democracy?*:

> The most serious threat to democracy stems from the depiction of a society as a system of absolute domination that is not content with exploiting and excluding the dominated but also deprives them of their consciousness or instills a false consciousness. . . . we see only victims . . . never actors. . . . The pessimism has always had a negative effect on democratic ideas, which are violently rejected or scorned as petit-bourgeois reformist.

After numerous instances where proponents of some supposedly true democracy—organic or socialist—took power only to carry out exclusionary policies, often genocidal in direction, against communities or a so-called bourgeoisie, it should be clear that what advocates of alternatives to "mere" procedural political democracy offer in practice is not fuller, truer democracy, but, instead, tyranny parading as democracy. Proletarian dictatorship is a reign of terror pretending to be a reign of virtue. Likewise, the discourse of full, direct democracy is more illusory than the discourses of liberal democracy which are initially almost invariably politically informed by exclusions that eventually can be exposed as most unfair and then, perhaps, only perhaps, after much effort, improved upon. It is crucial to keep the political system open to contention and reinterpretation, both a political struggle and a dialogue of continuous reexamination, something definitionally precluded in the presumed perfection of alternative "real" democracies, direct, organic, or people's democracies. It is worth being suspicious of those who tout some alleged virtue as more excellent than proceduralist gradualism. However unconsolidated, however incomplete, the project of procedural democracy is a liberating revolution in the interest of humanity. Yet it is a project.

That is, there is a kernel of wisdom inside the deadly poisonous chaff of the critique of liberal democracy by partisans of so-called direct or participatory democracy. The initial, very partial democracy of a fledgling democracy need not evolve into an inclusive democracy. No actual existing democracy has lived up to its billing. Most likely, none ever will. Perhaps, democratization is always partial because the continuing struggle and ongoing dialogue reveal illusions and exclusions that were previously invisible. Democratization seems a political trek with an ever-receding horizon.

As Benjamin Barber (1996) and numerous others have noted, democracy is a project. With democratization an endless quest, there is no static democratic content to consolidate. Consolidation at most any point in the trek would freeze much that is undemocratic and obstruct the process of further democratization. In fact, since the openness of the dialogue and the peaceful struggle in no way guarantee ever-greater movement in a more democratic direction, there is no sense to the idea of a consolidated democracy. So-called consolidation would murder the growth of the life project which is democratization. As with Britain and America in the century after the revolutionary achievements of 1688 and 1865, democracy could stagnate or decline. There is no escape from the risk that threatened groups can explode a particular balance of power they view as unsatisfactory and thereby destroy the procedures of further democratic expansion. Proceduralism is necessarily a discontinuous revolution.

In short, the standard two-stage comprehension of democratization as a transition is most misleading. In that conventional wisdom, there are democratic breakthroughs (or openings), followed by democratic consolidations (or institutionalizations). Most analysts who look at breakthroughs conclude that the sources of democratic openings are so diverse and particular that there is no possible general causal explanation of breakthroughs. One is studying the contingent tactics of political agents in building coalitions and reconciling previously irreconcilable blocs or interests or groups. What matters in democratization, therefore, is a politics of good crafting, compacting or constitutional engineering. A growing recent literature that wonderfully illuminates complex particular dynamics reflects on kinds of consolidation by focusing on the weight of elites and/or challengers in the process of institutionalizing the democratic rupture away from authoritarianism (Higley and Gunther 1992). But, historical contingency and political contention do not end, although prolonged cease-fires can wrongly create that impression. As explained above, consolidation is an incoherent notion.

The variety of breakthroughs is multidimensional. It includes institutional dilemmas of the moment, representing a spectrum running from post–World War Two Japan, where the military was institutionally disadvantaged, to post–Pinochet Chile, where the Pinochet military was protected and privileged. No useful general scheme explains the virtually infinite set of openings. National settings seem endlessly diverse. There is no singular Western solution to the dilemmas of democratization (Casper and Taylor 1996). There are useful schema, however, which suggest the variety of possibilities in this extraordinarily broad spectrum. Such schema allow analysts to identify the elements involved and the coalitions possible in diverse crafting projects.

Increasingly, the analysts' focus has been on the crafting of the initial democratic institutions in terms of how well they serve the long-run project of fuller democratization, although consolidation is an incoherent concept in an open and reversible process. Questions are asked about top-down or bottom-up or other kinds of crafting of the democratic institutions that will bring about a momentarily stable democratic polity. It would be more complete to conceive of good democratic crafting so as to include keeping the process advancing or at least open to advance.

But how? A huge literature has developed on the virtues of parliamentarianism versus presidentialism (Linz and Valenzuela 1994; Sartori 1997) and on first-past-the-post (or, actually, and very differently, majoritarian) voting versus proportional representation electoral systems, which come in a variety of forms. This literature often and tragically slights key issues, such as the conciliation of religious and other communalisms, rules for changing the rules, the division of powers between center and locales, how geographic boundaries are decided, and how the security forces are kept under the rule of democratically chosen civilians. These less-studied questions are truly core issues of any project of democratic crafting, as manifest clearly in the 1990s in Russia and South Africa.

One reason the non-West may look less democratic is because awareness of these core difficulties in the non-West—say, in India—is contrasted with their manufactured invisibility in the West. The conventional wisdom that romanticizes so-called Western civilization wrongly imagines Western democracies as states that were secular such that religion could not intrude on a supposedly rational process. Such thinking neglects the centrality of religion to the political struggle in seventeenth-century England or France after 1789 (or even its importance in U.S. or Israeli politics today). From Germany and Ireland to Canada and Japan, there is no secular state walled off from a purely private and societal arena of religion. The ideologized self-descriptions of the West which hide the complexities of democratization in the West will be of little help to crafters of democracy elsewhere (Friedman 1994).

Conventional academic wisdom, albeit rich in particular insights, is manifestly seriously flawed and grossly misleading. It omits too much that is decisive. That body of work is shaped by a deluding mythology of democratization that does not recognize sufficiently that: (1) democracy is a revolution, (2) the initial breakthrough to a fledgling democracy is almost inevitably far from fully democratic because of concessions made to entrenched elites, (3) political struggles inevitably ensue over the fairness of the original rules of the democratic political game, and (4) elites may be unwilling to budge from their initial and very limited notions of democracy (soon understood as an almost sacred heritage). Democracy therefore is an eternally contested concept and project, a tensely dynamic reality hidden by mechanical two-stage models of transition where the second step, an initial institutionalization is defined misleadingly as consolidation.

The lesson of this critical set of propositions, in contradistinction to the conventional wisdom, is that there is no such thing as a consolidated democracy. The standard two-stage model obscures the central fact regarding democratization in a fledgling democracy: the rule-bound initial process that is temporarily institutionalized in no way guarantees success for the open-ended project of further democratization. Indeed the eventually apparent unfairness of the original institutionalization readily becomes an incitement to a struggle whose outcome, as with post–Civil War America, often entrenches obstacles to continuing democratization. Struggle, indeed intense struggle, potentially explosive struggle, is virtually inevitable. A democracy, no matter how cleverly originally crafted, can be lost. Anywhere and everywhere, this painful, gradual, and discontinuous process of seemingly eternal democratization also is pregnant with delay, failure, and alienation, and, consequently, the possibility that democracy could one day be lost. As Abraham Lincoln explained at Gettysburg on November 19, 1863, "It is for us . . . to be dedicated to the unfinished work . . . a new birth of freedom . . . that government of the people, by the people, for the people, shall not perish from the earth." Yet it can perish. It has.

As people struggle endlessly over what constitutes fair rules of the political power game, their differences often lead to antidemocratic interventions. There is no intrinsic reason why antidemocrats in the United States (or Japan or any other nation enjoying political freedom) cannot win the ongoing debate and related struggle over power. They might do so by persuading ever more citizens, including elites, that the government entering the twenty-first century actually is the result of an antidemocratic coup that has betrayed the constitutional commitment to popular governance and imposed an unconstitutional order of judicial tyranny that, to take one political perspective, murders babies, frees criminals, privileges un-American alien elements, and is beholden to international elites ("The End of Democracy" 1996). It would, then, follow that a war of the white, Protestant, American community (and its allies) would be called for to purge the nation of threats to its cultural essence, just as Islamists try to purge Algeria of "alien" Western influences. In such an America, Anglo-Saxon racists would dub their enemies as threats to Western democracy, a categorization that enchants frightened Americans of certain European descent—even though the old, closed world of Europe, when American democracy was young, had seemed to many Americans an evil to be avoided in the new, open world of America. Eighteenth-century Americans used to believe they would be democratic precisely because of all the things that made America different from Europe (Hartz 1955).

Because of the uncertainty of outcomes that is inherent in the open-ended project of democracy, because it is impossible to give meaning to the notion of "consolidated democracy," therefore, the debate over fairness and inclusiveness never ends. Democracy is not some extant good set of institutions such as competitive elections, but is experientially fair rules for periodically choosing and holding publicly accountable governing officials so that people with incommensurable ultimate ends can live civilly with each other. What is fair is debatable. The debate never ends. While competitive elections may ordinarily be crucial to a democratic process, the substance of the proceduralism of democracy that includes elections is contestable. The result is a continuing struggle over what constitutes fairness and inclusiveness. The struggle has often been won by antidemocratic forces in "the West." This fact of uncertainty makes the fanciful notion of a consolidated democracy a mystification, an idea which obscures the reasons why democratization is painful, discontinuous, and not guaranteed. There is no way to know for sure the long-term result of Chile's democratization that still protects the military from democratic processes or of Japan's postwar discrediting of the military. As an uncertain and contingent project, a really existing democracy, replete with flaws and tensions—Israel as a Jewish state or India as a secular state—is in the hands of mere mortals who at any moment can act to botch up their political system of ordered liberty (Pantham 1997). That is why, I believe, it is important to comprehend the worth of an actually flawed but truly open democracy in contrast to all the allegedly superior but actually closed alternatives which present themselves as uniquely virtuous.

Let me illustrate the above points about the error in the conventional two-stage mechanical model of democratization with an instance of democratization well known in the United States. I want to highlight the different questions to be asked about democratization in a perspective that presumes that democratization is a gradual, painful, and loseable process with approaches to democratization that stress preconditions and find that a nation such as the United States, given its Protestant individualist political culture, and broadly dispersed (middling) property holdings was initially blessed by both the cultural and socioeconomic prerequisites of democracy. America, so the argument goes, was born free and truly democratic from its fortunate birth (Greenfeld 1992).

In contrast to that notion of a blessed and almost preternaturally well-crafted U.S. Constitution which culminated in George Washington's ascent to the presidency in 1789, the alleged beginning of a democratic machine that went on forever by itself, consider what is omitted by the mythology inherent in this well-meaning romanticization of the Constitution. In fact, the original crafting of the Continental Congress during the American War of Independence literally went bankrupt. The subsequent Articles of Confederation seemed such a source of chaos and economic confusion that they too were jettisoned. The Constitution implemented in 1788–89 is actually America's third republic. The American experience, already at its inception, reveals at least as much pain, disruption, and gradualness as French democracy. To survive a prolonged political crisis, the crafters made lots of compromises. Crafters usually do.

Some of the compromises that made possible that fledgling American democracy in 1789 turned out to be disastrous. The U.S. Constitution legalized slavery. The founders' belief that white Anglo-Saxon Protestants as a homogeneous political culture were uniquely suited to self-government also led to a virtual exclusion of Irish Catholics. In the years just before the racist exclusionary system broke down into a savage civil war of barbarous bloodletting, forerunners of the various Ku Klux Klan organizations came forward, describing themselves as the true preservers of American liberty in opposing the inclusion of both people from Africa and Catholics. Even abolitionists in the North agreed that blacks lacked a culture conducive to democratic self-government. Although slavery was immoral, many abolitionists nonetheless concluded that people from Africa had to be sent back to Africa. The logic of cultural preconditions for democracy is unadulterated, antidemocratic racism. It mystifies, magically presenting exclusionary European antidemocrats as the essence of inclusionary democracy.

The notion that people born and raised in America could all be citizens no matter where their ancestors came from was an invention of free blacks living in the north of the United States (Condit and Lucaites 1993). They argued that people became American citizens by living in American culture and being loyal to the American Constitution. The creation of an inclusionary American nationhood is a creation of people from Africa, not a construction of cultural chauvinists from Britain, not even of the real Protestant heroes of British descent who dominated the liberating abolitionist movement.

A debate on the content of national identity can obviously be won by groups committed to antidemocratic exclusiveness. In fact, it has. Indeed, after a decade of democratization in the American South in the wake of the Civil War, African-Americans were once again excluded from that region's polity. Actually, white Catholics were also initially lynched in the violent antidemocratic era that followed. African-Americans and their allies were murdered under color of law right into the 1960s. Some find that the continuing slaughter of unarmed black men by police reflects how far America is from inclusiveness even today. The pain of gradualness and proceduralism is best comprehended by focusing on the innocent victims whose lives can be made miserable or even snuffed out because democracy is still, in no small part, but a promise and a project. Democracy is better conceived of as a project than a fact, more a promise than the nostalgic essence conceived by exclusionary elites or antidemocrats who seek to freeze or reverse the process of democratization.

And yet America is usually deemed democratic since 1776 or 1789. This procedural constitutionalism is actually full of pain, rupture, and only gradual moral progress that enlarged the content of fairness in a continuing process of democratization. As in the struggle during the

1990s over creating districts with black majorities, the issue of fair rules is far from settled (Grofman 1992). Old elites regularly invent devices to exclude other groups and then treat those antidemocratic devices as natural or sacred, the better to dismiss the excluded as the irrational. Sadly for democratic progress, the tactic of procedural obstructionism quite often succeeds.

In a democracy, progress in inclusiveness best comes procedurally. Abraham Lincoln wanted slaves freed by constitutional amendment, not executive fiat. The danger of bypassing procedures to hasten progress in inclusiveness would threaten the whole system. Enslavement was prolonged to strengthen proceduralism. As the work of Barrington Moore, Jr.(1966 and elsewhere) has emphasized, there is a high cost to peaceful progress.

Dismantling the institutions of white racist resistance—white primaries, poll taxes, literacy laws, etc.—took decades even after a world war fought against racist fascism (Davidson and Grofman 1994). Further progress came in the 1960s only when the national government felt a need to woo newly independent African states in a cold war in which American apartheid was an embarrassing issue. This procedural progress required passage of civil rights and voting rights laws in 1964 and 1965. These then were massively resisted in parts of the American South by redistricting and switching to at-large elections. These procedural obstacles to inclusion were countermanded late in the twentieth century by crafting districts to permit Americans, many of whose ancestors came from Africa, to have a shot at winning seats even if virtually all whites, voting as a racist bloc, voted against African-American candidates. The Supreme Court, in its infinite wisdom, threw out this effort to end white racist rule, describing inclusion of Americans of African heritage as apartheid. The Court's language struck me as, at best, insensitive and inappropriate, and, in fact, an indication of the depth of European ethnocentrism which treats as natural districting that makes African-Americans a greatly unrepresented minority. Studies by David Canon (forthcoming) of voting and services provided show that African-American representatives are far more likely to represent all communities in their district than are European-American representatives.

But this continuing problem of pain, disruption, and gradualness in democratic progress is not peculiarly American. It arises any time the notion of nationhood and its attendant voting rules reflect a self-styled majority which takes itself as the nation. This reality prevailed in Japan. It threatens democracy in India, which the RSS (Association of National Volunteers) sees as a Hindu nation and calls Hitler lucky because he only had to get rid of 12 million Jews, whereas India's Hindus have to deal with 120 million Muslims. Indian democracy, as all democracies, can be maintained only by continually beating back antidemocratic challenges (particularly in the wake of the Hindu-Nationalist BJP's [Bharatiya Janta Party] 1998 parliamentary electoral victory). To gauge how well India is doing, one should remember how poorly America did. Accurately comprehending democratization in Europe and North America is a prerequisite for a comparative study of democratization.

As Donald Horowitz (1996) has shown for sub-Saharan Africa, British-style parliamentary systems, based on first-past-the-post voting, facilitate dominance by one community to the detriment of and exclusion of all others. Consequently, it may be more useful to see the British system not as it is romanticized by many, as the essence of democracy, but as reflected in the community politics of the United Kingdom in large matters such as the fate of Irish Catholics and the long alienation of Scot presbyters, a procedural system, as in the United States, which makes communalist exclusion easy, but which, consequently, can subvert the legitimacy of the democracy in the eyes of excluded communities, making the system appear inherently unfair.

This does not mean that proportional representation is better at legitimating democracies (Sartori 1997). It only means that the myths which treat some achievement, such as English parliamentarism, as the essence of true democracy cannot help being grossly misleading. There is no true democracy to emulate. There are merely a variety of polities at different points, paying different prices, in a continuous quest. There is no sense to the large body of literature which measures the real variety of non-Western democracies against an idealized imagining of Western democracies, whether parliamentary Britain or a presidential U.S., misleadingly understood as some impossible true model of authentic democracy.

However, once one understands how revolutionary democracy is, as it makes the power of elites uncertain, it becomes less of a mystery that democratic procedures are adopted precisely because they impose exclusions on challenging nonelites, thereby initiating a continual process of pain and gradual and discontinuous progress, in which the still-excluded struggle for inclusion. The struggle between elites and challengers is endless. The incompleteness of any really existing democracy is a continuing spur to antiliberal alternatives to representative democracy, including communalist fascism, Leninist dictatorship, and Athens-inspired direct democracy—alternatives for which the language of authentic inclusion actually legitimates exclusion and marginalization and perhaps even the annihilation of whole communities. These fraudulent alternatives are so regularly and pervasively attractive precisely because functioning democracies, flawed systems claiming to be truly consolidated democracies, can so easily appear as pain-inflicting, immoral frauds.

Thus it is no wonder that the wounded regularly seek alternatives to liberal democratic proceduralism which they understand as unadulterated hypocrisy. The literature which insists that constitutional governance establishing representative democracies is merely one of many kinds of democracy is, nonetheless, dangerously misleading. That literature uses the term democracy to legitimate antidemocratic projects, basing its agenda on the great degree of nondemocracy and of unfulfilled promise in real democracies. People in authoritarian regimes can sincerely conclude that their system is far more genuinely democratic than actually existing pluralist democracies. East Asian authoritarians invoked such legitimations in the 1980s (Bell et al. 1995). Nonetheless, those authoritarians are wrong.

In the fascist perspective, a community is essentialized so that any voting rule is seen as polluting its supposedly united community of authentic representativeness. Democracy is said to bring division when, to the communalist purist or fascist-oriented, national unity and survival seem a life-or-death issue. They assume an organic tie of the true people to authentic leadership. Fairness is defined to guarantee an outcome, the victory of a proper moral order embodied in "our" people, properly understood. In fascism, the real people rule in the truest of democracies.

But the decision rule of a democracy makes outcomes uncertain. It does not guarantee an outcome. Therefore fascism—organic, essentialist communalism—is obviously antidemocratic. It is also inhuman in its insistence that one dimension of personhood overrides all others, in eternally defining a democratic process that represents and is open to the multidimensional potential of humanity to be realized when only one element of the variegated and changing whole is embodied by the state. Antidemocratic communalists are correct to see that the open multivalence of democracy is a threat to a communalist project defined permanently in an exclusionary way. Fascist communalism is a war against most of what makes complex humanity human (Taylor et al. 1994; Appiah and Gutman 1996). But democratic procedures that seem grossly unfair to a community can legitimate the nondemocratic alternative.

Leninism likewise is deeply antidemocratic. It is an assault on representative democracy. It assumes that the essence defining all else in existing liberal democracies is an inhuman, exploitative, and oppressive economic base, called capitalism. As with fascist communalism, a deep inhumanity in the repressive Leninist project limits people to one dimension of their diverse potential. The logic of a liberationist economy is claimed by Leninists to guarantee political power in their hands alone, not to a gender, or to an ethnicity or people committed on an issue such as religion or community. Leninists consider the selection of government officials by supposedly fair, democratic rules to be a fraud that hides the secret truth known only to the revolutionary vanguard. That is, since capitalism supposedly dictates all, true democracy requires that capitalism must be extinguished and replaced by a poorly defined system called socialism which ends the economic basis of hidden domination and thus allows "authentic democracy" to prevail, authentic meaning the dictatorial imposition of "true knowers." People who do not accept this dogma as scientific truth cannot be allowed to rule or contest for power, since they will subvert socialism, imagined as the one and only base of true democracy and complete human liberation.

This Leninist project precludes open and reasoned debate and proceduralism. It guarantees who the rulers are. Hence only a self-proclaimed vanguard of the few who "know" can rule, tyrannically imposing an economic system that supposedly guarantees protection from economic exploitation and thereby providing the true essence of freedom. Political freedom is defined out of existence. That democracy is actually about an open politics of contestation without guaranteed results is thereby countered ontologically and coercively.

Leninism legitimates permanent rule by a self-replicating elite that supposedly grasps the essential truth of politics and economics. Like fascism, Leninism is an apologia for an antidemocratic project. It denies the premise of representative democracy, which is that citizens (not a self-defined elite of knowers, a group which can dismiss the masses as asses) in a fair political process regularly and by public rules choose officials whom they can hold publicly accountable and even replace. Leninism is antidemocratic to its core in ignoring the imperatives of public openness and public accountability. Like fascism, it legitimates dictatorial power in terms of a self-serving myth presented as the essence of political truth.

What makes alternatives to liberal democracy attractive is that constitutional democracy is a proceduralism that guarantees no particular outcome. Consequently, greedy, narrow winners can act in ways that—as in eighteenth-century Britain or the Philippines and Brazil entering the twenty-first century—allow major problems to fester or that injure and alienate large segments of society, thereby persuading many people that the proceduralism of democracy is not in their interest. Democracy, by its nature, is losable. It is worth taking seriously that, because of massive flaws experienced as unbearable unfairness, well-meaning people, in good conscience, can come to conclude that an antidemocratic project is somehow more democratic than today's palpably unfair proceduralisms.

Finally, there are opponents of representative democracy who insist that the only authentic democracy is direct democracy, as supposedly occurred originally in ancient Athens. Putting aside the historic Athens which, of course, had a higher proportion of slaves than societies in Africa which are frequently dubbed slave societies, and which denied citizenship possibilities also to women and aliens, even in its idealized form direct participatory democracy is not a desirable goal. The core argument for direct democracy defines true democracy as a system in which people rule themselves rather than being ruled by so-called representatives who, Rousseau claimed, only allow self-rule in the moment of electorally choosing new representatives. In Athenian direct democracy, in contrast to liberal democracy, the people—not representatives—were said to rule.

Proponents of direct democracy define democracy so that it has an inherently limited size, a population that can meet from time to time, discuss, and vote with all hearing each other. By definition, complex, large nation-states cannot be democratic in this sense since there is no way for all, beyond a certain small size, to discuss and decide in concert. Apologists for authoritarianism often use the notion that direct democracy is the only real democracy, in order to legitimate dictatorship as the same as "mere" procedural democracy.

Democracy is defined by direct democrats so that politics requires much free time for each and all to assemble, deliberate, and decide. As supporters of the American Confederacy argued in the mid-nineteenth century, the direct democracy of Athens required many to be slaves so that a leisured group could have the free time to rule. Slavery was the premise of such freedom. Democracy was defined to preclude participation by those whose lives were informed by imperatives of toil, art, religion, service, pleasure, etc. Politics was a time-consuming work. Direct democracy was a system which excluded from a say in the polity those who lacked a physical basis for ratiocination, people whose time, by choice or necessity, was devoted elsewhere. Again, humans are reduced to a single dimension as in communalist fascism or Leninist economism. There is nothing liberating in such a project where only deliberative participation makes people human. It is profoundly antihuman.

While there may be ways in which Athens' procedures can, in fact, be understood to make that city a great democracy, a focus on one dimension of the system, public participation in the debate, ignores the procedures of representation, fairness, and accountability that made Athens democratic in the ordinary way described in this essay. The key to Athenian democracy was the crafting of many precincts called *demes* so that those selected by lot from the *demes* would put representatives of the old oligarchical, entrenched, landed elite clans in a voting minority in all governing bodies. What made Athens democratic was its representativeness. That is, for its members, it was procedurally fair. To the extent that Athens was truly democratic, it was so in the standard manner of proceduralism. For democracy, there is no escape from the painful dilemmas of making procedural fairness work.

Entering the twenty-first century, the proponents of fascism, Leninism and direct democracy have dwindled. In fact, all three projects have been exposed as enemies of procedural democracy and opponents of limits on government that guarantee meaningful freedom and human dignity; they have been revealed as projects of despotism. And yet proponents of each and all of these alternatives to constitutional liberty correctly note that representative democracy is a very limited form of governance.

Democracy in no way guarantees the achievement of the good, let alone the solution of any particular problem. The politics of choice in representative democracy leaves in place lots of phenomena that can, quite reasonably, seem to many to be quite undemocratic evils, matters such as communalist injustice, economic inequality, and political alienation, the last a popular experience that those in power do not authentically represent "people like me." These flaws are real, not definitional. Enemies of democracy always can find proof that democracy is a fraud since actually existing democracies are regularly partial and often found to be most unfair. The challenge to really existing democracies never ends.

Yet in a world understood to consist of complex human beings with multiple and changing identities, a world in which expansion of wealth requires a market orientation, a world too large and complex to even entertain the notion that all citizens can assemble in one place at swiftly recurring intervals, the only viable and authentic democracy is representative democracy, the painful and continuing achievement and struggle over further achievement within proceduralism. It is misleading in the extreme, however, for propagandists of the most recent advance in the democratic project to see themselves as truly democratic and others who are elsewhere on this endless political road to be undemocratic. Amnesia parading as absolutism is not attractive or persuasive. Yet democrats quite often garb themselves in just such ideological garments.

All attempts to monopolize the term "democratic" to particular moments in the democratic quest are in fact undemocratic. There is always so much more democratizing to do, even though recent democratic gains are indeed achievements to be proud of. But why should a liberal and limited form of governance be considered authentically democratic when it can leave so many arenas of human action—family, workplace, religion—extremely undemocratic? Antidemocratic elements pervade functioning democracies. In the perspective of proceduralism and constitutional governments, these continuing authoritarian or unaccountable realms have to be seen, at best, as projects for the future, a future of open dialogue, struggle, persuasion, and changing notions of fairness. Within democratic proceduralism, people have the right to continue the endless, partial, and painful quest for ever more democracy. There is always such a long and uncertain path ahead that it is mind-boggling that theorists in the West conventionally present their flawed governments and exclusionary histories as truly democratic.

The key fact—which cannot be overemphasized in a world where the conventional wisdom obscures the actual dynamics of really existing democracy as continuous democratization—is that democracy is an ongoing and unfinished (unfinishable?) project, not a realized essence. It is a process of processes which guarantees no particular outcome, no particular solution to any pressing problem. Democracy thus can be rife with real injustices, contradictions, and irrationalities. It can seem a failure. It can exclude and alienate. It can actually fail. Democracy can produce cruel dilemmas that may lose a people their democracy, as in Algeria in the 1980s when a religious party seemed likely to use democratic decision rules to end the future use of such rules. What are democrats who hold sacred yesterday's or today's procedures to do when faced with a choice, in accord with the prevailing rules, of someone who seems a threat to the rules, imagined as a Hitler or an Allende, a Kishi or an Arbenz? In democracy, even in Europe, even in places with long constitutional histories, even in relatively prosperous nations, much is at risk. This permanent uncertainty is hidden from analysis in the conventional wisdom that conjures up the myth of a consolidated democracy.

Democracy tends to be institutionalized to err on the side of prudence. Challengers make concessions to elites to win new breakthroughs. How much democracy in all its fullness is humanly possible is a question the system regularly faces procedurally when those who feel disadvantaged by the prevailing rules—who can be elites as well as nonelites—try to persuade fellow citizens of the need to change the procedures, sometimes to end democracy. All that fascists, Leninists, and worshipers of Athens insist on as essence is thus treated as potential alternatives because critics can always point to failings in existing democracies and invent schema which falsely promise an end to the inevitable painful reality of democratic politics with so many unsolved problems, so much hypocrisy. The insightful analyses of the 1970s and 1980s asking, in response to military coups from South Korea to Greece to Chile, why democracies fail, have not lost their usefulness and, realistically, never will.

More people can always be included in the political community than is currently the case, thus redefining the nation. There are always people frightened of what a Song Jiaoren in China's 1912 republic or a Kerensky in Russia's 1917 democracy might do. Both leaders of fledgling democracies were overthrown by despotic regimes. Analysts who stress preconditions of democracy are of little help to democratic leaders trying to craft democracy, having to conciliate antidemocratic, old elites.

The revolutionary potential of democracy can terrify elites. Property or wealth can be differentially taxed or rewarded (e.g., minimum wage, guaranteed health care, pensions), thus redefining economic relations among groups. There are always powerful groups opposed to the next change in the system. This openness to improvement, which is not a guarantee that the greater and ever-reimagined promise of democracy can be realized, is a measure of how much democracy is both a procedural and prudential process and also a highly risky one, indeed, a revolutionary one that can alienate elites or challengers or both and thus threaten the "unconsolidable" system. Democracy is a risk and an opportunity. It can be lost. It can be frittered away.

How can a guarantee of no guarantees ensure the success of measures of greater democracy that previously would have been unthinkable—e.g. full participation for women, citizenship for aliens, economic security for nonowners of capital?

Democracy is difficult to define in terms of a particular content or a precise rule because it is forever in flux. An understanding of democracy that is more limiting than its actual unlimited potential for empowerment or failure will not be democratic. A definition of democracy cannot even include the notion of elections, since democratic Athenians did not always make use of competitive elections. There is nothing inherently undemocratic in appointing most officials rather than electing all. Fairness can lead citizens to prefer the appointment of technically competent leaders, rather than elections, to fill many powerful offices. Judges can serve for life. Senior military officials can serve at the will of the chief executive. The definition of democracy cannot say who or what rules, since procedures and notions of fairness can be made more inclusive, opening to other religions, to people without property, and to those with diverse places of origin. Democracy's fairness to the included must allow them to hear reasons for yet greater inclusiveness, including those once deemed beyond the pale—blasphemers, divorced, illegitimate, young, propertyless, foreign-born, female, illiterate, etc. A working definition of democracy which encompasses the actualities of this open-ended reality must include the changing notions of fairness of the politically active agents engaged in a never-ending dialogue about fairness and an open-ended process of continuous crafting and re-crafting, one whose discontinuous achievements necessarily, at any particular time, leave lots of innocents feeling cheated and in great pain. The process is endless.

Democratization is a challenging quest, one grossly misunderstood when any nation or region, such as "the West," holds itself up as an embodiment of an impossibility, a true and authentically embodied democracy. The braggart is a liar. And yet the achievement is real and wonderful, an achievement in no way diminished by the self-serving antidemocrats who mistake the long road ahead for proof that substantial progress has not been and cannot be made. It is easier to appreciate the glory of the partial democratic achievements of people everywhere if one is not fooled by the romanticizing and distorting mythologists of Western democracy who treat a democracy in the West as a natural, singular, authentic, and consolidated regime. The struggle for democracy is always partial, painful, and discontinuous.

REFERENCES

Appiah, K. Anthony, and Amy Gutman. 1996. *Color Consciousness*. Princeton, NJ: Princeton University Press.

Barber, Benjamin. 1996. "Foundationalism and Democracy." In Seyla Benhabid, ed., *Democracy and Difference*, pp. 348–59. Princeton: Princeton University Press.

Bell, Daniel A., et al. 1995. *Towards Illiberal Democracy in Pacific Asia*. New York: St. Martin's Press.

Berkowitz, Peter. 1996. "Liberalism's Virtue." *Perspectives on Political Science*, vol. 25, no. 4 (Fall): 183–91.

Canon, David (forthcoming). *Race, Redistricting and Representation*. Chicago: University of Chicago Press.

Carothers, Thomas. 1997. "Democratic Assistance." *Democratization*, vol. 4, no. 3 (Autumn): 109–32.

Casper, Gretchen, and Michelle Taylor. 1996. *Negotiating Democracy*. Pittsburgh: University of Pittsburgh Press.

Condit, Celeste Michelle, and John Lucaites. 1993. *Crafting Equality*. Chicago: University of Chicago Press.

Davidson, Chandler, and Bernard Grofman, eds. 1994. *Quiet Revolution in the South*. Princeton: Princeton University Press.

"End of Democracy, The." 1996. *First Things* (November): 18–42

Friedman, Edward. 1994. *The Politics of Democratization: Generalizing East Asian Experiences.* Boulder: Westview Press.

———. 1998. "Development, Revolution, Democracy, and Dictatorship." In Theda Skocpol, ed., *Democracy, Revolution, and History,* pp. 102–23. Ithaca: Cornell University Press.

Greenfeld, Liah. 1992. *Nationalism.* Cambridge: Harvard University Press.

Grofman, Bernard, et al. 1992. *Minority Representation and the Quest for Voting Equality.* New York: Cambridge University Press.

Hartz, Louis. 1955. *The Liberal Tradition in America.* New York: Harcourt, Brace and World.

Higley, John, and Richard Gunther, eds. 1992. *Elites and Democratic Consolidation in Latin America and Southern Europe.* New York: Cambridge University Press.

Horowitz, Donald. 1996. "Comparing Democratic Systems." In Larry Diamond and Marc Plattner, eds., *The Global Resurgence of Democracy,* pp. 143–49. Baltimore: Johns Hopkins University Press.

Huntington, Samuel P. 1991. *The Third Wave: Democratization in the Late Twentieth Century.* Norman: University of Oklahoma Press.

Levi, Margaret. 1997. *Consent, Dissent and Patriotism.* New York: Cambridge University Press.

Linz, Juan, and Arturo Valenzuela, eds. 1994. *The Failure of Presidential Democracy: Latin America.* Baltimore: Johns Hopkins University Press.

Moore, Barrington, Jr. 1966. *Social Origins of Dictatorship and Democracy.* Boston: Beacon Press.

O'Brien, Conor Cruise. 1994. *On the Eve of the Millennium: The Future of Democracy Through an Age of Unreason.* New York: The Free Press.

Pantham, Thomas. 1997. "Indian Secularism and Its Critics." *Review of Politics,* vol. 59, no. 3 (Summer): 523–40.

Rueschemeyer, Dietrich, Evelyne Huber Stephens, and John D. Stephens. 1992. *Capitalist Development and Democracy.* Chicago: University of Chicago Press.

Sartori, Giovanni. 1997. *Comparative Constitutional Engineering.* New York: New York University Press.

Schedler, Andreas. 1998. "What Is Democratic Consolidation?" *Journal of Democracy,* vol. 9, no.2 (April): 91–107.

Singer, Max. 1997. "What Is Happening in History." *PS* (March): 27–34.

Taylor, Charles, et al. 1994. *Multiculturalism.* Princeton: Princeton University Press.

Thomas, Alan. 1997. "Liberal Republicanism and the Role of Civil Society." *Democratization,* vol. 4, no. 3 (Autumn): 26–40.

Touraine, Alaine. 1997 [1994]. *What Is Democracy?* Boulder: Westview Press.

Contributors

Barry Ames: Heinz Professor of Political Science, University of Pittsburgh. His publications include *Political Survival: Politicians and Public Policy in Latin America* (University of California Press); *Rhetoric and Reality in a Militarized Regime: Brazil Since 1964* (Sage Publications). He has contributed articles to the *American Political Science Review, Journal of Politics, American Journal of Political Science,* among others.

Laurie Brand: Professor of Political Science, University of Southern California. Her publications include *Jordan's Inter-Arab Relations: The Political Economy of Alliance Making* (Columbia University Press); *Palestinians in the Arab World: Institution Building and the Search for State* (Columbia University Press).

Joseph Fewsmith: Professor of Political Science, Boston University. His publications include *Dilemmas of Reform in China: Political Conflict and Economic Debate* (M. E. Sharpe); *Party, State, and Local Elites in Republican China: Merchant Organizations and Politics in Shanghai, 1890–1930* (University of Hawaii Press).

Edward Friedman: Professor of Political Science, University of Wisconsin (Madison). His publications include *The Politics of Democratization: Generalizing East Asian Experiences* (editor) (Westview Press); *National Identity and Democratic Prospects in Socialist China* (M. E. Sharpe).

Howard Handelman: Professor of Political Science, University of Wisconsin-Milwaukee. Director, Center for Latin America. His publications include *Military Government and the Movement toward Democracy in South America* (coeditor) (Indiana University Press); *Mexican Politics: The Dynamics of Change* (St. Martin's Press).

341

Eric Hershberg: Social Science Research Council. His publications include *Constructing Democracy: Human Rights, Citizenship, and Society in Latin America* (coeditor) (Westview Press).

Farhad Kazemi: Professor of Political Science, New York University. His publications include *Peasants and Politics in the Modern Middle East* (coeditor) (Florida International University Press); *A Way Prepared: Essays on Islamic Culture in Honor of Richard Bayly Winder* (coeditor) (New York University Press).

Sunhyuk Kim: Assistant Professor of Political Science, University of Southern California. His publications include "Civic Mobilization for Democratic Reform," in Larry Diamond and Doh C. Shin (editors), *Institutional Reform and Democratic Consolidation in Korea* (Hoover Institution); "State and Civil Society in South Korea's Democratic Consolidation," *Asian Survey.*

Scott Mainwaring: Professor of Political Science, University of Notre Dame. Director of the Helen Kellogg Institute for International Studies. His publications include *Issues in Democratic Consolidation: The New South American Democracies in Comparative Perspective* (coeditor) (Helen Kellogg Institute for International Studies and the University of Notre Dame Press); *Presidentialism and Democracy in Latin America* (coeditor) (Cambridge University Press).

Augustus Richard Norton: Professor of Political Science, Boston University. His publications include *Civil Society in the Middle East* (editor) (Brill); *The International Relations of the Palestine Liberation Organization* (coeditor) (Southern Illinois University Press).

Jeffrey Riedinger: Associate Professor of Political Science, Michigan State University. His publications include *Agrarian Reform in the Philippines: Democratic Transitions and Redistributive Reform* (Stanford University Press); *Land Reform and Democratic Development* (co-author) (Johns Hopkins University Press).

Mark Tessler: Professor of Political Science, University of Arizona. Director, Center for Middle Eastern Studies. His publications include *Democracy, War, and Peace in the Middle East* (coeditor) (Indiana University Press); *A History of the Israeli-Palestinian Conflict* (Indiana University Press). He has contributed articles to *World Politics, Journal of Conflict Resolution,* and *International Studies Quarterly,* among others.

Index